Ireland and Scotland
in the Age of Revolution

Heard ye o' the Tree o' France?
And wat ye what's the name o't?
Around it a' the patriots dance,
Well Europe kens the fame o't.

'The Tree of Liberty', Robert Burns

Question: Are you straight?
Answer: I am.
Question: How straight?
Answer: As straight as a rush.
Question: Go on then?
Answer: In truth, in trust, in unity, and in liberty.
Question: What have you in your hand?
Answer: A green bough.
Question: Where did it first grow?
Answer: In America.
Question: Where did it bud?
Answer: In France.
Question: Where are you going to plant it?
Answer: In the crown of Great Britain.

Catechism as proof of membership
of the United Irishmen

Ireland and Scotland in the Age of Revolution

Planting the Green Bough

E. W. McFARLAND

EDINBURGH UNIVERSITY PRESS

© E. W. McFarland, 1994

Edinburgh University Press Ltd
22 George Square, Edinburgh

Typeset in Linotronic Garamond
by Speedspools, Edinburgh, and
printed and bound in Great Britain
by the University Press, Cambridge

A CIP record for this book is available from
the British Library

ISBN 0 7486 0539 8

Contents

PREFACE

Scotland and the Irish Crisis

For the Quaker Mary Leadbetter of County Kildare, Ireland in the months following the 1798 Rebellion was like 'the working of the sea after the storm'. She could hear the sound of the trees being felled at night for pike handles, and the creaking of the carts as they took them away. In Tyrone, meanwhile, the agitated inhabitants of Auchnacloy and Omagh rushed to pledge loyalty to their 'beloved Sovereign and glorious Constitution', and offered their patriotic services to the Volunteers and Yeomanry.[1]

The Revolutionary era in Ireland, although of short duration, was remarkable for the intensity of contemporaries' experiences. Such was the hightened tempo of change and conflict that many shared the sensation of living a lifetime in a year.[2] It was also, as Roy Foster comments, 'probably the most concentrated episode of violence in Irish history'.[3] Indeed, the 1798 Rebellion stands as a counter to the correlation between the importance and complexity of historical events, and their duration. Deep-rooted in the social and economic conditions of eighteenth-century Ireland, this sharp, intense political crisis was also to have a lasting impact on the subsequent course of Irish nationalism.

Its repercussions transcended the bounds of domestic politics and society. Demonstrating this, the central focus of this book is the interaction of Ireland's crisis with political developments in its closest neighbour, Scotland. In practice, this will involve analysing the development of the links at the end of the eighteenth century between Scottish radicals and the Society of United Irishmen, the group which posed the most inspired and energetic opposition to the Ascendancy domination of Irish politics. This is a considerable empirical task. However, it has been made less daunting in conceptual terms by recent shifts in historical orthodoxy.

For a number of years British and Irish historians alike adopted an isolationist stance on political reform pressures and insurrectionary threats in their respective geographical areas of interest. Radical movements in Ireland and on the mainland were traditionally placed in separate analytical compartments, and their links into the general political spasms which followed the American and French Revolutions were similarly addressed in an unfocused manner. To some extent this has reflected the isolationism and empiricism surviving in British historiography, identified with, but by no means exclusive to, conservative traditions of historical scholarship.

There were early dissenting voices. In 1955, A. W. Smith claimed in an ambitious footnote that 'Physical Force radicalism in England should in the last instance be traced back to the '98 Rebellion'.[4] Typically, Edward Thompson also offered a productive insight, identifying in *The Making of the English Working Class* important Irish connections in underground political movements in London and the North of England. Such co-operation he recognised as in some sense contributing to the 'secret revolutionary tradition', which, according to his seminal thesis, replaced the collapse of an open reform movement in the mid-1790s. Yet despite this preliminary groundwork, it is noticeable that in the encyclo-paedic bulk of R. B. McDowell's work, covering Ireland in the 1790s, analysis of the relationship between Irish and mainland radicalism remains undeveloped.[5] While this can perhaps be explained by his Irish starting point, it is more problematic in Thomis and Holt, who, in constructing a powerful and thought-provoking 'anti-Thompson' case for the limited threat posed by popular radicalism in the 1790s, largely confine their analysis to the British theatre of events.[6]

Reviewing the work of the last ten years or so, however, we can trace the emergence of a firmer 'internationalist' paradigm. Goodwin is a typical exponent of this, when he refuses to treat the revolutionary movement in England in isolation from events in Ireland and France, but it is Marianne Elliott who has provided some of the most creative and incisive work in the area.[7] Inspired by the American and French Revolutions, the United Irishmen, she argues, originally developed as an advanced extra-parliamentary reform body, operating on classically Whig-gish principles. The United Irishmen's fitful move towards anti-English, revolutionary republicanism also reflected 'the reaction of a general Euro-pean crisis upon the peculiar historical situation in Ireland'.[8] Thus, in 1795, following a wave of judicial repression at home, the confidence gained from their participation in a broader European reform movement led them to seek an alliance with revolutionary France. The dispatch of five invasion fleets is testament to the extent of French support, and the republican alliance became the mainspring of the United system. Crucially, she suggests, this 'externalisation' process involved the United Irishmen in building support among fellow democrats in England, resulting in the reconstruction of the remnants of English radicalism along the militant republican lines of the United Society.

Clearly, then, a useful initial basis for studying the dynamic and interlocking aspects of British and European radicalism has been established, and the constraints of a strictly national perspective recognised by a new generation of historians.[9] Inevitably, though, there remain gaps in our knowledge, and the picture of how Scotland fits into the network of international democratic politics is still shadowy and incomplete.[10] While existing studies offer several potential lines of investigation, the Scots–Irish radical alliance cannot be extrapolated a priori from these. In particular, the failure to disaggregate the Scottish experience systematically from the 'British' neglects how specific features of Scottish society and politics interacted with organisational and ideological importations from Ireland and the Continent to produce a unique synthesis.[11] This 'integrationist' framework tends to flaw Wells's otherwise useful analysis, but is particularly evident in Christie's emphatic restatement of the period's social stability.[12] Despite its subtitle *Reflections on the British Avoidance of Revolution*, his book's invocation of 'the Englishman's clubbishness' and 'the deep isolationist English love of country' as explanatory variables shows a customary metropolitan narrowness of vision.

Taken together, the antiquity of links between Presbyterian Scotland and Ulster, the evolution of a distinct Scottish democratic ethos, the nature of the Scottish 'proto-state', and not least, the differing salience of nationalism and sectarianism in the Scottish and Irish cases, all point to the value of a more locally-specific approach. The original inspiration for this book, indeed, originated in a study of a similar 'transplantation' into Scotland of a very dissimilar Irish political tradition – that of Orangeism. Here, despite a sympathetic ideological environment of militant Protestantism, the disjuncture between Ireland and Scotland, notably in terms of political and ecclesiastical structures, was sufficient to consign the 'unwelcome import' in question to the margins of Scottish society.[13]

The analysis of the Scottish experience offered in this book operates on two basic levels. On the one hand the involvement and influence of Irish radicals in Scotland raise a number of obvious substantive issues. The precise nature of the Irish contribution in England is itself still contested. On occasion, estimates seem to draw on national stereotypes. For Cassirer, the Irish provided a 'yeast' in radical movements, their contribution being more in terms of 'courage in direct action than consistency in organisation', while for Thompson their influence was most evident in a 'rebellious disposition' in communities and workplaces.[14] Meanwhile, Elliott's thesis on the nature and causes of English republicanism has been criticised for erecting Irish influence into a 'colossus', ignoring 'the scale and oscillating significance of popular "disaffection"', which may have existed independently.[15] In addressing similar questions for Scotland, an analytical distinction will be made, for example, between the *example* offered by the Irish crisis and the actual *involvement* of Irish personnel as agents and organisers.

Consideration of the Scottish dimension also helps clarify some issues of growing concern to historians of the Irish movement. The bicentennial of the foundation of the United Irishmen in 1991 encouraged a new burst of academic inquiry on the Society's origins and development. Attention has focused notably on the ideological and cultural antecedents of the Society, with A. T. Q. Stewart's *A Deeper Silence* emphasising the role of Freemasonry in Irish radicalism. There is also a greater awareness of the significance of internal tensions within the United Irishmen, and of the extent of continuity in tactics and personnel between the movement's 'constitutionalist' and 'underground' phases.[16]

The second set of issues are perhaps more reflective, and involve two interlocking controversies. The first surrounds the degree of unity and coherence in the developing consciousness of working people in the period of early industrialisation; the second concerns the extent to which plebeian radicalism posed a threat to the political order in Scotland. The longevity of these debates and the need to employ them as a reference point indicate the strength of the critical dialogue originally established by Edward Thompson. Some commentators are strongly polarised; the masses which are 'uninflammable' and 'remarkably unviolent' for Smout are Young's class-conscious working class, simultaneously revolutionary and nationalistic, 'made' in the context of industrialisation and a colonial relationship with England.[17] The difficulty here lies only partly with the patchy nature of evidence on underground radical movements. Even if copperplate minutebooks were available they would still be at the mercy of the historian's interpretation.

The nature of historical objectivity is, of course, an extremely complex and contentious area of historiography, and mercifully it is not intended to delve any deeper here. Suffice to say it is not the aim of this book to resolve the social order debate simply by presenting some piece of a 'definitive' new body of facts. Instead, in reassembling the pattern of relationships between Irish and Scottish radicals, we can begin to construct a fresh perspective for evaluating the divergent historical interpretations.

Scottish history has suffered as much as modern British and Irish history from isolationism; it is striking that one honourable exception to this, H. W. Meikle's pioneering *Scotland and the French Revolution*, originally published in 1912, was not reprinted until 1969, and then in New York. Yet, the nature of the revolutionary threat here can only be

grasped by placing Scottish radicalism in the context of the international
political crisis at the end of the eighteenth century. To take one important
instance, that of the underground United Scotsmen in the late 1790s,
Scottish democrats had historically much less success than their Irish
colleagues in constructing a mass-following, with their organisation experiencing chronic weaknesses as a result. Yet the significance of radicalism
in Scotland at this point cannot be inferred from its numerical presence
alone. For this was a determined insurrectionary minority actively linked
with like-minded brethren in Ireland and the rest of Britain. It was not
simply that the Irish provided 'inspiration'. Even more importantly, it
was through this medium that the Scots were brought into the orbit of
the wider European revolutionary movement, and presented with the
tantalising prospect of French assistance for their cause. When this linkage
is considered against the background of the major war being waged
between France and Britain, and continuous French invasion preparations,
the palpable unease felt by the traditional Scottish ruling élite of the
period does not seem flimsily based.[18] The external threat of the French
War, insurrectionary stirrings in Ireland, and the underground activities
of tenacious Scottish radicals were intertwining dimensions of the same
emergency, and their very interaction made the challenge to existing
mechanisms of political and military control a more dynamic one than is
often assumed.

However, this is not to understate the difficulties of the objective
context in which radicals in Scotland had to operate. Even the implications
of the Irish alliance were not uniformly positive for them. At times the
reality of 'international brotherhood' was to consist of squabbles between
the two sets of conspirators over whose claims for French military
assistance were the strongest. This was to be played out notably in the
Paris *émigré* colony. At home, Irish influence could also prove problematic, especially where sensitivity to specifically Scottish conditions was
lacking. This is most evident in the progress of the fledgeling Scottish
Friends of the People, but even in the late 1790s, not all Scottish democrats
were ready for the United Irishmen's subsequent brand of full-blown
revolutionary republicanism and covert organisation. The diversities, contradictions and shifts which were evident even within active movements
for political change of the period may immediately alert us to the dangers
of over-unitary interpretations of 'class consciousness'.

The structure of this book is dictated largely by the difficulties of studying
complex movements such as the United Irishmen and their counterparts
in Scotland. The relationship between the two sets of radicals was finely
balanced. Much of the analysis necessarily focuses on the impact of Irish

radicalism on the path of Scottish political development in the 1790s, but this was not the whole story. To illustrate the historic and reciprocal nature of links, Chapter One discusses the intellectual foundations of Irish radicalism, and the debt owed to Scotland through the cross-fertilisation of radical Presbyterianism with Enlightenment ideas taught at the Scottish universities. To begin to grasp the differing trajectories of radicalism in the two countries, Chapter Two adopts a comparative focus on economic and social developments in Ireland and Scotland, and examines their influence on the political process. Responses to the Revolution in France, and the subsequent development of popular movements for political reform are also presented as vital background to later events. More empirical issues are then tackled. Chapters Three and Four then trace the development of organisational links between the Society of United Irishmen and the Scottish Association of the Friends of the People in the years 1791–4, a period dominated by constitutionalist reform attempts. These are complemented by Chapters Five and Six, which focus on the relationships between the United Irishmen and the underground United Scotsmen, covering the uneven transition from reformism to revolutionary republicanism, culminating in the United Irishmen's alliance with France and the 1798 Rebellion in Ireland. Chapter Seven considers how the watershed of the Rebellion was received in Scotland, reviewing the responses of the press, government agencies and the radicals themselves. Finally, in Chapter Eight we examine the fate of political refugees from the Irish crisis, a group as diverse as the United Society's own composition, and in the Conclusion move on to trace the extent of their subsequent political involvement in Scotland up until the 'Radical War' of 1820.

NOTES

2. *The Leadbetter Papers*, p. 269, quoted in Key, *The Most Distressful Country*, p. 150; Lake Correspondence, 56, no. 175, National Library of Ireland.
2. For a vivid personal account, see the Diary of John Galt, a Methodist minister in Coleraine, D. 561, Public Record Office of Northern Ireland (PRONI).
3. Foster, *Modern Ireland*, p. 280.
4. 'Irish Rebels and English Radicals', pp. 78–85.
5. McDowell, *Ireland in the Age of Imperialism*, pp. 489, 598, 603.
6. Thomis and Holt, *Threats of Revolution in Britain*.
7. Goodwin, *Friends of Liberty*, pp. 30–1. For Marianne Elliott's work, see 'The "Despard Conspiracy" Reconsidered'; 'The Origins and Transformation of Early Irish Republicanism'; 'Irish Republicanism in England'; *Partners in Revolution.*; *Wolfe Tone*; and 'Ireland in the French Revolution'.
8. Elliott, *Partners in Revolution*, p. xiii. This is typical of a broader tendency developing in Irish historiography, which focuses on Ireland's role as an arena for the ambitions of larger powers. Modern treatments of the Williamite campaigns 1689–1691 are notable for this.

9. For a good example, see Smyth, *The Men of no Property*, p. 80.
10. Some theses hold interesting material. See Brims, 'The Scottish Democratic Movement'; Burns, 'Industrial Labour and Radical Movements'. Brims has also recently produced a short, but very useful overview which draws on his thesis, 'Scottish Radicalism and the United Irishmen'. Also important are Meikle, *Scotland and the French Revolution*; W. Ferguson, *Scotland: 1689 to the Present*; and Logue, *Popular Disturbances in Scotland*.
11. Wells, *Insurrection*.
12. Christie, *Stress and Stability*, p. 9.
13. McFarland, *Protestants First*.
14. Cassirer, 'The Irish Influence on the Liberal Movement', p. 570; Thompson, *The Making of the English Working Class*, pp. 469–85.
15. Wells, *Insurrection*, pp. 25–6.
16. See Dickson, Keogh and Whelan (eds), *The United Irishmen*.
17. Smout, *A History of the Scottish People*, p. 417; Young, *The Rousing of the Scottish Working Class, passim.*
18. Clarke and Dickson, 'The Making of a Class Society', pp. 168–77.

ACKNOWLEDGEMENTS

I would like to thank John Brims, Marianne Elliott and Graham Walker for their advice. I am also indebted to Jim Whiston, Ron, Marie, Maud and Keanu for uncritical support; and to my department for its financial assistance during the writing of this book. Thanks are due to the staff at Edinburgh University Library Special Collections, the Scottish Record Office, the Public Records Office Northern Ireland and the National Archives, Ireland; also to Andrew Reith of the Scottish Grand Lodge Library, Edinburgh. A final thanks should go to Rita Winter and the staff at Edinburgh University Press.

I

Irish Radicals and the 'Scotch Genius'

I am the son of . . . a Protestant dissenting minister, in the town of Belfast; the friend and associate of good, I may say, great men: of Bruce, of Duchal, and of Hutcheson.

William Drennan, leading publicist of the United Irishmen,
Fugitive Pieces in Verse and Prose, pp. 192–3

There existed in the eighteenth century an 'ideological community' between Scots and Presbyterians in the north of Ireland, a common ground of ideas and assumptions, firmly anchored in religious practice, education, culture and politics. Paralleling the relationship between Irish Catholicism and pre-revolutionary France, this demonstrated for contemporary observers the distinctiveness of the province of Ulster and the gulf between the worlds of the Plantation and 'Irish Ireland'. Yet, in hindsight, it was the Scottish connection which formed an important precondition for the formation and progress of the Society of United Irishmen, the very body which from the 1790s sought to bind Irishmen – regardless of religious confession – in a 'brotherhood of affection' towards a national and ultimately revolutionary movement.

The cultural and ideological interchange between Scotland and Ireland has received conscientiously thorough attention in ecclesiastical history, but its wider political implications have until recently been considered in much less detail.[1] It is certainly difficult to disentangle the various components which combined to shape Ireland's political crisis in the eighteenth century. The Society of United Irishmen, the main engine of that crisis, was itself a heterogenous body, 'a conspiracy operating at many levels'.[2] It comprised a tense alliance between various elements: the Presbyterians, a cohesive and intellectually vigorous community, concentrated in the north-eastern counties; a long-standing tradition of popular urban politics, centred on Dublin; Roman Catholic secret societies, also well grounded in the forms of agrarian protest; and finally, a much smaller number of Episcopalian renegades, such as Theobald Wolfe Tone and Lord Edward Fitzgerald, who attempted to give the movement leadership at critical stages.

The influence of the Scottish connection can be traced most strongly in the first element in this complex and protean picture. First, from the seventeenth century onwards came the importation of a radical brand of Presbyterianism in which religious and political dissent were fundamentally entwined. Prominently rooted in the Covenanting tradition, this reached its highest expression in the Covenanters' offshoot in Ulster, the Reformed Presbyterians. This denomination refused even to acknowledge the legitimacy of civil government as it abjured the sovereignty of Christ and were to be the most militant of those Presbyterians involved in the 1798 Rebellion.[3] Secondly and more importantly, the education of Ulster Presbyterians at Scottish universities also brought them into contact with the Enlightenment ideas which were beginning to flourish there from the 1720s, particularly under the tutelage of Professor Francis Hutcheson at Glasgow. The outcome was a refinement of the earlier Presbyterian ideas and their fusion with the broad current of European rationalism. This was voiced initially in the radical social values of New Light Presbyterianism, but later found expression in the United Irishmen's emphasis on religious tolerance and the right of resistance to tyrannical regimes. As we shall see, this 'fusion' contained its own problems and contradictions.

Scotland's earliest contribution to Irish radicalism lay in the linkage of the traditional stand for 'Christ's Crown and Covenant' with advanced European thought. However, the cultural transmission of radical Presbyterian ideas did not take place in a vacuum, nor was this a one-way process. The receptiveness of Ulster Presbyterians to these ideas can only be understood in accordance with their 'separateness' as a distinct community excluded from full social and political participation; their presence at the Scottish universities was precisely due to their effective disbarment from the Episcopalian Trinity College by the imposition of Religious Tests. Moreover, the flow of ideas from Scotland was met by those from indigenous Irish theorists such as Molesworth and Molyneux. Their development of the English 'Commonwealthman' or 'Real Whig' tradition of radical political thought had itself an important influence on teaching in the Scottish universities.[4] Above all, radical, enlightened dissent was valued not for its ideological purity, it existed instead to be used by people in real situations to highlight and combat perceived economic and political grievances. In this way the Scottish ideological legacy became welded to the Irish situation, and was shaped accordingly. In turn, Irish radicalism in terms of personnel, strategies and example was ultimately to have an important impact on the progress of its sister movement in Scotland.

We must now try to anchor the rather imprecise and troublesome idea of a Scottish 'legacy' or 'influence' on firmer empirical ground. This can be done by considering the emergence of accessible channels of communication, and how these functioned in practice. Of great importance here was the role played by university education, an influence acknowledged in existing literature, but seldom carefully analysed or explained.[5]

THE MECHANICS OF THE 'IDEOLOGICAL COMMUNITY'

A strong material basis existed for cultural contacts between Scotland and the north of Ireland, and contributed towards their vitality. Given the distance of barely 20 miles which separates the Antrim coast from Wigtownshire, the antiquity and intensity of communication is hardly surprising. This predated the formal Ulster Plantation in the reign of James VI. Indeed, the success of the planting may have rested less on official design than on earlier patterns of migration and settlement in Antrim and Down.[6] Scots, nevertheless, benefited amply from the distribution of Crown land grants, settling in strength on the north and east coasts of the province and the river valleys of Main, Lower Bann, Foyle and Erne.[7] Mercantile links had also been well established in the early seventeenth century, with Scottish merchants taking a leading role in the trade and municipal corporations of Ulster ports.

Building on this early foundation, material links strengthened in the next century, against the background of demographic growth and economic expansion in both countries. An advance was evident on three fronts: communications, trade and migration.

Communications in this context basically involved the cross-channel sea route between Donaghadee and Portpatrick; a service had been established in 1662 by Robert Main of Edinburgh, who had been granted a Commission for the purpose.[8] Already by 1695, a weekly service was being run by a privately owned, subsidised company, and considerable improvements followed in the next century, with daily services advertised in the *Belfast Newsletter* in the 1780s.[9] Finally, in July 1791, the Post Office further regularised the route by entering into a contract with a Donaghadee company headed by the Marquis of Downshire to run a daily mail service.[10]

This incremental improvement in the transport infrastructure reflected the growth of commerce between Scotland and Ulster. The relation between transport and trade here was a reciprocal one. The proximity of the two countries and their separation by sea itself stimulated commerce by the significant cost advantage it offered.[11] This, combined with the growing complementarity in Irish and Scottish production, sympathetic commercial legislation, and the general growth of trade within the territories of the nascent British Empire, assisted Scottish–Irish business relationships to flourish.[12]

A tangible product of increasing interaction between the two economies was, as Walker suggests, one of labour migration.[13] Again, this was a reciprocal process. Around 1789, for example, the future United Irish leader Henry Joy McCracken travelled to Scotland to engage calico printers and other mechanics for his father's firm.[14] The importation of Ulster weavers and bleachers into the Scottish linen industry – to give instruction to the native labour force – was also underway in the late eighteenth century. These were probably for the most part Protestants, prompted by the declining livelihoods offered by the north-eastern linen trade in the face of increased mechanisation in the 1790s.[15] They joined the earlier tradition of, initially seasonal, agricultural migration to Scotland in the 1790s by both Protestants and Catholics.[16]

Besides these plebeian migrants, who were to have their own role in the cross-fertilisation of Irish and Scottish radicalism from the end of the century onwards, a further group should be introduced. These were students, usually Presbyterians, and mostly the sons of Ulster tenant farmers or Presbyterian ministers, who received their education at the universities of Glasgow and Edinburgh.[17] They proved an effective conduit for the transmission of Enlightenment thought into Ireland, but we can begin by simply grasping the scale of their migration.

This is easiest in the case of Glasgow, the destination for most Ulster students. Matriculation albums here list all Irish students, with their counties of birth, although they understate the actual number of students in attendance, since not all students were required to go through the matriculation process. But the broad contours are still evident.[18] From Table 1.1, Bishop suggests that 'Irish' students over the years 1690–1809 numbered 1,846, 16.6 per cent of the total matriculating.[19] Where place of birth was indicated, these were largely from the four counties of Ulster where Presbyterians had predominantly settled. Indeed, despite periodic fluctuations, owing partly to temporary crises in agriculture, these students never accounted for less than 10 per cent of the total matriculating student body in any decade.[20]

For Edinburgh, evidence is very imperfect, as the university's matriculation albums do not yield the wealth of data of their Glasgow counterparts. Horn suggests that a great number of medical students were Irishmen who had studied elsewhere before coming to Edinburgh to complete a further

TABLE 1.1: Irish Students Matriculating at the University of Glasgow, 1690–1809.

Year	No. of Irish	Total no. of students	Irish as % of total
1690–1719	466	2,654	17.5
1720–49	306	2,056	14.9
1750–79	551	2,623	21.0
1780–1809	523	3,989	13.0
TOTAL	1,846	11,322	16.6 (average)

year of study.[21] Certainly the university's catalogue indicates 293 graduates from the whole of Ireland, 25 per cent of the total of Edinburgh MD graduates from 1740 to 1800.[22] Information is lacking for other courses, but the MD figures themselves suggest a significant Irish student population.[23]

Why did Irish students come to the Scottish universities?[24] As in most forms of migration, push and pull factors were involved. Presbyterians were, of course, excluded in practice from their nearest local university, Trinity College in Dublin. Here the Oath of Allegiance was required for matriculation and, more decisively, the Oath of Supremacy for graduation. Attendance at Divine Service was also expected, and the institution was marked generally by an Anglican ethos, and a rather languid intellectual climate, at least until the 1790s.[25]

More positively, Scottish universities offered distinct advantages in terms of accessibility and cost. This was particularly true in the case of Glasgow, where the fees for a complete course were estimated at half the cost of those at Edinburgh.[26] Both compared favourably with the expense of courses at the continental universities of Utrecht and Leyden, which were the only other viable educational alternatives for Presbyterians.[27]

Besides these practical features, parents were also attracted by the Scottish universities' rising academic status, and by their growing reputation for dispensing a progressive and above all useful education.[28] Their development reflected a responsiveness to the quickening of intellectual life in Scotland and beyond in the course of the eighteenth century. It was also the product of internal reforms beginning in Edinburgh in 1708 and in Glasgow some twenty years later. Most notable here was the shift away from 'regenting', a system based on individual tutorials, and its replacement by a professorial system of instruction by means of lectures.[29] While its success was uneven and depended on the inclinations and ability of individual professors, the shift had the effect of stimulating specialised, quality scholarship, a broader modernised curriculum and more effective teaching methods. The universities thus began to offer increasingly attractive subject areas: in Glasgow's case the broad-based Arts degree and Divinity; and in Edinburgh's, medicine. Aware of the Ulster Presbyterian market, by the 1790s the former was advertising its coming sessions in the United Irishmen's own mouthpiece, the *Northern Star*.[30]

To sum up, a Scottish university education was economical, progressive and in tune with Presbyterian sensibilities. Not surprisingly, a family tradition of attendance was to develop, sometimes extending to three generations. By the middle of the eighteenth century the effect of student contacts, taken together with the improved transport and commercial network, had firmly established the potential for sustained cultural interaction between Presbyterian society in the north of Ireland and Lowland Scotland. This was cemented by an increasing web of kinship and friendship ties which ensured that the 'Scotch–Irish' – or 'Scoto–Hiberni' as they were known in the graceful terminology of Glasgow University – were to form an identifiable community in the growing urban centres of Scotland as the century progressed.

EARLY INTELLECTUAL PRECEDENTS

While the most formative and direct development of Scotland's intellectual impact on Irish radicalism took place in Scottish universities from the 1720s onwards, the influence of these institutions was not an independent one. Instead, it reinforced an earlier pattern of complex reciprocal contact.

This had three interlinking components. The first was the original importation of Scottish Presbyterianism, and with it the Covenanting tradition, into Ulster. The second was the influence of Irish Episcopalian thought in the Scottish universities at the beginning of the eighteenth century. The final component was the contribution of Scottish university teaching to the development of 'New Light' Presbyterianism in Ulster in the century's opening decades.

THE COVENANTERS: 'COMING HOME TO GOD'

Irish church history is a fiercely partisan field of study. This is as true for academic contributions from both Presbyterian and Episcopalian camps, as it is for more popular accounts such as the Revd Hamilton's entertaining and splenetic *History of the Irish Presbyterian Church*, written at the height of the first Home Rule crisis. Yet there is agreement on one key point – namely the role of Scotland in developing Presbyterian forms of worship and church government in Ulster. As Hamilton quaintly expresses it, 'the Church of Scotland proved herself a nursing mother to the infant organisation'.[31] For a considerable period this was to result in Irish Presbyterianism's dependence on Scotland for both theological inspiration and for personnel, and its status as a self-governing offshoot of the Scottish national church.[32]

There was little preordained in this situation. Brooke indicates that the Scottish church at the time of the Plantation was, in fact, Episcopal rather than Presbyterian. The situation at the opening of the seventeenth century was complex and fluid.[33] Nevertheless, Presbyterian ideas were introduced informally by individuals such as Robert Brice, who became minister of Broadisland in 1613.[34]

In terms of formal organisation and the systematic exposition of doctrine, the establishment of Presbyterianism in Ulster owed more to the Scottish Covenanters and the upheavals of the Civil War period in the 1640s. The first National Covenant of 1638, signed in Edinburgh, represented an alliance between the Scottish nobility and Scottish military forces to overthrow the episcopacy.[35] It was also received with widespread enthusiasm as 'Scotland's coming home to God', an act of national rededication. Its scope was extended in the Second Solemn League and Covenant of 1643. By this treaty, the English parliament, in return for Scottish military assistance against Charles I, agreed to establish religious uniformity along the lines of Scottish Presbyterianism.

It is against this background of rising 'internationalist' ambitions that the Covenanters' concern for the spiritual and material welfare of Protestants in Ulster can be set. A Catholic rebellion had broken out in Ireland in 1641, which was felt to constitute a threat to Scotland's own security, as well as to the thousands of Scottish colonists settled there. The Scots army which landed at Carrickfergus in February 1642 to quell the rising was accompanied by regimental chaplains who proceeded to establish the basic framework of Presbyterianism.[36] Some ministers stayed on to take up Irish charges, and by June the first formal presbytery had been established. The Scriptural text preached on the occasion, Psalm 51, was eloquent on the privileged relationship with God in which Presbyterians saw themselves: 'Do good in Thy good pleasure unto Zion; build Thou the walls of Jerusalem'. Indeed this 'apartness' as 'a people alone among nations', and covenanted to God, was to remain a prominent theme of Presbyterian doctrine into the eighteenth century and beyond.[37]

The key point to take from this excursion into ecclesiastical history, besides the intensity of links between the two countries, is that from its earliest days Presbyterianism in Ulster was intertwined with ideas of the Covenanting movement. This in turn meant exposure to a certain contractual cast of thought stemming from the Covenanters' concern to define the relationships and obligations which bound parties together.[38]

The idea of a special 'covenanted' or contractual relationship between God and man had a long history in Christian theology. In the late sixteenth century Calvinist theologians such as George Buchanan accorded it a special place, resulting in the development of a specific 'federal' theology. For later theologians of this type, the Scottish Covenants were not strictly contracts, as this would imply that Free Will had ousted Predestination, but at the popular level the Covenant-contract link was highly probable.[39]

This was to find secular resonance, for example, in the Whig philosopher Locke's concept of a contract between ruler and ruled to preserve liberty and property, and eventually in eighteenth-century claims for parliamentary sovereignty and a balanced constitution, although, as Williamson argues, the Covenanting period itself produced highly developed spiritual politics, with theories of government emerging which linked Calvinism to a European tradition of 'civic humanism'.[40]

In Ulster, enthusiasm for the Covenants, with all their implications for constitutional thought, almost outstripped that in their country of origin. Ministers came from Scotland in April 1644 to administer the Second Covenant all over Ulster, 'where it was taken in all places in great affection'.[41] This enthusiasm was tested in the difficult years of state persecution which followed the Restoration.

This was a remarkable and formative period for Presbyterians, witnessed not only in their achievement in organising a unified Dissenting church, but also in shaping their future political culture towards a strong antipathy for state authority. Sixty-one out of 68 ministers in the Province were turned out of their parishes for their refusal to conform to the Episcopalian system, and there were even official suggestions that the Presbyterian population should be deported from Ulster to Tipperary.[42]

Indeed, this was probably the high point of unity for Presbyterianism in Ireland. Although the Revolutionary Settlement of 1689–90 tempered the active persecution, Presbyterians continued to suffer serious political disabilities, barred from public office, for example, by the statute of 1704 'To Prevent the Further Growth of Popery'. Resistance was now seriously fragmented, and Ulster in particular began to show increasing sensitivity to Scottish doctrinal disputes and schisms.[43]

The most trenchant opposition to the authority of the state was posed by the Reformed Presbyterian denomination. Again a Scottish import and part of the Covenanting tradition, this group provided one of the most important direct links into the radical Presbyterianism of the United Irishmen's Rebellion.[44] They derived from those Scottish Presbyterians who refused to accept the Revolution Settlement since it denied the Covenants' obligation 'to endeavour the extirpation of Popery and Prelacy'. Contact was quickly made with like-minded brethren in Ulster and close patronage of the fledgeling Ulster movement developed in the 1740s.[45]

According to their world view, civil government and the magistracy were in essence sinful as they had broken faith with the the Covenants. Consequently, these new Covenanters refused to take the Oath of Allegiance and adopted generally anti-authoritarian positions, thus building on the emphasis on civil as well as religious liberty expressed within the Covenants. Numerically weak – there were only twenty congregations in existence by 1800 – their influence in the progress of the Volunteer movement in the 1780s and the United Irishmen in the 1790s belied this.

The former movement was indeed a practical outgrowth of the contractual principle of a people's right to bear arms in defence of their liberties. It also followed the Covenanting tradition of 'public bands', self-created assemblies in opposition to central authority.[46] As such, it received enthusiastic support from some Reformed Presbyterian ministers and congregations. The Volunteers company at Knockbracken, for example, had the local minister William Stavely as its captain.[47]

Typical of Protestantism of the day, the Reformed Presbyterians were not a monolithic sect, and more conservative elements became alarmed at the course of political events in the 1790s. Illustrating their continued dependence as a Scottish satellite, Stavely was dispatched to Girvan to consult with the Scottish Reformed Presbytery to obtain instruction for the Irish church's future direction. The result was the issue of a 'Seasonable and Necessary Information' declaration which disclaimed any connection with 'any attempts to prejudice the peace of civil society'.[48]

Despite this, the church's members gave active support to the United Irishmen, although their opposition to secular oaths obstructed actual membership. As a result, ministers and probationers came under official suspicion and four were forced to flee to America. Stavely, who had been most deeply involved, was arrested and held on a prison ship at Belfast.[49] At least two members were executed, and a final enduring image of the doggedness of the Covenanting principle of dissent was the scene at the scaffold of Daniel English. The assembled crowd sang Psalm 119, the longest in the Psalter, with 175 verses:

> Blessed are they that undefiled'
> And straight are in the way;
> Who in the Lord's most holy law,
> Do walk and do not stray

THE 'REAL WHIGS'

An intellectual cross-current to the influence of Scottish Presbyterianism in Ulster also developed in the first half of the eighteenth century. This came with the spread of liberal ideas – on this occasion from Ireland *to* Scotland. The key figures here were the Irish Episcopal thinkers Robert

Molesworth and Bishop George Berkeley. The work of both was actively read in Scotland, although their ideas were also disseminated by young Presbyterians coming to Scotland for education.[50]

These so-called 'Real Whigs' were not original thinkers, but were linked to the English political tradition of Harrington and Locke, which preached the doctrine of 'natural rights': that is the common obligations of both ruler and ruled to obey the law of nature and the laws established in society.[51] Their ideas were also shaped by Irish conditions and extended to anti-mercantilism and claims for national self-determination.

Molesworth, politically active during the Glorious Revolution period and beyond, was, in Robbins's estimation, the most influential of the Liberal Whigs.[52] His abiding concern was to obtain a greater liberty of speech and religion, thus, he believed, securing the gains of the Revolutionary settlement and building on its constitutional reforms. He was also concerned with the threat of arbitrary government, stating that kings and ministers must be called to account by the constant vigilance of their people. Indeed, he maintained that to expel 'a tyrant or an idiot' could never be treason, and that motive determined whether a rebellion was treasonable or lawful.[53]

In contrast, the writings of Berkeley had a more authoritarian emphasis, stressing in works like *Passive Obedience* the role of the Established Church as a cement of the body politic.[54] Yet in practice he advocated similarly innovative economic reforms as Molesworth. In *The Querist* periodical, for example, he suggested that English policy towards Ireland should be modified to mutual advantage, with money, taxing and banking reforms to stimulate commerce. He also favoured an extension of education and a measure of toleration towards Roman Catholics.[55]

Both men had Scottish admirers who drew their own parallels for the 'Scotch Case'. Berkeley had various prominent correspondents in Scotland until his death in 1757: Dr William Wishart, Principal of Edinburgh University; the philosopher and theologian Robert Wallace; and the mathematician Colin McLaurin. Molesworth also had his Scottish disciples, such as George Turnbull at Aberdeen, as well as more indirect links at the Scottish universities. For despite his own Episcopalianism, he encouraged Irish Presbyterians – a constituency of course receptive to his libertarian ideas – to meet at his country house outside Dublin. Prominent among his circle were James Arbuckle, John Smith and Samuel Boyes. When these men left to attend Glasgow University in the 1710s Molesworth remained their 'mentor and patron', and they turned to him in a struggle against the autocratic management of the university, publishing *The Case of the Students* with a preface dedicated to him.[56]

THE 'NEW LIGHT'

The third historical component in the development of intellectual links between Scotland and Ireland is witnessed in the development of 'New Light' or 'Non-Subscribing' Presbyterianism in Ulster.

The term was first used in the north in the 1640s, but came into wider usage in the early eighteenth century to denote a belief in the centrality of personal conviction and individual conscience in religion, over adherence to man-made Confessions of Faith.[57] The main adherants of this view were the Belfast Society, a clerical discussion society founded in 1705. Their opponents were the upholders of orthodoxy in the Synod of Ulster, who had introduced subscription to the Westminster Confession as a requirement for ministers. Antagonism ultimately resulted in the 'Non-Subscription Controversy' of 1720–6 when amidst a war of words and pamphlets, the 'New Light' Presbytery of Antrim eventually separated itself from the predominantly orthodox Synod.

This was not merely an arcane theological dispute. The 'New Light' emphasis on subjective belief as the test of religious conviction was part of a broader liberalising current in European Protestantism. It drew also on the anti-authoritarianism of earlier Ulster Presbyterian thought, for its corollary was an attack on the church itself as a corporate institution, divinely ordained to interpret Scripture. In short, the 'New Light' Presbyterians have been cast as 'the most radical thinkers of eighteenth-century dissent'.[58]

The Scottish connection here may not be immediately apparent. On the contrary, Brooke suggests that given the continuing intellectual dependence of Ulster Presbyterians on Scotland, the lack of involvement is surprising.[59] In fact, it is necessary here to separate the theological genesis of the movement from its future course of development, and indeed from the personnel involved in it.

The early Non-Subscribers seem to have drawn, initially at least, on the theological literature of *English* Presbyterianism. As Bullock and Drummond note, the lack of a similar literature – a prominent exception to Scotland's 'Age of Achievement' – may reflect precisely the requirement imposed on otherwise progressive divines to subscribe to the various Confessions of Faith.[60] They could not thus publicly state their doubts without being suspected of unorthodoxy in Christian doctrine. Indeed, Scottish subscriptions were received from the synods of Ayr and Glasgow to fund the opposition to the 'New Light' position in Belfast.[61]

Nevertheless, the Scottish connection was vital to sustaining the movement in two key respects. First, a common link between the first wave of the Non-Subscribers was their Scottish education. Of the members of the Belfast Society, James Kirkpatrick, James Abernethy and Samuel Haliday were educated at Glasgow University; James Henderson, Alexander Brown, Andrew Colville, Thomas Orr, and, after his first graduation, Abernethy attended Edinburgh.[62] It is likely that it was here that they gained their first systematic exposure to English theology, as well as to the new ideas on science, philosophy and literature from England and the Continent. Certainly the influence of the anti-Trinitarian theologian Dr Samuel Clark, whose views had already caused controversy in England, were felt to be significant at Edinburgh.[63] Clark was also reputed to have influenced John Simson, Professor of Divinity at Glasgow from 1708 to 1729.[64]

Secondly, the University of Glasgow became important in the transmission of New Light ideas to a second generation of Ulster ministers. Or, as their orthodox opponents insisted, 'professors poisoning the fountainhead, the stream of the ministry'.[65] Central at this stage was the teaching of Professor Simson, himself a fellow student of Kirkpatrick and Abernethy at Glasgow, with whom he still corresponded.

Drawing on both Locke and Clark, Simson was a synthesiser rather than an originator of ideas. He nevertheless fell into repeated conflict with the church authorities over his 'rationalism' which it was felt challenged traditional doctrines of the Trinity and of Original Sin. As an advocate of the new 'enlightened' approach, which emphasised an empirically based spirit of enquiry, he attempted to teach students to use their powers of reasoning to consider how best to expound and defend these truths of Faith.[66]

The 'Simson Case' culminated in a lengthy enquiry and his eventual suspension from duties by the General Assembly of the Kirk, illustrating not only the penetration of new ideas into Scotland but also the barriers which they still encountered. Simson himself seems an evasive, vacillating figure, whose views – expressed in dubious scholastic Latin – were originally communicated with less than perfect clarity, and subsequently ineptly defended. Significantly, a further contribution to his downfall was his opponents' alarm over his contact with the founders of the Ulster Non-Subscribing tendency, and over the fact that its younger ministers and probationers had studied under him.[67] The danger seemed clear, namely that the Scottish universities would produce, 'men . . . whose legal sentiments were in direct antagonism to the Gospel and whose drowsy tinklings lulled the flock to sleep'.[68]

FRANCIS HUTCHESON AND THE SCOTTISH UNIVERSITIES

The action of the General Assembly against Simson was ultimately futile in checking the spread of advanced liberal ideas into the classrooms nominally under its jurisdiction. The universities were never again to be in Trevor-Roper's words 'the unreformed seminaries of a fanatical clergy'.[69] Indeed, within five years, Calvinist orthodoxy was to find a much more formidable academic opponent than Simson, in terms of intellect, eloquence, and indeed strength of character.

This was Francis Hutcheson, Professor of Moral Philosophy at the University of Glasgow from 1729 to 1746. In Hutcheson's thought, the intellectual themes of Covenanting, Real Whiggery and the New Light were powerfully united. In him we find the most pivotal link between Enlightenment thought at the Scottish universities and the tradition of Presbyterian Libertarianism which was to flourish in the Society of United Irishmen.

However tempting, this is not to suggest, with Carlyle, that 'history is but biography writ large'. Hutcheson's ultimate achievement in the dissemination of his ideas rested on complex antecedent conditions, such as the existence of accessible cultural channels, and intellectual cross-fertilisation between Ulster and Scotland from the seventeenth century onwards. By the time Hutcheson assumed his professorship, a pattern of 'spiritual succession' was already emerging, or, as sociologists would term it, more precisely 'generational socialisation'. This was a linear process, which we have already met in the example of John Simson, whereby one generation of thinkers and teachers transmitted their ideas to the next. From this second generation were drawn the academics, ministers and teachers who would in turn be influential as educators and theorists.

Accordingly, the large interval of time between Hutcheson's death in 1746 and the United Irishmen's rise in the 1790s is not unduly problematic. The power and clarity of Hutcheson's thought, the effectiveness of his teaching methods and even his progressive role in university administration ensured his legacy considerable longevity as part of the chain of influence. Above all, he helped set the broad context of assumptions and problematics which were part of the intellectual armoury of the educated Ulster Presbyterian.

LIFE

Hutcheson's life, thirty years spent in Ireland and twenty-two in Scotland, displayed in microcosm the material and cultural interaction between the two countries and the ties of kinship which bound them.[70] Yet he remained an Ulsterman at heart, considering Belfast superior to either Glasgow or Edinburgh, and conducting a constant correspondence to Belfast friends like Thomas Drennan – father of the United Irishman William Drennan – which is still lively and entertaining today.[71]

His grandfather was an Ayrshire man who had come to Ulster in the seventeenth century as a Presbyterian minister. His father John Hutcheson was also a minister and became a stalwart of orthodoxy in the Non-Subscribing Controversy. Francis was born in Armagh in 1694 and educated at a dissenting academy in Killyleagh, which he left for Glasgow University in 1710 or 1711, to pursue courses in Arts and Divinity – the latter under Professor Simson.

On graduation he returned to Ulster and followed a familiar clerical career route, becoming a probationer in his father's parish of Downpatrick. Straight from university, his high-flown theology left the congregation unimpressed, and although he was called to the parish of Magherally, he decided instead to set up a teaching academy in Dublin. Here he made contact with friends who were members of Molesworth's 'Classical' Whig circle, as well as with ex-classmates from Glasgow of a similar liberal Presbyterian persuasion as himself.[72]

It was also at this point that Hutcheson began to establish his literary reputation with *An Inquiry into the Origin of our Ideas of Beauty and Virtue*, published in 1725. This reputation, plus perhaps the hope that he would bring with him Irish students, prompted his election to the Professorship of Moral Philosophy at Glasgow University in December 1729, after a gruelling selection procedure. Despite the earlier failure of his pulpit powers, he swiftly became the most popular and distinguished professor of his day. His lectures were eventually edited in 1742 for *A Short Introduction to Moral Philosophy*. He died suddenly in Dublin in the Summer of 1746.

IDEAS

The bare facts of Hutcheson's life are insufficient to understand his inspiration across generations. History has not been unequivocally kind to him. Certainly, he has been widely hailed as the 'father of the Scottish Enlightenment', and accorded a seminal influence on Hume's ethics and epistemology, and on Smith's moral, legal and economic theories.[73] Yet, his originality as a philosopher was for a long period widely questioned. As his biographer Scott comments, 'he was a preacher, not a system builder'.[74] Elsewhere, with more asperity, he has been dismissed as 'basically a follower of Shaftsbury, but later eventually incorporating ideas from elsewhere', his originality reduced to a series of 'trifling innovations'.[75]

From the 1970s there has been something of a rediscovery of his pioneering role, but this has most commonly viewed Hutcheson exclusively as a moral philosopher, concentrating on his theory of 'moral sense' and his aesthetics.[76] Less attention has been paid to the political philosophy which flowed from his ethical doctrines. A very valuable exception is a body of research which traces the dissemination of Hutcheson's ideas by Scottish migrants to America, such as the Pennsylvania educator Francis Alison. Here it is argued that Hutcheson's philosophy played an active role in shaping the political theories of the American Revolution, as witnessed in the Presbyterian Libertarianism of the American Constitution.[77]

The evolution of Hutcheson's thought is revealing in itself. A formative influence came from his roots in the Covenanting Presbyterian tradition of Scotland and Ulster. For although he abandoned Calvinist orthodoxy, allowing only a restricted role to original sin and the innate degradation of man, his work retained a firm theological grounding. Forbes noted that implicit in Hutcheson's philosophy is the belief that an omnipresent and good God governs the world, and that 'the Deity is the original independent Being, compleat in all possible perfection . . .'.[78] More than this, his emphasis on personal conviction over dogma and on the contractual nature of the relationship between ruler and ruled reflected the older libertarian tendency of Presbyterian thought, and this may well have increased the receptiveness of the Ulster student audience to his message.

This radicalism in the politics of Hutcheson is indeed marked, and it is a radicalism which outstrips that of his academic successors such as Smith. As Robbins notes, the preface to his *Short Introduction* stated that it was written not for the learned, but 'for those anxious to study that way of life right reason required'. Hence 'the application of his theories to particular political and social problems was extraordinarily clear and explicit'.[79]

Hutcheson's key philosophical assumptions were the reasonable social and altruistic nature of man, and the existence of a natural law to which the laws of the state must bend and in which all free men were informed by their 'moral sense'. This sense can achieve the balance between liberty and necessity, and harmonious personal and general good. In this way he challenges Aristotle's view that some men were naturally slaves, and Hobbes's belief in the innate self-interested character of human action.

From this flowed two of Hutcheson's most important convictions, which were of vital relevance both to the American colonists and later to Irish radicals. These were the right of resistance to tyranny, and the unalienable right of freedom of opinion and religious tolerance.

When he came to establish the conditions for political rebellion, he carried the conception of a contract between ruler and ruled a stage beyond Locke. For Hutcheson, a contract was the normal form in which the political obligations of government were founded. This trust was broken if the potential 'utility' of civil society was not realised, 'utility' being the main criterion of government. If this were to occur, if in other words a government was no longer serving the general good, then its right to rule would lie forfeit. If government is oppressive, suggested Hutcheson, as in the case of poorly governed colonies, then civil war may be preferable to continued subjection. The 'moral sense' of educated men would, he believed, determine whether or not revolutionary action was necessary. Accordingly, Hutcheson was also warmly enthusiastic on the rights of citizens to bear arms, and on the tradition of militias for the maintenance of civil liberty. This position, as we shall see, was echoed in Ireland in the 1780s in the development of the Volunteer movement.

Hutcheson's endorsement of religious toleration also followed his belief in the centrality of 'natural liberty', or the right of doing everything that does not contravene the rights of others. Liberty was essential for human happiness and thus a wide measure of freedom should be allowed to religious belief and worship. Cautious in the wake of Simson's downfall, he still found space in his philosophical work to condemn the 'warm zealots of both sides' who represented all schemes of religion opposite to their own 'as opposed also to all goodness'.[80]

EDUCATIONALIST AND REFORMER

The successful transmission of Hutcheson's ideas was thus aided by their coherence and relevance to the problems of his day. This process also reflected the increased availability of his writings. The *Short Introduction* went into five editions after his death and was widely used as a teaching text in Britain and America.

A decisive role was also played by Hutcheson personally through the excellence of his teaching, his books being reputedly pale imitations of his lectures. This accorded with his conception of the pedagogic role. His aim, suggests his biographer, was not to give his students a system of morality which would bear the spotlight of logical scrutiny, but rather to saturate them with a code of ethics by which they could live or, if need be, die. In his own words, he aimed at 'touching the heart' and raising an enthusiasm for the cause of virtue.[81]

The surfeit of testimonials from former students, famous and otherwise, is eloquent as to his great physical presence, the conviction and power of his lectures, and above all on lasting influence on their lives. For Adam Smith he was 'the never to be forgotten Hutcheson'. Commending his 'manly zeal for promoting Civil and religious Liberty', his colleague William Leechman stated that his students 'panted to be like him'.[82] Even those students who were not won over admired him. Ramsay of Ochtertyre recalled that years after Hutcheson's death he had heard thoroughly orthodox ministers speaking of their old professor with enthusiastic veneration.[83]

It is difficult to grasp this impact, glancing at the stolid Hanoverian features in Hutcheson's portrait by Allan Ramsay the Younger, which still hangs at Glasgow University. A more vivid picture of the professor at work is given by Alexander 'Jupiter' Carlyle, the arch Moderate cleric who studied under Hutcheson at the height of his fame in the 1740s:

> He was a good-looking man of an engaging countenance. He delivered his lectures without notes, walking backwards and forwards in the area of his room. As his elocution was good, his voice and manner was pleasing. He raised the attention of his hearers at all times; and where a subject led him to explain and enforce the moral virtues and duties, he displayed a fervent and persuasive eloquence which was irresistible.[84]

His presence in the classroom was reinforced by a pastoral concern, especially for his Irish students, which reminds us that he remained an ordained Presbyterian minister. Financial difficulties were common for these students, and far from the eyes of their parents, they had an unenviable reputation for 'high spirits'.[85] Despite his temporary mortification at their 'vanity and foppery' and 'softness and sauntering', he continued to act as their friend and counsellor, and even – when the funds entrusted to him by their parents ran out – their personal financier.[86]

Hutcheson's influence, of course, spread beyond the cohort of students actually taught by him. In the most immediate sense, many of these students were to become Ulster's ministers and schoolmasters. As such, they were to be vital in providing leadership to the wider Presbyterian community.[87] More generally, Hutcheson's active role in university politics of the 1730s and 1740s also helped underpin a further process of spiritual succession, which allowed advanced liberal ideas to be communicated by university teachers to a new generation of Ulster, and native Scots, students.

Hutcheson was indeed vividly aware that the university was in a state of transition, and he attempted successfully to maintain the momentum of modernisation in the many committees on which he served, championing 'unmuzzled philosophy' against the religious zealots. At a practical level, this commitment to modernisation was evident in the encouragement he offered to the Foulis brothers – one a former student – to set up business as printers to the university.[88] This printing house subsequently had an important role in disseminating the works of the canon of radical political and religious thought, including Hutcheson's own works.

Even more decisive was the need to get 'sound' men into university positions. This was most evident in his campaign to the election of William Leechman as Professor of Divinity in 1743, against more orthodox, old school candidates. A similar struggle on which, Hutcheson believed, the very soul of the College depended was to push the progressive candidature of James Moor as Greek Professor. Although Hutcheson died within weeks of the successful conclusion of this contest, 'a Pisgah glimpse of the Promised Land', the process of liberalisation was now well advanced and in a sense his reforming work was complete.[89] This was confirmed by the increasing appointment of more of his ex-students and associates to chairs, the most famous being Adam Smith, who was to teach a moral philosophy course partly derived from Hutcheson's own model.

There was a final brief exception to Hutcheson's legacy as a successful university reformer, but one which may also have assisted the spread of liberal ideas to Ulster in a very practical way by boosting Ulster student numbers. For Hutcheson was also personally responsible for encouraging the university to allow students from Presbyterian academies in Ireland to obtain an Arts degree in only two years instead of the normal three. This continued to be a powerful incentive for Presbyterian-educated students, until worries over falling academic standards brought an end to the curious anomaly in 1782.[90]

There were of course many inspiring professors in eighteenth-century Scotland. Some like Leechman, Smith and Dugald Stewart, Professor of Moral Philosophy at Edinburgh, were even closer contemporaries of the radicals in the Society of United Irishmen. Yet, Hutcheson's contribution as a catalytic agent for political and intellectual development remains vital. In the first place, his political radicalism, where European neo-rationalism fused with the contractual emphasis of Presbyterian thought, was readily applicable to real situations in Scotland, Ireland and the Colonies. As regards the communication of these views, also significant was his abiding intellectual influence on successive cohorts both of university teachers in Scotland and Presbyterian community leaders in Ulster. Thirdly, Hutcheson played a prominent role in sustaining a more liberal climate at his university in which these professors could continue to teach Enlightenment ideas without fear of persecution. Finally, his eccentric but dogged method of swelling student numbers actually helped fill the classrooms of his academic successors with Ulster recruits.

THE 'SCOTCH IDEAS' AND THEIR INFLUENCE IN IRELAND

One such prominent recruit to the University of Glasgow was William Steel Dickson, the outspoken Presbyterian minister of Portaferry, who was arrested for United Irish sympathies in 1797. Dickson, writing as a broken man after years of exile and persecution for his radical beliefs, offers an unrepentant and affectionate testimony of the impact of his education at Glasgow under Hutcheson's distinguished successors, Moorhead, Smith, Leechman and Millar, during the 1760s. A note of hero worship still enters into his description of Dr Leechman, his professor of forty years before: 'A man, whose name will ever be venerated by the friends of religious liberty, learning, truth and unadulterated christianity. In my intercourse with him, I enjoyed every advantage which a youthful mind, engaged in the pursuit of knowledge, could reasonably hope for'.[91]

He accorded an even greater role in his intellectual development to John Millar, Professor of Law, who introduced him to Locke, Montesquieu and Puffendorf, and in so doing helped him lay the basis of his political credo:

> What particular effects his instructions then had on my mind, I cannot now pretend to say. This only I know, and this I acknowledge, that they, and a few books to which he directed my attention, produced a yet unaltered conviction that absolute monarchy is not the best possible government, except in the hands of absolute perfection – that aristocracy is, and must ever be, a bad government – that despotism under the *masque* of limited monarchy, a mixed government, or a free state, is worse – that any government, by *favouritism* is worse still – and, that a government, of what ever description, the administration of which is entirely submitted to a faction or sect – and particularly to upstarts and underlings of such a faction – subject to the influence, and liable to the control, of spies, informers, and mercenary clerks in office, is worst of all.[92]

Dickson's memoirs also illustrate that links with such distinguished teachers could be maintained long into adult life. Moorhead and Leechman 'honoured him with their correspondence as long as they lived'. Similarly, William Drennan, the Belfast physician and poet, who has been assigned the key role in the foundation of the United Irishmen, maintained a long-standing friendship and correspondence with his former mentor Professor Dugald Stewart at Edinburgh.[93] A. T. Q. Stewart notes how this 'curiously paralleled' that of his father and Francis Hutcheson in the previous generation, although given the process of generational socialisation sketched above, 'consistently patterned' might be more accurate.[94]

Indeed, Drennan's own case is another interesting illustration of cumulative contact with the 'Scotch genius' – as he himself termed the intellectual ferment of the period. He entered Glasgow University in 1769, aged fifteen, and after completion of his MA degree went to Edinburgh to study medicine, taking his MD in 1778. Although Hutcheson had been

dead over two decades, his influence clearly still weighed heavily in
family and university circles, helping mould the young man's politics.
Drennan was duly proud of his radical Presbyterian heritage, proclaiming,
'I am the son of . . . a Protestant dissenting minister, in the town of
Belfast; the friend and associate of good, I may say, great men: of Bruce,
of Duchal, and of Hutcheson'.[95] When he himself wrote in 1790 of the
need for some 'benevolent conspiracy' or 'plot for the people' to achieve
'the Rights of Man and the General Happiness of the Greatest Number',
the words were substantially Francis Hutcheson's.[96]

To move beyond these personal examples and try to quantify the impact
of educational experiences at Scottish universities on the subsequent course
of Irish radicalism is, of course, impossible. However, some idea of the
scale of the Scottish contribution can be gathered from a closer look at one
key group, the ministers and licentiates of the Presbyterian Church in
Ireland. These men are easily identifiable in official and unofficial accounts
of events surrounding the 1798 Rebellion, and their educational background can be traced from university matriculation albums and from the
Presbyterian Church in Ireland's *Fasti*.[97] An initial problem is the extent to
which ministers were involved in revolutionary activities. Ulster Presbyterian historians, following the realignment of Presbyterianism behind the
Loyalist standard during the nineteenth century are anxious to minimise
this, while their Episcopalian colleagues seem to take pleasure in their
embarrassment. From an examination of a range of sources relating to the
rebellion – most notably the *Black Book of Rebellion*, the *Rebellion Papers*,
the *State of the Country Papers*, and the *Lowry Papers* – we can estimate
that at least 23 licensed Presbyterian ministers and 7 probationers had some
form of involvement.[98] These range from the Revd James Porter of
Greyabbey and the probationer Archibald Warrick, who were hanged for
their participation, to less robust souls like the Revd Davidson of Tyrone,
who were merely suspected of concealing refugees. Of those implicated,
and whose educational background is available, 19 were educated at
Glasgow, 2 in 'Scotland', 2 in the home seminary of Strabane, one in
Edinburgh, and one Sinclair Kelbune at Glasgow, Edinburgh and for good
measure Trinity College, Dublin.[99]

If the above casts Scottish universities in a 'subversive' role, rather
akin to the much-maligned 1960s Sociology Departments, this is not the
intention. Most Presbyterian ministers were educated in Scotland, but
the universities did not unerringly turn out radical products. For every
libertarian such as Dr Dickson, they were also capable of producing a
Revd John Thompson, the rigid disciplinarian and sternly orthodox
theologian satirised in *The Ulster Synod* poem of 1807 for his disapproval
of frill cuffs for ministers. Similarly in the Non-Subscribing Controversy,

Glasgow University succeeded in providing the key protagonists on both sides. The strength of a Scottish university education, as we can see from Hutcheson's case, lay not so much in dispensing philosophies as in exposing students to an intellectual world restructured on an empirical and historical basis. The spirit of rational enquiry, for Hutcheson the only useful method in philosophy, thus encouraged students to think critically of received ideas from whatever source.

The classroom, moreover, was not the only source of radical ideas. For an important process of peer group socialisation was also taking place in the late eighteenth century, notably through the medium of student debating societies. Both Glasgow and Edinburgh were rich in these, though in the former case they proved more ephemeral. The political tenor of one of the Glasgow clubs can be guessed from its name 'Oceana', after Harrington's work of 1695, which advocated religious liberty and the extension of the parliamentary system.[100] A Friendly Debating Society for Scottish and Irish Covenanting students was also in operation from the 1770's onwards.[101] Meantime at Edinburgh, a Dialectic Society was formed in 1791 to discuss 'philological moral or political questions' at its fortnightly meetings.[102] Its proceedings were of an ostentatiously high-minded nature, with the French Revolution, established religion and parliamentary reform all featuring on its agenda, although the Society was eventually to share the chill of most middle-class reformers towards the course of events in France.[103]

More enduring and significant for present purposes was the Speculative Society at Edinburgh University. For Henry Cockburn this was the institution 'which has trained more young men to public speaking, talent, and liberal thought, than all the other private institutions in Scotland'.[104] The Society was an exclusive club originally established for 'improvement in literary composition and public speaking', but during its Golden Age at the end of the eighteenth century it drifted towards the discussion of more political and revolutionary topics, even acquiring a reputation for 'Jacobinism' which was hotly contested by its members.[105]

It is here we can trace some of the earliest involvement in the Scottish scene of personalities later to be influential in the development of Irish radicalism. For example, William Drennan was a member of the Speculative Society in 1778, during his period of study at Edinburgh University. His membership, he explained to his sister, gave him the weekly opportunity of 'venting some of my rancour . . . which I could not do in private company, and as most of them take me for an American I can do it with the greater safety'. As an 'honorary American', however, he expressed disquiet at a decision of the Society, taken in his absence, to subscribe one hundred guineas to the King of Great Britain to help pursue the war against the colonists.[106]

A more determined attempt was made to galvanise the Society by another future United Irish leader Thomas Addis Emmet, also at Edinburgh for medical training. This was by means of a formal reciprocal link between the Speculative Society and the Historical Society of Trinity College, Dublin, whereby members of either society would be permitted to attend each other's meetings. The point here is that Trinity College was at last opening up to modernising forces. While the Historical Society was never simply a 'radical' society, leaning more towards 'Real Whiggery', it proved an important intellectual forcing house not only for leading members of Grattan's parliament, but also for that most famous United Irishman Theobald Wolfe Tone, who joined the society in 1783.[107] Emmet's proposed link was agreed, also in 1783, and relations continued over the next twenty years, indeed outlasting Emmet's own membership which was forcibly terminated in the aftermath of the 1798 Rebellion.[108]

We are obviously concerned here with an educated élite, and the extent to which advanced ideas imported from Scotland permeated downwards to the ordinary Ulster Presbyterian is, of course, more open to debate. The eighteenth-century pulpit, to which many university products were called, does seem to have been a powerful instrument for the dissemination of ideas. Yet, Ulster was a literate society where a premium was placed on education as the path to a sound knowledge of the Scriptures.[109] The right to private judgement, a cornerstone of Protestantism, further permitted dissention from the minister's sermonising. This was dramatically demonstrated when one of William Stavely's congregation protested so violently at what he considered a seditious sermon that he later died of apoplexy.[110] Many families in W. S. Dickson's Portaferry congregation also left in disgust at his 'Scripture Politics'. There are contrary examples, though. A number of other members of Dickson's flock were arrested with him for suspected treasonable activities, while another preacher, Francis Pringle, was forced to resign when he refused to 'compromise his loyalty' in line with his parishioners' radical inclinations.[111]

Evidently, congregations could be divided, but these latter examples coupled with the widespread involvement of Presbyterian artisans and tenant farmers in political activity in the late eighteenth century – particularly in Antrim and Down – do indicate that in many cases radical middle-class views were received sympathetically. The pulpit was clearly not the only source of revolutionary ideas. News of the French Revolution and of Thomas Paine's writings spread even in remote rural areas through returning tradesmen and labourers.[112] Apocalyptic quasi-religious pamphlets were also popular in the northern counties, particularly those relating the persecutions and prophecies of the Covenanter Alexander Peden.[113]

The 'Scotch ideas' then appear to have enjoyed a generalised influence which extended beyond the university-educated. The Scottish universities, for example, were able to sustain Presbyterianism in Ireland in its period of adversity by training young men for the ministry who could offer leadership to the community. Even the sensitivity of Ulster to fissures in the Scottish churches had a positive result. For, the resultant divisions within Ulster Presbyterianism could paradoxically reinforce the community's vigour and self-confidence. Brooke, for example, notes that the Synod of Ulster, incorporating a range of political and theological currents, had the appearance of a national church, surrounded by a dissenting fringe comprised of the Presbytery of Antrim, the Covenanters and the Seceders.[114]

As regards the political dimension of Presbyterianism and its linkage with advanced liberal ideas, the 'ideological community' between Scotland and Ulster had a double impact. Scotland, in short, provided both a significant part of the message, as well as the medium of dissemination, in the shape of its universities. United Irish reading extended well beyond Hutcheson and the Scottish Whig philosophers Hume, Smith and Millar. It encompassed also indigenous writers such as Molyneux and Swift, the French *philosophes* – most notably Mirabeau – whose work was regularly serialised in the *Northern Star* – and contemporaries like Paine, Godwin and Price.[115] While the extent to which the universities provided this detailed bibliography remains open to debate, their more diffuse role in enhancing receptiveness to new currents of critical and innovatory thought seems evident.

In a more practical sense, education in Scotland had also acquainted radicals like Drennan with the Scottish political context, and would provide personal contacts among like-minded Scots. These were to be capitalised upon from the outset of the United Irishmen's history. In other words, Irish radicalism was never simply the creature of external events, a mere reflection of events in America or France; besides feeding on domestic grievances, it was able to draw on a long-standing core of beliefs in which the Scottish contribution was substantial.

Finally, however, it remains to trace a more negative and potentially divisive moment in intellectual influences from Scotland, and one which profoundly influenced the course of events in Ireland in the 1790s. There is an obvious point here. This discussion has concentrated on the interchange between Presbyterians in Scotland and Ireland, the group which in the latter case founded the United Irishmen, and were the motive force during its formative years. While some Episcopalian United leaders, such as Tone or the Emmet brothers, could happily identify with Presbyterianism's political content, contractual thought or 'New Light' libertarianism had little resonance with the Irish Catholics who were to form much of the movement's rank and file.

Ulster Presbyterians had indeed a rather alienating degree of pride in their own 'enlightenment', but the problem went deeper than cultural estrangement. Basically, between the twin strands of the Scottish intellectual legacy – Presbyterianism and Enlightenment – existed a dynamic tension. For the Scottish Presbyterian heritage had deeply exclusivist and 'particularist' elements which ran counter to the 'universalist' imperative at the heart of European Enlightenment thought. From its inception, Scottish Calvinism had, as Camic suggests, a tendency to erect barriers within the human community, and to rank the resulting sub-communities in accordance with its own Scottish version.[116] The Scottish kirk, 'the best reformed in Christendom', was viewed as particularly favoured by God – as were the people of Scotland. This reached its highest form of expression with the Covenanters during their persecution in the 1680s when they identified themselves with the sorrows and righteousness of the Children of Israel.[117]

One of the chief objects of this exclusiveness was Roman Catholicism, as evident in the Westminster Confession of Faith of 1643. This was influenced by anti-authoritarian sentiments, and by a belief in the primacy of individual conscience. Popery was associated with excessive, alien domination, and also represented for Calvinists a 'slavish fear', which betrayed man's free access to God and the liberty of conscience which Christ had won for believers. In Scotland these views proved resilient, despite their abstract quality in a country where the Catholic population was in reality small. They survived even the spread of Enlightenment ideas. Pillars of the Enlightenment such as Hume and Smith did decry 'the Bible's arbitrary choice of people – those people who are the countrymen of the author', but on this question Calvinist orthodoxy held the allegiance of the large part of eighteenth-century Scots.[118]

Nor could Ulster's case be one of simply and unproblematically importing libertarian ideas. Here the 'particularism' of Presbyterianism became a dynamic force. This was firstly through the independence and apartness of its Presbyterian community. Their experiences of persecution cast them easily in the role of 'a People among the Nations', their advanced thought itself a sign of their election. In addition, the presence of a large Catholic population in Ireland as a whole gave anti-Popery the practical focus it lacked in Scotland. This was increasingly the case following the Catholic Relief Act of 1778, which intensified economic competition, especially in Armagh and the other border counties.[119]

In this way, political libertarianism and religious sectarianism could coexist comfortably within Ulster Presbyterianism, both ideologies drawing on the Scottish intellectual legacy.[120] Contractual theory posed an important dilemma here, as Elliott indicates. At issue was the role of those who had no part in the making of the original contract. In Ireland's case, this meant the Catholics, the 'uncovenanted' of the population. Locke, whose basic assumption had been one of majority rule, provided little comfort.

For Irish radicalism, this was a dilemma only imperfectly and temporarily resolved, and wherever fear of Catholic encroachment outweighed the 'Brotherhood of Affection', sectarian consciousness was liable to assert itself over advanced liberal ideals of tolerance.

NOTES

1. See Reid, *History of the Presbyterian Church*; Brooke, *Ulster Presbyterianism*.
2. Elliott, 'The Origins and Transformation of Early Irish Republicanism', p. 410.
3. Loughridge, *The Covenanters in Ireland*, p. 43.
4. Robbins, *The Eighteenth-Century Commonwealthman*, pp. 167–266. The most recent body of work on the United Irish movement is beginning to bring the Scottish contribution into sharper focus: see Tesch, 'Presbyterian Radicalism', and McBride, 'William Drennan'; also A. T. Q. Stewart's *A Deeper Silence*, pp. 81–124.
5. Robbins, *The Eighteenth-Century Commonwealthman*, p. 17.
6. Foster, *Modern Ireland*, p. 73.
7. Crawford, 'Ulster as a Mirror of the Two Societies', p. 61; see also Perceval-Maxwell, *The Scottish Migration to Ulster*. Many Scottish settlers were from Gaelic-speaking areas, and by the 1790s Irish – by then quite distinct from Scottish Gaelic – was still used and understood by some Presbyterian congregations, see O'Saothrai Coiseam, *An Minister Gaelach*, Dublin, 1992.
8. Vogt, 'Portpatrick–Donaghadee: The Short Sea Route', p. 23.
9. *Belfast Newsletter*, 2 May 1783.
10. McHaffie, *The Short Sea Route*, p. 8.
11. Cochran, 'Scottish–Irish Trade in the Eighteenth Century', p. 151.
12. Ibid.
13. Walker, 'The Protestant Irish in Scotland', pp. 45–6.
14. Madden, *The United Irishmen*, ser. 2, vol. 2, p. 43.
15. Crawford, 'Ulster as a Mirror of the Two Societies', pp. 64–5.
16. Handley, *The Irish in Scotland*, p. 88.
17. Bishop, 'The Education of Ulster Students at Glasgow University'.
18. Innes Addison, *The Matriculation Albums of the University of Glasgow*. Medical students, for example, did not have to matriculate. Participation in Rectorial contests was one of the few benefits of matriculation.
19. Table adapted from Bishop, 'The Education of Ulster Students at Glasgow University'.
20. Ibid., p. 122.
21. *A Short History of the University of Edinburgh*, p. 46.
22. Compiled from, *Nomina eorum qui gradum medicinae doctoris*.
23. There was, for example, a large preponderance of Irish students in the period 1784–90 among Edinburgh graduates in the university's Chemical

Society. This was founded by Professor Joseph Black, himself of Belfast ancestry. See Kendal, 'The First Chemical Society', pp. 235–45.

24. Links with Glasgow had existed in the pre-Reformation period. It was hoped to attract Irish students at the time of the university's foundation in the fifteenth century. See Durkan and Kirk, *The University of Glasgow*, p. 383.

25. Stubbs, *The History of the University of Dublin*.

26. Ibid., pp. 126–7; for Edinburgh, see Horn, *A Short History of the University of Edinburgh*, p. 120. William Drennan was aware that he could have got his medical degree at Glasgow on 'so much easier terms' but that an Edinburgh degree was more 'credible', Drennan Letters, M. McTier to W. Drennan, 25 January 1778, no. 21, and W. Drennan to M. McTier, 7 February [1778], no. 22, T. 765 (PRONI).

27. Innes Smith, *English-Speaking Students at the University of Leyden*; Sarolan, 'The Golden Age of the University of Edinburgh', pp. 45–53.

28. Topham, *Letters from Edinburgh*, pp. 219–20.

29. For a general discussion of these developments, see Camic, *Experience and Enlightenment*. For Glasgow, see Coutts, *A History of the University of Glasgow*. For Edinburgh, see Emerson, 'Scottish Universities in the Eighteenth Century', pp. 453–75; Morrel, 'The University of Edinburgh in the late Eighteenth Century', pp. 158–71. Also interesting is Veich, 'Philosophy in the Scottish Universities', pp. 207–34.

30. Innes Smith, *English-Speaking Students at the University of Leyden*; Sarolan, 'The Golden Age of the University of Edinburgh'. Despite the process of modernisation, the life confronting eighteenth-century Ulster students was a very hard one by modern standards. See William Drennan, Drennan Letters, nos. 1–40, T. 765 (PRONI) and also the Revd Porter's memoirs in Porter, *Irish Presbyterian Biographical Sketches*. For typical advertisements, see *Northern Star*, 21 September 1793 and 31 October 1793.

31. Hamilton, *History of the Irish Presbyterian Church*, p. 12.

32. Beckett, *Protestant Dissent in Ireland*; Reid, *History of the Presbyterian Church*.

33. Brooke, *Ulster Presbyterianism*.

34. In a departure from Ireland's subsequent record of religious tolerance, ministers such as Brice who had fled to escape the 'prelatic' tendencies of the Scottish Church were received into the Established Episcopal Church of Ireland, which in an oddly expansive mood appointed them as prebendaries and allowed them to preach and conduct services in the Presbyterian manner. 'The Irish Episcopal Church has changed since those days – changed not for the better', commented Hamilton, *History of the Irish Presbyterian Church*, p. 38.

35. See Stevenson, *The Scottish Covenanters* for a useful précis of this rather confusing period.

36. Brooke, *Ulster Presbyterianism*, p. 29

37. Elliott, *Watchmen in Sion*, pp. 25–7. The theme is developed below.

38. Millar, *Queen's Rebels*, pp. 7–42 for a wider-ranging discussion on the influence of Covenanting.

39. Stevenson, *The Scottish Covenanters*, pp. 28–34.

40. Williamson, *Scottish National Consciousness in the Age of James VI*.

41. Hutchinson, *The Reformed Presbyterian Church in Scotland*; Adair, *A True Narrative of the Rise and Progress of the Presbyterian Church in Ireland*, p. 10.

42. Brooke, *Ulster Presbyterianism*, p. 39.

43. A. T. Q. Stewart, *The Narrow Ground*, p. 96.

44. T. A. Emmet considered them, 'the most active promoters of the system', in MacNeven, *Pieces of Irish History*, p. 100.

45. Loughridge *The Covenanters in Ireland*, pp. 10–11. See also Allen,

'Scottish Ecclesiastical Influence upon Irish Presbyterianism'. Allen also deals with the Seceders, another Scottish import. They emphasised Covenant renewal, but to a lesser extent than the Reformed Presbyterians. They took an anti-political stance in the 1798 Rebellion.

46. Elliott, *Watchmen in Sion*, p. 11.
47. Loughridge, *The Covenanters in Ireland*, p. 44. For Stavely, see S. Ferguson, *Brief Biographical Sketches*, pp. 38–59.
48. *Northern Star*, 10 October 1796, for full text.
49. Loughridge, *The Covenanters in Ireland*, p. 46.
50. Robbins, *The Eighteenth-Century Commonwealthman*, pp. 167–266 is the main source for the discussion which follows. See also her, ' "When it is that Colonies may Become Independent" '.
51. See Elliott, *Partners in Revolution*, p. 10. She also discusses the role of William Molyneux, who seems to have had less impact on Scotland.
52. Robbins, *The Eighteenth-Century Commonwealthman*, pp. 88–133.
53. Ibid., p. 108.
54. See Luce and Jessop (eds), *The Works of George Berkeley*, VI, pp.17–46.
55. Ibid., pp. 159–63.
56. Ibid., p. 197. Smith was eventually expelled for lighting a bonfire in Molesworth's honour. See A. T. Q. Stewart, *A Deeper Silence*, pp. 88–9.
57. See Brooke, *Ulster Presbyterianism*, pp. 63–111, and McBride, 'William Drennan', pp. 52–5. For a detailed treatment of doctrine, see Allen, 'Scottish Ecclesiastical Influence upon Irish Presbyterianism'; also McMillan, 'The Subscription Controversy in Irish Presbyterianism'.
58. Elliott, *Partners in Revolution*, p. 20.
59. Brooke, *Ulster Presbyterianism*, p. 99.
60. Bullock and Drummond, *The Scottish Church*, p. 103.
61. Hamilton, *History of the Irish Presbyterian Church*, p. 120. In gratitude, three pews were set aside for the use of Scottish visitors in the Rosemary Street church in Belfast.
62. Abernethy was a particularly influential figure. His sermon *Religous Obedience Founded on Personal Persuasion*, published in December 1719, was one of the first landmarks of the Non-Subscription controversy and attracted some fifty contemporary pamphlets in connection with it. For biographical details, see 'Life' by James Duchal, a preface to Abernethy's *Sermons*. For Kirkpatrick, see his *Historical Essay upon the Loyalty of Presbyterians*.
63. See Bishop, 'The Education of Ulster Students at Glasgow University', p. 89; for Samuel Clark, see Whiston, *Memoirs of Samuel Clark*.
64. W. Ferguson, *Scotland*, pp. 120–1.
65. Hamilton, *History of the Irish Presbyterian Church*, p. 128: 'It is not to be wondered that the pupils of the Synod of Ulster began to give a very uncertain sound on the verities of Faith and in some cases to ignore them altogether.' Reid, *History of the Presbyterian Church*, vol. iii, p. 300 was similarly in little doubt over the contribution of theological training at Glasgow University.
66. For details of the Simson Controversy, see Bullock and Drummond, *The Scottish Church*, p. 34ff. See also *The Case of John Simson*.
67. Witherow, *Historical and Literary Memorials*, pp. 158–68 and 192–204; D. Stewart, *The Seceders in Ireland*, p. 55.
68. A. Thompson, *The Origin of the Secession Church*, p. 28.
69. Trevor-Roper, 'The Scottish Enlightenment', p. 1636. The description is open to debate, even for the seventeenth century.
70. For fuller details, see W. Leechman, 'Some Account of the Life, Writings and Character of the Author', prefixed to Hutcheson's posthumous, *A System of Moral Philosophy*, Glasgow, 1775; Scott, *Francis Hutcheson*; Hutcheson's writings are in *Collected Works*. For a recent treatment of

his contribution, see A. T. Q. Stewart, *A Deeper Silence*, pp. 71–3 and 91–101.

71. Hutcheson, Letters to Thomas Drennan, dated 1737–46, Glasgow University Library Special Collections.

72. Robbins, *The Eighteenth-Century Commonwealthman*, p. 185.

73. Campbell and Skinner, *The Origins and Nature of the Scottish Enlightenment*, p. 167.

74. Scott, *Francis Hutcheson*, p. 185.

75. Dewar Gibb, *Fortuna Domus*, p. 106.

76. Campbell, *The Origins and Nature of the Scottish Enlightenment*, pp. 167–8. For examples of these treatments, see Blackstone, *Francis Hutcheson*; Kivy, *Francis Hutcheson*.

77. See Robbins, *The Eighteenth-Century Commonwealthman* and ' "When it is that Colonies may Become Independent" '; Norton, 'Francis Hutcheson in America'; Brock, *Scotus Americanus*.

78. Forbes, *Hume's Philosophical Politics*, p. 45; see Hutcheson, *Collected Works*, vol. 6, pp. 79–80.

79. Robbins, *The Eighteenth-Century Commonwealthman*, pp. 188ff.

80. Ibid., p. 149.

81. Scott, *Francis Hutcheson*, p. 286.

82. Leechman, 'Some Account of the Life'.

83. Ramsay, *Scotland and Scotsmen*, vol. 2, p. 264.

84. Carlyle, *Autobiography*, p. 78. Students were reputed to attend lectures, substantially similar in content, up to five times, for the pleasure of hearing Hutcheson speak.

85. 'To be an *Irish* medical student', commented Drennan, 'was the highest complication of disgrace', W. Drennan to M. McTier, n.d., no. 23, T.795 (PRONI). For the financial situation of Irish students, see Porter, *Irish Presbyterian Biographical Sketches* and *Christian Moderator*, II, p. 262, quoted in Scott, *Francis Hutcheson*, pp. 68–70. For a contrary view on the Irish, Bishop suggests that despite their 'wildness', the Irish accounted for over twice as large a proportion of graduates as they did matriculated students, 'The Education of Ulster Students at Glasgow University', p. 139.

86. Hutcheson, Letters: 31 January 1737 and 1 June 1741 (Glasgow Univ.). He took particular care of one Bob Haliday, son of Hutcheson's late friend, the 'New Light' minister Samuel Haliday. Bob's conduct fell short of that displayed by his high-minded father, and that of his brother Alexander, who was to be one of Belfast's most prominent liberals. He is described as 'conceited, pert and self-willed', and was repeatedly threatened with being sent home in disgrace to Belfast.

87. Bishop, 'The Education of Ulster Students at Glasgow University', p. 133 suggests that 484 out of 1,856 Ulster students matriculating between 1690 and 1770 entered the ministry. Of these, many would also be involved in schoolteaching during their probationary period and beyond. On the pivotal role of the minister, see Tesch, 'Presbyterian Radicalism', p. 40.

88. See Scott, *Francis Hutcheson*, pp. 78–95. He further details his involvement in the broader university reform process. This is also a prominent topic in Hutcheson's Letters (Glasgow Univ.).

89. Scott, *Francis Hutcheson*, p. 94.

90. The tightening of entry requirements may explain the marked fall in the numbers of Ulster students matriculating from the 1780s onwards. See Table 1.1.

91. Dickson, *Narrative of the Confinement*, p. 3.

92. Ibid., pp. 4–5. Dickson retained a life-long partiality for Scotland, spending four of his six weeks' leisure every year, 'renewing his intimacy and friendships'. Drennan Letters, W. Drennan to M. McTier, n.d. [July 1796], no. 621, T. 765 (PRONI).

93. Letters from Dugald Stewart and Mrs H. Stewart to W. Drennan 1807–8, D E. 1. 100², H5–8 (University of Edinburgh Library Special Collections); see also Drennan Letters, T. 765 (PRONI) for frequent mentions of his friend, including Stewart's romantic entanglements.

94. A. T. Q. Stewart, 'A Stable Unseen Power', p. 83.

95. Drennan, *Fugitive Pieces*, pp. 192–3.

96. W. Drennan to S. McTier, 21 May 1791, no. 54. T. 765 (PRONI); for a general discussion of Drennan's intellectual background, McBride, 'William Drennan', pp. 49–61.

97. McConnell (ed.), *Fasti of the Irish Presbyterian Church*.

98. The Black Book of Rebellion in McCance Collection, D. 272/1 (PRONI); Rebellion Papers, 620/1–67, National Archives Ireland (NAI); State of the Country Papers, 620/1015ff. (NAI); Lowry Papers, D. 1494 (PRONI); also Clelland MSS, MIC. 507 (PRONI); see also *Report from the Committee of Secrecy of the House of Commons of Ireland*, Dublin 1798. *The Records of the General Synod of the Presbyterian Church in Ireland* (pp. 216–17) for 1798 admit only eight participants, including licentiates, whereas the *Fasti* compiled in 1951 is able to recognise seventeen ordained ministers who were involved.

99. See Appendix I for full listing. Their years of matriculation range from 1759 to 1795.

100. Robbins, *The Eighteenth-Century Commonwealthman*, p. 237.

101. S. Ferguson, *Brief Biographical Sketches*, p. 29.

102. The Dialectic Society, Minutes, vol. 1, 1791–4 and vol. 2, 1794–1801 (University of Edinburgh Library Special Collections).

103. The Society is also interesting in offering an early example of a consumer boycott in 1792, when members renounced the use of sugar and rum, 'in consequence of the Society's determining that the use of the produce of the West Indies slave trade involves us in its guilt': The Dialectic Society, Minutes, vol. 1, 21 July 1792 (Edinburgh Univ.).

104. Cockburn, *Memorials*, p. 67.

105. *The History of Speculative Society*, pp. 8–12.

106. W. Drennan to M. McTier [April 1776], no. 3, T. 765 (PRONI). He assured his correspondent that the decision would not cost him personally a single farthing.

107. Elliott, *Wolfe Tone*, p. 32; for a full discussion of the History Society, see Dagg, *The College History Society*.

108. *The History of the Speculative Society*, p. 8.

109. Crawford, 'Ulster as a Mirror of the Two Societies', p. 64. For a detailed account of popular literacy in Ulster, see Adams, *The Printed Word*.

110. Loughridge, *The Covenanters in Ireland*, p. 45.

111. Bailie, 'William Steele Dickson', p. 248.

112. Smyth, *Men of no Property*, pp. 92–3; Elliott, *Partners in Revolution*, pp. 15–16.

113. MS. Book, *The Oakboys, the Hearts of Steel, the Volunteers, and the United Irishmen of Larne and Neighbourhood*, D. 2095/18 (PRONI).

114. Brooke, *Ulster Presbyterianism*, p. 112.

115. Elliott, *Partners in Revolution*, p. 27.

116. Camic, *Experience and Enlightenment*, pp. 15–18.

117. See Stevenson, *The Scottish Covenanters*, pp. 59–69.

118. Ibid., pp. 73–4.

119. Gibbon, 'The Origins of the Orange Order', pp. 135–66.

120. Elliott, *Watchmen in Sion*, pp. 12–13.

2

Ireland and Scotland
1700–1789

It has emerged with some force that learning experiences acquired in Scotland and the political ideas they helped foster were translated by Irish students in line with concrete situations in their country of origin. In this way, ideas and experiences became generalised beyond the specific settings of the Scottish universities, and acquired new capital in changing economic, political and religious conditions. The societies of Scotland and Ireland shared many important characteristics in the eighteenth century, and the attraction of Locke and Hutcheson's political thought in each case seems to have reflected a common spirit of uncertainty amid rapid economic development and political stalemate. However, the case of Ireland clearly stood out in two respects: the embattled position of Presbyterians and the presence of a large Roman Catholic majority. To grasp the future paths of intellectual and political development in the two countries, we must now press on with more systematic comparisons.

International comparisons of this type are of immense value as a source of new syntheses, questions and even, sometimes, answers. Through this method, overarching explanations of historical phenomena are challenged by the specificity of local cases, while theses which may fit comfortably in one society are tested by their application to a range of geographical situations.

Unfortunately, in applying these high-minded methological precepts to Ireland and Scotland, we encounter Louis Cullen's comment that the histories of both countries are obscured in 'whiskey, mist and misery'.[1] He might also have added 'mythology'. For one of the major tasks in pursuing a comparison is to cut through the propaganda of contemporary pamphleteers, and the romanticising tendencies of later historiography. This is particularly true of Ireland, where the theme of disappointed hopes has been a prominent one, but Scotland too shares something of the Jacobite preoccupation with regrets at the expense of realities.

The great degree of variation within the two societies is a further problem for building comparisons. At times 'Ireland' and 'Scotland' unravel as convenient analytic units. The Scottish Highlands often displayed stronger affinities with the western periphery of Ireland, in institutional and cultural terms, than with the Scottish Lowlands. As we have seen, Ulster too remained 'another Ireland', with closer practical links into the south-west of Scotland than with the southern Irish provinces.

Similarly, there is, a necessity to avoid fixed comparisons of the Scotland developed/Ireland underdeveloped, or the Ireland lawless/Scotland quiescent type. Contemporaries were adept at pointing to gulfs in national psychologies between 'the quiet and peacable habits of the instructed Scotch peasant' and 'the turbulent disposition of the ignorant Irishman'.[2] Such perceptions have a pervasive quality. To suggest, as one historian has done, that 'Violence characterised eighteenth-century Irish society', is a sweeping generalisation.[3] Ireland's reputation for violence and lawlessness owed a great deal to the perceptions of would-be civilisers, who had failed to root out the remnants of Gaelic society and practices.[4] This process of social construction actually concealed significant variations in the incidence of violence over time. Shifts in the relative positions of Ireland and Scotland with respect to social order are particularly instructive.

With this final caveat in mind, this chapter will explore one persistent comparative feature which does, nevertheless, emerge in the eighteenth-century landscape. This is the greater strength and maturity of what may be broadly termed 'protest' activity in the case of Ireland. Here, both rural unrest and extra-parliamentary political activity by the urban middle class were gaining momentum from mid-century. By the 1780s traditional mechanisms of control were being tested, and the authorities surveyed with anxiety the increasing alienation of literate public opinion from the parliamentary system. In contrast, radicals in Scotland had a narrower and more fragile base on which to build any political movement. The Scottish urban crowd could be ferocious when roused, but agrarian tensions and the tradition of middle-class political protest were each muted.

The eventual threat to social order in each case cannot be derived from these contrasting internal situations alone, and must be placed in a broader European context. The key point is, however, that the domestic eighteenth-century background in Ireland and Scotland not only helped structure the development of radicalism in the two countries, but also acted as a conditioning factor in the attitudes of Scottish and Irish radicals towards alliance with the revolutionary forces in France. For, while both groups could use their common ideological ground with the

French to legitimate their own movements as progressive and internationalist, the Scots were unable to use widespread discontent and alienation
to cast themselves convincingly in the role of representatives of 'the
Entire Nation' against a monarchical conspiracy. This, as Elliott demon-
strates, the United Irishmen were to accomplish with admirable *élan* and
political dexterity, while the Scots were destined to remain something of
a revolutionary élite in their own country.[5]

Why then was the political situation in Ireland more promising for
radical politics by the end of the eighteenth century? For this we have to
analyse developments on three levels: first, the role of economic change;
second, the nature of the social structure and social order; third, the
evolution of political institutions and processes.

ECONOMIC CHANGE

The late eighteenth-century upheavals in Ireland are commonly identified
with the political revolutions in America and France. Yet, the crisis in
these years was also grounded economically, and cannot be separated
from the revolution which had already begun to take place in the shape
of the rapid and uneven emergence of capitalist economic activities and
social relations, a process most marked in the Irish countryside.

The popular conception of Ireland as a stagnant, subsistence economy
has been comprehensively challenged by the 'revisionist' history of
Cullen.[6] The suggestion is that by the end of the eighteenth century,
two interrelated economies were in existence, a market economy superim-
posed on a non-money economy. The British connection was crucial
here, and McDowell perceptively contrasts Irishmen's acute consciousness
of the larger island with Britain's own intermittent awareness of Ireland.[7]
The development of Irish farming, for example, remained closely tied to
the fluctuations of demand across the Irish Sea. The rising demand for
dairy and beef products in the first half of the century had promoted the
creation of large pastoral farms, while continuing British inability to
produce sufficient cereals further intensified arable and mixed farming in
the east and Irish midlands.

These developments were to feed rural unrest in the next generation,
but for the present they served to stimulate the market orientation of the
economy. This was signalled in a variety of ways, including the production
of new crops, the rise in agricultural rents from the 1750s, and not least
the growth of a mercantile class, engaged in the production and export
of agricultural products. Change in agricultural production was also the
basis of the great growth of Anglo–Irish trade from the 1740s, ensuring
the quarter century of boom, described as Ireland's economic miracle.

The spearhead of prosperity was the province of Ulster, which had become heavily involved in linen production. Already marked out by its social and religious composition – following the settlement of English and Scottish Protestants in the seventeenth century – and enjoying a tenurial system unique in Ireland, the province now became distinguished by an interlinked domestic economy.[8] This was particularly true of its north-eastern corner, where a population of Scottish Presbyterian extraction predominated. Here it was Belfast, 'a practical little town with few embellishments', which stood to benefit most.[9] Building on the commercial advantage of linen, the town was on its way to becoming a major entrepôt for manufactured goods, and a centre for commercial and financial activity to rival Dublin. Already beautifully situated at the foot of the Antrim Hills, it became the subject of ambitious development schemes to match its new status, even including an early plan to make it 'a second Venice' by canalising the river network around Belfast Lough.[10] In the private language of Wolfe Tone and Thomas Russell's diaries it became 'Blefescu', the rival of Liliput in *Gulliver's Travels*.

The powerful and flexible economic base which was developing in the north-east was of lasting significance, ensuring continued industrial advance into the next century, but by no means was growth confined here. Elsewhere in Ireland, the wool and dairying trades stimulated the growth of the great harbours of Cork, Waterford, Limerick and Dublin, while state economic initiatives such as the Linen Board further stimulated commerce and industry. In short, by the 1780s, Ireland's economic potential appeared sufficient to cause stirrings of anxiety in the British manufacturing and mercantile world. This was not least in its Scottish outpost, where in 1778 the proposals of a government committee to permit Ireland direct trade with the colonies in most goods raised vigorous protest. Glasgow merchants, for example, offered their own diagnosis of Ireland's economic woes, which were the result of 'their narrow mean system of policy . . . their Protestant Popery and odious intolerance'. In return, a trade boycott of 'beggarly Glasgow' was called for.[11]

Here Scottish apprehensions appeared justified. In its own case, Scotland had inherited a widespread legacy of subsistence agriculture from before the Union of the Parliaments, with localised pockets of capitalist enterprise. The pace of change was quickening by the mid-eighteenth century, but there was still sufficient basis for the claim that 'Ireland seemed to hold out more promise of a bright economic future than Scotland'.[12] On the surface then, there was little cause to predict the divergence in the two countries' economic experiences. Nevertheless, by the end of the century Scotland was beginning to witness a well-rooted industrialisation with an efficient agricultural sector declining in importance, while most of Ireland,

Ulster being of course the exception, faced intense land hunger, famine and depopulation.

In fact, Scotland's superiority was not suddenly established. Nor is it simply the case that imperfect statistics prior to 1750 distort the countries relative economic standing.[13] Instead, the historic process of divergence fed off certain key structural weaknesses which lay behind Ireland's economic advance. For while Scotland was experiencing a more measured pace of development, its modernisation at least rested on sound foundations. Four points of economic comparison are particularly relevant here: the speed of commercialisation; population growth; living standards; and finally location within the imperial system.

For much of the eighteenth century, commercialisation displayed its greatest power in Ireland, where the process also had a longer history.[14] The very speed of the development of large-scale capitalist farming, with its emphasis on enclosure, put pressure on the stability of peasant communities by making less land available for proprietorship. Land outside Ulster continued to be let and farmed on the basis of an intricate tenurial system inhospitable to improvement. Agriculture was dominated by the tenant farmer, who could be fairly prosperous in the midland counties, but in the south and west was more likely to be an impoverished cottier. The latter group's lifestyle of subsistence farming, supplemented by internal migration, was put under further pressure by rising rents and prices. As in Britain and France, peasants were forced to invoke the 'moral economy' to stop merchants and market-orientated farmers exploiting consumers during subsistence crises.[15]

This penetration of market relations is clearly paralleled in the Scottish Highlands, where the resultant economic demands encouraged the rationalisation of estate management at the expense of concepts of family tenure.[16] Yet, even here the erosion of the traditional system was slower than in Gaelic Ireland, since the Highlands were less fertile and less well resourced, and lacked a pre-existing market network. The contrast was even more pronounced in the Scottish Lowlands, where changes in land use and landholding were prompted by the spread of market relations and the diffusion of commercial attitudes among landowners. Here the process was a piecemeal and evolutionary one, and when the consolidation of estates did develop from the 1770s it resulted in little systematic eviction, as in the Highlands or in Ireland.[17]

The tempo of change was not the only divergence between the two economies. A second force exacerbating the problems caused by the rapid capitalist orientation of rural Ireland was intensive demographic pressure. The revisionist thrust of Irish history has led to a reconsideration of the degree of regional variation in population growth, but it has not altered the fact that between 1780 and 1830 a very rapid expansion did occur, reflecting increased marital fertility.[18] The rise in Ireland's population was remarkable by general European standards, and certainly outstripped the Scottish experience of steady continuous growth.[19]

In Scotland, changes in agricultural land proprietorship thus coincided with a buoyant demand for agricultural labour. Its general level of economic development also helped sustain its modest population growth. For those unwilling to become farm servants in the new order, alternative modes of employment existed as a result of the process of urbanisation and industrialisation after 1760. By the end of the eighteenth century, towns contained over 20 per cent of the Scottish population.[20] A decade later, cotton textiles had become the leading industrial sector, transforming both the organisation of production and the social structure, with the rise of the factory system.[21]

Despite the degree of dynamism in its economy, Ireland, however, hovered around the Malthusian precipice. Already by the late eighteenth century, the result was land hunger, with increasing numbers forced to rent marginal plots or to work as seasonal agricultural labourers. The pressure on land also allowed landlords to increase money rents and step up enclosures, secure in the knowledge that alternative tenants were in ample supply. Nor were these profound effects on landholding mitigated by town and industrial development. While a measure of urbanisation did develop in the eighteenth century, the country remained dominated by Dublin and the three Munster ports, and lacked the middle-ranking regional centres which were a characteristic Scottish feature. Here too, industrialisation in the shape of textiles was a phenomenon insecurely based and liable to reversal, as witnessed in the last decade of the century.[22]

The population–resources ratio was in itself a contributory factor to the gap which existed between the two countries in terms of popular living standards. While the picture of a purely subsistence economy in Ireland has been qualified, the degree of poverty among those who did scratch out a subsistence living was intense. Again the pattern of poverty varied regionally and chronologically, but the strong impression remains that the Irish peasantry suffered a degree of destitution not experienced by their Scottish counterparts in a century of continuous, balanced economic growth. This was certainly expressed by the few contemporary foreign travellers who visited both countries. Cullen notes that De La Tocayne's accounts of his visits in the 1790s certainly viewed Scotland as the richer country.[23] On a less subjective level, from data on the relative level of real wages in the 1780s, it is also estimated that Scottish agricultural earnings were twice the level of the Irish, and that money wages more than doubled in the central Lowlands between the 1750s and 1790s, as farmers competed with manufacturers for a restricted labour supply.[24]

Briefly then, while eighteenth-century Ireland appeared the more 'advanced' economy in terms of commercialisation, this process had a superficial quality, for Scotland remained the more 'affluent', with higher popular living standards and an employment boom. While Ireland suffered successive subsistence crises, in Scotland – in common with much of the rest of Europe – shortages were countered by a greater agricultural surplus. These features were likely to have a general cushioning effect on the inevitable dislocations which accompanied the diffusion of capitalist relations in the countryside, though the pattern of capital-intensive, fact-ory-based industrialisation – eventually urban-based – was destined to create its own social tensions.

The final key feature in the pattern of economic differentiation between Ireland and Scotland had a lasting influence on their comparative social structures and political processes. This was the two countries' relationship with England.

It was a sensitive subject with the Irish Protestant Ascendancy, who had replaced the indigenous ruling class during the land confiscations of the previous century.[25] Their vigorous and assertive identity, expressed in a flourishing literature and architecture, belied the fundamentally *colonial* forces which had obtained and still secured their rule. The English economic connection had encouraged economic development up to the first half of the eighteenth century, but by the 1760s the benefits of what the Irish historian Leland called 'this mighty Empire' were beginning to wear thin.[26] There was a growing perception that Ireland's role in the imperial system was dictated by Westminster's needs rather than the country's own economic potential. The active interference of the English legislature in commerce and industry was resented as being onerous and exploitative, locking Irish trade and manufactures into an inflexible system.

Whereas mid-century Ireland was beginning to pay the price for the nature of its linkages into the imperial system, through the distortions of its economy, Scotland in the 1750s was now enjoying the commercial benefits of its 1707 parliamentary union with England. The relationship with England was not a simple colonial one, nor was it a bilateral merger, instead it assumed the form of a 'negotiated compromise'.[27] Here, in return for security guarantees against further Jacobite threats, Scotland's distinctive civil society was retained. Institutions like the Kirk and legal system were subsequently to function not only as aids to the definition of national identity, but also as stimuli of continued economic development. For the indigenous élite, the sacrifice of formal independence was rewarded both by material advance and the exercise of practical power.[28]

Admittedly, for the great majority of the Scottish people, the short-term economic advantages of the Union were not apparent. The equalisation of customs duties increased the taxation burden and meant increasing costs for Scottish producers, who were already encountering increased English competition.[29] In the longer term, the privileges of free trade within the Empire provided a favourable climate for capitalist enterprise to flourish, opening up the Atlantic colonial trade and reinforcing the commercial dominance of urban centres like Glasgow.

SOCIAL STRUCTURE

Ireland's colonial status and Scotland's 'civil autonomy' are essential factors in their separate pathways of development. Yet an analysis which remains at this generalised level of political economy is not sufficient to explain their distinctiveness. The form which the English connection assumed in each case also had a lasting impact on their respective social formations, and in turn, as Devine has convincingly argued, the indigenous social structure was itself active in determining the response to commercial association with England.[30]

Spared direct colonisation, Scottish society in the eighteenth century was less fluid than the Irish, and more cohesive, homogenous and developed. One contrast is particularly vivid and immediate: while in Scotland confessional identity was a unifying force, in Ireland religion drew the battle lines of social and political life.

The common Protestantism of most Scots, internal doctrinal and organisational quarrels apart, bound ruler and ruled. Anti-Catholicism was deeply engrained, and sanctioned by Calvinist doctrine, but in the late eighteenth century the actual number of Roman Catholics remained few, geographically concentrated in the Highlands and the north-east. In the Statistical Reports for Ayrshire, Lanarkshire and Renfrew in the 1790s, for example, only a sprinkling of 'unsheperded' adherents was noted; and in Glasgow, the 'Popish meetings' were 'conducted with such discretion' that they 'could not possibly give the slightest cause for offence'.[31] Consequently, 'No Popery' was powerfully witnessed in the formation of middle-class Protestant associations, and even in popular tumults to resist the extension of the 1778 Catholic Relief Act, but retained nevertheless a rather abstract quality of cultural rather than political significance.[32] The target was the papal system, defined as 'despotic' and 'authoritarian', but the real threat to the traditional order from the few thousand Scottish Catholics was very minimal.

In the Irish case, the complexity of its colonial status, and the resultant delicacy of the sectarian balance, were only imperfectly grasped by radical contemporaries in the late eighteenth century. The United Irishmen had themselves a fatally weak understanding of the aspirations of rural Catholics, and of the Protestant population's latent fears of rebellion and encirclement.

For dissident Ascendancy opinion from the 1780s onwards, colonialism was identified with intrusive mercantilist regulation of Irish commerce. Although Ascendancy politicians refused to accept the explicit 'colonial' label in the classic American sense, preferring their own self-definition as 'Irishmen with English civil rights', more distant observers could be more brutal about the reality of their situation. The English Solicitor General, Philip Yorke, for example, commented: 'The subjects of Ireland were to be considered in two respects, as English and Irish . . . the Irish were a conquered people, and the English a colony transplanted hither, and are a colony subject to the law of the mother country'.[33]

In other words, Ireland's situation could be described more accurately as 'double colonialism'. The ruling élite, while resenting English legislative interference, themselves held power through the conquest and repression of the Catholic majority, and ultimately remained dependent on English military support.

There was ample evidence of this status. Colonialism was directly apparent in the migration and settlement of Protestants from England and Scotland, in order to reinforce the subordination of the native population. The results were severe social and cultural fissures, not only between the Anglo-Irish élite and their tenants, but between the Protestant and Catholic peasantry, particularly in the border counties of Ulster.[34]

A further manifestation of colonial rule, the 'Penal Laws' were also potent sources of social tension. Closely following the English model, this legislation was the main mechanism for underpinning of the Ascendancy through the dismemberment of a Catholic landed power base. They reflected, however, more than political calculations, and at a more visceral level spoke eloquently of Protestant insecurities and contempt. By the 1770s the Penal Code seemed to many an unpleasant anachronism, but by this point its original objectives had been substantially achieved. It was calculated in 1776 that although Catholics numbered 75 per cent of the Irish population, they held only 5 per cent of the land.[35] The more humiliating Penal clauses, albeit unevenly enforced, had also ensured a pattern of alienation on the part of most of the population from the ruling élite.[36] Thus gradual repeal from 1788 produced resentment and heightened expectations from both Protestants and Catholics.

Suffering a more comfortable alienation were the Presbyterians in Ireland, numbering around half a million. Active harassment had ceased after the early eighteenth century, but Presbyterians continued to be excluded from Crown office and local government by the 'Test clause' inserted in the 1704 Popery Act. Like Catholics they were also bound to pay tithes to the established Anglican church, a further pillar of the Ascendancy, which represented less than a tenth of the Irish population. Geographically concentrated in Ulster, their material prosperity matched their political exclusion. Yet, considering themselves the very bulwark of Protestantism in Ireland, their position also encouraged a rather sceptical and critical perspective on the established order. In short, this group, 'could enjoy the feeling of being an outsider, without suffering the discomforts associated with the underprivileged'.[37]

Against this complex pattern of social and denominational disruption, Scotland, with its civil society intact, seems a model organic development. An obvious counter here might be the case of Jacobitism. Certainly, the 1715 Rebellion was a determined attempt to challenge the legitimacy of Hanoverian rule, and to alter social conditions in the Highlands, where the 'Old Cause' was still able to draw support in the succeeding decades. As Ferguson details, however, the 1745 episode was much more of a last 'Hurrah' before thinning ranks made a further attempt infeasible.[38] A major threat to government at the time, the Jacobite failure and its aftermath actually served to further cement the Union with England, and in the long term reinforced the stability of Scottish society. A series of legal and administrative reforms followed, but most importantly the old society of the Highlands, already disintegrating through integration with the British economic system, now faced a systematic process of destruction by a rigorously enforced policy of demilitarisation. In this process Scots themselves had a vital role, and so successful was the process that within a decade the Highlands were beginning to open up to the more adventurous tourist.

If Ireland and Scotland were distinguished by differing levels of social tension and polarisation, important contrasts also emerge if we deconstruct the social hierarchy and compare the positions of individual classes. Beginning with the aristocracy and peasantry which had traditionally dominated both societies, we can then consider the newer groupings which were beginning to be created in the process of modernisation and economic development.

The Anglo-Irish aristocracy's dependence on England and resultant cultural insecurity were discussed above. Besides their delicate structural position and consciousness, they also differed from their Scottish counterparts in terms of their basic composition. The larger number of small estates in the Scottish Lowlands seems to have permitted an important degree of mobility for merchants, lawyers, and what Ramsay called 'the fortunate adventurers' into landowning ranks.[39] This movement increased from mid-century, with one-third of Renfrewshire, for example, changing hands between 1760 and 1815.[40] This openness was largely absent in Ireland, with the translation of mercantile into landed capital comparatively rare. Indeed, the aristocracy displayed a well-bred distain for 'trade' as a respectable and useful occupation, and consequently lacked their Scottish counterparts' increasingly well-honed commercial inclinations.

An even more powerful source of differentiation was in the relationship between the aristocracy and their tenantry. It is now reckoned that Irish landowners had more engagement with the local economy than was previously supposed.[41] Even so, it is difficult to overlook the practical, religious and emotional divide which existed between this group and the native Irish peasantry. This situation compared unfavourably with the close personal ties of hierarchy and deference which existed between landlord and tenant in Scotland. These ties in turn reflected the considerable social and legal privileges which the lairds could exercise on their estates, including paternalistic influence on the church education and poor-relief. The latter was demonstrated to particular effect in the dearth of 1782, which was met with 'cheerfulness and patience' from the ordinary people, since, 'every precaution which human wisdom could suggest was taken by their superiors to procure a sufficient supply of provisions, and . . . the humanity of the rich never appeared with greater lustre . . .'.[42] Even the penetration of capitalist social relations in the countryside, which might have damaged their authority, had the opposite effect, for as demands for estates goods grew, landlords eagerly seized on the increased economic opportunities, implementing agricultural improvements and even pet industrial projects.[43] In short, unlike the Anglo-Irish, the Scottish landed gentry were a class firmly in the saddle and at the peak of their power in the late eighteenth century, displaying a self-assurance and certainty of their right to rule which Jonah Barrington's 'half-mounted gentlemen' would have found difficult to muster.[44]

The degree of contrast here is repeated in the case of the Irish and Scottish peasantries. Not only were their long-term futures very different, they also differed more immediately in their response to economic change, and in the form and significance of their protest.

Here Scottish history has been experiencing its own revisionism. With regard to the Highlands, Richards has questioned the standard interpretation of inhabitants as sullen and passive in the face of the Clearances.[45] More tentatively, Whatley has also begun to examine the 'orthodoxy of passivity' in the case of the rural Lowlander, depicted as the 'uninflammable' victim of change.[46] The 'eerie' silence of the Scottish countryside, he claims, was not broken by riot and tumult, but by other more informal patterns of resistance, secretive activities, such as sabotage and arson, as demands of the state and economy grew in the eighteenth century. Brown also suggests that rural congregations, while broadly accepting the arrival of 'free market forces' in church management, may have resented the attempts of local élites to reduce popular influence in parish churches.[47]

Conversely, the image beloved of nineteenth-century nationalist historians of the Irish peasantry as 'natural rebels' can also be qualified to some extent. The injustice of the Confiscations and land settlement was absorbed by the Roman Catholic population as a whole, but for most of the eighteenth century resentment was expressed in cultural forms such as bardic lament, rather than popular action.[48] The gulf between the peasantry and the remaining Catholic gentry may after all have been as wide as between them and the Anglo-Irish.

However, more recent developments in the eighteenth century did fuel rural discontent in Ireland, even if 'historic wrongs' did not. Above all, capitalist farming and resultant land hunger threatened the security offered by the old Gaelic landholding system. Disorder consequently assumed a different shape and severity from the Scottish experience. In Ireland, major outbreaks of localised agrarian violence took place in every decade from 1760 to 1840, often assuming a militaristic and desperately intense form through the medium of secret oath-bound societies.[49] In Scotland objective economic factors, such as rapid economic expansion and slow population growth, had a defusing effect on overt organised protest.

The sociological significance of unrest also differed between the two countries. In Scotland the informal rural protest which did materialise was, as Whatley suggests, far from a 'trial run' for working-class activity of the next century, but was intrinsically retrospective and conservative, essentially 'the product of its own times and conditions'.[50] Disorder in the Irish countryside was similarly unpoliticised and cannot simply be subsumed under the banner of 'proto-class politics'. Yet, it did hold out an important element of political potential, which made its contribution to future events crucial in three ways. First, it helped undermine automatic deference for the law and the authorities by substituting widespread popular notions of legitimacy. Secondly, it made rural violence part of a powerful popular tradition. Thirdly, and perhaps most importantly, for a class who had lost its traditional leaders in the Catholic gentry, it began to suggest alternative underground forms of discipline and popular action which did not require leadership from above. In the crisis conditions at the end of the eighteenth century, it was the Defenders movement, a more powerful, coherent and threatening version of the earlier agrarian secret societies, which was to benefit from these developments.[51]

Another means by which Irish popular discontent could be given shape and direction was through the new leadership of the middle class. The obvious candidates for this role seemed to be the rising Catholic bourgeoisie in the towns, whose growing economic power from mid-century was matched by an increase in social influence. Yet agressive assertiveness was not the hallmark of this class, although the foundation of the Catholic Association in 1759 to press politely for emancipation did slowly enhance its sense of identity and assisted later political education.[52]

The very quiescence of middle-class Catholics temporarily pushed the deeply entrenched fears of Protestants over Catholic 'disloyalty' to the edge of literate, educated consciousness. The ugliness of 'the Age of Religion', it was supposed, had been supplanted by progress and reason. Even in the Ascendancy this produced a novel sense of Irish identity and a more critical attitude to the English connection.[53]

An even more significant impact was made on the Presbyterian bourgeoisie. Already, as traced in Chapter One, their own peculiar situation in Ulster had fused dynamically with elements of libertarianism and independence in the Presbyterian thought, which had been imported from Scotland from the seventeenth century onwards, to produce a distinctive radical tradition of industry, reason and enlightenment, known to contempories as 'the Belfast Principle'.[54] Concentrated in Belfast and the north-eastern counties where Protestants predominated, they were also rather isolated from the dangers and complexities of the general Irish denominational situation. Again, the Presbyterians were not 'natural rebels', and exhibited impressive mental agility in combining Presbyterian respect for the social hierarchy with the practical grievances of their community.[55] But as an economically thrusting, prosperous and self-confident population, they resented both mercantilist restrictions on their commercial activity and the social and political disabilities imposed by the 'anti-Dissenter statutes'. It was indeed this group, rather than its Catholic counterpart, which was to become the vanguard of radicalism in the 1790s, channelling existing unrest into political crisis.

The Scottish bourgeoisie, like their Irish contemporaries, displayed considerable economic energy and prosperity. As in Ireland, the wish to translate their material power into attempts directly to influence other areas of social and political life was also beginning to crystallise. In fact, the Scottish and Irish representatives of this class on the surface shared more similarities than did the landed interest or peasantry. This was particularly evident in the cultural and doctrinal affinities of Presbyterian merchants and manufacturers in Scotland and Ulster. Yet, even here, distinctive features of the two social formations were to produce contrasting patterns of radicalisation.

At the most basic level, the Scottish bourgeoisie was more homogenous, lacking in the deep sectarian divisions which characterised Ireland. Also, although excluded from the parliamentary franchise, it remained free of vexatious and humiliating religious disabilities. Even more important was the nature of its relationship with the Scottish aristocracy. To some extent, this again reflected the broadly uniform religious heritage in Scotland, but there existed too a close functional fit between professional groups and the landed class here. Lawyers, for example, frequently drew a large part of their income from land-related work; ministers, doctors and dominies too were equally eager for this sort of work.[56] This relationship must also be set against the entrenched nature of aristocratic authority in Scotland, and the subtle and flexible manner in which this was exercised. While politically conservative, the landed class showed a commitment to economic change, which could help defuse middle-class protest.[57] This was symbolised in the Scottish legal system, whose changing conceptual basis from moralistic to practical definitions of property rights was in harmony with the needs of a rising urban bourgeoisie.[58] Finally, only financial barriers prevented the bourgeoisie themselves gaining landed status. Although the numbers who made the transition were small, as were the estates they purchased, the possibility remained a much more realistic one than in Ireland.

While the preceding comparisons point strongly to the greater degree of social stability in Scotland, this issue needs to be approached carefully. Scottish civil society displayed a pervasive and interlinking quality. Its institutions had in no sense been imposed on Scotland, and indeed, drew strength and legitimacy from their very Scottishness. Nevertheless, its associated mechanisms of social control had evolved from a closely knit rural society. The questions for the more intelligent members of the ruling élite were how the system would respond to the pressures of an increasingly urbanised and industrialised society, and whether in these conditions their own hegemonic position could be maintained. These issues also confronted the Anglo-Irish governing class, who too could be perceptive that not all disaffection was rural, and that not all rural disaffection was peasant-based.

The late eighteenth century was, of course, a transitional phase for the formation of a recognisable 'working class' in Scotland and Ireland. Scottish industrialisation was initially concentrated in rural settings, the major locational pull coming from raw materials and water power. Ireland indeed shared a similar experience, where the Defenders and later the United Irishmen were able to draw on the discontents of its, often highly mobile, rural industrial labour force to supplement the ranks of small peasant proprietors and rural craftsmen.[59] In the short term, the political significance of the industrial system was rather limited in Scotland. Cotton spinners and similar textile workers were not, for example, widely involved in radicalism until after the end of the Napoleonic Wars. This reflected not only the atomising effects of isolated workplaces, but also the effects of higher Scottish living standards, and the greater paternalism of Scottish employers. The organised militancy and unionisation of this group lay in the future as the rate of exploitation intensified, for just as Scotland was to prove more 'modern' than Ireland in terms of economic development, it was also destined in the nineteenth century to display more 'modern' forms of collective political and industrial activity, focused on class-based issues rather than nationalism.

For the moment, it was workers of the more traditional pre-industrial type – weavers, craftsmen, mechanics, small-workshop proprietors, with a growing component of wage-earning employees – who appeared to be the greater threat to the social order. Many were still in industrial villages, but an increasing number were also now in Scotland's expanding towns and cities. Protest in urban settings had a longer history in Scotland than commentators have traditionally allowed. Fraser's analysis of urban craft workers suggests that in the 1720s the incidence of strikes and combinations bore comparison with elsewhere in Europe.[60] Whatley, adopting a broader focus, traces the patterns of collective action on the streets of Scottish towns up to 1780, and while admitting that Scotland did not experience the great 'peaks of revolt', he identifies a significant measure of unrest and turmoil.[61]

Again, 'revolutionary' intent cannot be simplistically inferred here. Much of this community-based violence was in reaction to the perceived effects of economic change. By the last decades of the century, the process of change was indeed becoming increasingly evident in two spheres: the urban environment and the workplace. The process of class polarisation in Scottish towns intensified during the course of the eighteenth century. An early symptom was the gradual withdrawal of the middle and upper classes from popular customs such as town games, but from the 1780s the expanding pool of wage labour helped raise objective barriers in the form of residential segregation in the new urban centres.[62]

Meanwhile, emblematic of work-related changes was the position of the handloom weavers. The dramatic impoverishment of this group lay in the future. For the moment, this was a literate and seemingly independent community, displaying in particularly developed form a popular Scottish absorption in ecclesiastical and doctrinal issues.[63] In reality, however, like many 'independent producers', the autonomy of the group

was being subtly undermined by changes in the production and distribution system. From the 1780s Glasgow and Paisley merchants were beginning to dominate the weaving industry, with weavers in North Ayrshire,
Renfrewshire, Lanarkshire and Stirling being drawn into their putting-
out system.[64] To these new conditions, the confused artisan response
was destined to find a voice, not in theological disputation, but in public,
political activity. This lay not too far ahead, although, for the moment,
the political situation in Scotland presented the governing Dundas interest
with a remarkably untroubled aspect.

Ireland already seemed to be pointing the way. Dublin presented a
fine example of the pre-industrial urban crowd in action, though it has
not received as much attention as Irish agrarian unrest, possibly because
of its episodic nature, and the fact that it pales compared to the London
mob in full spate.[65] Reflecting the social and commercial functions, and
shifting denominational profile, of the Irish capital, its membership was
broadly Roman Catholic, artisan-based, with, like Scotland, a strong
representation of textile weavers. From the late 1750s these citizens
participated in a current of urban unrest, which peaked in three major
riots in 1759, 1779 and 1784. Superficially similar to events in Scottish
towns, as Smyth suggests, these disturbances were 'political' in the sense
that economic grievances were viewed as rooted in Ireland's problematic
constitutional relationship with England.[66] The 'anti-union' riot of 1759,
for example, revolved around allegations that a bill introduced to parliament was instigated by the English parliament to foist legislative union
on Ireland. These allegations, it was reported, 'were published in coffee
houses and all places of publick resort; . . . sung at corners of streets
and commented upon by coalporters'.[67] Such disturbances were serious
enough to warrant consideration of a 'rustication' of the city weaving
community, dispersing and resettling them in villages and towns at some
distance away. But, worrying also for the Dublin Castle authorities was
the practical alliance which was formed at such crisis points between
lower-class Dubliners and middle-class reformers, although, when the
immediate political struggle subsided, class tensions did tend to re-emerge,
notably over trades disputes.[68] These were precisely the inclinations and
experiences which were to be drawn on and shaped by the more determined radical movements of the 1790s.

POLITICAL DEVELOPMENTS

Economic and social divergences between Ireland and Scotland were
cumulative and structural, and as such were less likely to impress themselves on contemporaries than the more immediate contrasts in the two
countries' political life. Faced with the same inspiring set of events

internationally in the last quarter of the century, each indeed evolved its own response, which varied both in its degree of radicalism and breadth of popular support.

The absence of a lively and colourful political culture, particularly among the Scottish middle classes, had long puzzled witnesses who made explicit comparison with the neighbouring small nation of Ireland. The novelist Mrs Hamilton writing in 1782 commented:

> The people here are not such great politicians as in Ireland. There, politics engross the greatest part of discussion in every county, and man, woman and child enter as zealous in every debate, as if they had been perfectly acquainted with all the hidden springs of government. The people here pretend no such knowledge, but whatever changes happen they seem to adapt the maxim of Mr Pope that whatever is, is right.[69]

The contrast was well symbolised in the state of their respective media. In Scotland it took the French Revolution and the consequent hunger for information from Europe to stimulate the growth of newspapers. In 1782 there were only eight in the country, carrying mainly local news. By 1790, these had been joined by another nineteen titles, most being intensely partisan, though they lacked systematic comment on events.[70] To this can be counterposed the growing political influence and radicalisation of the Irish press, which had begun as early as mid-century. Assuming a 'modern' form, papers like *The Freeman* and *Dublin Evening Post* reported British and Irish parliamentary debates at length. By 1779, the Irish viceroy Buckinghamshire found them 'more terrifying than ten thousand soldiers', and attempts were accordingly made to bridle press freedom.[71]

The differing salience of politics in Irish and Scottish society were only partly the product of their specific political structures and institutions. Ultimately, features like the franchise, the electoral system and the very fact of Ireland's separate parliament were bound up with their historical relationship with England and the resultant balance of internal social forces.

Scotland's political system was more unrepresentative and subject to oligarchical control than Ireland's. Local government was notoriously exclusive: Cockburn described Edinburgh Town Council as 'Silent, powerful, submissive, mysterious and irresponsible, they might have been sitting in Venice'.[72] Parliamentary representation was little better. The fifteen burgh seats were managed by small municipal cliques of town council delegates, while the 30 county members in 1788 were elected by a mere 2,662 Freeholders.[73] The system was also famously corrupt, and since the Court of Session lacked the jurisdiction to review elections, manipulation and malpractice flourished in hospitable conditions. The Dukes of Queensberry, for example, specialised in the practice of openly rigging elections from the Act of Union onwards. An unusual opponent arose, however, in the shape of Robert Burns, when the then Duke, in a fit of pique, tried to force his candidate on the Dumfries Burghs in 1789. Burns's spirited account contains some poetic irony:

> Combustion through our borough rode,
> Whistling his roaring pack abroad,
> Of mad unmuzzled lions . . .[74]

The reality of the election was a typically narrow and squalid contest in which the town's 6,000 inhabitants had little direct role.

Such circumstances might have been expected to produce more vigorous agitation for political reform in Scotland. This was not the case for various interrelated reasons. First, the long-standing exclusion of most Scots from the political process had itself an alienating effect, meaning that only small reservoirs of political experience were in existence. Secondly, the issues at stake in elections, as in the Dumfries Burghs, were not those of principle, but remained largely personal to the major participants, or, as Wilkes expressed it, the strife of 'Goth against Goth'.[75] This feature reflected the development of a system of interest politics and ministerial privilege in the eighteenth century, a process which was hastened by the collapse of party. Here it is significant that, whereas in the last Scottish parliament embryonic groupings had existed, with some role for popular opinion, the removal of the legislative body to London ended this vestigial representation.[76] Ultimately, the deadening 'management' of Scottish politics was thus itself a natural reflection of the working of the Union, and of the political hegemony of the landed magnates which this ensured. Far from establishing English domination, the Union had accorded the Scottish ruling élite a real share of political power, by placing Scottish politics in a new national context while retaining the franchise and electoral system of the old feudal order. In turn, the landed interest's traditional local power bases and their new role as dispensers of patronage through their links to the London ministries produced a domestic politics characterised by servility and ties of obligation.[77]

In Ireland, the 'political nation' – those with a direct role in the business of government – was similarly small and exclusive. A key distinction was, however, the existence of a sizeable Protestant popular vote, which fed politicians' anxieties and militated against stultifying political management on the Scottish model. Irish politics presented a highly uneven, but often colourful aspect, and nowhere more so than in the case of the haphazard and often absurd electoral machinery, which had evolved from the medieval period.

The Irish House of Commons consisted of 300 members, chosen by 150 two-member constituencies, 32 counties, 117 boroughs and Trinity College. The Dublin electorate alone of 3,000–4,000 freemen outstripped the number of Scottish county electors.[78] Although the Irish counties, based on the 40-shilling freehold, were seldom contested and, as in Scotland, influence peddling was common, the general political process here was more complex and subtle than it first appeared. The Irish voting public were less poor and hence more independent than has commonly been assumed.[79] Important norms of political behaviour also existed, with career politicians anxious to avoid the taint of deference, and grandees equally aware of the dangers of too intrusive patronage. Likewise, borough constituencies varied in their openness, sometimes, as in the case of Dublin, reflecting vigorous and divided local political structures. Oligarchic control can also be overstated here, with no single 'borough-owner' returning more than nine members between 1777 and 1800.[80]

The electoral system in itself does not, of course, explain the greater politicisation of Irish culture. Even more decisive was the fact that, despite the colonial nature of its English connection, Ireland had retained the distinct legislature which Scotland had abandoned with the 1707 Treaty of Union.

The existence of a separate parliament was broadly stimulating for political development. Its physical presence in Dublin assisted in a positive, practical sense. The dignity and appointment of 'the Little House on College Green' compared favourably with its imperial counterpart. From the 1730s, Lords and Commons met in an impressive neo-classical build- ing, and the parliamentary process was accompanied by appropriate ceremony. Their deliberations had an important influence on Irish society, not least, as we have seen, on the press, but even the academic world was effected, with a high status accorded to oratory in the Trinity curriculum.[81]

A more seminal intellectual impact can also be traced. The existence of a separate legislature provided tangible support for the evolution of constitutional theories which began to question the nature of the English connection itself. A reoccurring concept among Ascendancy politicians and thinkers, drawing on the work of the seventeenth-century comment- ator William Molyneux, was that of a 'dual monarchy'. This implied that England and Ireland represented separate kingdoms, ruled over by a king who, since the time of Henry II, acted in a dual capacity. As a corollary, it was claimed that since homage was given to the king rather than to the imperial parliament, the latter could not bind the Irish parliament by any notion of 'higher authority'.[82]

The constitutional doubts implicit here were to receive ample confirmation. Originally the source of unqualified Irish pride, as the eighteenth century progressed the fundamental limitations of the Irish legislature became embarrassingly obvious, and it began to emerge as a public arena for growing political tensions. For behind the splendid figurative rhetoric of Irish parliamentarians, like Flood and Henry Grattan, parliament remained essentially dependent on Westminster. Under the 1720 Declaratory Act, the British parliament could legislate for Ireland, and under Poynings' Law, the heads of bills had to be submitted to England for approval; imperial and foreign affairs also remained Westminster's prerogative. As the economically punitive impact of its subordinate position within the imperial system began to force itself on the Ascendancy's consciousness, parliament grew restive.

The destabilising potential of this situation was fully realised in the century's closing decades as disenchantment with parliamentary pretensions led to extra-parliamentary forms of agitation. But already, English politicians, like North and Pitt, who were well tuned to these dangers, were considering that the most effective check on the constitutional uncertainty, which shrouded the Irish parliament, might be a straightforward and businesslike political union.[83] The clear precedent here was with Scotland, which union had rendered eminently 'manageable'. There by mid-century, the Union of parliaments had become accepted not just as a political *fait accompli*, but as a source of positive economic and social benefit. In addition, the survival of Scottish civil society had focused national feeling, while at the same time forestalling the development of a nationalist ideology. Although it was difficult for the dignified and loquacious Irish parliamentarians to grasp the fact, the two countries were already set on the path of constitutional convergence, which was to culminate in the 1801 Act of Union.

Parallels in the two countries' political experiences were also now being set in motion. As the repercussions of the American War and the associated imperial crisis began to dominate politics in the 1770s, both Ireland and Scotland shared a common sense of heightened expectations. This was particularly voiced in the middle classes' wish to see a broadening of the base of political decision-making. The existing contrasts in the countries' political cultures and structures were, however, sufficiently strong to promote much more active and developed pressure for reform in the Irish case.

Ties of sentiment, as well as commercial and constitutional issues, led to immediate Irish sympathy with the American cause: 'We are in water colour, what they are in fresco', commented one perceptive Irish MP in 1775.[84] This was particularly true in the north. Ulster emigration had assisted the development of a common Presbyterian heritage of independent thought, but this was grounded at a more practical level in resentment over the economic constrictions imposed by mercantilism. Not surprisingly, 'Americanism' became a fashionable stance in Belfast, and the *Newsletter* supported the colonists' rights with an enthusiasm which prefigured the *Northern Star*'s championing of revolutionary France a generation later. Glasgow-educated Presbyterian ministers were among the warmest advocates of the cause. In County Down, William Steel Dickson condemned government action as 'unnatural, impolitic and unprincipled', while in Stewartstown, Co. Tyrone, Thomas Ledlie Birch dispatched the good wishes of the town's Yankee Club to Washington.[85] Opposition to the war was also voiced elsewhere in Ireland. The Dublin *Freeman's Journal* reprinted Thomas Paine's classic apologia *Common Sense*. The colonists' manifestos were also widely circulated, and public-support meetings were held in Cork and other commercial centres, where parallels between the constitutional situations of Ireland and America were freely drawn.

The Irish response was finally made dynamic by the willingness of the parliamentary opposition on the mainland to cast the American struggle as part of their own anti-administration struggle, and their attempts to attract Irish support for their campaign. From the 1770s, escalating public discontent at commercial policy was to crystallise in the politics of 'Patriotism'. The term had multiple meanings, but essentially it was a form of gentry and bourgeois nationalism, with the key aim of obtaining a more advantageous position in the system rather than severing the imperial connection. Its central article of faith, however, was the winning of legislative independence for the Irish parliament, and by its very rhetoric it was bound to raise hopes which could not be met within the existing constitutional framework.

As for Scotland, the impact of the American War was probably more considerable than contemporary reformers, like Archibald Fletcher, were prepared to admit.[86] Nevertheless, it remained muted compared with Ireland, a fact which is another product of their distinct economic and constitutional status.

Initially, the war was popular in Scotland, where it was viewed as a just assertion of the rights of the Crown and the imperial parliament.[87] Even the commercial interests, whose trade was disrupted as a result of the conflict, displayed little of the sympathy for the colonists which was so evident from their Belfast and Dublin counterparts. The turning point in public opinion did not become apparent till 1779–80, and then only when the British defeat at Saratoga led to questions about the ability of British arms actually to achieve victory. The result was not a focused burst of political activity, but more a general quickening of interest in political affairs. Nor were Anglo-Scottish constitutional relations questioned as a result, instead discontent centred on charges of ministerial mismanagement and corruption, with even Scotland's political manager, Henry Dundas, growing peeved at the lack of patronage baubles from Lord North's beleaguered administration.

For the young William Drennan, then a student in Scotland, the political scene was frustrating for one attuned to the repercussions of the war in Ireland. Drennan was absorbed by the cause of America, 'the promised land I wish to see before I die', to the extent that he delighted in being taken as an 'Irish American'. He commented bitterly:

> Nothing is going on here [Edinburgh] at present, but raising regiments to be devoted to destruction in America. Every order of men from the highest to the lowest, are emptying their pockets (and what more could be asked of Scotchmen) in support of the war; and even the caddies of Edinburgh . . . have subscribed 30 guineas for the aid and assistance of the King of Great Britain.[88]

In more reflective mood, he realised the barrier presented by the entrenched position of the Scottish landed interest, 'who do not deem to regard how heavy their yoke may be, if their burden is light'.[89] Drennan's sister, also on a Scottish visit, did detect more positive, albeit limited, developments. More generally, she took a positive delight in the effects of the war in Glasgow, most of whose inhabitants were also damned by their ignorance of Irish affairs:

> in spite of resentment, the cold contempt and sneers of Age, and all the political caution of the learned Clergy here, there is a spark of a spirit got into the young men . . . and while they honour the Irish, they wish much to follow their example. But nothing can exceed the ignorance and resentment which the Glasgow people possess in regard to us. What pay did our Volunteers receive and from whom? were common questions. They are smarting severely from the war, bemoaning their ruined trade . . . I cannot help saying I enjoyed the sight, supposing it only to be a change from purseproud luxury.[90]

Her sensitivity on the subject of the 'Volunteers' is revealing. For it is the Volunteer movement, the most tangible product of the American War in Ireland, which also provides the strongest evidence for the vigour and maturity of middle-class political protest there.[91] Drawing on a tradition of northern volunteer initiatives which stretched back to the Rebellion of 1641, this 'self-embodied army' now represented patriot politics in action. The formation of volunteer military detachments began formally in 1778, as a spontaneous 'free market' response to the ramshackle nature of Irish defence preparation, as invasion from France or Spain, by now American allies, was threatened.[92] Gentry-led, they also had a large mercantile, professional and artisan component. By 1780 they had rapidly grown to 30,000–40,000 men, in some areas – particularly the north-east – including Catholics in their ranks. In the circumstances, the authorities had little option but to incorporate these insistent defenders.

The Volunteers' contribution to Irish politics in the 1780s far out-weighed their military value.[93] Soon after their foundation they began to establish their own agenda for reform. Ideologically, the Volunteers drew for this on an amalgam of classical republican notions of civic and natural virtue, and on the libertarian strain of Presbyterianism, which posited the right of lawful resistance to tyranny. In tactical terms, they have been described as the reformers' battering ram, employing a highly public campaign of levees, reviews and assemblies, which culminated in the great Convention at Dungannon in 1782. Here, 143 Ulster corps assembled and proceeded to pass a series of resolutions which asserted the legislative rights of the Irish parliament.

These activities achieved apparently striking success. A series of bank failures, revenue deficits and a crisis in defence arrangements combined with the Volunteers' own external pressure to force the granting of Free Trade to Ireland in 1779. Three years later, partly in the wake of Dungannon, but also in response to the political crisis in England, a process began which seemed to guarantee the removal of the Westminster parliament's interference. In July 1782 the Declaratory Act was repealed and Poynings' Law amended so that Irish Bills could no longer be altered in England. Thus began 'Grattan's parliament', so called for its most florid orator.

These political triumphs had an invigorating effect on the psychology of 'the Protestant nation', cultivating pride and self-confidence in their to ability use peaceful mass protest to circumvent parliament. A more critical gaze also began to be directed on parliament itself and on the system of parliamentary representation. Indeed, the euphoria of the early 1780s was soon dissipated as reform-minded Irishmen became more sensitive to the reality of supineness and corruption in the College Green parliament. The new 1782 constitution had, in fact, left the executive sufficient power to dictate its will to the supposedly independent parliament, and this influence was actually to increase steadily over the next decade. This feat was accomplished most commonly through jobbery and patronage, practices particularly offensive to the public virtue of the Volunteers' tradition.[94]

Not surprisingly, parliament itself became the next great target for reform. Here the Volunteers were influenced by the examples of the parallel constitutional campaign in England and were in active communication with its leaders. The Convention at Lisburn in 1783, for example, addressed enquiries to Cartwright, Jacob, Price and Wyvill.[95] Beyond this important bridge-building, the Volunteers' strategy was fatally exclusive and unfocused. The question of the political representation of the Catholic majority of the Irish population was simply not addressed. Convinced of the rectitude and reasonableness of their cause, they were content simply to reapply the same direct pressure which had been effective in 1782. This reliance on 'the popular will', expressed in concrete form by the Volunteers, was a high-risk strategy. Eminently law-abiding, the movement was unwilling to press home its military muscle, nor were contingency plans made should mass reviews and petitions fail to achieve their aims.

In the event, the Volunteers' plan for reform was incorporated into a bill presented to parliament by Flood in November 1793, but their prestige was not sufficient to prevent its rejection. Volunteer protest at their convention meeting concurrently in Dublin quickly evaporated, and splits over the projected political role of Roman Catholics rapidly beset the movement. The mood of anti-climax which followed was well expressed by Wolfe Tone, then a student at Trinity, who had formerly thrilled to the Volunteers' magnificent public displays on Stephen's Green. Now he commented bitingly on the patriot gentlemen of Ireland, 'flying like deer to their counties, to return no more, after making a foolish profession of pacific interest'.[96]

The heady days of the 1780s had little equal in Scotland. The Scottish reform movements for county and burgh reform which, like the Volunteers, emerged from the general climate of discontent following the American War were cautious and colourless. Absent from their political agenda were the great 'theoretical' or constitutional issues which were exciting Irish opinion.

This was particularly true of the county reform movement, founded in 1782, which pressed for unambitious concrete measures, such as the abolition of fictitious votes, to check some of the worst excesses of the existing electoral system.[97] The movement began to gather momentum in the north of Scotland, and a general meeting of reform-minded freeholders was also called in Edinburgh, representing all but ten of the Scottish counties. From this English reformers such as Wyvill, who had founded the Yorkshire Freeholders Association to agitate for similar administrative reform, expected useful support. But they were to be disappointed. Manifestos of the Yorkshire body circulated in Scotland, but the Scots clung to their specific localised grievances and, unlike the Irish reformers, were unwilling to make common cause with movements beyond their own national boundaries. On the contrary, they were anxious to distinguish themselves from the English reformers in order to stress their own 'reasonableness'. The English plan, they suggested, was much more radical, representing, 'a compleat new modelling of the whole system of representation, and even of the constitution of parliament itself'. Their own, however, was, 'only a moderate extension of the privilege of voting . . . to a respectable and independent body of proprietors'.[98] Coupled with this timidity, the movement remained too narrowly focused in its own country to build much popular support, and the issues it raised were precisely those which the system could contain without unduly disturbing the entrenched positions of the landed élite.

A more significant and determined movement was that for reform of the Scottish burghs. This drew strength from the slowly developing shift of economic power from rural to urban settings, and reflected the wealth and confidence of the rising bourgeoisie. This movement also began in 1782, initiated largely by a prosperous Edinburgh burgess, Thomas Macgrugar, whose *Letters of Zeno*, drawing on the ideas of Montesquieu, contrasted the bribery, threats and myopic mismanagement of town councils with the ideals of the intelligent propertied middle class.[99] A committee was formed, drawing particularly on merchants and young advocates, to press for reform of both municipal government and the method of selecting MPs. The movement made steady and continuous progress, and by 1784 was able to call a convention in Edinburgh, at which half the Scottish burghs were represented.

This Scottish movement had, nevertheless, basically limited aims and vision. The burgh reformers were pragmatists, not ideologues. There was little conscious appeal to 'American ideas', and they quickly moved on to the defensive when faced with conservative counter-claims that Britain possessed a 'perfect', and hence unreformable, constitution.[100] Having rejected universal suffrage, they were unable to capture the popular imagination, and found the realities of Scottish interest peddling difficult to overcome. Nor were their internal problems balanced by external alliances. Like the county movement, they also failed to support the English reformers, who by 1785 had Pitt under some pressure in parliament to grant concessions. Instead, when British reform initiatives stalled, they dropped their planned Bill on parliamentary representation, and substituted it with a less ambitious measure to reform municipal elections.

After an undignified scrabble after a sponsor, this was championed by the playwright Sheridan to little eventual effect.

Clearly, the stirring motto of the Irish Volunteers, 'Go on persevere, nothing is impossible . . .' was lost on these earnest, but eminently careful reformers.

Using broad brushstrokes, we can identify a good measure of common ground between Ireland and Scotland on the eve of the French Revolution. Economic dynamism contrasted with political deadlock, much to the chagrin of the rising bourgeoisie. However, the pace and form of economic change, Ireland and Scotland's specific social structures, and their unique constitutional positions combined in distinct pathways of political development.

Most importantly, the economic strains of Ireland's colonial status and the uncertainty of Anglo-Irish constitutional relations produced a political reform movement which was initially at a more advanced stage of development than its counterpart in Scotland, where the political and social hegemony of the landed élite carried more decisive weight. This contrast had a number of key implications.

Foucault's idea of a growing preoccupation with order and 'rationality', closely bound up with the acquisition of political power by the middle class, has been used to effect to conceptualise the 'ordering' of middle class protest in Scotland from the 1780s onwards. The new middle-class protest movements, argues Nenadic, employed novel techniques, such as national co-ordination, the provision of statistical data, and formalised public demonstrations.[101] These functioned both to differentiate their own activity from the emotional and physical protest of the 'lower orders', and to construct an alternative definition of legitimate protest, which could effect change without threatening their own collective interests as a class.

The open, painstaking and practical conduct of the Scottish Burgh Reformers, as Nenadic suggests, casts them well as one of the early British examples of this process. Yet, it is the Volunteers in Ireland who clearly predate them, and who are even more developed advocates of 'ordered protest'. Not only were their leaders expert disseminators of information in support of their cause, but the body's military organisation was itself testament to their commitment to open collective political activity and formal order, ironically enough without the use of physical force. The Volunteers saw themselves as an enlightened *corps d'élite* rather than as the forerunners of mass democracy; as McDowell comments, 'If by supplying political confidence, cohesion and camaraderie to the respectable sections of Irish society they anticipated anything, it was the Reform Bill of 1832, the great charter of the respectable middle class.'[102]

The higher level of maturity evident in bourgeois political activity in Ireland had implications both for the future course of Irish radicalism, and for relations between Irish and Scottish radical movements. The Volunteers movement contributed to the growing gulf between the middle class and parliamentary institutions. This was a process particularly evident in the years 1782–5, and one which entailed questions concerning parliamentary reform and the British connection, which were eventually taken up and given a more developed articulation by the United Irishmen.

Even more importantly, the Volunteers contained in their ranks many of the actual personalities who were to be instrumental in the foundation and progress of the United movement. Indeed, the movement's fate was vital to the political education of a generation. For younger radicals, like Tone and Drennan, the Volunteers' climb-down and frustration in 1785 seemed to indicate the limitations of formal middle-class pressure, and acted as a forcing house for the development of new ideas and methods. Organisationally, the impact was not immediately apparent, the United Irishmen themselves started life as open constitutionalists, and developed pragmatically and unevenly into a conspiratorial form in the mid-1790s. Yet, already in 1784, Drennan was writing that he would like much:

> The institution of a society as secret as the Freemasons, whose object might be, by every practical means, to put into execution plans for the complete liberation of the country. The secrecy would surround the proceedings of such a society with authority and majesty, and the oath of admission would inspire enthusiasm into its members.[103]

The public discourse of Irish radicalism was also shifting significantly in the 1780s. Two issues were integral to this process. First, it was becoming increasingly apparent to its more thoughtful adherents that the Protestant population alone could not accomplish any just and meaningful degree of reform in Ireland. Instead, they recognised that the growing wealth and education of Catholics, coupled with their rising ambitions, necessitated the incorporation of this group into a progressive political partnership. Secondly, this was allied with a broader realisation, again prominent in William Drennan's political and poetic work, that Ireland could not continue slavishly to follow English examples, such as the Whig model of politics, but must begin to look to its own cultural and intellectual heritage.

Finally, the very 'precociousness' of the Irish radicals here also had its negative moments. Notably, it bred a sense of psychological superiority, which could find expression in a rather patronising air – evident in much of Drennan's correspondence while in Scotland – towards those who could not boast such advanced organisations or ideologies as their own.[104] In a sense this condescension was misplaced, since it overlooked the contradictions and traditional sectarian tensions which were still present in their own movement, notably surfacing over Catholic political participation. The Scottish democratic movement might have been less vigorous and 'modern', but it was also less prone to sectarian polarisation.

There was also a graver danger stemming from Irish self-confidence. This was to be realised in the next few years at some cost to both movements. It was that the Irish would offer ideas and strategies, appropriate in the context of their own country, but less suited to Scotland. For, from their superior vantage point, the Irish were liable to overlook that the economic and social basis for linking political radicalism with nascent nationalism was historically specific, and as such could not be unproblematically exported.

NOTES

1. L. Cullen, 'Incomes, Social Classes and Economic Growth', p. 248.
2. Malthus, *An Essay on the Principle of Population*, p. 419.
3. Wells, *Insurrection*, p. 6.
4. Vaughan (ed.), *Ireland after the Union*, pp. 78–9.
5. Elliott, *Partners in Revolution*, p. xv.
6. Cullen, *An Economic History of Ireland*; id., *The Emergence of Modern Ireland*. A useful recent overview is contained in Smyth, *Men of no Property*, pp. 23–7.
7. McDowell, *Ireland in the Age of Imperialism*, p. 4.
8. Foster, *Modern Ireland*, p. 213.
9. McNeil, *Mary Ann McCracken*, p. 50 for a good account of eighteenth-century Belfast; see also Crawford, 'The Belfast Middle Classes', pp. 62–73.
10. McNeil, *Mary Ann McCracken*, p. 49. These schemes perhaps overlooked the more obvious problems of a rapidly growing market town. Pigs rooting in the streets brought down the civic authorities' wrath, *Northern Star*, 28 November 1793.
11. McDowell, *Ireland in the Age of Imperialism*, p. 252; *Hibernian Magazine*, 1779, pp. 246 and 307.
12. Cullen and Smout, *Comparative Aspects*, p. 4.
13. See Devine, 'The English Connection and Irish and Scottish Development', pp. 12–23.
14. It had been heightened by Cromwell's land revolution following the 1641 Rebellion. See Mitcheson and Roebuck, *Economy and Society*, p. 3.
15. Christianson, 'Secret Societies and Agrarian Violence', pp. 369–84; Bartlett, 'An End to the Moral Economy', pp. 41–61.
16. Burgess, 'Scotland and the First British Empire', p. 93. For a full discussion, see Smout, *A History of the Scottish People*, pp. 205–12.
17. Devine, 'Unrest and Stability in Rural Ireland and Scotland', pp. 126–39. For a contemporary's view on the slow and uneven process of change, see Ramsay, *Scotland and Scotsmen*, vol. 2, pp. 46–133.

18. See Connell, *The Population of Ireland* for a classic account. More recent critical perspectives are contained in O'Grada and Mokyr, 'New Developments in Irish Population History', pp. 437–88.

19. Lenman, *An Economic History of Modern Scotland*, pp. 102–3. He cites the 1801 Census which indicated a growth rate of only 0.6% per annum from the preceding century.

20. Devine and Dickson (eds), *Ireland and Scotland*, p. 266.

21. W. Ferguson, *Scotland*, p. 185.

22. Foster, *Modern Ireland*, p. 225.

23. *Rambles through Ireland*, Cork, 1798, and *Promenade d'un Français dans la Grande Bretagne*, Dublin, 1798, quoted in Cullen, 'Incomes, Social Classes and Economic Growth', p. 251.

24. Cullen, Smout and Gibson, 'Wages and Comparative Development', pp. 105–14; and Morgan, 'Agricultural Wage Rates', pp. 181–201.

25. This group has been succinctly described as 'defined along social and political rather than ethnic lines and comprising those who sat in the Irish Parliament or who exercised significant influence over the return of the 300 members of the House of Commons'. See Malcolmson, *John Foster*; Hill, 'The Meaning and Significance of Protestant Ascendancy', pp. 1–22.

26. McDowell, *Ireland in the Age of Imperialism*, pp. 209–38.

27. McCrone, *Understanding Scotland*, pp. 42–9, for a recent review of debates in the area.

28. Devine, 'The English Connection and Irish and Scottish Development', p. 14.

29. Whatley, 'How Tame were the Scottish Lowlanders', pp. 11–12.

30. Devine, 'The English Connection and Irish and Scottish Development', p. 16.

31. *Statistical Account for Scotland*, vol. VII, pp. 312; for Ayrshire vol. VI, pp. 500.

32. Black, 'The Tumultuous Petitioners', pp. 183–211.

33. Quoted in McDowell, *Ireland in the Age of Imperialism*, p. 132.

34. See Millar, *Peep O' Day Boys*, pp. 1–7.

35. The effects of the Laws are considered at length in Power and Whelan (eds), *Endurance and Emergence*.

36. Catholics were officially not permitted to own a horse of more than £5 in value, a good horse being the mark of a gentleman. Bells and steeples on their chapels were also forbidden.

37. McDowell, *Ireland in the Age of Imperialism*, p. 173; Tesch, 'Presbyterian Radicalism', pp. 33–48.

38. W. Ferguson, *Scotland*, pp. 147–55.

39. Ramsay, *Scotland and Scotsmen*, vol. 2, p. 247. He is also a useful source on the gentry's changing manners following the 1707 Union, including the minutiae of diet, drink and wigs: pp. 46–133.

40. Sommerville, *My Own Life and Times*, pp. 359–360.

41. Laye, 'The Wealth of the Greater Irish Landowners', pp. 15–30; for an overview of the issues, see Foster, *Modern Ireland*, p. 179–80.

42. Ramsay, *Scotland and Scotsmen*, vol. 2, p. 259.

43. See Devine, 'The Failure of Radical Reform in Scotland in the Eighteenth Century', pp. 51–64.

44. Foster, *Modern Ireland*, p. 169.

45. Richards, 'How Tame were the Scottish Highlanders during the Clearances?', pp. 35–50. In 1792, for example, the inhabitants of Rosshire combined to drive a thousand sheep before them as a protest against enclosures. See 'Thoughts on the Present Conditions in Rosshire' in *The Bee*, vol. 10, 1792, pp. 297–302.

46. Whatley, 'How Tame were the Scottish Lowlanders', pp. 1–30. For the traditional viewpoint, see Houston and Whyte, *Scottish Society*, p. 25. The classic statement is in Smout, *History of the Scottish People*, p. 417.

47. Brown, 'Protest in the Pews', pp. 83–105.

48. Elliott, *Partners in Revolution*, pp. 4–6.

49. These movements dominated Irish peasant life, and were not confined to Catholics. The Oakboys, set up in 1763 to oppose taxes for road building, included Catholics and lower-class Presbyterians. The Steelboys of South Antrim also included Presbyterians, but had strong sectarian overtones. See Millar, *Peep O'Day Boys*, pp. 1–7; Philpin (ed.), *Nationalism and Political Protest in Ireland*, Cambridge, 1987.

50. Whatley, 'How Tame were the Scottish Lowlanders', p. 23.

51. Foster, *Modern Ireland*, pp. 244–5. Smyth offers a very useful recent assessment of agrarian societies, *Men of no Property*, pp. 33–51. For Defenderism, see also Elliott, 'The Origins and Transformations of Early Irish Republicanism', pp. 405–27.

52. Elliott, *Partners in Revolution*, pp. 16–17 suggests that middle-class Catholics and church leaders operated on the principle that submission to the system would eventually better their lot.

53. Ibid., pp. 9–10.

54. The 'Belfast Principle' was personified in the Joy–McCracken families. Francis Joy, an attorney, took over the *Belfast Newsletter* in 1737 and turned it into a flourishing liberal organ. His sons Henry and Robert Joy continued the family proprietorship, but also extended their activities into printing, paper manufacture, and, following reconnoitring trips to 'North Britain', cotton spinning and weaving. Their grandson Henry Joy McCracken was one of the most prominent and enlightened of the United Irish leaders. See McNeil, *Mary Anne McCracken*; also Joy MSS (Linen Hall Library, Belfast). The papers of Henry Joy contain much interesting incidental material on Belfast history.

55. McDowell, *Ireland in the Age of Imperialism*, pp. 172–3.

56. Clarke and Dickson, 'The Making of a Class Society', p. 153.

57. Devine, 'The Failure of Radical Reform in Scotland', pp. 57–8.

58. Burgess, 'Scotland and the First British Empire', pp. 107–113.

59. Elliott, *Partners in Revolution*, pp. 15–20. She has, however, been criticised for over-emphasising this element in the Defenders' composition, see J. Donnelly, 'Republicanism and Reaction', pp. 94–100. See also Smyth, *Men of no Property*, p. 26.

60. Fraser, *Conflict and Class*.

61. Whatley, 'How Tame were the Scottish Lowlanders', p. 3; see also Logue, *Popular Disturbances in Scotland*.

62. Whatley, 'How Tame were the Scottish Lowlanders', pp. 159–68.

63. See Brims, 'The Covenanting Tradition and Scottish Radicalism', pp. 50–1.

64. Brims, 'The Scottish Democratic Movement', p. 11; N. Murray, *The Scottish Handloom Weavers*.

65. Smyth, *Men of no Property*, pp. 121–56.

66. Ibid., pp. 126–31. Fiscal changes stemming from the 1707 Anglo-Scottish Union had given rise to violent protest in Scottish towns in the early eighteenth century, but Whatley suggests that overt opposition to customs and exise impositions was already dying down by the 1740s, possibly as a result of economic growth and rising living standards, see 'How Tame were the Scottish Lowlanders', p. 12.

67. James, *Ireland in the Empire*, p. 260.

68. D. Dickson, *New Foundations*, pp. 166–7.

69. *Memoirs of Mrs E. Hamilton*, quoted in Meikle, *Scotland and the French Revolution*, p. 44. 'Hissing' was heard for the first time at a Glasgow public meeting over proposals to send a loyal address to Pitt: ibid., p. 5.

70. W. Ferguson, *Scotland*, pp. 250–1.

71. Foster, *Modern Ireland*, pp. 239–40.

72. Cockburn, *Memorials*, pp. 87–90.
73. Meikle, *Scotland and the French Revolution*, pp. 9, 20–1.
74. 'Election Ballad addressed to Robert Graham of Fintry 1790', in J. Burke (ed.), *Poems and Songs of Robert Burns*, pp. 321–6.
75. Meikle, *Scotland and the French Revolution*, p. xvii.
76. W. Ferguson, *Scotland*, p. 137.
77. MPs, it was reported, received ten guineas for dutiful attendance at the House: Ferguson, ibid. For some, like Lord Bute or Pitt's lieutenant and drinking companion Henry Dundas, an independent role in English politics was also possible. See also Fry, *The Dundas Despotism*, pp. 31–53.
78. For a very full account of the Irish electoral system, see McDowell, *Ireland in the Age of Imperialism*, pp. 107–20.
79. Foster, *Modern Ireland*, p. 253.
80. Ibid.
81. McDowell, *Ireland in the Age of Imperialism*, p. 127.
82. The 'two kingdoms' argument was put into action at various points. Typical were Flood's angry claims in 1766 that Ireland had a 'distinct and separate executive', and it was improper for the King to be directed, 'to advise with his British Privy Council with respect to an act . . . in which he is concerned merely as the King of Ireland': ibid., pp. 127–8.
83. Foster, *Modern Ireland*, p. 253; See, Johnstone, *Great Britain and Ireland*.
84. McDowell, *Ireland in the Age of Imperialism*, p. 241. For a full account, see Doyle, *Ireland, Irishmen and Revolutionary America*; also O'Connell, *Irish Politics and Social Conflict*.
85. A. T. Q. Stewart, *A Deeper Silence*, p. 54.
86. Former leaders, such as Fletcher, later keen to rationalise their conduct and free it from the taint of French revolutionary excesses, were quick to distance their activity in the 1770s and 1780s from the influence of external events: Fletcher, *Memoir Concerning the Origin and Progress of Burgh Reform in Scotland*, p. 128.
87. W. Ferguson, *Scotland*, p. 237.
88. W. Drennan to M. McTier, 20 January 1778, no. 20, T. 765 (PRONI).
89. W. Drennan to W. Bruce, Drennan–Bruce Correspondence, 28 October 1782, no. 20, D. 553 (PRONI).
90. M. McTier to W. Drennan, 10 October 1782, no. 46, T. 765 (PRONI).
91. The 'Volunteers' in Scotland were a very half-hearted effort. They were, Drennan remarked, 'neither numerous or well-disposed', Drennan–Bruce Correspondence, 28 October 1782, no. 20, D. 553 (PRONI). See also note 104 below.
92. Smyth, 'The Volunteer Movement in Ulster'. See also McDowell, *Ireland in the Age of Imperialism*, pp. 264–74 and Stewart, *A Deeper Silence*, pp. 4–6. For a contemporary account of 'the spirit now springing up in the place for self-defence', see Lawless, *The Belfast Politics*, p. 138.
93. Their only actual experience of active service ended successfully when a French privateer anchored off Larne, and the town's Volunteers kept it covered from a strategic point on the bay until a frigate of the line drove it off: *The Oakboys*, MS. Book, D. 2095/18 (PRONI).
94. McDowell, *Ireland in the Age of Imperialism*, p. 288.
95. Foster, *Modern Ireland*, p. 255.
96. Tone, *Life of Theobald Wolfe Tone*, vol. 1, p. 351.
97. Meikle, *Scotland and the French Revolution*, pp. 8–12.
98. *The Proposed Reform for the Counties*, pp. 30–1.
99. Meikle, *Scotland and the French Revolution*, pp. 16–17.
100. Reform, according to conservatives, 'is a fairly small matter, which can be left to the renovating principle in the constitution which has always filled up breaches': see, *A Few Thoughts on Political Subjects*. In the

same pamphlet it was suggested that since political power in the small burghs had already such 'unhappy effects', it was probable best not to extend it.

101. Nenadic, 'Political Reform and the "Ordering" of Middle-Class Protest', pp. 65–82; Foucault, *The Archaeology of Knowledge,* London, 1972.

102. McDowell, *Ireland in the Age of Imperialism*, p. 261.

103. Drennan–Bruce Correspondence, 28 October 1782, no. 20, D. 553 (PRONI).

104. Witness his comments: 'They have made some attempts at Volunteers in this country, but they are rude and imperfect sketches . . . Time will show. I wish these defensive Caledonian bands all possible success.': W. Drennan–M. McTier, September 1782, no. 44, T. 765 (PRONI).

3

The Politics of Optimism
1789–1792

The press was suffocated with their addresses, and letters of fraternity, which were swallowed by *the mob*, for whom they were intended, with an appetite which generally characterises that class of citizens.

William Cobbett, *Elements of Reform*, p. 8

The historiography of eighteenth-century Scotland has been locked into a powerful Whiggish paradigm, which judges the past by present standards and casts history as a progressive pathway towards currently respected ideas and institutions.[1] Typical of the school is the 'political awakening' approach of Henry Meikle and William Mathieson, but perhaps equally responsible for its lasting vigour is the single-minded analysis and eminently quotable prose of Cockburn and his friends. Testament to the power of this reasoning is its mirror image in the attempts of some Marxist historians to construct an equally unilinear and teleological model of a working-class formation.

Seminal and cumulative processes were clearly at work in Scottish economy and society, but in reality these were translated into the political sphere in the early 1790s with less than deterministic force. The detail of political history of these years is one of unevenness, more episodic than evolutionary, and studded with complex cross-currents of radicalism and reaction, militancy and accommodation. Nowhere is this more evident than in the words of participants. These oscillate between triumphalism, apathy and fear to such an extent that the modern observer may find them difficult to fathom. In particular, the landscape between 1789 and 1794 was inhabited by two politics: the politics of optimism – faith in the inexorable victory of a just cause, which peaked at the end of 1792 – and the politics of defiance – which gained momentum from the summer of 1793, in the face of escalating anti-reform measures from the government and its supporters. The history of the democratic movements in Scotland and Ireland cannot be understood independently of these processes; thus we can trace in the early 1790s the transition from the principled fraternity of euphoric public addresses – mocked so effectively by the young William Cobbett – to the forging of formal organisational links as a practical defence mechanism in a hostile political environment.

THE FRENCH REVOLUTION

Optimism was a hallmark of European society in the eighteenth century. As John Galt's Mr Balquidder saw it, 'the minds of men were excited to new enterprises; a new genius, as it were, had descended upon the earth, and there was an erect and outward looking spirit abroad'.[2] This found its highest expression in the tide of liberal and radical opinion, and nowhere more so than in Paine's prediction: 'From what we now see, nothing of reform in the political world ought to be held improbable. It is an age of revolutions in which everything may be looked for.'[3]

Ireland and Scotland shared this self-confident spirit. In both cases, radicals were to place their faith in the power of reason and the force of enlightened public opinion to shake the foundations of the old order. Particularly in Ireland, radicals were gripped with an overwhelming conviction that their time was at hand, with the elaborate pageantry of the annual Bastille celebrations in Belfast and Dublin appearing to herald the dawn of the new age of progress.[4] Albeit less exuberantly, Scottish radicals shared this easy confidence. As the Edinburgh Friends of the People reassured themselves in September 1792, 'the cause is good and it is the public *weal*, and the end must be great and successful. Though at present the attempt is arduous, the excitements to perseverance are growing and powerful.'[5]

Such optimism had an impressive intellectual pedigree and drew on a variety of sources, but undoubtedly the most spectacular and energising impetus came from the unfolding of the Revolution in France. Initially, for the 'Death-Birth of a World', as Carlyle typically termed it, this had been received with a surprising measure of puzzlement and dismissive benevolence. The reaction of the British government, for example, was disengaged and non-committal, but by no means hostile at the prospect of a reduction of French territorial pretensions. The two features of the Revolution which were to pose the greatest potential threat, the challenge to Britain's European commitments and attempts to export the Revolution abroad, were absent in its early stages.[6] This attitude was set to change rapidly, as the Revolution itself, less an 'event' than a process, underwent a series of fundamental social and political shifts.

For contemporaries, perhaps the most immediate sensation was a speeding-up of the tempo of political events. A vignette of the period is provided in the literary career of James Mackintosh. A young man of twenty-six, he had received a liberal education at the Scottish universities and had tried a variety of careers before suddenly becoming, in his own words, 'the lion of the place', on the publication in April 1791 of his *Vindiciae Gaulicae*, an early home-grown rebuttal to Burke's *Reflections*. The work bears the marks of being finished in a great hurry to keep up with the pace of change. Three editions followed in rapid succession, the first part going to press before the second was written. Yet, within two years Mackintosh was already tasting 'indignation, grief and shame' at the outcome of the Revolution. He now became an admirer of Burke, and withdrew 'from political contemplation to the contemplation of his own prospects in life'.[7]

Less apparent than the change in political tempo, but of more lasting significance, was also a subtle dialectical process in which the crisis in Europe was reacting with pre-existing domestic tensions. In both Ireland and Scotland, the impact and legacy of the French Revolution was decisively shaped by their own unique political and historical situations.

The spontaneity and vigour of the Belfast *Northern Star*'s coverage of French developments was symbolic of the general Irish response which, after a sluggish start, by 1790 was enthusiastic even by British standards. Belfast was particularly inspired. This was displayed in addresses to the French National Assembly which declared that 'it was good for humanity that grass now grew where the Bastille once stood', and even stretched to a fashion for 'Bastille hats'.[8] Dublin too witnessed the rounds of parades and dinners, with their interminable toast lists, which commemorated the secular festivals of the new French regime.[9]

This partly reflects the close cultural and commercial connections which existed between Ireland and France. These were most evident in the case of Catholic Ireland, but also extended to leading northern Presbyterian families such as the McCrackens, who repudiated the francophobia of the Anglo-Irish élite.[10] Still more significant than any diffuse empathy was the recent history of Irish politics. The French Revolution burst upon the Irish imagination after a decade of struggle and debate over the country's constitutional position and the question of parliamentary reform. With expectations already heightened, the reformers were now able to place their efforts in the context of a general European struggle against tyranny, corruption and obscurantism. Their attitude was more complex than slavish emulation. Admiration for the French stemmed from the perception that they had won in the course of a single year the combined gains of the Glorious Revolution and the Volunteer *annus mirabilis* of 1782. The Irish reformers also believed the Revolution had achieved their own ultimate goal, the rationalisation and modernisation of the entire political process.

This identification had two major effects, which were to have an important bearing on the future course of events. The realisation that French Catholics could create a Revolution, and that Irish Catholics might support it, now made the prospect of a radical-Catholic alliance for reform more palatable. Catholics might after all be fit to receive admission to political rights. More negatively, by setting up France as a measure of what enlightened liberated men could achieve, Irish radicals now associated their own movement, not with an abstract ideal, but with the fortunes of a real political system, inevitably flawed and more hard-pressed than most.[11]

Turning to Scotland, Cockburn's image of everything 'ringing' and 'soaked' in the Revolution has proved a convenient and popular one, despite the fact that, aged ten at the Revolution's outbreak, his comments are more the product of youthful impressions than participant observation.[12] In fact, the nature of the Scottish response was a very accurate indication of the divergent hopes and aims, which were destined to open up even among the broad spectrum of those favourable to change.

After an initial hiatus, Whig opinion was galvanised by the downfall of despotism and the enlightened transactions of the National Assembly over the next two years; this was not least because they discerned a flattering debt to their own Glorious Revolution. Luminaries such as John Millar and Dugald Stewart competed in their admiration for 'the dawn of universal liberty', and their enthusiasm was further fuelled by the great Burke-Paine debate on the political and intellectual significance of the Revolution.[13]

And yet while the pattern was similar to Ireland, in the Scottish case the Revolution was being received in a nation where political debate remained largely underdeveloped, and where the movements for reform in the 1780s had remained socially exclusive, operating amid a general climate of apathy. Accordingly, the response of the professional and commercial bourgeoisie and their few gentry allies, while warm, was altogether cautious. Only one address was sent to France from Scotland, that of the Dundee Whig Club in September 1790.[14] An exercise in studied moderation, not to say smugness, this was as much a vindication of their own cherished 'Revolution Principles', as an active attempt to link current Scottish grievances to French achievements. Correspondence was not maintained.

Less dignified, but more invigorating, was the effect which events in France had on latent popular discontent in Scotland. The early summer of 1792 was marked by a series of disturbances in Scottish towns and their hinterlands. It would be simplistic to view these as the Scottish people suddenly shuffling on to the historical stage, given that riots and popular protest had been recurrent features of the urban scene earlier in the century.[15] It also seems the case that some of the unrest still stemmed from localised economic grievances: in Berwickshire from turnpikes, in Lanarkshire from enclosure, or most seriously in Easter Ross from the encroachment of sheep farming.[16] What was novel about the riots in the larger Scottish towns – Perth, Dundee, Aberdeen and Edinburgh – was the linking of more general economic issues, notably the tax burden and the new Corn Act of 1791, with explicit 'political' overtones.[17] Despite the fears of the authorities, these owed less to Painite ideology than to the perception that the governing classes were showing an ill-judged and arrogant disregard for popular feeling. Evidence was found in their opposition to local-government reform and to the abolition of the slave trade, and by their proclamation against seditious writings in May 1792.

These were demonstrations directed against Henry Dundas, the figure who was identified as Scotland's own incarnation of despotism and corruption. Indeed, by the end of the year, the Lord President must have grown accustomed to having himself burned in effigy.[18] What the demonstrations underlined was the contrast already developing between the vigour and immediacy of popular action and the restraint of middle-class reformers. Above all, for nervous government representatives, they also held out the prospect that familiar types of popular disorder – such as food riots, which had operated within an intellectual framework shared with the established order – might now be fusing into something new, and hence distressingly unfamiliar and incomprehensible.

The French Revolution had two further consequences in Ireland and Scotland. The first was a deep and bitter polarisation in political thought, and an intensification of the extremes of radicalism and reaction. The second, and bound up in the process of polarisation, was the channelling of discontent into the form of advanced reform societies and clubs, a development hardly surprising in view of the vital role of similar bodies in France.

Although relatively shortlived, two of these societies were destined to be of lasting historical significance. These were the Society of United Irishmen and the Scottish Friends of the People. It is the relationship between them in one short but dramatic period, between 1791 and 1792, on which the discussion now focuses.

THE SOCIETIES

Both the United Irishmen and the Friends of the People were amorphous, and indeed rather confused groups. Having grown out of the intellectual ferment which marked the European crisis, the detailed circumstances of their birth again reflected local circumstances. This fact was voiced not so much in their composition and political ideas, which shared considerable affinities, but in their strategies and tactics.

The origins of the United Irish Society lay in the impatience of radical Ulster Presbyterians, already schooled and active in the Volunteers tradition, towards existing movements for reform.[19] High hopes for the opposition group formed in the Irish parliament had been met by insipid tameness. From 1789 to 1790, the Whigs in parliament, led by the sound and fury of Grattan's oratory, had pressed the Irish administration on legalistic issues, but had failed to champion parliamentary reform with the necessary determination. Similarly, the Whig Clubs, including even the more radical Belfast variant, were still faltering over the association of Catholic emancipation with the reform movement.

In this climate of hesitancy, more advanced reformers like Drennan and Tone were able to seize the initiative. Drennan had, of course, already conceived of a more streamlined and committed fraternal association, his a 'plot for the people'. Meanwhile, Tone's pamphlet *An Argument on Behalf of the Catholics of Ireland* helped finally clear the ground for an alliance between liberal Protestants and the more politically educated sections of the Catholic bourgeoisie. Plans for a political club as a focus for progressive opinion had been laid in Belfast during September 1791, and Tone was invited northwards the following month to participate in its actual foundation on 18 October. Resolutions on that occasion emphasised the new society's objective: parliamentary reform and the means to achieve it – a union of the Irish people, Protestant and Catholic, which would challenge venial Ascendancy politics and the obduracy of Westminster.[20] Details were immediately communicated to Dublin, where a sister branch was formed. This was soon to be regarded as the United Irishmen's most influential, or at least most conspicuous, outpost. As early as November, its very founding declaration had been brought to the attention of Westmorland, the Lord-Lieutenant, who felt that its contents would probably bring the Society under House of Commons observation.[21]

This was an auspicious beginning. For Tone the new club was no less than 'the first step to the reconciliation of the two great sects, the Catholics and the Dissenters, by whose disunion the power of England . . . has been hitherto too well-served'.[22] Part of the United Irish Society's original rationale was clearly to cut loose from timid temporising spirits, but their growing momentum as a political and intellectual force further reduced the need to conciliate. Rapidly, in the course of the year following their foundation, they bypassed the sedate liberalism of Charlemont and his ilk as a political irrelevancy. Political differences were present in United Irish ranks, Catholic political rights remained the major divisive issue, and there also existed geographical tensions, evident in the north's contempt for the Dublin branch's flamboyant oratory and practical indecision. Yet, the Society was not in any simple sense an unstable coalition of political viewpoints. Instead, those nervously unable to swallow emancipation or advanced reform tended to remain aloof from membership, clinging rather to the Whig clubs or the Volunteers. Crucially, this did not prevent the United Irishmen enjoying a fruitful association with the latter body, and in partnership with a revival in Volunteering in the north-east and Dublin, they were able to advance their own cause in the course of 1792.[23] They showed similar skill in utilising other existing channels of popular opinion, such as Freemasons' lodges, Presbyterian congregations and parish meetings.[24]

The United Irishmen were not the most politically extreme of Irish radical groups – this honour belongs probably to the Belfast-based Irish Jacobin Club, formed late in 1792.[25] They had, however, the great advantage of being a vanguard organisation relatively free from the inhibiting bonds of 'moderate' opinion, yet able to use the organisational muscle of older well-established reform bodies. To the more restlessly-minded spirits in the Scottish Friends of the People the situation of their Irish brethren in this respect must have appeared enviable. In their own case they were entitled to feel they had the worst of both worlds.

Far from providing a progressive and vigorous alternative to caution and moderation, one of the main motivations of the Scottish movement was to damn the rising tide of popular unrest and physical protest in the summer of 1792, and in particular to place solid constitutionalism in the stead of dangerous Painite doctrines.[26] From the outset the aim was not to short-circuit the traditional burgh and county reform movements, but on the contrary to unite them in a truly national reform movement. As a result, the aims of the organisation, as formulated at its inaugural meeting in Fortunes Tavern on 26 July 1792, were kept highly generalised, committing it to secure 'an Equal Representation of the People', and expressing 'warmest sentiments of veneration and regard' for its Foxite London namesake.[27]

In the face of continued rejections, a polite mating ritual with the burgh reformers was maintained throughout the year. The vital effect of this was that the new movement was kept firmly on the pathway of self-conscious restraint, without actually ever achieving its goal. More complex problems were also raised. While the burgh reformers as an organisation did not affiliate to the Friends of the People, owing largely to hostility from its leader Henry Erskine, individuals from its ranks did. Foxite

Whigs such as Colonel Dalrymple, Lord Daer, and William Morthland were to have a decisive influence on the tone and content of the movement's initial proceedings. Despite much handwringing, they were unable to quench the more radical and openly Painite positions which did inevitably surface among the Friends of the People. The end result was a mutually abrasive alliance between moderates and radicals united on the need to reform the traditional political system, but at odds on the extent of reform required and the methods to be used to achieve it.

Despite these specific origins, the broader forces of political development and the constellation of accumulated grievances at work in the eighteenth century did ensure that the United Irishmen and the Scottish Friends of the People shared a more comparable social and ideological profile. Both were cross-class movements, although their leaderships did not reflect this fact. Indeed, their social make-up was not a particular source of worry for participants, for whom they were movements of 'The People', rather than the preserve of any one class. The original Belfast United Irish club was dominated by Presbyterian merchants and well-established business proprietors.[28] Its Dublin counterpart had a landed sprinkling, but similarly represented the educated bourgeoisie, with a particular following from medicine and the law, and from textile merchants, anxious for protectionist measures.[29] As the movement grew in the north-east involvement from the 'lower orders' – artisans, mechanics, and tenant farmers – also increased. In this case, the United Irishmen seem to have been tapping a pre-existing inclination towards radical politics; clubs of 'Journeymen, artificers and tradesmen . . . something above the common rabble', with titles such as 'The Liberty Boys' and 'The Sons of Freedom', were reported to be taking shape after 1789.[30]

This sansculotte element was also shared by the Scottish Friends of the People, as they too expanded in the latter half of 1792. Low subscription rates ensured a significant membership from urban tradesmen and shopkeepers. Shoemakers and weavers particularly featured among radical occupational groups, but in contrast to the Ulster countryside, the political conservatism and loyalty of farmers was much stressed, reflecting the material prosperity and social aspirations of this group in Scotland, but also pointing to the difficulties of radical organisation in rural areas where the landowners' personal hegemony was decisive. Meanwhile, the leadership of the Scottish movement featured some aristocratic reformers, but more commonly drew on the same disgruntled professional and mercantile constituency as the United Irishmen.[31]

For both movements reform was a matter of providing political solutions to what were viewed as political problems. It was not only the language of Whig constitutionalism they shared in their early days, but also their key historical doctrine of the 'Ancient Constitution'. Figures like Drennan, Dalrymple and Daer argued that the people had historic as well as natural rights, and that political participation had been a feature of national life before the Norman conquest. Now a purifying process was required to modify, not overthrow, a constitution which, although sound, had become encrusted with the dead weight of corruption and executive privilege.[32]

To this traditional position, and much to the distaste of the extreme constitutionalists, there became welded a selective interpretation of Thomas Paine's work. The popular impact of *The Rights of Man* in both countries was initially constrained by its price, but perversely the Proclamation against Seditious Publications seems to have encouraged its spread in Scotland, with attempts already being made by September 1792 to apply its doctrines to the Scottish political situation.[33] In Ireland, its eventual diffusion was also assisted by rural migrant workers.[34] The more highly educated among the Irish and Scottish radicals also had a good measure of ideological sympathy with Paine, whose own style seemed influenced by the reasoning and rhetoric taught at the Scottish universities.[35] His concepts of an unmediated compact between God and man, and of sovereignty resting with the individual, struck home also to Presbyterian sensibilities. At the same time, the threat of persecution, and in the Scottish case also the fear of alienating potential allies, meant that their regard had to be tempered with caution. Nevertheless, after tortuous debates in both organisations during 1793, a commitment to a universal manhood suffrage emerged.

This position, coupled with the sociological model which emerged from their reading of Paine – of two classes, one wealth producing, the other wealth consuming – immediately led to charges of social egalitarianism and economic 'levelling'. Conservatives, indeed, seem to have been more perceptive than the radicals themselves on the practical link which held between social and economic equality. Following Paine, most of the middle-class leadership of the Irish and Scottish democrats held poverty not to be the result of an unequal distribution of wealth, but a symptom of political malaise, the product of the type of government produced by a restricted franchise. Economic individualism and property rights were held inviolable, a point underscored by the Dublin United Irishmen when they stated that by equality they did not infer 'the equality of property or the destruction of subordination'.[36]

Nor did the majority of the original United Irishmen or the Friends of the People display any enduring interest in meaningful social reconstruction. Both wished a reduction in the burden of taxation to be accomplished directly through restructuring in favour of wealth produ-

cers, and indirectly through the abolition of corruption and the advent
of cheaper government. There also seems to have been shared support
for any reformed parliament to provide a national system of education
to ameliorate the situation of the common people.[37] Beyond this, part
two of *The Rights of Man* which contains most of Paine's social welfare
proposals was studiously neglected. On the contrary, often their sympathy
with and understanding of urban and rural protest appeared rather limited,
especially where this threatened to undermine their own efforts for
peaceful constitutional reform. There were important exceptions, however, which are harder to find in Scotland. After the turmoil of the
1790s, James Hope wrote bitterly: 'None of our leaders seemed to me
perfectly acquainted with the main cause of social derangement, if I
exempt Neilson, McCracken, Russell and Emmet. It was my settled
opinion that the condition of the labouring class was the fundamental
question at issue between the rulers and the people'.[38]

As suggested by Hope's remarks, some of the leadership, particularly
in Ulster, appeared less willing to accept the consensus of moderation,
pushing instead for the expansion of the Society's membership base. The
Journals of Thomas Russell confirm this and highlight his own key role,
which was conferred by a unique 'social and spatial mobility'. As the
climate for reform worsened in the next few years and radicalism began
to restructure itself, this more determined cadre was destined to assume
considerable significance. In these circumstances, 'Adieu to Property!'
might after all find its way on to the political agenda.[39]

The other element of the Painite canon which was more generally
omitted, even by the most committed social reformers, was his religious
scepticism. This was to be expected and emphasises the genuine and
pervasive piety of eighteenth-century Irish and Scottish society. Both
movements had deep religious well-springs, tinged with Presbyterian
egalitarianism. The contributions of an enduring Covenanting tradition
in Ulster, and the more modern 'scripture politics' of the United Irishmen
have already been described. The Friends of the People also had an
important input from orthodox Covenanting Calvinism, including members of the Old Dissent in the Relief Church and the Anti-Burgher sect.
The new Rational Dissenters, including Unitarians, were less evident
numerically, although they did make an important local contribution in
areas such as Tayside.[40] Similarly prominent individual radicals like
Thomas Muir, who quarrelled with Paine over religion when they were
both in Paris, did not find their political principles incompatible with a
practical religious commitment.[41] This was also true of Drennan, Russell,
McCracken and many of the United Irish leaders; Drennan, for example,
could praise Neckar's 'excellent, useful and agreeable book [*Compte*

Rendu]', while noting with distaste that it seemed to be addressed to 'a nation of atheists'.[42]

Where the movements differed was not in the extent of religious belief, but in the actual salience of confessional issues. The United Irishmen accepted the need of Catholic emancipation with resignation rather than enthusiasm. For without emancipation, representation would not be 'free equal and entire'.[43] There was sympathy and even a degree of fellow-feeling from Presbyterians concerning Catholic disabilities, but little sympathy or understanding for Catholicism as a creed. Pragmatism nevertheless dictated that their cynicism and apprehension be kept for private consumption.[44] In Scotland, where Catholic involvement in radical politics was slight, and where Catholic political rights had enjoyed little bearing on the political agenda since the storms of 1778, opposition to 'Popery' was more routinely expressed as part of the radicals' general distaste for despotism, temporal and spiritual.[45] Thus, in his 1792 Address to the People and their Friends, James Tytler could argue quite unselfconsciously that: 'As the Popish Priests absorbed in the worship due to the deity by sticks and stones and rascally saints, so have the House of Commons artfully drawn the attention of the people of Britain from the king to themselves'.[46]

In short, neither the Irish nor the Scots were atheistic republicans, unless 'republican' is meant, as Drennan intended, in the Real Whig sense as a limited monarchy, governed in the interests of the majority. So reasonable did this aim appear to them that less attention was paid to the actual mechanics of how to achieve it. Both groups shared important first precepts here, most notably on the efficacy of enlightened public opinion, when brought to bear constitutionally on parliament. Accordingly, propaganda was seen to be vital, and one of their first endeavours was to found sympathetic newspapers, though the sound business sense of the Belfast Presbyterians ensured that the *Northern Star*, founded in 1792, proved a more successful proposition than its nearest Scottish counterparts, the *Edinburgh Gazetteer* and the *Caledonian Chronicle*.[47]

Important too was the expression of massive public support for their cause. Yet, it is here that the Irish and Scottish situations diverge, and the sense in which the former movement was more 'advanced' becomes clearer. This turns on the existence of a separate parliament, and on the more firmly grounded tradition of radical middle-class political campaigning in Ireland. On the one hand, their semi-independent legislature allowed the Irish authorities more room for manœuvre over the granting of minor reform measures than government representatives were permitted in Scotland. In 1793, for example, four bills were passed, incorporating reforms previously advocated by opposition Whigs, such as the reduction of the Pension List.[48] While this further reinforced the conviction of Irish radicals that the tide of history was running in their favour, it did little to mitigate the basic contempt in which the institution of parliament had been held since the constitutional struggles of the 1780s. For, the hallowed Volunteering tradition had not only legitimated extra-parliamentary reform activity, it had also promoted a strategy of brinkmanship, which held out the powerful temptation of casting public-reform conventions in the role of sovereign assemblies of 'The People'. Their position contrasted strongly with the Scottish Friends of the People, who had only the mild legacy of the Scottish local-government reform movements to draw upon, and who remained set on attracting the burgh reformers to their standard. Despite their awareness – following the failure of the latter group's petition to parliament in 1792 – that Westminster was unlikely to respond positively to their demands, their moderate leadership could still hardly bring itself to consider the alternatives if campaigning through constitutional channels failed.[49]

Finally, the association of the United Irishmen with the Volunteers had the additional important result that the Society indirectly became an armed organisation from its very inception. Although a formal decision to resort to force was not to be taken until 1795, this was a fact which immediately exercised the minds of the Irish authorities. In December 1792, Westmorland was already warning Henry Dundas that the United Irishmen were raising a Volunteer battalion, armed with flintlocks and pikes, and with cannons ordered for two of its corps.[50] Whatever hellish designs spies like Robert Watt might impute to the Scottish Friends of the People, it is difficult to imagine them being the source of apprehensions of quite this gravity.[51]

CONTACT

Contact between individual members of the United Irishmen and the Scottish Friends of the People began within weeks of the Scottish group's establishment. According to the government agent Thomas Collins, present at a meeting of the Dublin Society on 31 August 1792, correspondence with like-minded societies in Great Britain had just been discussed, whereupon:

> A member present said he had private letters from members of a society lately established in London, called the Friends of the People, and also from some Scotch delegates lately assembled in Edinburgh who are determined to give up the idea of a partial reform of their burghs and join in demanding a *radical reform* of the whole *representation* of the *people* . . .[52]

These individual links were swiftly translated into more formal correspondence. At the United Irishmen's next meeting, a draft of a letter to the new 'Scotch Reform Society in Edinburgh' was read and referred to the Committee of Correspondence, with the final version ordered to be forwarded immediately at the meeting of 2 November.[53]

The individual participants in the original exchange of letters remain elusive. The methodological problem here is interesting in itself. Given the fate which awaited radical movements in the two countries, and the allegations of conspiracy which lay at the heart of the government's reaction, there were perhaps few brave enough to claim the honour of forging the original link. We do know that a correspondence was begun in 1792 between Thomas Muir, Vice-President of the Friends of the People societies in and around Edinburgh, and Hamilton Rowan, Secretary of the Dublin Society of United Irishmen, which, as Rowan remarked, increased in frequency towards November of that year.[54] Some commentators go further. Donnelly suggests that Muir was responsible, 'acting upon his own initiative' for making the link, while Bewley writes that he entered into correspondence with Rowan *and* Drennan 'through common friends in Glasgow'. In neither case is evidence provided for these claims.[55] Perhaps the willingness to lionise Muir's role in Scottish political history also serves to boost his profile as its earliest leading 'internationalist'. In fact, if Muir was involved, it is likely that he was not acting alone. Collins's report clearly suggests that more than one 'delegate' was in touch, and the papers of the Friends of the People Committee of Finance from 31 July to 21 November 1792 also include three payments for postage received from 'Dublin' or 'Ireland'.[56]

Yet, in a sense the precise detail of the initial contact between the Edinburgh and Dublin societies is less revealing than the impression it conveys of the intensely personal character of much of the radical activity of the period. The Rowan–Muir correspondence suggests men who could confidently address each other from the vantage point of broadly similar social status, upbringing and education. Rowan, from an Ulster landed family had, indeed, Scottish Covenanting forebears. On eventually meeting, they were also to strike up a warm and immediate friendship on the basis of sympathetic personalities, for both were flamboyant, eloquent and given to political posturing as modern-day *Gracchiae* or 'tribunes of the plebs'.[57] Also revealing are the potential chains of connection which bound radicals. Muir, for example, attended Edinburgh University from 1785 to 1787, and there joined the Speculative Society where his membership overlapped with Thomas Emmet, a colleague of Rowan's in the Dublin United Society. Just as the 'political nation' was small and byzantine in the late eighteenth century, so was the world of those who aspired to join it.[58] Rowan was also a Freemason, a member of the First Volunteer Lodge of Ireland, and while there is no evidence of Muir's affiliation to the Craft, we cannot rule out the possibility of Freemasonry as an additional contact medium at this stage, given its role among other Enlightenment influences on radicalism.[59]

Beyond these personal considerations, and the broad social and ideological empathy between the two movements, what were the motivations for building links? From the vantage point of 1799, the authorities had little doubt that the previous decade had witnessed a uniform conspiracy. Radicals, they stated:

> considered themselves as engaged in one common cause, as far as related to the destruction of the existing constitution; all looked to the success of the disaffected in each country, as forwarding their common views; and each was ready to support the other in any resistance to the lawful government; a frequent intercourse between them was therefore considered important to their ends.[60]

In fact, this analysis greatly overstates the planned and systematic nature of the shift from constitutional to conspiratorial policies in the 1790s. In the process, it also attributes purely instrumental aims to an alliance which was founded originally from a confused mixture of idealistic and pragmatic motives. Indeed, it was not until the summer of 1793 that doctrinal inspiration was to become supplanted by the practical imperative of defensive solidarity. Even then the result was not yet the 'revolutionary conspiracy' of official propaganda.

The large component of idealism in the relationship between Irish and Scottish radicalism drew strength from the climate of 'international brotherhood' which accompanied the French Revolution, and from radicals' consequent sense of belonging to a European-wide movement for reform. In the very midst of this cosmopolitan upsurge, Irish, Scots and English reformers in Paris had combined, after an excellent dinner, to send a warm fraternal greeting to the French National Convention.[61] At home, the Irish were similarly inspired, as the Belfast United Irishmen expressed it, 'Liberty is the desire of *all* nations! The birthright of *all* men!'[62] Already in the 1780s, the Irish had been more willing than the Scottish county and burgh reformers to identify themselves with wider reform movements. Now in late 1792, the United Irishmen were busy addressing their radical counterparts in England, and also, with graver consequences, in Scotland.[63] As usual, the Scots movement officially showed greater restraint in its fraternal feelings, still wary of scaring off potential supporters by associating with high-coloured international radicalism.[64] Yet this line was not followed unquestioningly, and local Friends of the

People societies, as in the case of the Partick branch which had been set up in response to a local 'Burkified' society, were proud to proclaim their 'co-operation with the immense host of reform associations in Scotland, England and Ireland for the glorious purpose of vindicating the natural rights of man'.[65]

New French-inspired ideas of fraternity were only one impetus for Irish–Scottish links. There also existed more traditional ideological precedents. Not least was the pre-existing cultural interchange, which was symbolised in the *Northern Star*'s fondness for printing the poems of Burns, and other less illustrious productions in unadorned Doric, for the consumption of its Belfast readers.[66] We must also remember the seminal influence of the Scottish universities, and the common Presbyterianism of many radicals. The Belfast United Irishmen were well aware of both linkages, and in an address to the Scottish radicals in 1793 diplomatically praised 'the seminaries [which] have provided the world with statesmen, orators, historians and philosophers', while simultaneously invoking 'the solemn ties of religion and blood [with] which many of us are connected with you'.[67] Not only did this situation lay down a basic common ground for the relaxed exchange of ideas, their temporary sojourn in Scotland may also have given Irish radicals, like Drennan, the impression of familiarity with Scottish affairs, and encouraged concern for further political developments in Scotland. The problem was, as in Drennan's own case, that their impressions could be based on experiences of over ten years before.[68]

On the Scottish side the situation was more complex, and some of those active in the radical interest seem to have felt the need to clear the ground of lingering anti-Irish sentiment before the ties of shared religious principles and political convictions could take effect. The pro-government *Glasgow Courier*, for example, was prone to this unsubtle brand of humour, with the Dublin Volunteers parade to celebrate Bastille Day on 15 July serving as a typical target. 'We presume', commented the *Courier*, 'that this is because this is *leap year*'.[69] In an attempt to counter this tendency, the reformers' *Glasgow Advertiser* reminded its readers that all 'natural inflections are ungenerous'. It was also prepared to print prominently a letter from an Irish student, complaining about another of the *Courier*'s attempts 'to rekindle the dying embers of national prejudice, and groundless animosity'.[70]

More practical factors also lay behind the establishment of links in 1792. The establishment of an efficient and co-ordinated national movement was one of the characteristics of the ordering of middle-class protest in the late eighteenth century.[71] The next stage of bringing together reformers in the three British kingdoms was not then some unparalleled aberration. Contact benefited the morale of societies in Ireland and Scotland by promoting an awareness that they were not campaigning in uncongenial isolation. In the beginning, the mechanisms involved were public resolutions and solemn fraternal greetings, but to dismiss these loftily, like Ehrman, as 'touching, sometimes rather absurd and sad' is to neglect their psychological contribution in bolstering a sense of shared grievance and common cause.[72]

Even more enduring and effective was the contribution of the radical press in promoting mutual awareness and reciprocal support. Through this medium, news of the progress of the other's movement was directly available. The *Northern Star*'s extensive distribution network included Edinburgh, while the *Caledonian Chronicle* had separate subscription arrangements for Ireland.[73] This did not represent a circulation war; the Star was happy to welcome the appearance of a new radical Edinburgh paper, the *Gazetteer*, in November 1792, and besides, the high cost of postage meant that a more common source of information on the broader political situation was in their own house journals. The *Star*'s coverage of non-Irish affairs was impressive generally, often at the expense of Irish events outside Ulster. Its attention to Scotland was quite painstaking, with Edinburgh-based correspondents sending regular reports. Popular protests towards the end of 1792 were given detailed coverage, and when some in Belfast considered this 'alarmist', the *Star* replied in superior tone that the calling-out of the militia in the counties bordering Scotland was 'tolerable confirmation of the authenticity of our intelligence respecting commotions in that quarter'.[74] Closer interest was shown in the early progress of the Scottish Friends of the People, with the *Star* often appearing more interested and better informed than Scottish papers like the *Courier* and the similarly loyal *Glasgow Mercury*. From 'several letters received from different parts of Scotland', it assured its readers that 'the people are seriously occupied about the means of obtaining a reform in parliament'.[75] This was confirmed by reports of the formation and resolutions of individual Friends of the People societies throughout central Scotland.[76]

The Scottish radical papers reciprocated by following Irish affairs, and it is a good rule of thumb that the more 'advanced' the paper's politics, the better their Irish coverage. The *Gazetteer* had correspondents in Dublin and Belfast, and its very first edition of 16 November featured a lengthy analysis of the Irish political situation, suggesting that the goal of the 'creatures of government' in that country was 'in some unguarded moment [to] hurry the country into that state on which their hearts are fixed, but which all other Irishmen ought most to depreciate – a UNION with Great Britain'.[77] This interest carried through into the heart of the paper. In a typically outward-looking inaugural editorial which reviewed the present state of Europe, Ireland was looked upon as an extreme case of the system of corruption by pensions and sinecures which they condemned in their own country. In arguments very similar to William Drennan's on Ireland's geographical and economic potential, they argued that, 'If Ireland obtains a Free Constitution, and an equality of political rights, she must rise to the highest pitch of commerce and political consequence. Her situation, her internal resources, her fertility and population must unite to create an importance not inferior to Holland'.[78] Scottish reformers could also take heart that the political scene in Ireland was particularly vibrant, and that, before a few months elapsed, Ireland might boast of 'a free, not mercenary, army of eighty thousand volunteer citizens'.[79]

This latter point brings us to a second major impulse which drove Scottish radicals to look to Ireland, namely the superior political experience and self-confident buoyancy of their Irish counterparts. One striking example of this was the case of the Paisley reformers. Here, reported a government informer, the French Revolution had 'stimulated a spirit of political investigation which has been conducted with an ardour unequalled in any former period'.[80] Yet, when it came to translating this spirit into a more concrete form, the radicals turned to an example closer to home. Thus, at the beginning of August:

> A few individuals agreed to publish an account extracted from an Irish newspaper, of the military review at Belfast, being the day appointed for celebrating the annual anniversary of the French Revolution. This pamphlate [sic], besides an account of the parade and review contains an address from about 5000 humble inhabitants of Belfast to the National Assembly of France and another to the People of Ireland.[81]

This material, the former Address penned by Drennan, the latter by the young Wolfe Tone, and breathing 'the same bold, masculine spirit', seems to have had the desired effect.[82] Immediately after its publication, 'a regular society was formed, slow at first, but soon divided into four daughter societies'.

It was not only the Scottish grass roots who were inspired, nor was it the splendid public displays of the newly resurgent Volunteers which were solely responsible for the inspiration. In an open letter to the Scottish Friends of the People, the moderate reform leader Norman Macleod M P recommended 'constant patience and endeavour, while seeking to maintain the momentum for reform'. In this piece, he searched for a definition of 'The People' in order to silence those conservatives who argued that 'The People' had no place in the British Constitution since no law book definition of this concept existed. Macleod found his definition in the political thought of the United Irishmen, and this provided him 'with as eloquent, as concise and as perspicacious a definition of the word and the thing PEOPLE as ever was given of any of the objects of the science of government'.[83]

The definition he quotes, although lacking in the conciseness he claimed for it, is a final forceful statement of the universalist spirit which enthused the radical politics of the day:

> If we are asked who are the people? We turn not our eyes here and there, and cry Lo! The People; but we look around us and without partiality and predeliction, and we answer 'The Multitude of Human Beings, the living mass of humanity, associated to exist, to subsist and to be happy'. In them and them only we find the origin of social authority, the measure of political value, and the pedestal of legitimate power.

THE FIRST CONVENTION: 'A CIVIC UNION'

The first formal public contact between the United Irishmen and the Scottish Friends of the People came with the Address *To the Delegates for Promoting a Reform in Scotland*, sent to Thomas Muir to be read at the Society's inaugural national convention in Edinburgh in December 1792.[84] While on the one hand, this stands as a laudable instance of the United Irishmen reaching out to wider currents of reform, it can also be viewed, in more negative terms, as an ill-judged intervention into a delicate political situation in Scotland. The problem was only partly the different levels of tactical and ideological development which marked the two reform movements. More importantly, the Address was sent from a country reaching a crescendo of optimism in late 1792, to one where reaction was already gathering momentum, and where, critically, the authorities had the appropriate judicial machinery to strike immediately against the fledgeling Scottish democratic movement. Such was the speed of events, that the high-flown combative rhetoric which Irish radicals had been accustomed to use for a generation was shortly to be regarded as 'treason' and 'sedition' in their own country. The hostile reception of their Address in Scotland should perhaps have provided them with food for thought.

The idea of the first Scottish national reform convention may itself have owed something to the Irish example in the first place.[85] Scotland had its own venerable tradition of public assemblies bound up with its

Covenanting past, but this had found only a pallid reflection in the county and burgh reform conventions of the 1780s. In contrast, Ireland, and particularly Ulster, which shared the Covenanting heritage, had enjoyed a spectacular recent history of extra-parliamentary displays of public opinion. At the very point at which the Scottish reformers were meeting in Edinburgh, a Catholic congress met in Dublin in 'a bold attempt to redress the balance of Irish politics, and typically snubbing the Irish admin-istration and parliament, resolved to petition the King directly'.[86] Mean-while, William Drennan was pressing Belfast radicals to hold a convention of parochial delegates at Dungannon, the site of the great Volunteer triumph of 1782. Here he appears to have been attempting a compelling link between the indigenous convention tradition and modern ideas from the Continent concerning popular sovereignty. There had already developed in France, argues Gwyn Williams, a need for a new political dis-course to express this new sovereignty. A major concept which emerged was that of 'embodiment', in other words, the function of popular assemblies to give form and expression to the people's General Will.[87] There is a strong echo of this in Drennan's desire for the Dungannon Convention to 'embody and ascertain public opinion' and to draw up comprehensive principles on the Rights of the Nation. At first, he sug-gested that the Convention should not disperse until it was given the guarantee that reform would be granted – with appropriate subsistence allowances provided. Later, his position was modified to recommend a permanent executive committee and the dispatch of delegates to a per-manent reform convention, which would convene if parliament would not accept reform.[88]

For some of the more restless spirits in the Scottish reform movement, particularly Thomas Muir, the role of their own convention was simil-arly to inspire and concentrate the reform process. In recommending a general convention, Muir began diplomatically by choosing the precedent of the Scottish County Reformers, but his later military metaphors were indicative of the much more vigorous campaigning role he actually envisaged:

> The general of an army might well propose to storm an enemy's trenches by detailing small parties to fire platoons at the distance of a week, as a Friend of the People might imagine that Parochial or even County Associations could obtain a civil reception on such a subject in the British House of Commons.[89]

The Irish input was not the only one. Other more diffuse aims also lay behind the decision to hold a convention. Moderates too saw the practical opportunity in 1792 to produce a co-ordinated national policy, and to consider the fine detail of how and with what Address to petition for reform. In the event, it was the misfortune of both the moderate position and Muir's own strategy to be overtaken by a series of developments which lay outside the privileged and petulant world of the middle-class reformers.

By late 1792, the French Revolution had reached its second phase. In the face of attack from the coalition of European powers, popular sansculotte movements took on a new key political role. The Revolution also became more bloody. In particular, the 'September Massacres' against remaining aristocrats, clergy, and other perceived enemies within received detailed coverage from the Scottish press. The *Glasgow Mercury* excelled itself in its accounts of the upper half of the Princess of Lamballe placed on a pike, 'still reeking', or of the Paris pastry cooks making pies out of Swiss Guards and priests.[90] These were the images which were to be firmly fixed in the minds of Scotland's ruling élite, and it is little wonder that they sent the young Cockburn to bed shuddering.[91]

Yet, almost incredibly against the odds, the rag-tag citizens' army was able to throw back the allies under the Duke of Brunswick. This victory, coupled with the formal internationalism of the Revolution, as voiced in the Decree of 19 November 1792, which offered fraternity and aid to all peoples seeking liberty, touched popular Scottish opinion just as the events of 1789–91 had caught the imagination of their liberally-minded social superiors.[92] This was only partially channelled into a spurt of growth for the Friends of the People. The current of triumphalism and optimism also resulted in November in a wave of spontaneous riots in Scottish towns. In Perth, Dundee, Leith, and Aberdeen, demonstrations, complete with the usual smouldering Dundas effigies and Trees of Liberty, took a more violent and openly political form than elsewhere in Britain, or for that matter in Ireland. The nervous attitude of the Scottish authorities was summed up in Vaughan's comment, 'The thief has entered in'.[93]

Saddled with a military establishment which was well below strength, a legacy of the pacific 1780s in Scotland, the riots confirmed Henry Dundas in his belief that the Friends of the People Association was strongly linked to the climate of unrest, and that he himself was a prime object of their attentions:

> I am more and more satisfied that unless something effectual can be done by parliament to check the indiscriminate process of association, they will spread the fermentation of the Country to such a height, that it will be impossible to restrain the effects of them. They stop

at nothing, it would appear they intend to either murder myself or
burn my house.[94]

A series of official measures, formal and informal, was the result. The
first response was a traditional one, stemming from the belief that social
disaffection could be viewed in directly economic terms. Thus in late
November and December, Dundas was apprehensive at the prospect of
a grain shortage, and sent an exploratory circular to provosts and sheriffs.[95]
Intertwined with this tactic was also a growing awareness that new
mass-communication techniques might be required to counter the
reformers' attempts at orchestrating public opinion. Accordingly, the
authorities themselves began to address a wider audience, and to employ
the emergent arts of propaganda, welcoming a flurry of loyal addresses
and resolutions, and subsidising a sympathetic press.[96]

Not surprisingly, following Dundas's earlier remarks, a central feature
of the exercise was the implication of the Friends of the People in the
popular disturbances. The fact that this largely succeeded, despite the
dearth of actual evidence, suggests that the authorities were harnessing,
rather than creating, nervousness among Scotland's propertied classes.
As Dundas could assure his parliamentary audience after a jibe from
Grey on his 'well-earned popularity in Scotland':

> With respect to his popularity, if those who had laboured to create
> prejudices against him had meant to occasion him uneasiness, they
> had certainly succeeded. During his summer in Scotland . . . he had
> been visited from every quarter by the great manufacturers, by
> Magistrates and by gentlemen, all expressing their alarm at the situ-
> ation of the country; and requesting the interference of government
> to check a spirit which threatened to be attended by such dangerous
> consequences.[97]

The concern of these groups was further expressed in their bombarding
of the authorities with largely unsolicited advice on probable carriers of
'sedition'.[98] These *ad hoc* channels of information, supplemented by a
handful of paid informers, now formed the rudiments of a local intelligence system for Scotland.[99] The national authorites in Britain, who
had faced similar challenges in gearing up to the new radical threat, were
also eager to offer advice and assistance, and by early November 1792
had already called on the vigilance of loyal postmasters at Glasgow and
Edinburgh.[100]

For the Foxite leaders of the Scottish Friends of the People, the
loyalist reaction and the closing of propertied ranks seemed to be the
most severe threat to date to their much desired alliance with the burgh

reformers. When their Convention met at last on 11 December, after six turbulent weeks, high-minded ideas of 'embodiment', or even more routine concerns for the content of the reform petition, had become supplanted by the more pressing need to refute loyalist calumnies, and pursue a path of compromise and moderation.

It was into this highly delicate situation that the United Irishmen stretched the hand of fraternal greeting. It has been suggested that Thomas Muir himself requested the Irish Address, but again here evidence is lacking.[101] Certainly as far as William Drennan was concerned, he considered himself to be a moving spirit behind its production. As President of the United Irishmen, but 'bearing his honours meekly', he 'proposed a letter to the Scots delegates which was received with great acclamation, and Tandy etc. bedaubed me with praises'.[102] He continued to display an inordinate pride in the piece which resulted as a fine specimen of his rhetorical gifts, and enclosed 'the letter to the Scotch' to his sister so that she could also marvel at its stylistic conceits.[103] She, in turn, assured him that it had been printed in the *Northern Star*, without introduction, and that 'many of the proprietors have declared it to be one of the finest papers [that] ever was written'.[104]

It is hard to escape the impression that Drennan considered the Address to be a literary exercise, as much as a political statement. Interestingly, when the time finally came for the United Irishmen to produce a specific reform manifesto, it was drawn up clearly and concisely by Thomas Emmet, using Drennan's material, for his own pen was deemed 'too florid and refined for the people'.[105] Nevertheless, practical political motivations also lay behind its dispatch. The 'Irish Address' must be set against the background of the gathering momentum for reform in Ireland during the winter of 1792–3, but it also reflected internal conflicts becoming increasingly evident within the Dublin United Society. Louis Cullen has recently pointed to the tactical debate being fought out between those like Drennan, Rowan and Simon Butler, who saw the Society as a high-profile public campaigning body, and those like Thomas Russell and Wolfe Tone, who prioritised the building of a broad radical network beyond the Dublin élites.[106] For the first grouping it seemed that at last the cause was about to triumph. The Volunteers had revived throughout Ulster; middle-class Catholics were using open constitutional methods to push for emancipation; liberal plans were laid for a symbolic show of strength at Dungannon; even the parliamentary Whigs, Ponsonby and Grattan, were said to be pledged to reform. The Drennan–Rowan clique were also able for the time being to monopolise the leading positions of the Dublin United Irish Society, and the Address was only one of several important productions, as they tried to clarify ideas and objectives in response to events and throw down a final challenge to the government. To this extent, its contents were as much for home consumption as for a Scottish audience – hence publication in the *Northern Star*.[107]

There also seems to have existed a hope, if Drennan's sister can be relied upon, that the extravagant and uplifting sentiments of the Address would 'flatter' the Scots into engaging in further correspondence with Ireland, perhaps even tempting them from their accustomed tactical timidity. She wrote to him:

> You have attacked them on their weak side. The Edinburgh society, I hear, is founded on the strictest pr[inc]ples. Every member admitted must have two credible witnesses to his character. In case of misbehaviour he is to be expelled but in any attack made on him he is to be supported. All they fear is the ardour of the people, and their every effort is to keep them from any irregularities or riotous proceedings.[108]

Not only did this rather condescending analysis omit the complex circumstances which were now intensifying the traditional circumspection of the Scots, it also disingenuously neglected the warning words which McTier could have read in her own *Northern Star* a few weeks earlier: 'the Scots seem not to be behind hand in the pursuit of Freedom; but we would be sorry to find that they would thus prematurely push into violent measures without making application to the legislature for redress'.[109] Ironically, at the last moment, the Address was almost not sent. The spy Collins had alerted the Irish authorities that it far exceeded 'anything produced by our Jacobines, for stile, art and boldness [*sic*] . . .', and there were rumours that the post would be stopped, but Hamilton Rowan managed to beat the ban, enclosing the 'Scotch Address', as it was known to the United Irishmen, and paying seven shillings for it.[110]

Following its arrival in Scotland, the Dublin Society was soon basking in the warmth of two highly gratifying letters. The correspondents here were Thomas Muir and William Skirving, Secretary of the Edinburgh Friends of the People: 'Both of them highly approving of our principles and pursuits and promising the most strenuous support and co-operation of the *whole Scotch nation*, observing that although Ireland has proceeded Scotland in the present struggle, yet the latter will be equally zealous in bringing matters to a happy conclusion . . .'.[111] The fact that this promise proved an extravagant one was partly the result of the real political situation of 'the whole Scotch nation', but probably also reflected Muir and Skirving's own injudicious handling of the document.

The Address was introduced by Muir on Wednesday 12 December, the second day of the Convention, to an audience which had already retrenched, and where the internal divisions of the Scottish reformers were now uncomfortably public. Muir or Skirving must also have unwisely circulated copies of the Address prior to its public debut, for the response was immediate, and served to open the movement's splits even further. The moderates, Daer, Dalrymple and Morthland, at once opposed its reading on the grounds that 'it contained treason or at least the misprision of treason [concealing knowledge of treason]'.[112] 'A universal cry to hear it', however, arose, and with Muir gallantly taking upon himself 'the whole responsibility and danger of the measure', he read it out and moved an answer be sent. A fierce debate ensued, which placed earlier disputes over standing committees and the wording of various resolutions firmly in the shade.[113]

What was there in the Irish Address to produce this reaction? The veteran Glasgow reformer, Peter Mackenzie, writing in 1831, could find nothing in it to substantiate its description as 'a species of wicked and abominable SEDITION', and on the contrary felt that nothing 'could be more beautiful and gratifying to the feelings of a Scotchman . . .'.[114] A nearer contemporary of Muir's was probably more accurate when he described the Irish Address as 'conceived in the language of enthusiasm, figurative, bold, but unhappily exposed to misconstruction and abuse'.[115]

Sadly, Drennan's flamboyant prose, running to nearly three thousand words, has not stood the test of time. The broad outline is straightforward. The Scottish reformers were first hailed 'in a spirit of civic union, in the fellowship of a just and common cause'. The piece then went on, apparently quite innocuously, to pay tribute to the progress of the cause of reform in Scotland and to its supporters there, suggesting that some competitive emulation might be valuable, a struggle of 'noble animosity' in place of 'puerile national antipathies', to determine 'who shall first obtain that free constitution from which both are equidistant'. It expanded on the latter point with an analysis of the political balance of forces in both countries. In each case the inadequate parliamentary franchise was outlined, with the Irish being given particularly detailed treatment. Drennan recounted how in 1782, inspired by Grattan, 'the angel of our deliverance', Ireland ceased to be a province and became a nation. But British supremacy in Ireland presented changing aspects: first rule through direct oppression, and then through systematic corruption. Now, despite attempts to divide and rule, Catholics and Protestants under United Irish leadership, had come together to win reform and emancipation. There followed some practical recommendations. Drennan suggested that in each country – Scotland, England and Ireland – the people should meet in constitutional conventions, and send delegates to discuss a plan for reform, 'best adapted to the situation and circumstances of their respective nations', and then petition parliament 'with a unanimous voice'. The Address concluded with a request for an answer – 'and quickly'.

Beyond this, Drennan's production was problematic in a number of major respects. First, a general difficulty sprang from the Address's highly coloured 'nationalistic' tone. This was voiced in Drennan's pride in the regenerative powers of a union of Irish people, but was most evident in the opening paragraph of the Address, destined to be its most controversial passage:

> We greatly rejoice that the spirit of freedom moves over the surface of Scotland, that light seems to break from the chaos of her internal government; and that a country so respectable for her attainments in science, in arts and in arms; . . . now rises to distinction, not by a calm, contented, secret wish for a reform in parliament, but by openly, actively and urgently *willing* it with the unity and energy of an embodied nation. We rejoice that you do not consider yourselves as merged and melted down into another country, but that still in this great national question you are still – Scotland – the land where Buchanan wrote, and Fletcher spoke, and Wallace fought.[116]

These sentiments were difficult to stomach for some Foxite delegates, like Robert Fowler, a friend of William Morthland, who considered that it contained 'high treason against the Union betwixt England and Scotland'.[117] In fact, the United Irishmen, as firm cosmopolites, were themselves edging, only gingerly, towards nationalist positions in late 1792. It was to take the events of the next three years to strengthen their perception that the pathway to Irish political rights remained blocked by English-sponsored officials, and ultimately by the English connection itself. For the moment, aware of the practical ties which bound them to England, many, including Drennan, still hoped for a modification rather than rupture in the relationship. Nevertheless, an ideological shift had already begun. Most importantly, this was set against the background of the previous decade of constitutional uncertainty and discussion in Irish politics. Consequently, there was little inhibition among Irish radicals in raising the prospect of separation of the component parts of the British Isles, at least as another hypothesis worthy of earnest testing.

For all Drennan's enthusiasm, this speculative, forward-looking spirit was much less evident in Scotland. Here, the Anglo-Scottish Union, with its perceived links into native economic prosperity and national security, had gathered legitimacy in the course of the eighteenth century, becoming thus an unlikely subject for serious political debate. There did exist an ample supply of pride in Scotland's surviving civil and cultural institutions, and a certain Scottish 'patriotism', elegiac and nostalgic, to which 'The land

... where Wallace fought and the rest' might have appealed, but this was a doubtful basis for future political activity to secure 'national rights'.[118]

As Brims suggests, it is difficult even to view the battle in the Convention over the Address as one between nationalist and unionists *within* the Scottish reform movement, as it has been popularly represented.[119] Muir's own position as a 'radical nationalist' did not crystallise until towards the end of his eventful life. In the First Convention he was probably more critical towards the Union than some of his moderate colleagues, but, like W. S. Dickson, his ideas still seemed to have owed something to the teachings of his old law professor, John Millar, himself a firm unionist. In this way, when Muir avoided the usual Anglo-Saxon precedents for claiming the people's historic political rights, and stressed instead the purity of the ancient Scottish institution, he was apparently following Millar's argument in his *Historical View of English Government*, that England's 'uniqueness' was the product of natural resources rather than constitutional precocity.[120]

A further, more specific, concern of the opponents of the Irish Address was that any greater formal linkage between the Scottish and Irish reform campaigns might have restricted the Scottish movement's freedom of action. A similar fear had already moved delegates earlier in the Convention to express disquiet over a general statement of objects, which would have helped commit the Scottish Friends of the People to a co-ordinated campaign with their London namesakes. On this occasion it was the diffidence and hesitancy of the ultra-constitutionalist English group which was the sticking point; in the Irish case it was conversely their reputation for radical extremism which raised violent antipathies.

For some, the strength of the language in the Address was enough to confirm their worst prejudices. In particular, Drennan's use of the 'embodiment' concept at the outset of the Address alarmed moderate Whig constitutionalists, such as Fowler. To these figures, when read along with a later passage which stated that 'it is not the Constitution, but the People which ought to be inviolable', it appeared to cast their own meeting in the undesired role of a sovereign assembly, threatening the integrity of the British Constitution and the Rule of Law. This was illegal, or at best inexpedient in late 1792. To this objection, Muir could initially only reply with the optimistic assertion that Scotland *was* an embodied nation, for , 'Have we not distinct courts, judges, juries, laws etc.' Besides, he argued, the peoples of Ireland and Scotland willed a reform and were merely petitioning parliament to translate that will into a reality, and to petition parliament was not treasonable. Finally, he suggested, not to send a reply to the Address would leave the Irish a scapegoat.

These rather feeble attempts were not enough to convince his opponents, whose appraisal of the political situation in Scotland was perhaps more acute than Muir's own. Well-founded fear of the loyalist reaction was one factor here. Another, voiced by Colonel Dalrymple, was the divisive impact a reply to the Address would have on their own movement, and by implication on the last-ditch attempt to involve other 'gentlemen reformers'. Many members must have listened with anxiety to a county delegate, who emphasised he was also a royal burgh reformer, when he said that, 'if such a paper was read before his constituents, they would withdraw themselves from the association'.[121]

Despite repeated attempts by some Edinburgh delegates to reopen the issue, and a vocal minority, who chaffed at the meeting's restraint and consistently supported the Address, the Convention decided that passages were too extreme. Muir agreed to withdraw it, and return it to Drennan for 'smoothing'.

After two days and evenings of debate, many in the Convention may have sympathised with the delegate who expressed the view that the Irish Address should have been 'smothered in the cradle'. Many too, as they moved on to other lengthy discussions on the petitioning campaign, may have assumed that the matter was at an end.

In this they were sorely mistaken. For with the new year, the implications of the Irish Address for the authorities, for the radical societies, and not least for Thomas Muir himself rapidly became clear.

NOTES

1. See Fry's provocative essay, 'The Whig Interpretation of Scottish History', pp. 72–89.
2. Galt, *Annals of the Parish*, p. 118.
3. Paine, *The Rights of Man*, see especially pp. 68–9 and 159–62. An echo of Lafayette's phrase, 'For a nation to be free, it is sufficent that she wills it'.
4. *Northern Star*, 12–14 July 1792 for Belfast celebrations.
5. *Minute Book of the Edinburgh Society of the Friends of the People*, Justiciary Papers, JC 26/280 Scottish Records Office (SRO). See also Jacob, *The Rise of the United Irishmen*, pp. 193–206.
6. Note Pitt's cautious, but still hopeful statement in February 1790, 'The present convulsions in France must sooner than later, terminate in harmony and regular order; . . . it might also make her less obnoxious as a neighbour . . .': *The Parliamentary History of England*, vol. xxxvii, pp. 78–90.
7. Mackintosh, *Life of Sir James Mackintosh*, vol. 1, p. 84.
8. For the *Northern Star* see February to November 1792 *passim*. Helpfully, it printed for its readers a handy guide to converting the new revolutionary calender into the more conventional Julian version. Typical Irish coverage in the *Dublin Evening Post*, 15 November 1792; Bastille hats in Elliott, *Wolfe Tone*, p. 18.
9. *Dublin Weekly Journal*, 16 July and 12 October 1791 for examples.
10. For background, see de la Poer Beresford, 'Ireland and French Strategy';

for Ulster links, McNeil, *Mary Ann McCracken*, p. 4. For the Ascendancy view, O'Brien, 'Francophobia in Later Eighteenth-Century Irish History', pp. 40–51.

11. McDowell, *Ireland in the Age of Imperialism*, p. 335.

12. Cockburn, *Memorials*, p. 73.

13. See Meikle, *Scotland and the French Revolution*, pp. 49–61.

14. *Caledonian Mercury*, 2 September 1790; for other celebrations in Edinburgh and Dundee, see *Caledonian Mercury*, 16 July 1791.

15. See preceding chapter; see also Whatley's recent paper, '"An Uninflammable People"', pp. 51–71.

16. For anxious offical correspondence on the latter outbreak, see Home Office Correspondence (Scotland) RH 2/4/4/64 (SRO).

17. A comprehensive discussion of economic grievances is given in Brims, 'The Scottish Democratic Movement', pp. 135–47. The Corn Act provided for bounties and import restrictions which benefited southern landlords, but which went against the living standards of those in manufacturing towns.

18. Pitt was sufficiently concerned at 'the outrages at Dundee' to request full details from Henry Dundas: W. Pitt–H. Dundas, 4 July 1792, Arniston Papers (SRO).

19. For details, see McDowell, *Ireland in the Age of Imperialism*, pp. 379–89; Elliott, *Partners in Revolution*, pp. 21–2. Note also Cobbett's vituperative account: 'Soon after the ever to be regretted epoch, when God in his wrath, suffered the tinkers, butchers, harlequins, quacks, cut-throats and other modern *philosophes*, to usurp the government in France, their bretheren in Ireland tempted by the successful example, began with wonderful industry to prepare for taking the government of that country into their own hands' (*Elements of Reform*, pp. 8–11); see also, *Porcupine*, vol. ii, pp. 8–9.

20. See Tone, *Life of Theobald Wolfe Tone*, vol. 1, pp. 367–8. For a discussion of the relative roles of Drennan and Tone, see Stewart, '"A Stable Unseen Power"', pp. 80–92; and id., *A Deeper Silence*, pp. 149–63.

21. Westmorland to Grenville, 16 November 1791, Private Official Correspondence, CSO LB417 (NAI). For a first-hand account of the formation, W. Drennan to W. Bruce, n.d. [1791], Drennan–Bruce Correspondence, D. 553 (PRONI)

22. T. W. Tone to Citizen Minister De la Croix, 26 February 1796, Tone MSS.2050 & 3807 (Trinity College Dublin).

23. For these developments, see *Northern Star*, 22–5 February 1792, and 9–11 May 1792.

24. Curtin, 'The Transformation of the Society of United Irishmen', p. 464. For a different interpretation, see A. T. Q. Stewart, *A Deeper Silence*, pp. 164–78.

25. *Northern Star*, 15 December 1792 for their inaugural address. For further discussion, see Curtin, 'The Transformation of the Society of United Irishmen', pp. 471–3.

26. See Brims, 'The Scottish Democratic Movement', and id., 'The Scottish Association of the Friends of the People', pp. 33–6.

27. Caledonian Mercury, 28 July 1792.

28. A. T. Q. Stewart, '"A Stable Unseen Power"', pp. 80–92.

29. McDowell, 'The Personnel of Dublin Society of United Irishmen', pp. 12–53.

30. See Howell and Howell (eds), *A Complete Collection of State Trials*, vol. xxxi, col. 395; Madden, *The United Irishmen*, vol. 1, p. 116.

31. Brims, 'The Scottish Democratic Movement', pp. 201, 206–8.

32. See Elliott, *Partners in Revolution*, pp. 24–34.

33. Howell and Howell, *State Trials*, xxiii, col. 27 has a reprint of a broadsheet forwarded to Henry Dundas, containing the first part of Paine's work

      to which is appended an account of Dundas's handling of the burgh
      reformers' petition.
34. Elliott, *Partners in Revolution*, p. 16.
35. Ehrman, *The Younger Pitt*, vol. 2, p. 114n.; Paine was elected an
      honorary member of the United Irishmen, McDowell, 'The Personnel
      of Dublin Society of United Irishmen', pp. 12–53.
36. *Procceedings of the United Irish Society of Dublin*, Dublin, 1793, p. 45.
37. Brims, 'The Scottish Democratic Movement', p. 227ff.; Emmet saw this
      as perhaps the most significant boon of a reformed legislature, see
      MacNeven, *Pieces of Irish History*, p. 222. Russell characteristically was
      one of the first to highlight the practical advantages of some manner of
      educational provision for the poorest, Woods (ed.), *Journals and Memoirs
      of Thomas Russell*, p. 36.
38. Madden, *Antrim and Down in '98*, p. 108, and see Hope MSS. 7253–6,
      Trinity College Dublin (TCD). For another viewpoint on the social
      radicalism of the United Irishmen and their appeal to a plebeian audience
      before 1795, see Smyth, *Men of no Property*, pp. 75–9.
39. Russell was expressing this view by July of 1793, Woods (ed.), *Journals*,
      pp. 87–8.
40. Brims, 'The Covenanting Tradition and Scottish Radicalism', pp. 50–63.
41. Religion played an important role in Muir's upbringing. He was an
      elder in his local church at Cadder until he resigned in 1791, possibly
      over a patronage dispute. He continued to have a lively interest in Kirk
      affairs. See Marshall, 'Thomas Muir', pp. 1–42.
42. Drennan Letters, W. Drennan to M. McTier [September 1788], no.
      262, T. 795 (PRONI). He also disapproved of the 'atheism' of David
      Hume, whose mind 'had been distorted by his own sophistry' (letter
      no. 8 [May 1777]).
43. *Proceedings* (1793), p. 24.
44. For examples, see, Drennan Letters, nos. 351 and 463 (PRONI), and his
      comments to his sister Martha McTier.
45. David Downie, implicated in the 1794 'Pike Plot', was one of the few
      Catholics in radical politics: Anderson, 'David Downie and the Friends
      of the People', pp. 165–79.
46. Printed in Howell and Howell, *State Trials*, xxxiii, cols 2–3.
47. For the *Star* see Biggar, 'The Northern Star', pp. 33–5, and McDowell,
      Ireland in the Age of Revolution, pp. 384–6. The paper was very effici-
      ently established and managed by a team of ten investors. In contrast,
      the *Gazetteer* had a sole proprietor (Captain Johnstone), and seemed
      undercapitalised from the outset. It was the object of various survival
      bids. See *Edinburgh Gazetteer*, 16 November 1792 where Johnstone, a
      half-pay officer, reminds readers of his own £700 investment, and JC
      26/280 (SRO) for the establishment of a committee of support. Less is
      known about the *Chronicle*. Only one edition appears to have survived
      in the Mitchell Library Glasgow: 7 December 1792 (bound in with the
      Gazetteer).
48. McDowell, *Ireland in the Age of Revolution*, pp. 435–6.
49. They were unwilling to listen to calls which were already being made
      in 1792 that they should petition the King directly and by-pass parlia-
      ment. J. Pringle to H. Dundas, 24 November 1792, RH 2/4/65/37
      (SRO) raises divisions in opinion over the issue.
50. Westmorland to H. Dundas, 5 December 1792, Westmorland Corres-
      pondence, 1/78 (NAI).
51. For one of Watt's early hysterical dispatches, see R. Watt to H. Dundas,
      31 August 1792, RH 2/4/64/303 (SRO).
52. Rebellion Papers, 620/19/97 (NAI).
53. Contact was also initiated with the London Friends of the People:
      Rebellion Papers, 620/19/97, 620/19/100, 620/19/104 (NAI).

54. Drummond (ed.), *Autobiography of Archibald Hamilton Rowan Esquire*, p. 170.

55. Donnelly, *Thomas Muir of Huntershill*, p. 9. He suggests that this was in September 1792. Bewley, *Muir of Huntershill*, p. 70.

56. JC/26/280/6/1–24 (SRO). Muir himself, writing in April 1794, stated that Rowan had introduced him to the United Society, a fact that he considered to be 'his highest pride', *Northern Star*, 17 April 1794.

57. For Rowan, see Drummond (ed.), *Autobiography*, and also Nicholson's unreliable, but occasionally illuminating, *The Desire to Please*. Particularly valuable for Scottish links is the copy of his *Memoirs*, probably a transcript of the original, MS 24 K 28, held in the Royal Irish Academy (RIA). For Muir, Marshall, 'Thomas Muir' is a personal memoir by a contemporary, probably Robert Forsyth, see particularly pp. 161–245. Also useful though heavily polemical, is Mackenzie, *Life of Thomas Muir*. The best short modern account is Logue, 'Thomas Muir': pp. 21–31 are most useful on Muir's famous trial.

58. James Mackintosh was well aware that this phenomenon has its ironies. Three of his old friends in the Edinburgh Speculative Society were Baron Constant de Rebeque, Charles Hope and Thomas Addis Emmet. Their subsequent fortunes were 'a curious specimen of the revolutionary times' in which he had lived. 'When I was in Scotland in 1801, Constant was a tribune in France; Charles Hope was Lord Advocate; and Emmet his former companion, a prisoner under his control': Mackintosh, *Life of Sir James Mackintosh*, vol. 1, p. 27.

59. Smyth, *Men of no Property*, p. 175; A. T. Q. Stewart, *A Deeper Silence*, pp. 176–8.

60. *Report of the Committee of Secrecy of the House of Commons*, 1799, p. 11.

61. See, *A Collection of Addresses*. For a first-hand account, see Ceasar Colclough to John Colclough, 19 November 1792, McPeake Papers T. 3048 C/10 (PRONI), and Sheares Letters MS 4833 (TCD); see also Seaman, 'British Democratic Societies', pp. 223–61; Alger, *Englishmen in the French Revolution*, and id., 'The British Colony in Paris', pp. 672–94.

62. Lawless, *Belfast Politics*, p. 102.

63. *Proceedings*, pp. 15–19 for 'Address to the Friends of the People at London'.

64. Brims also follows this interpretation, 'Scottish Radicalism and the United Irishmen', pp. 154–5.

65. Howell and Howell, *State Trials* xxiii, pp. 33–4.

66. See *Northern Star*, 14–16 April 1792. It published his Address to Francis Grose, 'in which the ideas, like most of Mr Burns' productions are singular and eccentric'. *Northern Star*, 27–30 October 1794 also has a Burns pastiche, 'An Address to Mr Pitt in GUID BRAID SCOTCH'.

67. Copy in JC 26/280 (SRO), also reprinted in *Belfast Politics*, pp. 100–4.

68. W. Drennan to W. Bruce, 28 October 1782 for one of his early analyses of the Scottish scene: 'It is truely amazing to observe the effects occasioned by the spirit of party... The truth is, I believe, that the Stewarts fear the consequences of the democratic spirit... they with some others of the gentry are endeavouring to collect the reins which have lain floating on the necks of the multitude, and to accustom them once more to that proper discipline which the distance of ranks, when well-presented, produces in civil society', D. 553 (PRONI).

69. *Glasgow Courier*, 17 July 1792.

70. *Glasgow Advertiser*, 7 March 1794.

71. Nenadic, 'Political Reform', pp. 65–82.

72. Ehrman, *The Younger Pitt*, p. 75.

73. *Northern Star*, 29 December–2 January 1792–3; *Caledonian Chronicle*, 7 December 1792, it cost £2 by post.

74. *Northern Star*, 5–8 December 1792; for coverage of disturbances, see *Northern Star*, 28 October–2 November, 28 November–1 December; 8–12 December.

75. *Northern Star*, 24–28 November 1792.

76. *Northern Star*, 12–15 December for Penicuik, Glasgow and Galston; 15–19 December for Linlithgow; 2–5 January 1793 for Perth; 16–20 March for Paisley; 30 March–3 April for Water of Leven.

77. *Edinburgh Gazetteer*, 16 November 1792.

78. Ibid.; note Drennan's lines:

> The vast Atlantic tide,
> Has scooped thy harbours deep and wide.

Also his remarks, in *Second Letter to Rt. Hon. William Pitt*, 1799, quoted in McDowell, *Ireland in the Age of Imperialism*, p. 369.

79. *Edinburgh Gazetteer*, 23 November 1792; for further reports on Irish affairs, see 30 November 1792 and 28 December 1792.

80. Grand Lodge of Scotland Miscellaneous Papers, GD/1009/16/1–5 (SRO). The first report is dated Paisley, 21 January 1793.

81. Ibid.; for the Bastille celebrations, see *Northern Star*, 12–14 July 1792, from which the extract may have been taken. The two Addresses are contained in *Proceedings* . . .

82. Tone, *Life*, vol. 1, p. 40.

83. *Glasgow Advertiser*, 14–18 January 1793. The full text of the letter is also reproduced in *Two Letters to Chairman of the Friends of the People*, Edinburgh, 1793. Evidence again of the tightly knit world of radicalism is the fact that United Irishman Thomas Russell served under Macleod in India in the early 1780s, Woods (ed.), *Journals and Memoirs*, p. 16.

84. Reprinted in Howell and Howell, *State Trials*, xxiii, cols 154–160; and in *Proceedings* (1793), pp. 19–25. It was also widely reported in the Irish press: *Dublin Evening Post*, 6 December 1792. See Appendix B for text.

85. Brims, 'The Scottish Democratic Movement', p. 269.

86. McDowell, *Ireland in the Age of Imperialism*, p. 409.

87. Williams, *Artisans and Sans-Culottes*, p. xvi.

88. McDowell, *Ireland in the Age of Imperialism*, p. 425.

89. *Glasgow Advertiser*, 23–6 September 1792.

90. *Glasgow Mercury*, 11–18 September 1792. Their own correspondent had been present when these pies had been consumed in a restaurant to cries of 'Vive la Nation'.

91. Cockburn, *Memorials*, p. 41.

92. *Edinburgh Gazetteer*, 7 December 1792 for another heady editorial.

93. Vaughan to E. Nepean, 30 November 1792, HO 42/22 (PRO). A more determined response is contained in Arniston MSS RH 4/15/5/no. 75 (SRO), C. Long to H. Dundas, 10 November 1792:

> I am sorry to say that spirit of discontent prevails so much in Scotland. It has increased here since the failure of the Duke of Brunswick and nothing but the most vigorous efforts of govt. I think are enough to suppress it, but such efforts I think are, and such efforts I think must be used – are wont to require a degree of activity equal to that of our opponents. The Attrny. General is determin'd to prosecute every libel that appears . . . Pitt supports this and believes punishment should follow the offence as quickly as possible.

94. H. Dundas to E. Nepean, 30 November 1792, RH 2/4/64/364 (SRO).

95. RH 2/4/65 and 66 (SRO) for correspondence.

96. For examples of the former, see RH 2/4/65/241–2, and 28 (SRO). The *Edinburgh Herald* was financed by £400 from the Secret Service Fund, RH 2/4/66/313 (SRO).

97. *Parliamentary History*, xxx, col. 45; the speech was also widely reported in Scotland, *Glasgow Advertiser*, 17–21 December 1792.

98. For examples, RH 2/4/64/367, RH 2/4/67/438 (SRO).

99. Robert Watt began as an informer, 'out of attachment to the constitution of this country', but within a few months he was getting 'something in hand to reward and encourage him', RH 2/4/64/313 (SRO), R. Dundas to H. Dundas, 12 November 1792. The most valuable spy, J.B. also had a healthy appetite for money, see RH 2/4/70/1–2 for his unsubtle demand, 'Send me five guineas!'

100. Arniston MSS RH 4/15/4 (SRO), C. Long to H. Dundas, 10 November 1792.

101. M. Donnelly, 'Thomas Muir', pp. 330–4.

102. Drennan Letters, W. Drennan to M. McTier, 25 November 1792, no. 351, T. 765 (PRONI).

103. Ibid., W. Drennan to M. McTier, November 1792, no. 353, T. 765 (PRONI): 'You may laugh at my expression of "away from us and from our children", and say how *unlike* me, and . . . you may smile at the expression "smiling" with scorn and say how *like* me.'

104. Ibid., M. McTier to W. Drennan, 8 December 1792, no. 356, T. 765 (PRONI).

105. McDowell, *Ireland in the Age of Imperialism*, p. 367; see also Rebellion Papers, 620/20/82 (NAI).

106. 'The Internal Politics of the United Irishmen', pp. 181–8.

107. It was also printed in the *Dublin Evening Post*, 6 December 1792.

108. Drennan Letters, M. McTier to W. Drennan, 8 December 1792, no. 356, T. 765 (PRONI).

109. *Northern Star*, 24–8 December 1792.

110. Drennan Letters, no. 357 (PRONI). Collins's report in Rebellion Papers, 620/19/120 (NAI), dated 15 December 1792.

111. Rebellion Papers, 620/19/120 (NAI).

112. Morthland's original, hastily scrawled, protest against 'the Irish paper' is in JC 26/280 (SRO).

113. The minutes of the First Convention are reprinted in Meikle, *Scotland and the French Revolution*, pp. 239–73; originals are in RH 2/4/66/342–8 and 350–60 (SRO).

114. Mackenzie, *Life of Thomas Muir*, pp. 8–9.

115. Marshall, 'Thomas Muir', pp. 241–2.

116. See Appendix II.

117. RH 2/4/66 (SRO).

118. This reaches perhaps its highest expression in Burns romanticism. Nor was Scottish patriotism the preserve of radicals. In a letter to Henry Dundas, 'a warm friend of government' protested that a reply of Lord Grenville to the French, which had used the term 'England', had given 'great offence to the foes of government and much distaste to its friends – why not "Great Britain"': RH 2/4/68/199 (SRO).

119. Brims, 'The Scottish Democratic Movement', p. 332.

120. Muir remarked that in the reigns of Edward I and III, 'in Scotland a free man was even more free than in England', RH 2/4/66 (SRO).

121. RH 2/4/66 (SRO).

4

The Politics of Defiance
1793–1794

As the votives of liberty are of no country, or rather of every country, and the destruction or establishment of the rights of mankind in one nation conduces a similar consequence in its neighbour state, I should hope ceremonial may be thrown aside and a frank and ingenious correspondence take place between the Friends of the People in our Nations.

Hamilton Rowan Esq. to Colonel Macleod MP,
Dublin, 25 July 1793[1]

The history of these years is the history of a colder climate for radical politics. The transforming factor was the outbreak of war between the British Crown and France in February 1793, for in this instance government proved as sensitive as its opponents to international events, and proceeded to cast attachment to 'French Principles', and cries of universal brotherhood, in an altogether more sinister light. This in turn had a damaging impact on radical self-confidence. For democratic movements in Ireland and Scotland, as well as for their English brethren, the solution was now to turn the 'just and common cause' of 1792 into reality, through the construction of more formal organisational bridges. For the moment in Scotland both the radicals and their opponents had also the immediate aftermath of the first National Convention of the Friends of the People to consider.

TAKING STOCK

From the early autumn of 1792, the Scottish authorities had experienced a sense of growing anxiety. At the same time, they had also begun to gather information on the source of their unease, the targets being the most prominent members of the Friends of the People. By November, the letters of Macleod, Captain Johnstone and Dalrymple were being stopped at the Post Office, and in the same month, the spy Watt was dispatched on a tour of Dundee and the north.[2] Yet, Dundas and party were on no account despairing. On the contrary, the reformers' internal fissures and their painfully correct and constitutional attempts had actually raised their spirits. Now the letters of the Lord Advocate Robert Dundas to the Lord President, his uncle Henry, were injected with a quavering note of triumph. The Burgh Reform Bill had earlier been 'universally laughed at', but even better was the Friends of the People Convention and the sight of 'Dalrymple frightened out of his wits'.[3]

Glee apart, the prime object of official attention was not the discomfited Dalrymple, but the more unabashed radical, Muir, whose open organisational role in the democratic movement made him a splendid catch. The judicial weapon was also at hand in the shape of the Irish Address. This had failed to attract the attention of government-inclined newspapers, usually hungry for hints of 'sedition', but the eyewitness reports of spies were full of the debates over 'the treasonable letter, conceived in the stile [*sic*] of the Jacobine tendency'.[4] On reading these, Robert Dundas realised, without even seeing the text, that Muir's championing of the piece now offered the prime opportunity to secure him on a charge of treason.[5] Sheriff John Pringle was already doing some determined rooting to get hold of the 'treasonable' Address, hampered by the fact that only a very few copies had come into Scotland.[6]

Muir was not long spared. Subsequent incriminating material from his dealings with Kirkintilloch radicals strengthened the authorities' case, and he was arrested on 2 January 1793.[7] Characteristically, he took a belligerent stance from the outset, refusing to answer questions and declaring his commitment to parliamentary reform, but regardless was released on bail.[8] After a week, he left on an ill-judged peregrination around London, Paris, and eventually Dublin, where he was to develop a much closer personal acquaintance with the United Irishmen.

The incidents surrounding the reading of the Irish Address had also engaged the more benevolent attentions of radicals in both Scotland and Ireland, promoting a sharper awareness of the realities of each other's situation. Initially, William Drennan did not seem too concerned at the lack of a reply to his masterpiece, for having heard the two letters sent by 'the principal persons in the Scotch Convention, Muir and Skirving' to Dublin, he was comforted by the belief that 'it was to be read in future, and copies distributed throughout the kingdom'.[9] Events at the Convention and the government's response swiftly deprived him of this hope, and brought home to him that 'the terrors of legal torture was the form'd design through all the three kingdoms, and it has already had its effect in Scotland for the present'.[10] Possibly as a reward for his championing of the Irish

Address, and as an act of solidarity on his arrest, Muir was elected *in absentia* a member of the United Irish Society of Dublin.[11] In Ulster the *Northern Star*, which had covered the Scottish Convention with its customary diligence, now also followed his fate and that of the Scottish Friends of the People with growing concern.[12]

In turn, the focus of Scots radicals on Irish affairs also intensified. In its first defiant editorial of the year, the *Edinburgh Gazetteer* proclaimed that 'Scotland and Ireland in their political sentiments are unanimous. What a blessing it is to see general harmony pervade a nation'.[13] It proceeded in the coming months to draw political parallels between the two, showing keen interest in the difficulties of the *Star*'s proprietors with the law.[14] The profile of the United Irish Society was also a beneficiary of this closer attention. Even a Foxite moderate like Colonel Macleod, in his letter otherwise urging restraint on the Friends of the People, was uninhibited in praising 'this body of men in Ireland, distinguished by the love of liberty, and closely united in the same glorious cause of reform with the Friends of the People in Britain'.[15]

There is a paradox here. For all the mutual goodwill which followed the Scottish Convention, the first half of 1793 marks a hiatus in the development of practical links between the radical societies. Three related reasons existed for this. First, the Scottish democrats were themselves at a low ebb in these months, reflected in the severe financial difficulties of their newspapers, and in the fall of recruitment and attendance at the meetings of the various Societies. The spy J.B., for one, seemed thoroughly bored at an Edinburgh meeting at which the 8–10 members present passed three hours in a procedural wrangle, and sarcastically reported 'much ado about nothing'.[16]

Secondly, Scottish diffidence reflected in good measure the success of the intensified loyalist offensive, which had commenced at the beginning of the year. Although Muir was the most famous victim, his arrest coincided with a wave of indictments against the 'small men', who were involved in the publication and distribution of radical literature. Here judicial pressure was also reinforced by freelance efforts at economic harassment by local enthusiasts.[17] A developing aspect of this reaction was apprehension over the possible effect of a concert of reformers in the three kingdoms. This was clear in Lord Advocate Dundas's firm conviction that England, and especially Ireland, might become havens for fugitives from Scottish justice. The test case was that of the publisher and pioneer balloonist James Tytler, who had jumped bail in January and was already reported to be in Ireland. One William Stewart, a Leith merchant tried for sedition, was also missing and suspected to have taken the same route.[18] Writing to his uncle, Dundas pronounced himself 'indifferent' as to whether such a little fish as Tytler was apprehended, but realised: 'It would have the most beneficial effects on the minds of the people if both of these persons were advertised in the *London* or *Dublin Gazette*; as it would prove to them the determination of the government to proceed to the ultimate extremity – the *Dublin Gazette* particularly'.[19]

The Scots were not alone in their difficulties with the authorities, for the third factor inhibiting closer relations in early 1793 was precisely the preoccupation of the United Irishmen with their own problems. Detailed information on the Dublin Society had been built up by government spies such as Collins, and although he was personally inclined to dismiss them as 'meare swaggerers',[20] in Ireland official reaction to the radical challenge gathered momentum in tandem with the approach of open conflict with revolutionary France. Initially the response was less severe than in Scotland, with its more responsive and repressive legal system, and it remained unclear whether the Irish administration could continue to meet the threat from the Volunteers and United Irishmen, and also settle rising Catholic demands. Soon, however, legal harassment had brought a virtual halt to Volunteer activity in Dublin, and although Northern radicals were initially scathing about the Dubliners' collapse, by March their own battalions had dispersed in a quiet and law-abiding fashion. This was complemented by a series of arrests and celebrity trials in January–February, which targeted the United Irishmen. Hamilton Rowan was charged with seditious libel for distributing copies of the Society's 'Address to the Volunteers'. Simon Butler and Oliver Bond, the United Irishmen's chairman and secretary, who had protested the illegality of action by the Irish House of Lords, were fined and imprisoned for six months, their extravagant living in Dublin's Newgate Prison causing the Society great financial embarrassment. A fortnight later, Napper Tandy, one of the most popular United leaders, although of dubious ability, fled Ireland under threat of more severe punishment.[21]

Against this general background, it is hardly surprising that the United Society made no intervention in the Second National Convention of the Friends of the People in Scotland, which met on 30 April 1793, or that its proceedings were attended by few of the histrionics which had surrounded the reading of the Irish Address. Despite the protests of Foxites who had wanted the movement to 'ly by' and the Convention to be deferred, it went ahead, distinguished by copious moderation. To accomplish this, a screening process may have already taken place in the Convention's Committee of Overture. Here, attempts were made to raise a motion of sympathy for Butler and Bond, and other sufferers for 'so great a cause', which expressed the hope that their example would be followed by similar behaviour 'in all those whose duty prompt them to oppose illegal unscrupulous power in this country'. The initiative was speedily quashed as 'imprudent if not seditious'.[22]

Despite its cautious proceedings, this new assembly was important for the future of the radical movement. It meant the final withdrawal of the most circumspect moderates, such as Morthland and Fowler. While hardly giving way to the 'extremist leadership', which Meikle suggested, this did mean that the principal personalities who had opposed a closer working relationship with the Irish were no longer in evidence.[23] The United Irishmen were not alone in benefiting. The decision of the Convention to back a co-ordinated British-wide petition campaign in support of Lord Grey's parliamentary motion for reform now also necessitated a more outward-looking attitude generally, and brought the Scottish reformers into contact with the London Corresponding Society and other provincial English reform bodies.[24]

The potential of these developments was to be realised in the summer of 1793, a watershed for the democratic movement in Britain and Ireland. The failure of their petitioning initiative in May, with the arrogant rejection of Grey's anodyne motion for an enquiry into the state of parliamentary representation, had already meant a further loss of reformers' morale in Scotland. The search now began for new strategies to win reform. At the same point, government repression too entered into a new heightened phase, this time seeming to contemporaries to strike at the very heart of radical organisation. This was symbolised in two events: the passage of the Irish Convention Bill in July 1793, and the arrest and trial of Thomas Muir in August. Closer co-operation with fellow radicals, it was felt, was no longer a pious article of internationalist faith, but a strategic necessity.

RE-ENTER MUIR

The year 1792 had been a period of easy optimism for the radical movement, but with 1793 their addresses and other public productions began to exhibit a greater air of defensiveness. Fading too were hopes of reform by strictly constitutional means, though the alternatives were not yet clearly focused. In Ireland the shift was particularly profound, since government retribution had followed so fast on rising hopes.

The entry of Britain and Ireland into the Coalition's war with France had, of course, been vital in altering the political terrain. War contributed to the economic distress on which political radicalism might feed, but at the same time raised official fears over internal security and widened the definition of 'treasonable' activity. Behind the government's reaction was the realisation that they were fighting a new sort of war. As the

Sheriff of Edinburgh explained to genteel volunteers for the new local Fencible Cavalry, 'The enemy we have to contend with was no common kind, and their war was not only to deprive us of our foreign possessions, but everything most dear to us at home, our lives, our Constitution and the very existence of our nation'.[25] Even though France did not intend to export revolution in the early months of war, the November Decree of Fraternity had already coloured images of dangerous internationalism. Their response took the familiar forms of judicial and economic pressure, but a new legislative emphasis also became clear.

The cornerstone of the Irish parliament's contribution was their Convention Act. The central fact behind this measure was the constitutional precariousness of their own institution, and the low esteem in which it was widely held in Ireland. This had been irritatingly underlined by the decision of the Catholic Convention of December 1792 to bypass the Irish administration and petition the King directly for the repeal of remaining penal legislation.[26] A more serious threat was the Convention of radical delegates, originally projected by Drennan, which eventually met in February in the old Volunteer haunt of Dungannon. This, proclaimed the *Northern Star*, demonstrated to the whole world that the whole province is 'one great society of United Irishmen'.[27] In fact, it drew on the wider constituency of Volunteers and the remaining Northern Whigs, and was strictly constitutional and anti-republican in its aims, but its call for a national reform convention was sufficient to prompt the authorities into legislative action.

The resulting Bill duly declared unlawful, conventions and other assemblies 'which may be made use of to serve the ends of factious and seditious persons to the violation of the public peace and the great and manifest encouragement of riot tumult and disorder'.[28] While not ostensibly seeking to remove the 'undoubted rights' of His Majesty's subjects to petition the King and parliament, it in practice removed the machinery for doing so. Thus, in Ireland, executive power was firmly restated and the whole tradition of 'out of doors' protest stopped in its tracks. It achieved an immediate victory with the cancellation of a huge Volunteer Convention at Athlone, planned for once parliament was prorogued.

The thoughts of Scottish and English radicals were at once inflamed by the suspicion that similar action was planned for the British mainland. For, although their own extra-parliamentary tactics were much less dramatic and confrontationalist than the Irish, the health of their Societies likewise depended on their ability to organise and energise mass public opinion. The situation indeed held a certain irony. The democratic movement, which had been so often accused of subversive and unconstitutional behaviour, was now confronted with a government which, they were convinced, was using basically *unconstitutional* means to stifle reform.

There was great need for news on the actual working of the Act in Ireland. Even conservative newspapers like the *Glasgow Mercury* seemed taken aback by the Convention Bill's 'very restraining nature', but justified it on the grounds of the existence of, 'mutinous assemblies in different parts of the Sister Kingdom and the outrages they have committed'.[29] Radical press coverage was, however, forced by the climate of reaction to be more oblique and circumscribed than was usual. The *Gazetteer*, facing major financial and production difficulties, had only limited copy, but the *Advertiser* printed the full text of 'a Bill of so much importance [which] cannot fail to be of interest to our readers'.[30]

In these conditions, eyewitness accounts were at a particular premium, and it was on just such a mission that Thomas Muir now reappeared on the Scottish scene.

After leaving Scotland a week after his initial arrest, Muir had received a head-turning welcome from the London Friends of the People. Then, from a mixture of rational political motives, curiosity and pique, he embarked for France. Again, in Paris he was welcomed by 'an amiable and distinguished' circle, and, despite his protests to the contrary, had apparently little inclination to remove himself to Edinburgh and to the sedition trial which awaited him there.[31] But, the favourable situation for foreign guests like himself swiftly evaporated with the onset of war with Britain, and the eclipse of the Brissotin party from which Muir's circle was largely drawn. In May, he managed to get a French passport, and boarded the *Hope* at Le Harve, his destination – depending which version is accepted – being Scotland or America.

Whatever his original intentions, the temptation of another splendid reception, this time from the United Irishmen of which he was an honorary member, coupled with the prospect of actually meeting his fellow campaigners, Rowan and Drennan, proved overwhelming. The *Hope* was due to call at Belfast *en route*, and when it docked on 17 July, Muir set off for Dublin. The days which followed again spoke eloquently of the small and intimate world of bourgeois reform in the 1790s, and also illustrate the role that individual 'personalities' were to have in the broader course of the democratic movement.

Muir met Drennan and was entertained to dinner, soon after his arrival in Dublin. Drennan found him 'a very sensible, honest intelligent man', but no particular rapport seems to have been established.[32] This may reflect the poet's cold and diffident manner, which was belied in the flamboyance of the Irish Address. He was described as passing in appearance, 'the demure minister of some remote village-congregation of the Scotch kirk'.[33] Contemporaries, like Barrington, noted the contrast with his patrician friend Hamilton Rowan. A tall and commanding presence, with impeccably courteous manners, Rowan was accustomed to stride about Dublin, carrying a large knotted club and with a Newfoundland dog at his side. Drennan was initially enthusiastic hailing 'a man whose body and mind does honour to Ireland . . . a true patriot, excellent in head and heart'. However, on mature reflection and perhaps becoming more acquainted with Rowan's streak of arrogance and demagoguery, he found him to have more 'personal' than 'political' courage.[34]

A similarly favourable first impression was made on Thomas Muir. The acquaintance made through their correspondence now grew into a warm friendship, and Muir was invited to Rowan's estate at Rathcoffey.[35] It may be that Rowan had a personal role in Muir's decision to return and stand trial in Scotland, but the extent of this cannot be specified with any accuracy. Muir's behaviour throughout his Irish visit is highly ambiguous. It had been reported in radical circles as early as March that he was bound for America, and this was still apparently his aim on reaching Belfast on 17 July, but by the 20th Drennan was writing that he intended to return to Scotland, 'to stand his ground'.[36] For Rowan to have effected this change of heart, his impact must have been instant and overwhelming. Brims cautions against casting Rowan in a Svengali role, Muir being hardly an innocent 'victim', but a man who had already made an impressive mark in his own legal and political career, yet there remains an insistent note of hero worship in Muir's correspondence with the older man, which proudly continued after his trial and sentencing. Entreating Rowan to write to him frequently, he explained to him that he had held off writing himself till his trial was terminated, 'in order that you may from that investigation judge whether or not I merited your friendship'.[37] In the event, however, it is unlikely that Rowan can claim sole credit for Muir's choosing the path of 'duty' over safety. He had introduced him to various contacts and, as in London and Paris, the warmth of his formal installation as a United Irishman may also have swayed him.[38] All the more so since this took place in an atmosphere of crisis and heroic defiance, which followed the Volunteers clamp-down and the Convention Act.

Once he had made up his mind to return, the eloquence of his new Irish friends was no doubt useful in reinforcing his sense of mission. On one level, Muir's task was simple. Rowan entrusted him with a package of various United Irish literature, including copies of the resolutions and proceedings of the Dublin Society and several squibs produced by Rowan himself on 'the Liberty of unlicensed printing'.[39] He was also given a number of letters to take to contacts in Scotland, most notably to the

Unitarian minister, T. F. Palmer, with whom Rowan had been a fellow student at Cambridge, and to Colonel Norman Macleod MP. It is these, in fact, which suggest the deeper motivation for Muir's return. This had two main components. First, Rowan was anxious to give these important contacts 'an account of the present state of Ireland', hoping that Muir would communicate 'the little insight I have been able to give him'.[40] Second, this political situation made it necessary to improve communication and co-ordination between reformers in Scotland and Ireland, 'each of them oppressed, and neither of them bearing oppression tamely'. For Rowan argued:

> As the votives of liberty are of no country, or rather of every country, and the destruction or establishment of the rights of mankind in one nation conduces a similar consequence in its neighbour state, I should hope ceremonial may be thrown aside and a frank and ingenious correspondence take place between the Friends of the People in our Nations.[41]

The request for a 'frank and ingenious correspondence' was particularly aimed at Macleod, who may have raised Muir and Rowan's hopes by his public affection for the United Irish Society in the open letter to the Friends of the People in January 1793. To Macleod, Rowan explained that the Convention Bill had been 'hurried' through, 'to prevent the people from acting by deputies in obtaining the redress of grievances or even applying to the King or parliament . . . leaving a melancholy but plain alternative; unconditional surrender or defiance'.[42] In short, the establishment of executive despotism in Ireland could mean the beginning of the same process in Scotland soon.

What finer 'votive of liberty' to rally Scottish radicals to the need for closer linkages beyond their own borders than Thomas Muir? And what better platform for him to do so than the dock of the High Court of Justiciary in Edinburgh? An acquittal would seize the popular imagination and the moral high ground for the radicals after months of retreat. A conviction would still re-invigorate the movement by its vivid illustration of encroaching despotism. As an advocate, Muir must have been aware that the Scottish legal system held greater dangers than the Irish or English in this respect, but observing the fairly mild sentences handed out by Edinburgh courts earlier in the year, he had grounds to hope any penalty was not too severe. Besides, as Butler and Bond could have assured him, six months in prison could be spent in reasonable profit and comfort. In this spirit of judicious martyrdom, Muir landed at Portpatrick on 30 July, and was promptly arrested and committed for trial.

Muir's subsequent trial in August 1793 has held a hallowed place for radical polemicists from Peter Mackenzie down to the present, but there has also developed a reassessment, which is perhaps more useful in illustrating how consistently Muir was to pursue his outward-looking radicalism, strengthened through aquaintance with the United Irishmen.[43] The splendidly coarse Lord Braxfield is usually cast as the villain of the piece, though he himself falls victim to Cockburn's distaste for such 'Scotch' survivals.[44] In reality, while Braxfield was unashamedly partisan and the jury carefully selected, and while the prosecution case rested on fairly dubious testimony, a large part of the problem also lay with the nature of Muir's own defence. Events in the lawcourts in the early 1790s were already proving the importance of obtaining the best defence counsel possible. Men such as James Curran, whom Muir had met in Dublin, were to perform great feats of damage limitation in the cases of the leading United Irishmen; for a relieved Drennan, the Irish barrister was 'that marmoset of genius'.[45] Scotland had its own 'Currans' in the shape of Archibald Fletcher and Henry Erskine – the latter offered to undertake Muir's defence – but Muir, either trusting his forensic skills or still holding fast to his role of political martyr, decided to become his own counsel. The way was now clear to present a *political* defence to what he believed, rightly, to be a *political* trial.[46]

Muir began badly by arriving late, and made his situation worse by a series of initial tactical errors, failing most notably to challenge the relevance of the indictment. There was little argument that he had committed the acts alleged, but he could have protested that this did not amount to the crime of sedition. The Scottish law of sedition was poorly defined, and an incisive legalistic defence could have capitalised on this. The costs of the alternative political approach were even more evident in Muir's handling of the Irish Address, the reading of which formed one of the main indictments against him.[47] The Address was described in court as 'a paper of a most inflammatory and seditious tendency, insiduously representing the Irish and Scottish nations as in a state of downright oppression, and exciting the people to rise up and oppose the government'.[48]

Muir had already gravely compromised his position here by his visit to Ireland, even though, as he insisted, he had remained no longer than nine days, and had been perfectly open in his movements. This insensitive trip, following on the heels of his equally defiant French visit, seemed to confirm the Scottish authorities' worst fears of an international revolutionary conspiracy. Already in December 1792, the Home Office had been informed from Ireland that Mr Archdeacon of London and Mr Muir were expected there in the course of a short time for the purpose of establishing 'a more intimate correspondence of the English, Scottish and Irish'.[49] The Lord Advocate similarly had little doubt that he was witnessing the fruits of such meetings, and that Muir was 'an emissary from France or the disaffected in Ireland'.[50]

Now, in a powerful courtroom peroration, which put the summing-up of the Lord Advocate, 'a poor brisk speaker', in the shade, Muir 'gloried' in reading the Irish Address, and was prepared to defend every sentence from charges of sedition. To this end, he read most of the Address, 'the work of an immortal pen', pointing out to the jury where the indictment had mutilated the original passages to change their meaning. The first paragraph, which had so outraged William Morthland and his Foxite allies, and which it was now claimed contained treason against the Union between England and Scotland, was, in fact, 'strictly constitutional'. For while the indictment broke off the passage, 'You are still Scotland', inferring that the United Irishmen wished a dissolution of the Union, the rest of the sentence continued the sense in which the Society understood 'still Scotland', namely as 'solely expressing their idea of her still being distinguished by her former lustre'.[51]

Such fine textural exegesis was less the problem than Muir's provocative defence of the United Irishmen themselves:

> The prosecutor has represented that Society as a gang of mean and nefarious conspirators; and their diploma of my admission into their number, and an aggravation of my crime. Let me tell the Lord Advocate of Scotland, that Society stands too high to be affected by his invective, or to require the aid of this defence. I am a member of that society; and in the last moments of my life to have been so shall be my honour and my pride.[52]

These inspiring and uncompromising words did much, as no doubt intended, to link the 'Good Cause' in the sister kingdoms, and his whole closing address in much the same high tone was met with 'indecent applause'. Later, writing to Rowan, Muir was indeed keen to highlight his performance with regard to the Society, hoping that he had acted upon that occasion 'as anyone of their number would have done'.[53] Yet, all this did nothing for Muir's own case. He had himself provided the collateral evidence which the prosecution required to prove he had contact with a dangerous organisation. Braxfield was irritated at his impertinence. 'Instead of denying the address,' he commented, 'Mr Muir had asserted the innocence of it, and enlarged upon its merits.' Considering it himself to be 'most seditious', he gave it to the jury to make up their own minds.[54] This they did, and having considered the rest of the evidence against him, when the court reconvened at noon 1 September, they found Muir 'guilty of the crimes libelled'. In an exemplary sentence, designed to remove Muir from the Scottish scene, Braxfield sentenced him to transportation to Botany Bay for a period of fourteen years. 'The Sidney of his Age', as the *Northern Star* described him, was conducted to the Tolbooth to await the execution of his sentence.

Although his health was soon to suffer, Muir initially was elated by his experience. He sent copies of Robertson's edition, which he considered the best account of his trial, to Drennan and 'Sheares', and commented proudly that demand for it was 'altogether unexampled'.[55] It may be that he could not quite grasp the gravity of the situation, having convinced himself that such a drastic and unexpected punishment either could or would not actually be carried out. Palmer, who was to suffer the same fate, being found guilty of sedition at Perth and sentenced to transportation in September, was likewise 'sanguine enough to hope that the time is not far distant, when I shall be recalled with honour to my country'.[56]

This air of unreality extended beyond the immediate participants. In Ireland, where the case had been given extensive coverage, the severity of Muir's sentence caused great alarm.[57] Among the Dublin United Irishmen concern for his personal welfare was accompanied by an acute appreciation of the episode's political value. Drennan's reaction was characteristic. On hearing that his Address was read out in court, he, 'really could not help thinking it an elegant little piece of rational declaration,' though in mitigation, he too felt the trial would be proved illegal, and an appeal made possible.[58]

In Scotland, Muir's fate confirmed radicals in their fears over the unconstitutional intentions of government, and actually gave new life to the Friends of the People societies. As Muir assured Rowan, 'The cause of truth and freedom derives strength from persecution – The apathy of the public mind is fast melting away – In number and respectability our friends are daily increasing'.[59] Soon, the spy J.B. was reporting standing-room only at Edinburgh meetings, and the Scottish movement began a new phase of regrouping. Here, the broad example of Irish radicalism and the personal intervention of individual United Irishmen were again to be formative influences.

RE-ENTER ROWAN

The linkage between Scottish and Irish radicals in late 1793 was only one component of a general process of *rapprochement* or, as William Skirving expressed it, 'affiliation in one great indivisible family'.[60] Strong political links were now also being formed between the Scottish and English societies after the failure of polite petitioning. The simple fact that both these movements were seeking redress of grievances from the same parliament gave this a great practical impetus, and a potential for effective joint work which was not always evident in Scots–Irish solidarity.[61]

Skirving, in his official capacity as secretary of the Friends of the People in Edinburgh, had been convinced that both the new, common threat from government, and the original 'ennobling principle of universal benevolence', prompted an approach which crossed the petty national boundaries of Scotland and England.[62] This personal commitment from key personnel, coupled with contacts made in the earlier petitioning movement in the spring, meant that when overtures were made from the London Corresponding Society requesting 'a renewal of correspondence . . . and a more intimate cooperation', they were not resisted.[63]

The instrument of this new co-operation was to be a new convention, projected to meet in Edinburgh on 29 October, which it was hoped would press a full democratic agenda on the British parliament. The concept of a British convention of national delegates to draw up a true constitution had been advanced by the Belfast radicals in the Irish Jacobin club as early as December 1792, and the Irish were not intended to be left out of Skirving's scheme.[64] On the contrary. His interest in the United Irish Society had been engaged the previous year, and he appears to have been as implicated as Muir in the receipt of the Irish Address. Now, on 23 October, less than a week before the Convention was due to sit, he wrote eagerly to Hamilton Rowan, seeking United Irish representation. Supposing that the Scots could hardly flatter themselves with Rowan's own august presence, he hoped that some of his Dublin friends could come over without delay; the 'Messrs. Sheares, Butler, Bond, McNally and Dowling' would be specially welcome.[65]

Skirving's fraternal intentions do not seem to have been matched by his administrative capabilities. Despite his assurances that there was still sufficient time, six days were clearly not enough time for the legalistically-minded Dublin Society to ponder suitable delegates and dispatch them to Edinburgh. The same logistical problem faced the English delegates who had been invited at similarly short notice; they arrived too late to attend the assembly, which carried on regardless, without its international sprinkling.[66]

The *Northern Star* keenly defended this Third National Convention of the Scottish Association of the Friends of the People from its loyalist detractors. It reassured its Belfast readers that:

> The truly respectable appearance must at once silence the false aspersions of their enemies, that the Friends of the People are comprised of the wretched outcasts of society. The solemn manner in which

they opened and adjourned their sittings by prayer, the regular and orderly conduct during all these sittings, will show to the world that they are neither void of religion or good sense.[67]

In fact, the proceedings had the opposite effect, and the resolutions passed marked a departure from the hesitancy of the previous two Scottish conventions. Annual parliaments and universal male suffrage were accepted, and the desire for a closer working relationship with English radicals forcibly expressed, but one further hallmark of the new defiant, confrontationalist mood was again the reading of a new 'Irish Address', this time from the four Belfast Societies of United Irishmen.[68]

The letter's sentiments were more forthright and pugnacious than the original paper. At the very outset, the United Irishmen's cosmopolitan vision was expounded, as they beheld:

The vivid glow of patriotism which brightens the face of other nations, and the irresistible elasticity, with which man, long bent down into a beast of burden, shakes of the yoke of despotism and resumes his form erect in neighbouring kingdoms. We exult in the triumph of humanity which regenerated Gaul exhibits; . . . We accompany with raptures, the steps of freemen traversing the mountains of Savoy, erecting the standard of liberty on the strongholds of despotism . . .[69]

These were brave words indeed since Britain had been at war with 'regenerated Gaul' for the past eight months, but on the domestic front their hope was for 'a *voluntary, immediate*, and *radical Reform*', since this would avert 'the awful experiment of a contested revolution'. Perhaps not all the Address was as welcome to Scottish ears. The past intellectual glories of Scotland, 'where a Reid and a Beatty broke the spells of an annihilating philosophy', were contrasted to 'her present degenerated state, as a nation sleeping over her political insignificance . . .', and with a characteristic touch of Ulster Presbyterian hubris the audience were reminded that however humiliating their own situation in that Province, 'the Protestants and the reformed among us, in the sense of freedom, were much superior to the Scottish people'.[70] Although the Address received no formal reply, the very fact that this spirited piece could now be read without the drama surrounding its predecessor illustrates the path by which radical solidarity was coming to be accepted as a political necessity by the Scots.

By such gestures, the Scottish delegates were not only clearing the ground for a genuine British convention, but were also once again confirming the worst suspicions of the authorities. The Lord Advocate and his agents were well aware of the proposed British alliance, and in a state of some excitement had daily awaited delegates from England and Ireland from early November. Muir, still in the Tolbooth, was also believed to be preparing material for the coming assembly.[71] The delegates' non-arrival for the Third Convention was thus a great disappointment for those present, but a temporary relief to government.[72] When the English did eventually arrive, and preparations got underway to recall the Convention for 19 November, 'the Union of Wills', as Skirving called it, became the focus of renewed official scrutiny.

Hamilton Rowan now also chose to arrive in Edinburgh, accompanied by Simon Butler, the new secretary of the Dublin United Irishmen, a man described by the fastidious Drennan as 'a young lawyer of lascivious character'.[73] If not exactly *dei ex machina*, these visitors were at least active irritants. This odd incident created a sensation both in Ireland and Scotland at the time, but is perhaps one of the less productive and edifying moments in relations between the two democratic movements.

Immediately suspicious, the authorities were convinced that Rowan and Butler were visiting as delegates. Accordingly, in his judicial examination held on the day of his arrival, Rowan was closely questioned on whether he had been invited to the Convention, or to any other reform meeting in Edinburgh.[74] Later Secret Committee Reports stated that Rowan had acknowledged, by voluntary declaration, that 'he had been solicited from Scotland by letter on the subject of sending delegates', which was correct.[75] If contemporary press reports can be credited, however, he seems to have been more economical with the truth at his interview, denying that any invitation had been received. He was more accurate when he stated that he was not a delegate to the Convention. Indeed, the issue of formal delegation was irrelevant, as he and Butler had decided to come to Edinburgh on another, far less prosaic, mission.

The facts of Rowan's short but eventful visit are fairly well established. Most of the relevant correspondence between the two men has survived, also throwing light on the character of Rowan, and on the relationship between his main adversaries Robert and Henry Dundas.[76]

In the course of Muir's trial, although it does not appear in the official transcripts, Lord Advocate Dundas had made a typically bad-tempered, off-the-cuff remark, in which he referred to the Irish Address as 'A paper penned by some wretches, who have like himself [Muir] fled from the punishment which awaited them'.[77] This was more correctly a reference to Napper Tandy who had fled bail, than to Rowan who was still patiently awaiting trial following his arrest in January. Quickly, after Muir's trial, an infuriated Rowan wrote to the Lord Advocate, asking if the obnoxious 'wretches' phrase applied to him, as only his own and

Drennan's names were appended to the Irish Address.[78] When no response was received to this or a second letter, Rowan and Butler set out for Edinburgh to demand satisfaction, if necessary by challenging Robert Dundas to a duel.

The Lord Advocate's failure to respond masked a period of anxious consultation regarding how he should handle 'his Irishman'. From a spy's information from one of the Edinburgh Friends of the People societies, and from a letter from a gentleman in Dublin, he was well aware that Butler had made a similar challenge to the Irish Lord Chancellor, Lord Fitzgibbon. He now fully expected a similar visit.[79] Behind the scenes, his father and brother now sought the advice of the family patriarch Henry Dundas, who in turn prescribed a form of words to counter Rowan, which the Lord Advocate obediently employed.[80]

The object of this concern was meantime occupying himself in Edinburgh. Soon after arrival at the Dumbarton Hotel, Rowan sent a note to Dundas, announcing that a full letter would follow shortly. From there he went with Butler to visit Thomas Muir, still captive in the Tolbooth. After half an hour in Muir's cell, Rowan was arrested. He was then given a lengthy legal examination, and only released on the bond of Colonel Norman Macleod.[81] The following day, the promised letter was at last delivered, but the Lord Advocate contributed to a growing sense of anti-climax by repeating his uncle's polite formula of non-accountability. Realising it was perhaps unwise to press the point, Rowan gave a select dinner at Hunter's Tavern for the leading figures of the Scottish Friends of the People, and set off for home the next evening, 8 November.[82] From the safety of Dublin, and still fuming over his arrest in Scotland, Rowan wrote – abusing the Lord Advocate – that 'The epithet usually applied by a person asserting a falsehood respecting another is that he is a lyar [sic]'.[83]

These antics were taken very seriously by the government. Pitt, for example, was kept informed of the unfolding correspondence, and expressed his personal concern to Henry Dundas.[84] To some extent, Henry's own response reflected worries over his nephew's personal safety. A fairly talentless lawyer, Robert Dundas was still 'a gentleman' and 'a man of spirit', who might well rise to Rowan's taunts.[85] Yet, more decisive at the level of national policy was the fear that 'publick men acting in the course of their duty should be supposed amenable as individuals to every man who thought it proper to be offended'. The present case was particularly intolerable, 'when it would appear to be part of a lawless confederacy that strikes at the heart of all order, law and legitimate authority'.[86] Thus linking the Edinburgh episode back to the challenge made to Fitzgibbon, Henry Dundas saw Rowan's mission as part of a concerted plan to intimidate public figures, and make key law officers desist from their duty by means of personal threats. He moved entirely in line with this interpretation, acting as the guiding spirit behind Rowan's detention, thus stopping any duel in its tracks.[87]

This type of reaction underlines the authorities' sensitivity and willingness to see plots behind every action of the reformers, but Rowan's actions were in fact a very literal expression of the tactic espoused by his clique in the Dublin leadership of offering public challenges to government at every opportunity. Personal motivations may also have influenced him. One of his correspondents was probably near the truth when he wrote, 'You are a perfect Quixote in politics, or you would not have ventured into Scotland'.[88] His visit was certainly a brave one, given the apprehensions of his friends and family earlier in the year that the authorities intended to have Rowan tried under Scottish law to facilitate a sentence of transportation to Botany Bay.[89] Still in touch with Muir after his trial, and possibly experiencing some guilt for encouraging his friend in his own Quixotic venture, he may have viewed a duel with the Lord Advocate, not as a stratagem for undermining the judicial process, but as a means of personally avenging Muir. His political career was indeed marked by such behaviour.[90] In this he was warmly supported by Drennan, eager as ever to urge others on to action: 'If ever a duel was called for,' he wrote, 'it is here, for the sentence was all from personal vengeance, and can only be met by the same'.[91] Again suggesting some of the distance in spirit and tone between Irish and Scottish radicals, Colonel Macleod had little time for these flamboyant 'gesture politics', and communicated to Rowan his disapproval of the idea of appealing to the principles of private honour in public transactions. 'I am sure you wish to serve the public cause of liberty, and give me leave to repeat that a duel or challenge to a duel, never will be useful to in Great Britain'.[92]

However politic or noble its original inspiration, Rowan's brief visit, like the reading of the Irish Address the previous year, was to have important consequences for Thomas Muir, and for the Scottish radical movement as a whole. The visit had gained wide press coverage, and Rowan and Butler on their return to Ireland were hailed as the heroes of the hour. At Belfast, on 11 November, they were 'elegantly entertained' at dinner and the evening spent 'with the conviviality and heartfelt pleasure, which the patriotic and the virtuous alone experience'. Muir was not forgotten, and his health was drunk among 'eighteen and many other toasts'.[93]

Unfortunately for Muir, Rowan's visit had proved the last straw for the authorities. Rumours of an escape bid had been circulating for weeks, and now the sight of him cordially entertaining Rowan and other notables, allied with the prospect of a recalled radical convention, convinced Robert Dundas that his removal to London was 'essential for the peace and quiet of this city'. Besides, the incident had also made up his mind that in the event of an application for the mitigation of Muir's sentence, the request should not be yielded to.[94] In consequence, on 14 November, three days after Rowan's celebration dinner, Muir, now showing signs of a consumptive illness, was placed aboard the excise yacht *Royal George* for dispatch to the Hulks on the Thames.[95]

There now followed the customary exchange of elegant addresses between the United Irishmen and Muir. The Irish addressed him in a homily again penned by Drennan, the intent of which, commented the spy Collins, 'is not to console or compliment that delinquent, but to be dispersed with all imaginative industry throughout this kingdom . . .'.[96] Approaching Muir, 'as men in sympathy with a man suffering', they consoled him:

> You ought then dear associate! You ought to extract comfort from your present situation. Pleasure often sickens, but there is sublime and permanent delight in struggling with unmerciful misfortunes . . . Is it not sweet to think that your confinement or exile may in any way, tend to the liberty of others.
>
> We feel much at your illness; we hope there are many years before you, but if otherwise, be satisfied, for you have not lived in vain. If death be, as we believe it, but a pause in existence, your happiness is yet to come; and if death be, as we trust in God it is not, an eternal sleep, are not the dreams of such an honest man infinitely preferable to the perpetual incubus of a guilty conscience.[97]

By this time the wretched Muir might have been forgiven for thinking that the United Irish Society was something of a 'perpetual incubus' itself. Yet he gallantly showed no regret at having read out their 'Immortal Address'. Instead, in lines that suggest that he was now moving to a more unadorned nationalist position, he presumed in the name of his country to entreat the continuation of their esteem for the great mass of the people in Scotland. 'They deserve your esteem; in the holy cause of national freedom they are actuated by the same spirit which animates you. Towards you their hearts burn with affection. Those barriers . . . to separate nation from nation are now broken down'.[98]

For the moment, contact between them now ceased, but was to resume a few years later in Paris, the revolutionary capital itself. By this time the spirit of harmony and mutual admiration had begun to wear more thin.

By the time Muir was removed from Edinburgh, the more general ramifications of the United Irishmen's visit were also becoming clear. Sheriff William Scott was surprised when, despite the denials in his earlier legal examination, Rowan and Butler attended a General Committee meeting of the Friends of the People on 6 November, being 'introduced and received with acclamation'.[99] Their presence here was important. Official reports correctly stressed the major influence of the English delegates, Gerrald, Margarot, Brown and Sinclair, in the setting-up of the British Convention.[100] This is also echoed by later historians like Goodwin, who credits the English with 'the far-reaching claims and pretensions' which accompanied its proceedings.[101] Yet, as indicated by the meeting of 6 November, the Irish role, though not an independent one, was still significant.

At the meeting, the London delegate Maurice Margarot began by inspiring the Scots with an up-tempo assessment of his own movement's numerical strength. 'In some parts of England,' he assured them, 'whole towns are reformers. In Sheffield and its invirons [sic] there are 50000. In Norwich there are thirty societies in one'. This emphasis accorded with the English intention to shape the Convention into a demonstration of radical strength, and a lesson to government as to what 'out of doors' pressure might mean. For, as he continued, 'If we could get a convention of England and Scotland called, we might represent six or twelve hundred males . . . and the ministry would not dare refuse our rights.'[102]

It was now the task of the Irish to describe the political situation in their own country. In doing so, they tempered Margarot's assurances of the power of mass pressure with a chilling picture of the onslaught on democratic rights which might be to come. Samuel Butler reported that in Ireland:

> The executive part of the government were almost omnipotent – The landed interest almost aristocratic – The manufactures idle. The last parliament was expected to have given Ireland emancipation, however that portent was flattering, a few weeks changed the scene. An infamous coalition took place between the opposition and ministry – The Catholics retired with what they had got. No longer opposed by them the Government turned their oppressive measures against the friends of Reform . . . In Scotland they met yet in convention – in Ireland the parliament had enacted laws against it. When a law like that should take place here, he was afraid freedom would vanish.[103]

No doubt this was much the same message on the implications of the Convention Bill, which Muir had hoped to convey on his return from Ireland. Now in the wake of his trial, it had an even greater impact on the Scots audience, with Alex Callander retorting that those who would pass such a bill should be forced to 'eat it'. The Englishman Gerrald was also much affected by this live testimony, and was to return to the subject frequently during the coming days. With sentiments similar to Rowan's, though more pungently expressed, he argued:

> If our neighbour's house is on fire the greater should be our vigilance to prevent the flame seizing our own. A parchment piece of Justice has been presented in Ireland . . . If ever it was passed here, we should throw it in the face of our oppressors. Everything the people gained here was thro' conventions . . . A citizen of Ireland has told you as soon as the alarm bell was rung, the opposition joined the ministry, party is ever a bird of prey, and the people their banquet.'[104]

As the Convention eventually met and began to deliberate on 19 November, the Irish influence was still evident in two major respects, even though Rowan and Butler had long since departed for home. First, their picture of political opposition crushed by legislative intervention bolstered the delegates in their conviction that their own assembly should function as a bulwark against any similar government encroachments on civil liberty on the mainland. After several days' debate, the Convention resolved to appoint a small 'Secret Committee' which would reconvene as a 'Permanent Emergency Convention' at the first notice of a Convention Bill, or any bill for the suspension of Habeus Corpus, or of various other contingencies, such as the import of foreign mercenaries into Britain or Ireland.[105] Again this was justified by Gerrald by explicit reference to the Irish Convention Bill:

> Surely despotism could not be more strongly expressed even in Turkey: There every Bashaw listens to the petitions of his trembling slaves; yet that privilege is denied the people of Ireland . . . this Bill was in fact passed in Ireland to feel the pulse of the people in Britain, that our rulers might know if it beat high with indignation, or if the blood run coldly in our veins . . .[106]

The second aspect of the United Irishmen's influence followed on from this perception of the united front of reaction which faced reformers. Now the closer correspondence and co-ordinated response by the various democratic movements, projected by Rowan in July, were becoming a reality. Practicality dictated the first consideration to be that the Scots and English persist in their joint efforts to reform the British parliament.

Thus, in the opening session of the Convention, Margarot moved that before an Address to the Public was published, a committee should be set up to draw up a plan of general union between the two.[107] Again, the United Irish Society was soon also drawn in, as the touchstone of fraternal bridge-building. In an emotional atmosphere, becoming more effusive by the hour, Charles Sinclair – a young Edinburgh-born delegate from the London Constitutional Society – moved that henceforth the assembly be known officially as 'The British Convention of the Delegates of the People, associated to obtain Universal Suffrage and Annual Parliaments', thus sailing closer to Drennan's 'embodied nation' than any previous reform convention.[108] Having heard the universal acclaim which greeted this bold and 'revolutionary' change of nomenclature, Sinclair proceeded to move that:

> The British Convention: taking into consideration the oppressed state of their brethren in Ireland and the unconstitutional Act of the last session of the parliament of that kingdom, called the Convention Act; and feeling with indignation that by it the people of Ireland were deprived of those rights cheaply [sic] purchased with the blood of our common ancestors, and which are confirmed and secured to us in the Great Charter of our liberty, resolve that 'all or any of the patriotic members of the Society of United Irishmen of Dublin shall be admitted to speak and vote in this Convention'.[109]

Sinclair's motives here might be doubted, as his reputation has suffered from Cockburn's charges that his eventual escape from prosecution suggested his role as a government spy.[110] There is, however, no official evidence to support this, or to suggest that the United Irish resolution was the work of an *agent provocateur*. It is possible that he was not working in isolation; he knew Thomas Muir, for example, visiting him in Newgate shortly before his own trial in 1794; he is also likely to have been present at the dinner given by Rowan and Butler while in Edinburgh.[111] More importantly, the enthusiastic reception his motion received when it was transmitted to the sections for discussion indicates that it was at one with the general current of feeling in favour of an Irish alliance. After the most prominent voices in the Convention had supported Sinclair's resolution, it was agreed on 25 November, and guaranteed by the solemn joining of hands.[112]

The contrast with the First Convention was complete, and we have here another excellent illustration of the rapid pace of political life in the 1790s. The United Irishmen, delighted by this outcome, were well aware of sea-change which had taken place. The resolution was transmitted and read out at the Dublin Society's meeting of 3 December. Now, Butler could not resist calling the company's attention:

> to remark the change of public sentiment in Scotland. Nine months ago the Address of this Society to them went unnoticed; but such has been the progress of truth that this day the public virtue of this Society has been recognised by them and we are now collectively and individually members of the British Convention.[113]

More practical initiatives to consolidate this new closeness were also soon initiated. An Address was dispatched to the British Convention, reciprocating their gesture by considering its delegates, and members of its constituent societies as United Irish members, with speaking and voting rights.[114] The proceedings in Edinburgh clearly held special appeal for the more radical and internationally-minded members, like the Sheares brothers. Both men had joined the Jacobin club while in Paris, and their vociferous support for things French alarmed cautious colleagues.[115] John Sheares now moved 'with great warmth' that delegates be appointed to attend and confer with the Convention. Speed, he stressed, was of the essence, as 'perhaps another *opportunity* for the people obtaining their rights might never *offer* . . .'. It was generally agreed that two or three members would immediately set off, John and Henry Sheares among their number, as they had come from Cork with the express purpose of attending the meeting.[116]

Their visit was not to take place, for the trip itself and the high spirits which had surrounded it were rapidly overtaken by the speed and severity of a renewed government counter-offensive. This embraced both Britain and Ireland, thus confirming radical fears of a concerted strike. The immediate effects were most critical in Scotland. Here, the authorities' finally dispersed the British Convention on 6 December as 'illegal and unconstitutional'. This came as little surprise to literate public opinion, already alienated by some of the delegates' more confrontationalist conduct. Even sympathetic newspapers, such as the *Caledonian Mercury*, now joined diehards, like the *Glasgow Courier*, in their condemnation of the 'enthusiasm and madness which had usurped the place of reason'.[117] More specifically, the Scottish authorities, like their Irish counterparts, were antagonised by the threat of unconstitutional popular assemblies aimed at challenging the authority of parliament. For although the British Convention does not seem to have considered itself a sovereign assembly – along the lines of the type prescribed by Paine – it gave the contrary message through its use of revolutionary forms of address and procedures of the French National Convention. No doubt, had they arrived in time, the Sheares brothers would have added extra zest to these borrowings, and to the authorities' case.

A round-up of the leading voices in the Convention also began. As in Muir's case, some displayed a remarkably poor grasp of the reality of their legal position. Skirving, for example, informed Hamilton Rowan on 10 December that any prosecutions against 'the Friends of Reform' would be 'directed against the Rock of Truth', and that 'any prosecution against me will add greatly to my reputation and to their disappointment'.[118] This was not the case. Rearrested two days later, he was subsequently indicted, along with Margarot and Gerrald, on charges of sedition. Tried and found guilty in early 1794, they were handed down the sentences of fourteen years' transportation, which was now becoming customary.[119]

These reverses in Scotland caused disagreement in United Irish ranks. Despite his warm words of a few weeks before, Butler now stated that 'he had as poor an opinion of the Scotch for suffering the *wreath* to be torn from over the head of Mr Margarot, as he had of the mob of Dublin for suffering their champion to be dragged like a felon to a common prison . . .'.[120] The 'champion' in question was Rowan, whose case had at last come to trial in January, now able to play the role of 'patriot martyr' for himself. His sentence, in marked contrast to those of his erstwhile Scottish correspondents, was two years in prison. Other members, notably two Ulster visitors, were more phlegmatic, and sympathised with the Scots plight. Dr James Reynolds of Tyrone defended them, saying that they 'only waited for the proper time', as indeed did his own people of the North. Meanwhile Samuel Neilson, the *Northern Star*'s editor from Belfast, was insistent that correspondence be maintained. Not wishing to transact business through the Post Office, in the light of possible measures against 'treasonable correspondence', he suggested that he had 'some very *confidential friends* in Edinburgh, happy in forwarding any United Irish papers to any part of Scotland'. These views prevailed and Reynolds and Neilson were added to the Society's Committee of Correspondence.[121]

Rowan's prosecution, however, had signalled the start of a sudden, but determined official campaign against the United Irishmen. The Sheares brothers were openly branded French agents by the Irish Lord Chancellor.[122] Drennan was tried in June as the author of an address to the Volunteers. Acquitted through the good offices of Curran, the fright he had received plus 'a certain nausea or indifference to politics' assisted his withdrawal from radical activity to calmer literary pursuits.[123] Six weeks later, Rowan too was in fresh trouble. He was severely compromised by the visit of a genuine French agent, Revd William Jackson, while in prison and forced to make a typically dramatic escape from Ireland.[124] Although the Society's initial response was to stress its commitment to a legal and open reform agenda, with key leaders out of circulation and members cowed, Irish radicalism quickly seemed a spent and discredited force. Finally, on the evening of 24 May 1794, the remaining Dublin United Irishmen were dispersed and their papers seized. The loss of purpose and momentum which resulted was described by Thomas Emmet: 'The expectations of the reformers had been blasted. their plans had been defeated, and decisive measures had been taken by government to prevent them being resumed. It therefore became necessary to wait for new events, from which might be formed new plans'.[125]

Samuel Neilson's plans for the secret passage of material between Ulster and Scotland already hinted at what these 'new plans' might be, but a more vivid foretaste was offered within Scotland itself. Here the operation of the political societies was largely curtailed as government repression bit in earnest. Some, like the Third Cannongate Society, passed brave resolutions against the dispersal of the British Convention, setting at their head, in good Covenanting style, Psalm 23, 'The Lord is on my side, I will not fear; what can men do unto me?'[126] By January, J.B. was, nevertheless, reporting the decline in 'seditious meetings', and that those formerly involved in them were most disconcerted.[127]

If middle-class radicalism dwindled in organisational terms, still there persisted among the 'lower orders' a more inchoate spirit of rage and despair at government actions and economic hardship in early 1794. Drawing on this atmosphere of crisis, the ex-spy Robert Watt conceived an ambitious insurrectionary plan to seize the nerve centres of government in Edinburgh.[128] A classic case of the hunter captured by the game, Watt's conspiracy was probably not as far advanced as he wished to convey. It was, besides, aborted by the authorities' chance discovery of 'abominable instruments, half-spear, half-hatchet' in the house of an Edinburgh bankrupt.[129]

The 'Pike Plot' was ill-starred, but significant. First, it indicated how far the union between 'The swine of England, the rabble of Scotland, and the wretches of Ireland', as the popular toast went, had become a commonplace in radical calculations. The uprising in Edinburgh was to be only one part of a concerted assault 'in three metropolisses [sic]'. 'There remained nothing to do', claimed Watt in his dying *Declaration*, 'for the execution of the whole, but a visit to England and Ireland by intelligent and confidential persons.'[130] Second, Watt's escapade marked the close of one chapter in radical politics. The 'polite' era of open constitutional campaigning and the sense of 'living in a great era of reform' were most certainly over. The future of radical movements in Scotland, and in Ireland, now lay in the hands of an embattled revolutionary underground, a conspiratorial élite.

'A JUST AND COMMON CAUSE'?

The reform movements of Ireland and Scotland had a basic ideological and social identity in their early years, and although their trajectories were to diverge later in the 1790s, this was not immediately apparent to observers or participants. It is also likely that both could have been diverted from the intrigue and violence of later years by 'firm but mild and judicious treatment and a little reliance on the tendency of the time to abate epidemic follies . . .'.[131] Instead, it is a tragedy of the period, if a predictable one, that government proved unable to recognise the early bourgeois societies' hunger for openness, legality and orderly protest, and that both sides became locked in a dangerous cycle of provocation and retaliation, each fuelling the other's sense of crisis.

What contribution was made by the developing relationship between Scottish and Irish radicals in these years? In drawing up the balance sheet up to 1794, it is clear that its practical implications, for better or worse, fell on the Scottish side. Although more strategic considerations were later to emerge, for the United Irishmen's part, contact with Scotland originally grew out of their self-perception as 'advanced cosmopolites'. There was also the more specific 'sentimental' reason, that many of their members, like Drennan, Rowan and Neilson, shared ethnic, cultural or educational links with those in the developing movement in Scotland. For the Scots part, we have seen that at some times the *élan* and vigour of Irish politics proved and inspiring example; at others, a portent of what government might have in store for their own organisation.

The symbiotic nature of links had its limits. In the first place, the example of Ireland might be initially galvanising when translated into a Scottish setting, but a lasting momentum was more difficult to maintain, and could even be stifled by local conditions. We have seen, for example, that vivid reports of reformers' activities in Belfast helped the formation of Friends of the People societies in Paisley in 1792, but these were not enough to prevent the Paisley radicals falling into a labyrinth of obscure procedural and doctrinal wrangles, which sprang from settled rivalries between local dissenting sects.[132]

A more pressing problem was also implicit, as already seen in the case of the reformers and France: the linking of their own cause with evolution of a real political situation over which they had no control. Ireland too could do sterling service as an 'energising myth', but difficulties arose for the Scottish radical movement when 'Ireland' became a real presence in their counsels, and the rhetoric of fraternity and civic union was translated into practical political initiatives.

It is too simplistic to say at this point in the early 1790s that the Irish were a divisive influence on Scottish radical politics. Important fault lines existed quite independently between Foxites and more Painite-influenced radicals, and had been in evidence from the first formation of the Scottish Friends of the People. What the United Irishmen's intervention did achieve at the First Convention was to bring these fully into the open in a most acrimonious fashion, though, it could be argued, this was bound to happen when the elegant formulae which clouded the details of the reform programme were swept away.

The linkage of Irish and Scottish campaigning was even more problematic in the official onslaught it brought down on the heads of the Scottish reformers. Just as fears of a conspiratorial union of radicals were sharpening in government consciousness, the Addresses from the United Irishmen in Dublin and Belfast, and Rowan and Butler's visit to Edinburgh were active goads to nervous officials. Again in mitigation, these were not the only sources of apprehension regarding the Scottish Societies who were quite capable of acting provocatively in their own right. Nor, as Revd Palmer's trial in September 1793 indicates, did there need to be evidence of Irish links before a conviction was secured. Palmer was a correspondent of Hamilton Rowan, but although Rowan's letter to him was raised at Thomas Muir's trial, there was no attempt in his own trial to raise the type of 'incidental and collateral' evidence of involvement with the United Irishmen which had so damaged Muir.[133]

It is also most important to distinguish carefully between the United Irishmen's *intentions*, which were presumably within their control, and the *effects* of their actions, which generally were not: thus, Drennan and Rowan cannot be simply 'blamed' for the government's reaction. A note of personal culpability is more evident in their headstrong and intemperate disregard for the sensitivities and complexities of the Scottish political scene. The embodiment theme and the nationalist strains of the first Irish Address, coupled with Rowan's flamboyant challenge to the Lord Advocate, are testament to an arrogant and provocative vein running through the conduct of the early United Irish Society. Not only did this have an impact in Scotland, it also contributed to an overconfident and imperfect grasp of their own political situation. Drennan cuts a particularly poor figure, sheltering behind the bravado of his pen, whereas Rowan was at least willing to accept the personal consequences of his actions. The prime victim of the government's response to the Irish alliance was, however, another of its main architects, Thomas Muir.

Inevitably, the actions of the authorities formed a vital backcloth to the events of the early 1790s, and this brings us to a final set of issues. Why was the government's repression in Scotland so successful?; or, to put this another way, how great a threat was posed by the link-up of

Irish and Scottish radicals? The fact that astute politicians like Pitt and Henry Dundas were willing to exploit the political situation for their party ends does not mean that their fears for the existing political order were less than genuine. Nor were these fears incompatible with the hegemonic position enjoyed by the Scottish landed interest at the end of the eighteenth century. The basis for the existing social and political order was a peculiar mixture of latent strength and precariousness. As subsequent events were to prove, it could accommodate considerable pressures, but these pressures themselves gave rise to alarm and a gathering crisis of confidence.

Once more, the Scottish authorities' fears stemmed from the novelty of their situation, and from the sheer speed of events in the 1790s, which followed on the torpor of previous decades. It was above all the double danger of an interlocking of domestic and international events which made the familiar outlines of popular protest seem alien and threatening. The challenge of the Friends of the People societies was not so much in what they achieved, as in what they signified. Official alarm in Scotland was intensified by a consciousness of the scanty resources available for maintaining order, another legacy of the quiet life. The absence of a Scottish militia was a constant concern, reinforced by fears that the Fencible corps and the other existing soldiery 'from their education are liable to sedition'.[134]

There was another explanation for government nervousness, but this in itself concealed the residual strength of their position. As we have seen, with the exception of a few paid spies, such as Robert Watt and the much more painstaking J.B., the Scottish authorities had to rely on a voluntary network of informers. These were the many 'respectable gentlemen' who wrote to Henry Dundas and his nephew, the Lord Advocate. The flood of freelance information which resulted, sometimes highly coloured and alarmist, made it difficult to weigh up the evidence. Dundas tended to take admonitions seriously, though others felt that fears in London of a Scottish insurrection in these years were ridiculous.[135] Whatever the reality of the situation, the very fact that this network existed says a great deal about the difficult terrain for radicalism in Scotland, where the government were clearly able to rely on the co-operation of the propertied classes, both the landed gentry and lesser propertied groups in the towns. Here, radicals were left to attempt to reform the existing order from the outside. Indeed, as 1793 progressed, they were forced to do so in increasing isolation, as 'respectable' reformers closed the door and took shelter in protestations of devotion to King and Constitution. While the upper ranks of society thus fused into a loyalist coalition, no comparable fusion took place among the numbers of the discontented. The alliance with Irish radicalism, or for that matter with the English societies was not sufficient to compensate for this failure.

For the moment then, the Scottish authorities could relax. The 'Pike Plot' had been a brief scare, but this was followed by a quick recovery: as the Lord Provost of Glasgow assured Henry Dundas, 'The mob of this town is *Loyal* by a good majority – Long may it continue so!'[136] In Ireland too, the administration had recovered its poise after its own crisis of confidence. Dictated by local imperatives, its strategy and tactics were quite distinct. Faced with the settled hostility of Presbyterians and Roman Catholics, and by the more general alienation of educated public opinion from the Irish parliamentary process, it was required to proceed against a combination of reforming sentiment much more strenuously than the Lord Advocate had ever to contemplate. Fortunately, the existence of the separate legislature and the fact of deep sectarian fissures also gave the Irish authorities more room to manœuvre than their Scottish counterparts. The object was not so much to consolidate pro-administration forces, than to divide anti-government opinion. Accordingly, the first targets were the Protestant reformers, and in a climate of fear and legal repression the activities of the Volunteers and the United Irishmen were curtailed. Accompanying this was a series of conciliatory measures designed to buy off the more prosperous Roman Catholics with a partial emancipation package in the 1793 Catholic Relief Act. To secure the government party a broader popular platform, four bills were also passed, including anti-corruption measures, which were inspired by the suggestions of leading parliamentary Whigs.[137] By the following year, this adroit blend of coercion and compromise appeared to have succeeded.

In reality, deeper political processes were at work which were shortly to undermine official peace of mind, and lead to greater apprehension than had ever been evident in the 'polite' era. These developments were also to change the whole context of radical activity in Ireland, and in Scotland. In the first place, issues of agrarian discontent and Catholic political rights in Ireland had not disappeared because the government had decided to concentrate their assault on the radical Protestant middle class. From 1792 onwards, the Catholic Defenders societies had also been spreading rapidly, resulting in a widespread co-ordinated system, which gave traditional demands a new revolutionary tone. The alliance of a reorientated United Irish Society with the Defenders in 1795 was to produce precisely that type of radical union which played most on the minds of the Irish administration.

Ultimately, the broader European context was destined to have a further vital role in shaping events. The government had been convinced from the November 1792 Edict of Fraternity onwards that an international revolutionary conspiracy was afoot.[138] For the moment, there was as little evidence for this as for Gerrald's desperate remarks that the sentence against Thomas Muir would not be carried out as the French would be in the country before it was possible. This was an opinion delivered at the Friends of the People meeting in Edinburgh, 'so wild' that J.B. could hardly believe his ears.[139] Yet soon, as the war on the Continent intensified, evidence began to filter through that the French *were* beginning to turn their eyes to the British home front, a development signalled by Hamilton Rowan's visit from the French agent Jackson in the spring of 1794. Offers of French military assistance and the spread of underground radical movements were soon to give the government grounds for genuine concern. In this light, a piece of intelligence given by one of Henry Dundas's respectable correspondents, who had spent time as a captive of the French in St Malo, was most alarming.

> I heard much talk of invading Britain for which there is mighty preparations making at this port. I heard them frequently mention Scotland and Ireland and saying that if the English fleet was once a few leagues to the west of Scilly, they would eat roast beef in Sussex . . . they intended the expedition chiefly in Scotland, as they know there was no regular militia there to oppose them.[140]

NOTES

1. JC 26/276/8 (SRO).
2. R. Dundas to H. Dundas, 12 November 1792, RH 2/4/209/1; RH 2/4/66/313 (SRO).
3. Ibid.
4. Robert Watt's Report, RH 2/4/209/12–15 (SRO).
5. R. Dundas to H. Dundas, 15 December 1792, RH 2/4/66/340–1 (SRO).
6. Ibid. Clearly, discussion at the Convention on the need to print more had come to nothing.
7. J. Pringle to H. Dundas, 16 December 1792, RH 2/4/66/362 (SRO); W. Scott to R. Dundas, 3 January 1793, RH 2/4/68/13 (SRO).
8. RH 2/4/66/401 (SRO).
9. Drennan Letters, W. Drennan to M. McTier, 15 December 1792, no. 360, T. 765 (PRONI).
10. Drennan Letters, W. Drennan to M. McTier, 18 December 1792, no. 366, T. 765 (PRONI).
11. His original membership certificate found in his possession when he was rearrested on his return from Dublin in April 1793 is in JC 26/276 (SRO). *Report from the Committee of Secrecy of the House of Commons* (1799), p. 12, was in no doubt that, 'his zeal . . . commended itself to the conspirators in Ireland'.
12. The profile of the Scottish organisation seems to have risen generally in Ireland from this point in early 1793. 'The Scottish Society of the Friends of the People', for example, became a feature on radical toast lists: *Northern Star*, 17–20 April 1793 for a 'Civic Feast' in Cork.

13. *Edinburgh Gazetteer*, 1 January 1793.
14. *Edinburgh Gazetteer*, 18 January 1793. Their own problems with the Scottish authorities became shortly apparent, see *Edinburgh Gazetteer*, 26 February 1793. For examples of their Irish coverage, see 22 January for the formation of 'The Friends of Parliamentary Reform' in Belfast, and 2 April 1793 for coverage of Napper Tandy's latest escapades.
15. *Glasgow Advertiser*, 14–18 January 1793. 'A wonderful production', commented the Lord Advocate who sent a copy of Macleod's letter to Henry Dundas to see whether it was actionable and outwith parliamentary privilege: RH 2/4/68/154 (SRO).
16. RH 2/4/70/139 (SRO).
17. Brims, 'The Scottish Democratic Movement', pp. 378–85; for the broader British perspective, see Walvin, 'English Democratic Societies and Popular Radicalism'.
18. Laing MSS Add. 7 (University of Edinburgh) for a copy of Tytler proceedings; *Glasgow Advertiser*, 25 February–1 March for sentence of fugitation passed on him. The Lord Advocates fears were well founded. Tytler reached Belfast, and, as we shall see, offered his services as a United Irish agent to Scotland. For Stewart, see Howell and Howell, *State Trials*, xxiii, cols 25–34.
19. R. Dundas to H. Dundas, 13 January 1793, RH 2/4/68/151 (SRO). Returning to the point tenaciously a week later, he suggested that advertising rewards would also have 'the great effect to satisfy the country that within Britain's dominions, none of these fellows are safe', R. Dundas to E. Nepean, 21 January 1793, RH 2/4/69/212 (SRO).
20. Rebellion Papers, 620/20/77 (NAI).
21 McDowell, *Ireland in the Age of Imperialism*, pp. 439–40.
22. J.B.'s report, 1 May 1793, RH 2/4/70/191–2 (SRO).
23. Meikle, *Scotland and the French Revolution*, p. 134.
24. Goodwin, *The Friends of Liberty*, pp. 284–5.
25. *Glasgow Advertiser*, 19–20 June 1793.
26. H. Dundas to Westmorland, January 1793, Westmorland Correspondence, 1/86 (NAI).
27. *Northern Star*, 15–20 February 1793.
28. *Glasgow Advertiser*, 19–22 July 1793.
29. *Glasgow Mercury*, 16–20 July 1793.
30. *Edinburgh Gazetteer*, 30 July 1793, the paper had been suspended due to official pressure following its edition of 7 June 1793, and had only reappeared on 2 July; *Glasgow Advertiser*, 19–22 July 1793.
31. His trial was fixed for 11 February, with a sentence of fugitation later produced, *Glasgow Advertiser*, 25 February–1 March. J.B. was most concerned to report Muir's correspondence with his radical colleagues, see reports 21 January 1793, RH 2/4/69/216–17, and 27 March, RH 2/4/70/139 (SRO).
32. Drennan Letters, W. Drennan to M. McTier, 20 July 1793, no. 436, T. 765 (PRONI).
33. Lady Morgan, *O'Brians and O'Flahertys*, vol. 3, p. 75, quoted in Elliott, *Wolfe Tone*, p. 104.
34. Drennan Letters, W. Drennan to M. McTier, 30 November 1792, no. 346, T. 765 (PRONI). His sister Matilda was less inspired from the outset, this was possibly connected with Rowan's past romantic dalliances, 'especially with marry'd women'.
35. Drummond (ed.), *Autobiography of Archibald Hamilton Rowan Esquire*, p. 139.
36. RH 2/4/71/139 (SRO), J.B.'s Report; Howell and Howell, *State Trials*, xxiii, cols 168 and 185. The letter to Muir's father is contained in JC 20/276 (SRO). Drennan Letters, W. Drennan to M. McTier, 20 July 1793, no. 436, T. 765 (PRONI).

37. Brims, 'The Scottish Democratic Movement', p. 429. T. Muir to A. H. Rowan, 17 September 1793 (copy), *Memoirs*, pp. 295–6, MS 24.K.48 (RIA).
38. 'Maxwell, Higgision and Hamilton' were among these, T. Muir to A. H. Rowan, 4 February 1794 (copy), *Memoirs*, pp. 301–2, MS 24.K.48 (RIA).
39. Declaration of George Williamson and inventory of Muir's papers: JC 26/276/8/6x (SRO). The full package contained: Proceedings of the United Irishmen Dublin (10); Roman Catholics of Ireland Address (29); Resolutions of the United Irishmen, 15 July 1793 (5); Rowan Slip (84); Abstract of Trial of Francis Graham, instrumental in the Tandy case (24); Copies of 1787 Act against Tumultuous Risings (11). Clearly the distribution circle was not intended to be very wide initially.
40. Dated 25 July 1793, JC 26/276/8 (SRO).
41. Ibid.
42. Ibid.
43. See Donnelly, *Thomas Muir of Huntershill*, pp. 10–11, for the former approach; for a more revisionist angle, W. Ferguson, *Scotland*, pp. 256–7, and Logue, 'Thomas Muir', pp. 24–31.
44. Commented Cockburn, 'Except in civil and Scotch law, and probably two or three works of indecency, it is my doubt if he ever read a book in his life', *An Examination of the Trials for Sedition*, vol. 1, p. 87. A more sympathetic memoir is in Laing MSS 113 (University of Edinburgh). One of the few books he had actually read was by Swift.
45. See Davis (ed.), *Speeches and Memoirs of J. P. Curran*.
46. For the trial see Howell and Howell, *State Trials*, xxiii, cols 115–251.
47. *State Trials*, xxiii, col. 181.
48. *State Trials*, ibid.
49. R. Hobart to E. Nepean, 19 December 1792, HO 100/38 (PRO).
50. R. Dundas to H. Dundas, 2 August 1793, RH 2/4/71/381 (SRO).
51. Howell and Howell, *State Trials*, col. 225; for original indictment, xxiii, cols 124–5.
52. Ibid., col. 224.
53. T. Muir to A. H. Rowan, 17 September 1793 (copy), Memoirs, pp.295–6, MS 24.K.48 (RIA).
54. Howell and Howell, *State Trials*, xxiii, col. 230.
55. T. Muir to A. H. Rowan (Second Letter), n.d. [1793] (copy), Memoirs, pp. 297–8, MS 24.K.48 (RIA). This was either Henry Shears or his younger brother John, two of the most radical-minded of the Dublin Society.
56. T. F. Palmer to A. H. Rowan, 7 November 1793 (copy), Memoirs, pp.312–14, MS 24.K.48 (RIA).
57. *Northern Star*, 7–11 September 1793, for 'A more correct and full account of the trial . . . than has appeared in the English or Irish papers'. At a Dublin United Irish meeting in September, Rowan produced a letter from Muir, who was 'glorying in the punishment inflicted on him', and hoping that the United Irishmen were 'ready to suffer the same or a severer punishment in so great a cause', Rebellion Papers, 620/20/77 (NAI).
58. Drennan Letters, W. Drennan to M. McTier, 11 October 1793, no. 445, T. 765 (PRONI).
59. J.B. Report, 6 September 1793, RH 2/4/72 (SRO); T. Muir to A. H. Rowan (Second Letter), n.d. [1793] (copy), Memoirs, pp. 297–8, MS 24.K.48 (RIA). Dublin Castle was well aware of this correspondence. Rowan was also suspected of being in contact with France, Rebellion Papers, 620/20/63 (NAI). The Scottish authorities seem to have been less well informed.
60. Howell and Howell, *State Trials*, xxiii, cols 24–30; *Parliamentary History*, vol. xxxi, pp. 816–18.

61. Not all Irish radical groups shared leading United Irishmen's appreciation of a distinct 'Irish Consititution'. As early as 1792, the Irish Jacobin Club were denying that such a thing existed and called for a national convention of English, Scottish and Irish delegates to agree to a 'true constitution': *Northern Star*, 15 December 1792.
62. Howell and Howell, *State Trials*, xxiii, col. 36.
63. Ibid.
64. *Northern Star*, 15 December 1792.
65. Skirving to A. H. Rowan, 23 October 1793, Memoirs, pp. 301–2, MS 24.K.48 (RIA). The letter was highly flattering to Rowan: 'Permit me to assure you of the high respect with which we in Scotland regard your character . . . we regard you as one of those men whom Providence has peculiarly filled to save the country in the present tempestuous period.' The barrister Leonard McNally by 1794 had become so afraid of being implicated in treasonable activities that he became a paid informer and the authorities key source of information on the United Irishmen. Mathew Dowling was a prominent Catholic lawyer, who remained loyal to the Society and, following imprisonment in Scotland, went into exile in 1802.
66. Howell and Howell, *State Trials*, xxiii, cols 401 and 412. See also Brims, 'The Scottish Democratic Movement', pp. 437–9.
67. *Northern Star*, 7 November 1793.
68. Howell and Howell, *State Trials*, xxiii, cols 401 and 412. For the Irish Address, ibid., col. 395. The original was composed in February and sent to Muir in May 1793. Copies are also among Skirving's papers concerning the Third Convention, JC 26/280. The Address is reprinted by Lawless in his *Belfast Politics* collection, pp. 100–4, but dated December 1792, giving rise to the confusion that this was the Address sent to the First Convention. See Appendix III for full text.
69. JC 26/280 (SRO).
70. Ibid.
71. W. Scott to R. Dundas, 1 November 1792, RH 2/4/92/102–3 (SRO); W. Scott to R. Dundas, 11 November 1792, RH 2/4/92/107 (SRO).
72. Ibid.
73. W. Drennan to W. Bruce, n.d. [1791], Drennan–Bruce Correspondence, D. 553 (PRONI). He also noted that Butler and Rowan disliked each other 'as men, tho' they associated as politicians': Drennan Letters, W. Drennan to M. McTier, 25 November 1792, T. 765 (PRONI).
74. Howell and Howell, *State Trials*, xxiii, cols 751–7. See also coverage in *Edinburgh Gazetteer*, 12 November 1793 and *Northern Star*, 18 November 1793.
75. *Reports from the Secret Committee of the House of Commons* (1794), col. 731; *Report from the Committee of Secrecy of the House of Commons* (1799), p. 12.
76. Laing MSS 500–1 (University of Edinburgh). See Kay, *A Series of Original Portraits*, for a cartoon of Butler and Rowan in Edinburgh. Rowan is depicted with his famous club, inscribed 'A pill for a puppy' – the 'puppy' in question being Robert Dundas.
77. Mackenzie, *Life of Thomas Muir*, p. 75.
78. A. H. Rowan to R. Dundas, 14 September 1793, Laing MSS 500–1 (University of Edinburgh).
79. R. Dundas to H. Dundas, 28 October 1793, RH 2/4/72 (SRO).
80. W. Dundas to R. Dundas, 29 October 1793. Robert had been told to write, 'Sir, I received your first and second letters: and I have only to inform you I do not hold myself responsible to you or any person for any observations, which in the course of my official duty, I feel it proper for me to make . . .' His brother Francis had though it best to have 'no correspondence whatever with the blackguard in Dublin', F.

Dundas to R. Dundas, 4 October 1793, Laing MSS 500–1 (University of Edinburgh).

81. Drummond (ed.), *Autobiography of Archibald Hamilton Rowan Esquire*, pp. 171–2.

82. For the dinner, see W. Scott to R. Dundas, 8 November 1793, RH 2/4/72/137 (SRO). The waiters, who were inevitably government spies, reported present Captain Johnstone, Skirving and William Moffat, and three other persons, who were reckoned to be the English delegates to the Convention, Gerrald, Margarot and Sinclair, only recently arrived in Edinburgh.

83. A. H. Rowan to R. Dundas, 15 November 1793, Laing MSS 500–1 (University of Edinburgh).

84. W. Dundas to R. Dundas, 29 October 1793, Laing MSS 500–1 (University of Edinburgh).

85. H. Dundas to R. Blair, 2 November 1793, RH 2/4/72/117–18 (SRO). Cockburn has the usual cutting pen portrait. The Lord Advocate was a small man, 'with a slightly animated look and manners', popular, but then, 'power and agreeableness and claret will make any man a favourite', *An Examination of the Trials for Sedition*, vol. 1, p. 91. See also Fry, *The Dundas Despotism*, p. 156.

86. H. Dundas to R. Blair, 2 November 1793, RH 2/4/72/117–18 (SRO).

87. Radicals in Ireland and Scotland both suspected that the Lord Advocate was responsible: *Northern Star*, 18 November 1793; *Dublin Evening Post*, 26 November 1793; *Edinburgh Gazetteer*, 12 November 1793. In fact, Henry Dundas had liaised with the Procurator Fiscal apparently without his knowledge, see RH 2/4/72/117–18 (SRO).

88. Drummond (ed.), *Autobiography of Archibald Hamilton Rowan Esquire*, p. 181.

89. Drennan Letters, W. Drennan to M. McTier, 22 February 1793, no. 391, T. 765 (PRONI).

90. He had first entered Dublin politics by defending a servant girl wrongly imprisoned. Even at the end of his life, aged 74, he was ready to duel with an MP who had referred to him as a convicted traitor.

91. Drennan Letters, W. Drennan to M. McTier, 18 October 1793, no. 440, T. 765 (PRONI).

92. Drummond (ed.), *Autobiography of Archibald Hamilton Rowan Esquire*, p. 178.

93. *Edinburgh Gazetteer*, 26 November 1793.

94. R. Dundas to H. Dundas, 2 November 1793, RH 2/4/72 (SRO).

95. *Northern Star*, 28 November 1793.

96. Rebellion Papers, 620/20/79 (NAI).

97. Lawless (ed.), *Belfast Politics*, pp. 477–81. In a more practical vein, they also raised a collection of forty guineas, which was much needed since the trunk containing his clothes had been arrested for non-payment of booksellers' bills: Rebellion Papers, 620/20/78 (NAI); W. Moffat to A. H. Rowan, 13 November 1793, Memoirs, pp. 305–6, MS 24.K.48 (RIA).

98. *Northern Star*, 17 April 1794.

99. W. Scott to R. Dundas, 8 November 1793, RH 2/4/72/137 (SRO), 'from what passed at the examination of Hamilton Rowan, I never supposed that he would be present at any meeting of the People'. The meeting is reported in Howell and Howell, *State Trials*, vol. xxiii, cols 413–16.

100. W. Scott to R. Dundas, 17 November 1793, RH 2/4/72/156 (SRO).

101. Goodwin, *Friends of Liberty*, pp. 297–8.

102. Howell and Howell, *State Trials*, vol. xxiii, col. 416.

103. Ibid.

104. Ibid.

105. RH 2/4/72/158–91 (SRO) for debate.

106. Howell and Howell, *State Trials*, vol. xxiii col. 457.
107. RH 2/4/73/203 (SRO).
108. Howell and Howell, *State Trials*, vol. xxiii, col. 457.
109. Original of resolution in JC 26/280/31 (SRO). See also coverage in *Edinburgh Gazetteer*, 3 December 1793.
110. Cockburn, *An Examination of the Trials for Sedition*, vol. 2, pp. 34–40. Sinclair's success may have had more to do with his highly skilled counsels Fletcher and Erskine, whose Jesuitical reasoning thoroughly confused the *Glasgow Mercury* court reporter, 18–25 February 1794. See Brims, 'The Scottish Democratic Movement', pp. 545–7, and W. Ferguson, *Scotland*, pp. 256–7 for fuller discussion.
111. RH 2/4/74/157 (SRO) for list of Muir's visitors in London; see note 82 for Edinburgh dinner.
112. Howell and Howell, *State Trials*, vol. xxiii, col. 428.
113. *Edinburgh Gazetteer*, 10 December 1793; *Northern Star*, 16 December 1793.
114. Rebellion Papers, 620/20/78 (NAI), report of meeting 20 December.
115. Sheares Letters, MS 4833 (TCD) for some of Henry's correspondence while in Paris.
116. Rebellion Papers, 620/20/78 (NAI).
117. *Caledonian Mercury*, 7 December 1973; *Glasgow Courier*, 14 December 1793.
118. W. Skirving to A. H. Rowan, 10 December 1793, Memoirs, pp. 303–4, MS 24.K.48 (RIA).
119. For Skirving's trial, Howell and Howell, *State Trials*, vol. xxiii, cols 391–471; for Margarot's, cols 604–778; for Gerrald's, cols 803–1012. Gerrald's defence drew on the Irish Address from the First Convention, col. 992.
120. Rebellion Papers, 620/21/27 (NAI), report of meeting of 1 February 1794.
121. Ibid. United Irish material was reported to be circulating in Scotland in the spring of 1794, *Dublin Evening Post*, 17 May 1794.
122. Rebellion Papers, 620/42/18 (NAI).
123. Larkin (ed.), *The Trial of William Drennan*. For his later romantic nationalism, see *Fugitive Pieces in Verse and Prose*.
124. His first stop was France, where he was sobered by some of the worst excesses of the Reign of Terror. From there he went to America. Despite constant rumours of his imminent arrival at the head of a conquering French army, he did not return to Ireland for over a decade. By the time of his pardon in 1803, he had moderated his political opinions.
125. MacNeven, *Pieces of Irish History*, p. 70, quoted in Elliott, *Partners in Revolution*, p. 50.
126. *Edinburgh Gazetteer*, 24 December 1793.
127. RH 2/4/74/111 (SRO).
128. *The Declaration and Confession of Robert Watt*, pp. 10–20; see also *Reports from the Secret Committee of the House of Commons* (1794), cols 696–794.
129. *Glasgow Advertiser*, 19 May 1794.
130. *The Declaration and Confession of Robert Watt*, p. 14.
131. Cockburn, *Memorials*, vol. 1, p. 74; Elliott, *Partners in Revolution*, p. 26 similarly suggests that the United Irishmen could have been 'rescued' by a measure of reform before 1794.
132. Grand Lodge of Scotland Miscellaneous Papers, GD/1009/16/4 (SRO). Some members, possibly from the Cameronian sect, protested at the number of unnecessary oaths in the Friends of the People's constitution. In true uncompromising Covenanting style, they considered this issue paramount, since, 'They regarded the Reform as a person resting his whole care upon a scratched finger, when a dangerous wound on the head was totally disregarded.'

133. His prosecution instead focused on his responsibility for an Address to the Friends of the People in Dundee, Howell and Howell, *State Trials*, vol. xxiii, cols 378–82.

134. H. Dundas to W. Pitt, 12 November 1792, 30/8/157 (PRO). R. Dundas to H. Dundas, 21 January 1794, RH 2/4/74 (SRO). For further examples, see A. Gordon to R. Dundas, 19 and 21 January 1794, stressing the desirability of building barracks at Glasgow and removing troops from quarters in the town. See also Melville MSS 172, National Library of Scotland (NLS), for General Gordon's early worries on the state of Dumbarton Castle, garrisoned by some 'old invalids', but 'a post of much importance if any disturbances arise in the West of Scotland or from Ireland'.

135. Writing of the fear of insurrection in December 1792, Sir Gilbert Elliot wrote, as regards the Borders, 'this is certainly ridiculous to those who live in Scotland and know the truth', *Life and Letters of Elliot*, vol. 2, p. 81, quoted in Ehrman, *Pitt the Younger*, p. 219.

136. J. Dunlop to H. Dundas, n.d. [July] 1794, RH 2/4/74/83 (SRO).

137. McDowell, *Ireland in the Age of Imperialism*, pp. 435–6.

138. *Parliamentary History*, vol. xxx, col. 46. Dundas believed that, 'The example of France had been held out for invitation, not only with regard to their object . . . those societies held a correspondence with France, for the purpose of overturning the Constitution, and even sent members to Paris to procure instructions.

139. J.B.'s report, 9 February 1794, Melville MSS 172 (NLS).

140. G. Young to H. Dundas, 15 February 1794, RH 2/4/209/67–8 (SRO).

5

Underground
1795–1797

We still have swarms from Ireland, but have sent back as many as
we may and indeed more persons than in strict law we are entitled
to do. But we must not stop at trifles.

Robert Dundas, Lord Advocate of Scotland,
to James King, 14 July 1797[1]

The year 1795 opened with most of the chief actors who had shaped the
alliance between Irish and Scottish radicalism in exile or confinement.
Paradoxically, while its former champions languished, the alliance itself
was destined to develop and advance. It had always possessed a powerful
momentum, independent of the elegant addresses of William Drennan
and his associates. Not only had the popular experiences of the early
1790s helped undermine habits of deference and quiescence, they had
also instructed radicals in the three kingdoms in the wisdom of concerted
effort against their common foe – the British government. Now this
strategy gained a further practical imperative from the promise of international support held out by the French Republic's switch to the military
offensive at the end of 1794, and from the impact of official repression
on the home front.

The parallel escalation of European and domestic crises had a transfigur-
ing effect on the nature of the connection between the two democratic
movements. As both shifted towards oath-bound conspiracy and an
unambiguous republican ideology, secrecy and intrigue became the hallmark of their relationship. The weight of the new politics was borne not
by charismatic 'personalities', but by the faceless 'disaffected' who popu-
lated the correspondence of Lord Advocate Dundas and his nervous
subordinates; what Edward Thompson has referred to as the social and
political 'apartheid' of the nascent working class was now established.
Along with the social status of participants, the geographical axis of

contact also switched, with the main channel of communication now between Belfast and Glasgow rather than Dublin and Edinburgh. Even the language of association took on a more urgent and prosaic turn, as 'civic union' gave way to 'the planting of Irish potatoes', as the democrats of Perth mischievously termed the adoption of underground methods.[2]

The United Irishmen's links with Scotland in this period were only one component of a determined attempt to extend their new conspiratorial system and insurrectionary tactics throughout Ireland and on to the British mainland. Here, Scottish radicalism stood out as apparently well placed in organisational terms to make the shift into an effective political underground. For all its limitations, the Scottish Friends of the People Association had entailed a centrally co-ordinated nationwide structure which compared favourably with the more diffuse English pattern of metropolitan and provincial societies. Ideologically too, the Presbyterian legacy of independent thought suggested a closer approximation with conditions in Ulster.

These initial advantages still did not guarantee success and the paths of development of the two radical movements were set to diverge to an even greater extent than in the era of high-profile propagandising. One key feature was the slower pace of transformation of democratic political life in Scotland towards more desperate tactics. But even more significant was the failure of the United Scotsmen, as the new covert organisation was to become, to anchor themselves in the sort of mass consciousness which would have secured for them a meaningful social base.

The historical problem of how to account for Scottish radicalism's uncertain political future immediately presents itself. Was this the inevitable product of objective social and political conditions, or did the specific circumstances surrounding the birth of the United Scotsmen also intervene?; or, to put it more bluntly, was the very 'Irishness' of the new radicalism to blame? Addressing this, discussion again begins from the basic dynamics and evolution of this latest incarnation of Irish–Scots alliance. For although the principle of mutual assistance had been established, the new political conditions by the mid-1790s meant that practical links had to be actively sought and negotiated anew.

1795–1796: A MASS MOVEMENT LOOKS OUTWARDS

Roger Wells has pointed to 1796 as the year of greatest dissimilarity between radicalism in Ireland and Britain.[3] Alternatively, when the Scottish case is taken separately and when recent work on the United Irishmen's shift to mass revolutionary tactics is considered, the years 1795 and 1796 *both* stand out as marked by striking contrasts.

After the alarms of the British Convention and the Pike Plot, Home

Office correspondence on Scottish affairs was quick to settle into the smooth accustomed grooves of patronage and jobbery. The *Glasgow Courier* complained in March 1795 that the news had become 'so dumb and sterile, as hardly to lend . . . one judgement for political cognition'.[4] Beneath this apparent calm, a *frisson* of anxiety was at work. One source was the country's preparedness to withstand the predatory attentions of French forces, the east coast and the Minch being seen as notably lacking in adequate naval protection.[5] Domestic tensions also re-emerged. As elsewhere in Britain, 1795 and 1796 were years of dearth and high food prices.[6] The pattern of resultant unrest was highly uneven, but meal mobs appeared in Ross-shire and Aberdeenshire, and helped to shift the traditional paternalistic methods of conciliation into gear. Lord Swinton, one of Muir's judges and a man 'distinguished by his liberality to the poor of his neighbourhood', reminded law officers of their duty to enquire into instances of profiteering and hoarding in grain and bring supplies to be publicly sold at fair prices.[7] At Perth, 'very liberal subscriptions' from the town's inhabitants lowered meal prices in favour of the labouring poor who were bearing high prices particularly hard.[8]

For the present, Scottish democrats were not in the position to hammer material distress into a political weapon. Whereas elsewhere in mainland Britain, 1795 had marked the re-emergence of radicalism as a vehicle for public protest, with mass meetings to articulate popular grievances, the Scots seem to have quietly turned in on themselves after the dispersal of the British Convention and the Treason Trials of summer 1794.[9] Gentlemen reformers continued to meet discreetly under government surveillance. An informer reported in February 1795 that a dinner had taken place in Fortune's Tavern, Edinburgh, featuring some of those 'looked upon as the most decided Republicans in the country'.[10] There is understandably little information regarding the rank and file's activities, but it is highly unlikely that the political ideals and organisational experience gained during the preceding reform agitation simply expired, however much the authorities might have willed it to do so. Indeed, in the winter of 1795 some radicals were stimulated into renewed activity with the passage of the 'Two Acts' against Treasonable Practices and Seditious Meetings. These were hailed by the conservative press 'as giving force to the law and vigour to the Constitution', but in effect restricted the rights of free speech and public assembly. In this way, 'the British Convention Bill', balefully intimated by the United Irishmen in 1793, was finally in place.[11] In Glasgow, resistance took the familiar form of cautious remonstrances and petitioning; but, more interestingly in Perth, an old Friends of the People centre, more covert techniques were employed. Here 'seditious papers' were distributed, apparently originating from the visit of one George Rutherford, a journeyman tailor from London.[12] Admittedly, such activities were not always appreciated by the population at large. One strolling lecturer in 'Modern Political Philosophy,' while attempting to make converts, was forced to take refuge in a cow-house.[13] Yet, however feeble these efforts may appear, they are still a significant reminder that later United Irish missionising to Scotland was not directed at a completely barren political landscape, but to an enduring, if submerged, tradition of indigenous radicalism.

The comparison with the situation of the democratic movement in Ireland is striking nevertheless. The problem for the historian in the Irish case is less one of information than interpretation. Plentiful testimony exists of the United Irishmen's vigorous new profile as a mass revolutionary movement in the two years following the formal extinction of the Dublin United Irish Society in May 1794. In making sense of this, commentators have tended to follow the contemporary account of the Dublin leader Thomas Addis Emmet.[14] This states that one of the Belfast United societies and another radical club escaped attention, owing to the humble social situations of their members, and continued to meet. As constitutional reform channels were now shut off, they became determined on forming secret associations, and in the autumn and winter of 1794 adopted a new oath-bound form. As the title 'United Irishmen' was 'dear to the people' and suited their needs, they adopted it, but, Emmet explained, it was not a continuation of the old open society, and middle-class reformers in Belfast and Dublin only joined this reconstruction 'from the bottom up' in the spring of 1795.

The overall picture of two successive United Irish organisations, with bourgeois leaders like Emmet himself being carried along by popular passions, has at last become the subject of increasing critical attention. Curtin and Smyth both stress a central continuity in terms of organisation and personnel in radical developments in the mid-1790s, with the latter also advocating a populist social-radical reading of United Irish ideology.[15] Cullen too has detected elements of secrecy from as early as 1793.[16] Emmet, it seems, was not familiar with the working of the northern societies, some of whom were flirting discreetly with seditious activity, such as the acquisition of arms, within months of their initial organisation in 1791. Use also continued to be made of the network of more obscure radical clubs, such as the Irish Jacobins, coexisting with the United Irishmen from the the early 1790s. Even in his own Dublin base, radical societies had never, as Emmet implied, ceased to meet; in July 1794, for example, the Sheares brothers were able to re-emerge in a public meeting to receive messages from Dundee and Glasgow.[17]

This new revisionism has great merit, not least methodologically: it underlines the dangers of decontextualising crisp and convenient eyewitness accounts such as Emmet's. Anxious to distance himself from the eventual violent climax of the Irish revolutionary movement, he was unwilling to admit any 'radicalisation from within' process in his movement. The traditional notion of a sudden unprecedented switch to insurrectionary politics, with 1795 as the caesura, also neglects the ideological grounding of such a step in the libertarian Presbyterianism and advanced Whiggery which had been filtering into Ulster from the mid-eighteenth century through the medium of Scottish university education. Concepts like 'the right of resistance to tyranny' were to prove powerful solvents to strictly constitutionalist positions.

'Continuity', however, should not be equated with a path of unproblematic linear development, a rather inhuman phenomenon which historians are sometimes anxious to attach to movements like the United Irishmen. There are various empirical difficulties with this model. The diaries of one of the leading 'radicalisers', Thomas Russell, reveal the continuing oscillations between apocalyptic certainty and bitter despair which debilitated the societies, especially in 1793 and 1794. Russell considered emigration to America 'the only attraction' as reform was now out of the question, yet soon he was revelling in the divine retribution which would surely follow official repression.[18] Inevitable differences of opinion and personality were also liable to shatter any consistent and unitary route towards radicalisation. Even the politically sympathetic editor Samuel Neilson commented that Russell's ardour induced him to '*bore us with politics, but few pay any attention to him . . .*'.[19] More important was the gap between rhetoric and action which coloured much of the United Irishmen's proceedings. McDowell has noted how the *Northern Star* editorials of the spring of 1796 combined theorising on how to oppose government actions with disapproval of local attempts to actually do so.[20] This reflected the enduring hope among some United men that pacific external pressure would work the same magic as in the golden years of Volunteering, thereby eliminating the need for real physical force.

The flexible and uncertain quality of Irish radicalism should therefore not be underestimated. Indeed, the same mixture of good intentions and hesitancy was shortly to manifest itself in its attempts to reactivate a Scottish connection. Rival discourses flourished within the same movement, and no doubt coexisted in the minds of men like Russell and Neilson. The fascination of the years 1795 and 1796 in Ireland is how political, social and economic structures specific to that country combined to ensure that the options of conspiracy and armed struggle eventually prevailed.

The first step in this process was the shift by Pitt's administration and the Irish authorities towards a policy of outright coercion. This was in turn the product of the consolidation of conservative opinion among the upper ranks of Irish Protestantism, a phenomenon accomplished later than in Scotland but attended with much greater violence.

The forcing house was the inglorious 'Fitzwilliam episode' of February and March, which also reawakened all the old constitutional uncertainties and humiliations of the Anglo-Irish relationship. The arrival of the new Whig Viceroy, Earl Fitzwilliam – a figure of known liberal and pro-Catholic sympathies – had been hailed by radicals as 'one of the brightest in the Annals of our Country', while for the Ascendancy it seemed about to undermine the very basis of their power.[21] Hardly a political animal, his viceroyalty was the pragmatic product of Pitt's wartime coalition with the Portland Whigs, and fell far short of the febrile expectations it had raised. The major success of Fitzwilliam's hasty attempts at a reform programme lay in uniting the King, the Prime Minister, and the Irish grandees Beresford and Fitzgibbon against further instalments of Catholic emancipation. He was abruptly recalled to Whitehall on 25 February, leaving democrats and Catholics disappointed and the Protestant gentry in an apprehensive and excitable state. Dublin was draped in mourning on his departure, and the *Northern Star* remembered it as 'the most ominous and fatal to the interests of Ireland that had occurred in the present century'.[22] There was some justice in this contemporary perception of a turning point, as from the spring of 1795 the British cabinet became increasingly receptive to Irish administration demands for pacification by military force. Political polarisation, open disaffection, and official counter-insurgency shortly became intertwined in a downward spiral.[23]

Participants' sense of a closing-off of options in this year was reinforced by another Irish political *cause célèbre* – the trial in April of Revd William Jackson, the French agent whose mission to Dublin in 1794 had incriminated Rowan. Jackson was found guilty of treason and took poison to escape the inevitable sentence, but the importance of the trial was less in its victim's fate than the publicity it gave to French offers of military assistance in the event of an Irish rebellion, an alternative which presented itself to political radicals and dissatisfied Catholics alike at the very moment when repression was beginning to bite.[24]

By the early summer of 1795, developments on the political level had encouraged the evolution of the United Irishmen as a militant revolutionary movement, making use of the network of existing United Irish societies, but also expanding the movement's numerical and geographical profile. In Dublin, a narrowly based but revitalised grouping now operated and continued to attract the most advanced radicals in the capital. In the north, a centrally led, clandestine system of affiliated societies was emerging, forming in theory a pyramid of societies, each 35 strong, and higher delegated baronial and county committees.[25] The movement's ideological character was similarly remodelled in line with the new exigencies of security and possible French intervention. As Curtin notes, the United Irish oath now dropped parliamentary reform as a central objective in exchange for 'an equal full and adequate representation of all the people in Ireland', signalling the movement's revolutionary turn both for domestic consumption and with an eye for international opinion.[26]

An enthusiastic membership drive was now aimed at the Presbyterian and Episcopalian 'lower orders' in towns and commercial centres, and in the Ulster countryside, a strategy which was shortly to alienate many traditional propertied supporters of the radical cause. Women too seem to have assumed a role in the Societies at this point.[27] By far the most rapid short cut to expansion was the coalition with the Catholic Defenders, worked out from mid-1795.[28] That this relationship was achieved at all stands as a reminder that Ireland's eighteenth-century crisis not only encompassed politics, but was also grounded in the contradictions of a fast developing cash economy and in an unfavourable land–population ratio. The Defenders had their origins in 1780s' County Armagh where they articulated the Catholic frustrations, but by the next decade, feeding off government repression, they had spread impressively into north Leinster, Munster and North Connaught in a loose horizontal federation of 'lodges'. The social basis also broadened to some extent beyond the peasantry, to include radical artisans, shopkeepers and school teachers.[29] Already penetrated by democratic doctrines even before the rise of the United Irishmen, their system continued to show an admirable facility for adjusting its ideological mix to suit local conditions. Unmistakably, by 1795 the weight of their agenda had shifted from immediate agrarian grievances to mass economic and political disaffection. In this, they were informed both by Painite ideas and ancient grievances, the result being a potentially revolutionary amalgam of elemental republicanism and pro-French Catholic nationalism in which an invasion was looked for to restore Irish land to Catholic ownership.

For democrats of a more secularised persuasion, the Defenders were a puzzle. A few years before, the Scottish radical press had dismissed them as 'those unfortunate people . . . who act evidently at random, without object or motive'.[30] This was understandable given their lack of exposure to rural discontent and popular alienation on a similar scale, but Ulster Presbyterians shared their problems of comprehension. While advocating that the government should try to understand what the Defenders' grievances actually were, for their own part they were less interested in making sense of the movement than in exploiting its potential for mass mobilisation.[31] This entailed a consistent under-estimation of the sectarian content of Defender ideology and practice and of the salience generally of sectarian conflict in Irish society. Displaying flashes of that sense of superiority and provincial élitism which were so characteristic of Ulster Presbyterian thinking, they were confident in their ability to mould the Defenders to suit their own purposes. Indeed, such was their confidence, that they were able to swallow their abiding distaste for Catholicism in the drive to swell numbers.[32] When in September and October 1795 a grass-roots campaign of terror against Catholics in Armagh, the so-called 'Armagh Outrages', resulted in the flight of thousands of Catholics southwards, the United Irishmen even consciously played on fears of an Orange terror to promote the coalition of the two movements.[33] Their success was dramatic, as was the ease with which they could harness the economic grievances and anti-Ascendancy stance of almost the whole of the class and confessional spectrum in Ireland. The full working of the internal contradictions which this process concealed were yet to become apparent. In the interim, more practical dilemmas presented themselves over the geographical scope of the United Irish mission.

'POOR TITLER'

In August 1795, Wolfe Tone, who had left Ireland after being ensnared along with Rowan in the Jackson affair, arrived in America and was soon attempting to impress the French minister at Washington, Pierre Adet, with the information from Belfast that 'Scottish agents' had recently been in Ireland.[34] The facts behind Tone's claim are unclear. The breadth of disaffection throughout the British Isles and the United Irishmen's ability to focus and harness this was to become a convention in their dealings with the French. What determined with greater certainty is that the Belfast radicals at this very juncture were earnestly debating whether to extend their operations to Scotland. From the information of the government agent William Bird, 'the Committee of Belfast' had deputed one individual 'Titler' to travel to Scotland:

> thinking the People ripe for revolt and this a fit citizen for their use, and in consequence of a *Plan* provided by the B. Com[ee] [Belfast Committee] he was to traverse Scotland as a *Highland Piper*. He learned the tongue and was to have gone from town to town to organise a General Insurrection, from there to the South of Ireland (Cork), hence to *Paris* to enlist the French.[35]

In the event, Bird reported, 'Titler', under the alias Donaldson, went as far as Donaghadee, ready to make the crossing to Scotland, but 'the Committee was afraid to persevere and recalled him hence'. Relations then became soured.

> When this project was given up, they neglected poor *Titler*, and he was very ill-used, he used to *damn* the club altogether, and was suddenly taken to *America* . . . No one man of the Club would go with him to his ship, and he went away with great anger at the Societies . . . He wrote a severe satire of the *Irish Democrats*, entitled 'Manners and Principles of the Belfast Jacobines' . . .[36]

Another Belfast agent, Maxwell, records a similar story, but with some important additional detail. He suggests that William Putnam McCabe, Samuel Neilson and Henry Joy McCracken were among those who were to have made the rendezvous with the agent at Donaghadee and given him instructions for Scotland, but 'thought better of it and afterwards sent him themselves to America as an "excuse"'.[37]

While all this might sound like typically fanciful spy material, particularly the notion of a lone piper rousing a Highland rebellion, the most important particulars have a compelling ring of truth. First, as regards 'the Belfast Committee', the leaders who are mentioned are precisely the cadre who have been identified as giving direction to the radicalisation of the Societies during 1795.[38] Neilson, as we have seen, had been advising the Dublin United Irishmen as early as February the previous year to transmit their material through his 'confidential' Scottish friends. McCracken, one of the most socially radical of the United leaders, was reported to be touring Ulster in December 1795, 'to unite Defenders with United Irishmen'.[39] McCabe, who according to Bird was 'Titler's particular friend', was one of the United Irishmen's travelling emissaries and recruiting sergeants. 'A person of great energy and character, gifted with some talents as a speaker', and 'an ardent republican', he was himself sent by the Belfast Committee in 1795 to proselytise in rural Ulster, and later performed this task in Scotland.[40]

Second, the 'Titler' referred to in the reports is, in fact, James Tytler, the polymath Scottish radical who had fled Scotland for Belfast in January 1794: Bird describes him as 'a man of genius but very poor . . . a compiler of the Branch of the Scottish Encyclopaedia'. The *Northern Star* reported his eventual arrival in Boston, and a fragment of his correspondence from Salem, Massachusetts, dated 7 September 1795, found its way into the hands of the Irish authorities.[41] Here Tytler spoke warmly of the increasing community of Irish exiles in America, including Rowan, Tone, Reynolds and Tandy, but he remained extremely bitter over his ex-friends in Belfast, dreading 'the unstable disposition of most of those who call themselves "Friends of Liberty" there'.[42] Also enclosed was a copy, now lost, of his squib against them, showing 'he was not a better-humoured politician than formerly'.[43]

It is impossible to reconstruct what actually had occurred between them. It is possible that the services of Tytler, as a seasoned pamphleteer, were offered or solicited for an exploratory expedition to Scotland in order to disseminate reworked United Irish doctrines and organisational techniques among surviving radical groupings. This is more likely than the 'General Insurrection' which Bird supposed.[44] From Tytler's recriminations it seems that some understanding had indeed been reached with the Belfast leadership and that the project had advanced beyond the planning stage, reaching the point of execution when the Committee drew back.

Their motives stemmed probably from personal and political considerations. Tytler under closer acquaintance was perhaps not the ideal undercover agent. The poet Burns viewed him as 'an obscure, tippling though extraordinary body'.[45] Nor was the relative quiet in Scotland during the year very encouraging; the speculative venture may also have appeared inauspicious at the point when United recruitment and work towards the extremely delicate Defenders coalition were still getting underway in Ulster.[46]

This is an odd, rather amateurish interlude, and perhaps provides the basis for Tone's talk of 'Scottish agents'. Yet, it is significant that such a scheme as Tytler's could be given serious consideration by the Belfast United leaders. That it was suggests simultaneously the breadth of their ambitions for recruitment and the 'timid step', as MacNeven expressed it, with which they attempted to give them practical expression.[47] At this point in 1795, it was necessary to weigh up the demands of exporting their system with those of internal expansion and radicalisation. In the turmoil of the next year, the distinction between the two appeared increasingly academic.

EXPEDITIONS

The Tytler episode was not enough to dissuade United Irishmen in the north from building Scottish links. Instead, this option received an important boost in 1796 as a by-product of the latest escalation of government repression.

Whereas coercion in Ireland had previously to rely on a fairly flimsy legal foundation, *de facto* procedures – such as disarming and detention without charge – were now regularised by an Indemnity Act in February (which sanctioned magistrates' extra-legal operations), and by an Insurrection Act, in which the British Cabinet again found a discomfiting reminder

of Irish loyalist hysteria in pursuit of security. The Act made the administration of 'seditious oaths' a capital offence and facilitated the proclamation
of martial law. In districts where magistrates deemed this necessary,
special powers were permitted to search houses, suspend meetings and
send untried prisoners to the fleet. These measures were rapidly put into
effect, but Ulster, in particular, remained highly disturbed. By the summer,
the Irish administration was forced to push through another set of repressive measures to manage the crisis.

This process reacted positively on the export of the United system.
Coercion strengthened the resolve of the Belfast Committee to persevere
with expansion as both a practical and a moral bulwark, with Scotland
an early object of their concern. Efforts here followed the organisation
of the borderlands of Ulster and developed simultaneously with preliminary missionising work in Connacht and Munster. In this respect, the
thinking of the Belfast men probably reflected cultural as much as geographical proximity, Scottish radicals providing a more comfortable reference point than the Catholic Defender bands in the south of their own
country.

Whatever the precise motivation, the old battle-cry of radical solidarity
was resurrected. The spy Bird was soon reporting that Samuel Neilson
and Samuel Kennedy, chief compositor of the *Northern Star* and founder
of the Irish Jacobin Club, 'were connected with Jacobin Clubs in Kinsale,
England and Scotland'. Neilson had been especially inquisitive over the
number of 'citizens' they could muster, while Kennedy admitted that
'men of confidence' had already been sent over.[48] This later information
seems correct, for by July 1796 a formal approach *had* been made from
Belfast to Glasgow, with two delegates – Joseph Cuthbert and Thomas
Potts – sent 'with new Irish constitutions for the inspection and approba-
tion of the Scots'.[49] They returned in high spirits, but this initial contact
was not an unqualified success, and some of the old condescension
which had clouded Irish–Scottish radical relations in the past crept into
the delegates' reports to a Northern Provincial meeting. Another Belfast
United man, John Simpson, contrasted the Scottish situation with the
good news from Dublin and Connacht, complaining that they had found
'the Scottish willing and ready to act with the Friends of Liberty in
Ireland, but the Scotch were not possessed of sufficient energy . . . their
was [sic] decent fellows among them and they had come on surprisingly
. . .'.[50] Deputations sent to England around the same time conveyed
similar lukewarm impressions of 'spirit' tempered by a lack of real organisational and numerical muscle.[51]

The impact of these visitations on the Scots is not recorded, but later
official investigations into the spread of organised disaffection traced

this in some cases to the year 1796. It was suspected, for example, that the United Scotsmen leader George Mealmaker of Dundee began the administration of secret oaths at this point.[52] The claim was also made that during the course of the year, individuals, particularly in Ayrshire and Renfrewshire, had formed themselves into 'secret and illegal associations . . . after the model of the United Irishmen'. A key figure was Archibald Grey, a warehouse keeper of Irvine, who was accused of swearing in members in the town from September onwards.[53]

Some progress then seems likely, but this was after a rather modest fashion, especially when compared with the United Irishmen's own efforts at building up their movement. In the latter half of 1796, radicalism in Ireland seemed positively to thrive on the authorities' attempts to crush it. The arrests of the main Belfast leaders, including Neilson, during September, and the suspension of Habeus Corpus the following month only served to propel the Societies into military forms of organisation. Orders were sent out from Belfast for every member to take up arms, and county committees were instructed to modify their hierarchical structures accordingly.[54] Ulster's call to arms was readily answered, with the Scottish connection now being employed to secure gunpowder, which the authorities were convinced was being smuggled via Larne.[55] On 6 November, most of the Province was placed under the Insurrection Act.

These feverish preparations were not only driven by domestic pressures, but also by rising confidence in the reality of French offers of military assistance. The activities of unsolicited French agents had encouraged the popular impression that the French would gladly assist their struggles, when invited to do so.[56] In fact, since his eventual arrival in France in early 1796, Wolfe Tone had been working assiduously to ensure that Ireland was the destination of any French expedition. The political climate in France fortunately assisted him, with Anglophobia at its height after an English-sponsored civil war in the Vendée, but Tone himself proved a skilful diplomat, fully exploiting the personal intrigue of the Directory regime. His efforts were bolstered by the agency of two further Irish emissaries, Arthur O'Connor and Lord Edward Fitzgerald, both wayward scions of the Irish Protestant ascendancy.[57] They impressed French representatives by saying that their intervention in Ireland was imperative to save the people from further military confrontations. An invasion, they claimed, must proceed any rising, and in secret consultations details were drawn up of the forces required. On their return to Dublin in October, they revitalised the United organisation with news of the expected expedition. Meanwhile in Ulster, some of the extravagant optimism of earlier in the decade was reviving, and among the United Irishmen and the Defenders alike, 'very considerable preparations were making *in a quiet way* to further [the French] descent'.[58]

Tragically for United Irish hopes, when the French expeditionary force did arrive in Bantry Bay on Ireland's south-west coast in Christmas week 1796, it came as much as a surprise to the radicals as to the authorities.[59] Its timing was unexpected, and it had arrived off a province where the United system had hardly penetrated.

1797: MISSIONISING AND CONTAGION

For loyalists like the Methodist minister John Galt, January 1797 was a time to rejoice; as he recorded in his diary, 'Hallelujah! the Lord omnipotent reighneth and by his strong arm and without our aid has wrought our deliverance. By a storm he has dispersed the French fleet'.[60] Whether the work of Divine Providence or a 'Protestant Wind', the authorities had little space for triumphalism. Although the French fleet's appearance had not given rise to sympathetic shows of strength on land, the Irish administration was determined to disarm and crush the disaffected before a second force could arrive. Bantry Bay, however, had given the United Irishmen their most powerful stimulus to date and in the north membership doubled between January and April.

Still, progress was flawed, for tensions now grew within the expanding radical movement. Despite their hopes of further landings in the near future, the Dublin leadership counselled delaying any home-grown military effort until French assistance had assumed a concrete form. This was an unfortunate stance, since the French had by now reverted to their previous position of seeking a rising before risking new troop commitments. Meanwhile, Ulster leaders chaffed at the apparent drift of policy, and the lower levels of the Society began to display a growing capacity for independent action. Their dissatisfaction peaked in the first week of June when the Dublin section of the United executive again rebuffed the call of many of the Ulster leaders for an immediate rising. Returning to their own Province, it was now the turn of the Antrim colonels to refuse to act without French aid. In the next few weeks, facing the threat of arrests, eight of the Ulster militants – among them James Coigley, a Catholic priest from County Armagh, and a Presbyterian minister, Arthur McMahon – fled into exile. After landing on the Scottish coast, most dispersed southwards, and after a brief but productive visit stimulating United Irish membership in England, they were reunited in France.[61]

In this way 1797 slipped by, with the United movement in Ulster increasingly sapped by forcible disarming, arrest and exile. Internecine dispute also allowed the authorities to retake the initiative through military measures and by means of their spy network. At the height of their powers, the United Irishmen were already a diminishing force.

This was the depressing context of the next major extension of the

United system to Scotland and the rest of the British mainland. While the *Northern Star* publicly applauded continuing attempts at mass petitioning in Glasgow and Edinburgh, United strategy in reality had forsaken such open methods.[62] Their external involvement was not restricted to the exchange of formal deputations from higher committees, but also entailed an active and systematic policy of covert communication by missionaries 'all negotiating by parlance'.[63] For the societies in Ulster, such activity offered an outlet for their restless energy, which the cautious policy of the centralised Dublin leadership denied them. Not only did external contact raise their spirits in a period of enforced inactivity, it might also prove useful in negotiations for French support, if they could hold out the prospect of a diversionary uprising on the mainland.

Although it was English population centres which proved the greatest magnet for the work of the most prominent agents, such as James Coigley, the Ulster United men had various advantages in their more discreet efforts to externalise their movement across the North Channel. The first of these was simply their experience of popular proselytising work. The Belfast leadership had been making full use of emissaries to boost numbers and spread their political ideology at home since 1795. McCabe, McCracken and the self-educated James Hope are the best-known examples in an extensive network of agents, financed by the subscriptions of Society members.[64] To escape official detection, a series of imaginative, and sometimes bizarre personae were adopted; preachers, 'lapsed papists', muslin sellers, silk weavers, beggars, itinerant astronomers, farmers and pedlars all carried the United message.[65] Bearing certificates which empowered them to 'take tests and create new clubs', they also distributed a mass of 'seditious papers', handbills, tracts and broadsheets.[66]

United work at home was assisted by the fluid communications network, which sprang from the Irish linen industry. While these conditions were not fully replicated within Scotland, the established educational and commercial channels which existed between the two societies were open for exploitation. One obvious conduit for United Irish ideas was the flow of Ulster Presbyterian students into the Scottish universities. In May 1796, for example, Alexander Carson, from Stewartstown, County Tyrone, won a prize at Glasgow University for his Latin oration on 'The Claims of the Catholics of Ireland and the Expedience of the Union of Irishmen'.[67] While Carson's audience was clearly limited, another Tyrone student, James Boyle, was bound for the university with a more explicit mission, and 'a purse, collected from the local United men, for the purpose of making United Scotchmen'.[68]

Economic links between Ulster and the west of Scotland were also at a premium. A tradition of seasonal labour for harvest time was well established in the western counties by the end of the eighteenth century. Elsewhere in Scotland, peripatetic hawkers of Irish linens and cheap cloth were a familiar sight, as were a swelling complement of Irish beggars and vagrants.[69] This itinerant population could provide a useful cover for United work, much as they did in Ireland, where pedlars and packmen were also employed directly to disseminate radical literature. Some government supporters, such as Revd James Lapslie, were keen to seize on the dangers of 'these strolling agents of the seditious and the treasonable', most of whom, he remarked, were Irish and 'however low . . . well qualified to produce an effect on the minds of the peasantry'. In his parish of Campsie to the north of Glasgow, they had employed the usual ingenious techniques, some claiming to be ex-prisoners of the French, 'who when asked about their treatment, said the French were much better than represented in the newspapers'.[70]

Besides these transients, the United Irishmen were also able to benefit from a developing process of permanent migration and settlement in Scotland. To a large extent this was a response to the pull of rising wages in a developing economy, just as the linen and woollen industries were declining at home. While in Wigtownshire, Kirkcudbright and Dumfries there had been 'some mixture from time immemorial', large numbers of Irish had begun to settle in Ayr and surrounding parishes from the 1770s, with Girvan and Maybole becoming major receiving centres for migrants towards the century's end. In Glasgow, the population was sufficient by 1792 to sustain a Hibernian Benefit Society.[71] The west was not alone in this respect, and Irish linen weavers also contributed to a sudden rise in the population of Fife around the same time, with Perth and Forfar also affected.[72]

The resultant migrant communities could be pressed into service as operational bases for underground activity. One of the most energetic propagators of the United system in Perth, James Craigendallie was not an 'emissary', but an Irish weaver, who had been settled in the town for a considerable time. Another activist, George Murdoch was a County Down blacksmith, resident in Scotland since 1787.[73] Similarly in south Ayrshire, the Lord-Lieutenant reported that those gathered as weavers in villages in the locality formed 'a serious body of disaffected, who would take the first opportunity upon alarm of trying everything in their power to bring on mischief'.[74]

These were not simply introspective Irish enclaves. Migration from Scotland was mainly from those counties, Antrim and Down, where Protestants predominated.[75] Correlating the admittedly piecemeal information on settlement patterns – provided by the *Statistical Account* – with the denominational profiles of relevant parishes', most settlers at this point were probable Protestant, the religion of the receiving society; in St Quivox in Ayrshire, for instance, despite 'a considerable number of Irish' settled as weavers and day labourers, no Roman Catholics were reported in the area.[76] This was in contrast to the situation in London and the north-west of England, also set to become United strongholds. Here, barriers of religion and ethnicity stood between Catholic Irish migrants and the indigenous population. While conducive to the creation of United Irish cells, and helping resistance to government surveillance, these conditions were more problematic for making links into local radicalism.[77]

Voluntary labour migration was only one dimension of population movement from Ireland. The litany of legally-sanctioned repression in Ulster had continued from the previous year, but in 1797 reached a new intensity. Military reinforcements poured into the Province in January, and the commander General Lake was given an unrestricted mandate to arrest suspicious persons. On 13 March, Martial Law was proclaimed and disarming began in earnest. Despite protestations against 'unjust and tyrannical practices', the military campaign again intensified in May, now unhampered by the need to co-operate with the civil power.[78] By June, 103 of the main Ulster leaders had been detained.

The government strategy of targeted coercion ensured that the growing tide of migrants to Scotland from the end of 1796 was to become a flood. Some were motivated by the generally unsettled state of Ulster, and by familiar economic imperatives. For others, these general considerations were reinforced by the need to flee from direct persecution. For these men, the passage to Scotland was cheap, speedy and, if the domestic situation improved, reversible.[79]

The migration process was vital for the fortunes of the United system in Scotland. It meant that the conscious policy of the Belfast leaders of selecting and financing agents was no longer the only means of propagating their beliefs and tactics. It was now complemented by the spontaneous testimonies of those who had experienced at first hand the military campaign in Ulster. There was a clear parallel here with the logic and momentum of the spread of the Defenders in 1795, when persecution and flight had merely created a diffusion of disaffection in the southern Irish counties.

Friends of government in south-west Scotland, which was the initial point of contact for this turbulent influx, were quickly alive to the security implications. In February 1797, the 'general opinion' was already reported to be that 'in the event of an invasion, even of a very distant part of the kingdom, which might occasion the withdrawal of the regular troops we have in this corner, this part of the country so left to itself would be in danger from the Irish . . . as from the French'.[80] These concerns had already been anticipated at Cabinet level, and the official response which resulted was evidence of increasing co-ordination and information-sharing between the branches of government.[81]

Pitt's nightmare of the concerted pressure of foreign and domestic enemies had apparently communicated itself to Henry Dundas's successor at the Home Office, the Duke of Portland, an ex-Viceroy of Ireland and a practised alarmist in his own right. Acting on information from the Irish administration at Dublin Castle on the scale of emigration from Ulster to Portpatrick, the Duke directed the Lord Advocate to implement immediate checks.[82] This evolved into a two-pronged strategy. The names of those arriving were to be remitted back to Whitehall, and then passed on to the Irish Chief Secretary Thomas Pelham, to allow him to pick out any for 'special watch'. At the same time, those carrying on a secret correspondence between the two countries were to be identified and their mail intercepted. Underlining the importance of these steps, money was to come from the Secret Service Fund, 'utility outweighing expense'.[83]

Lord Advocate Dundas diligently complied with these instructions. An *ad hoc* refugee policy thus emerged and Portpatrick became a listening post for developments in Ireland and beyond. This was not simply Dundas's answering the call of Whitehall. For although the Scottish authorities at this point faced much less of an internal radical challenge than their Irish neighbours, the fear of 'contagion' became a constant theme in their calculations. As the Laird of Dalquharran expressed it:

> That part of Ireland nearest to us is in the very worst situation, I believe, in respect of its principles of any part of that Kingdom; I cannot help thinking it an object well worthy of the attention of government to diminish by the most active means possible all communication between this country and such dangerous neighbours.[84]

An insistent worry was that the 'highest men' in the United system and 'people of very great property from Belfast' had become domiciled in Scotland.[85] This was the case, though not to the extent which the authorities feared. One of the most interesting refugees was Major Robert Rollo Reid of Saintfield County Down, who had fled along with Coigley, McMahon and the other Ulster leaders in June.[86] He had landed from an open boat at Girvan and stayed there three or four weeks but, finding it too public, removed to Kirkoswald, where the Lord-Lieutenant had him placed under strict surveillance.[87] A related concern was that United men were coming over from Ulster to subvert the military; two soldiers had already been approached in May 1797 and offered twenty guineas and plain clothes to desert, to prevent them from giving evidence at the Carrickfergus Assizes.[88]

More generally, the effectiveness of these security and intelligence measures was limited by practical considerations. First, the sheer scale of communications between Ireland and Scotland was in itself problematic. Portpatrick acted as the main entrepôt for trade with the north of Ireland and not every traveller was obligingly suspicious as Major Reid. As the postmaster of Belfast explained, there were 'a number of boats about Ballycastle, Cushendun and Larne, employed in carrying on some kind of traffick [sic] . . . which afford fugitives opportunities of correspondence by letter or otherwise'.[89] A census taken at the Home Secretary's request between 4 December 1796 and 26 January 1797 revealed a host of horse and cattle dealers, students, herring purchasers and, of most concern to the authorities, '289 persons of the common rank of life and whose purpose was professed to be bartering in old cloathes [sic], begging and seeking work'. 'With these people', the authorities believed, 'corres-pondence probably takes place.'[90]

More delicate difficulties arose from trying to separate 'the very good people leaving Ireland' from 'those leaving it to avoid punishment,' and also from the limited legal powers available to enforce this vital distinction. The Lord Advocate complained that 'magistrates were labouring under the difficulty of a want of power to stop persons who do not fall under the legal description of vagrants', but in practice, he admitted himself 'not to be bound by the strict letter of the law in such an area of expediency'.[91]

By the summer of 1797 then, the number of persons fleeing from Ireland continued to rise in line with the intensification of military action. From April to June, the Sheriff of Wigtown reported that 83 vessels, carrying cattle and passengers, had arrived, over and above the normal number of packet and lime boats. On board were over a thousand passengers, including 912 hold passengers 'of low condition and mean appearance'.[92] The total rate of arrivals was considerably greater, often amounting in one day from '100 to 150 men in a Body', who then were liable to melt away in every direction through the western counties.[93] In these circumstances, the Lord Advocate was forced to rely on the energy and initiative of local officers who found that civility could be more effective than any violent measures. Some revenue officers even returned 'miserable looking wretches' at their own expense. Since the majority of passengers were going on to Glasgow, Paisley, Ayr, Kilmarnock and Irvine in search of employment as weavers, the Wigtown Sheriff took the precaution of writing ahead to warn his colleagues in those towns, and contacted JPs in Down, Antrim, Armagh and Tyrone to request that they be more stringent in the issuing of certificates of good character to emigrants. Coercion remained the ultimate sanction, for hearing that some Irish were sneaking in along the coast, the local Galloway militia were also alerted.[94]

And yet, despite all their efforts and anxieties, the authorities knew that rudimentary quantification and control of this type were not enough. Faced with the visible evidence of Irish refugee settlement, they could now only speculate on how it would bear political fruit in Scotland.

NOTES

1. Lord Advocate's Papers, RH 2/4 80 f. 133 (SRO).
2. W. Scott to H. Dundas, 22 July 1797, Melville MSS GD 51/5/29 (SRO).
3. Wells, *Insurrection*, p. 44.
4. *Glasgow Courier*, 15 March 1795.
5. J. Stirling to R. Dundas, 21 February 1795, RH 2/4/78 f. 35 (SRO), and A. Macdonald to Sir John Grant, 25 May 1796, RH 2/4/79 ff. 197–8 (SRO).
6. W. McDowell to Lord Pelham, 9 September 1796, RH 2/4/79 f. 239 (SRO). A boll of oatmeal had risen from 16/- to £1. 6/- in a short period in McDowell's district of Renfrewshire, and he worried about the effect on the dependent manufacturing population. For background, see Stern, 'The Bread Crisis in Britain', pp. 168–87; Wells, *Wretched Faces*, pp. 35–52.
7. *Glasgow Courier*, 25 March and 23 April 1796.
8. Duke of Atholl to Duke of Portland, 2 April 1796, RH 2/4/79 ff. 78–9 (SRO).
9. Goodwin, *Friends of Liberty*, pp. 359–95.
10. In fact, the company included the Earl of Breadalbane, the Whiggish reformers Erskine and Fletcher, and the former Friends of the People moderate William Morthland: Melville MSS 7 f. 12 (NLS).
11. *Glasgow Courier*, 29 December 1795 for a typical pro-government response: 'Let those look to it who are guilty.'
12. Burns, 'Industrial Labour and Radical Movements', pp. 163–4; Duke of Atholl to Duke of Portland, 8 November 1795, RH 2/4/78 (SRO).
13. *Glasgow Courier*, 30 April 1796.
14. MacNeven, *Pieces of Irish History*, pp. 76–7; Elliott, *Partners in Revolution*, pp. 67–8; McDowell, *Ireland in the Age of Imperialism*, pp. 443–4, 470–3.
15. Curtin, 'The Tranformation of the Society of United Irishmen'; Smyth, *Men of no Property*.
16. Cullen, 'The Internal Politics of the United Irishmen', p. 188.
17. HO 100/52/159 (PRO).
18. Woods (ed.), *Journals*, entries for 4 April 1793 and 19 January 1794, pp. 71, 141–2. Dr Reynolds of County Tyrone, who had been so confident in January 1794 that the people of Scotland and Ulster were simply biding their time, left for America later that year: Madden, *United Irishmen*, ser. 1, vol. ii, p. 25.
19. S. Neilson to W. Drennan, 10 June 1793, D 516 (1) (PRONI).
20. McDowell, *Ireland in the Age of Imperialism*, p. 486.
21. *Northern Star*, 5–9 April 1795.
22. *Northern Star*, 26–30 March 1796.
23. MacNeven, *Pieces of Irish History*, pp. 74–6; Smyth, *Men of no Property*, pp. 109–10.

24. Elliott, *Partners in Revolution*, pp. 69–74. Just to underscore the lesson that conciliation had ended, on 5 May 1795 a new Catholic Bill was defeated in the Irish House of Commons.
25. McCance, D. 272/6 (PRONI) for a first-hand account of the process; see also McDowell, *Ireland in the Age of Imperialism*, pp. 471–2.
26. *Report from the Committee of Secrecy of the House of Commons* (1799), p. 112, quoted in Curtin, 'The Tranformation of the Society of United Irishmen', p. 475.
27. Some of the United Irish leaders, such as Thomas Russell, had more positive ideas on women's role than most of their contemporaries: 'Women in public offices as clever as men. Queens Poetesses, etc. etc.', Woods (ed.), *Journals*, 11 July 1793, p. 86. McSkimmin suggests that 'societies of Irish *women* were among the novelties of this day', their chief business being to gather information and further the common cause by subscription. The clubs were facetiously called *Teapot Societies* and their members were generally violent in their threats. 'Recollections of the Most Important Events which Took Place in the County of Antrim', MS 12.F.36 (RIA). Martha McTier was suspected of involvement: J. Whinnery to J. Lees, 25 May 1795, 620/30/194 (NAI) and W. Drennan to M. McTier, 10 June 1797, no. 665, T. 795 (PRONI).
28. Curtin, 'The Tranformation of the Society of United Irishmen', pp. 486–8. For the origins and development of the Defenders, see Elliott's classic study, 'The Origins and Transformations of Early Irish Republicanism', pp. 100–20 gives an interesting recent interpretation based on contemporary propaganda materials.
29. In the south, some urban Protestant artisans were also attracted to the Defenders as a revolutionary vehicle, and served as a bridge between them and the United Irishmen, Smyth, *Men of no Property*, p. 152.
30. *Edinburgh Gazetteer*, 13 August 1793.
31. *Northern Star*, 14–18 May 1795. The *Star* at this stage saw the Defenders' impetus as purely economic, 'the price of labour too low – the price of everything else too high'.
32. Officially United Irish anti-Catholicism was directed against Catholicism as a system, rather than individual Catholics, but in private their hostility could shade into unreconstructed racism. William Drennan, on meeting two expatriate Irishmen arrived from France, commented: 'It is singular that such men, both of the most ancient strain of Ireland and both in foreign courts the whole of their lives, should smack so strongly of the bogtrotter.' W. Drennan to M. McTier, 29 April 1795, Drennan Letters, no. 553, T. 765 (PRONI).
33. *Northern Star* 22–5 February 1796, for typical coverage. Fears were even orchestrated of an Orange attack on Belfast: *Northern Star*, 24–8 March 1796.
34. Tone (Dickinson) MSS, W. Tone–P. Adet, 10 August 1795, cited in Elliott, *Partners in Revolution*, p. 265.
35. Rebellion Papers, 620/27/1 (NAI). Bird was an English merchant who had some skill in purloining United documents, see W. E. H. Lecky, *A History of Ireland in the Eighteenth Century*, vol. 3, p. 400.
36. Rebellion Papers, 620/27/1 (NAI).
37. J. Maxwell Notebooks, Rebellion Papers, 620/34/54 (NAI).
38. Curtin, 'The Tranformation of the Society of United Irishmen', p. 470.
39. Madden, *United Irishmen*, ser. 1, vol. ii, pp. 400–1.
40. Madden, *Antrim and Down*, p. 160; id., *United Irishmen*, ser. 3, vol. i, pp. 257, 312, 333; Frazer MSS II 18, 19 (NAI).
41. *Northern Star*, 13–18 October 1795; Sirr MSS 868/2 ff. 182–3 (TCD).
42. Sirr MSS 868/2 ff. 182–3 (TCD).
43. Ibid.
44. The extension of the trip to Munster and France seems much more

ambitious. Munster did not become 'organised' until late 1797, Musgrove, *Memoirs of Different Rebellions in Ireland*, vol. 1, p. 175.

45. Tytler seems to have been destined to become a historical footnote. It was on his way to defend him that Thomas Muir had been arrested in 1793. For biographical details, see Meek, *A Biographical Sketch*; and J. Ferguson's rather unreliable *Balloon Tytler*. A further uncontroversial fragment of his correspondence is in Add. MSS 22.4II f. 38 (NLS).

46. The financial and legal resources of the Societies were shortly to be offered to the victims of the Armagh persecutions: *Northern Star*, 18–20 August 1796.

47. MacNeven, *Pieces of Irish History*, p. 176.

48. Rebellion Papers, 620/27/1, Smith/Bird Information (NAI).

49. Newell's Report, 21 July 1796, HO 100/62/141 (PRO); Frazer MSS II 23 (NAI).

50. Ibid.

51. Newell's Reports, 21–9 July 1796, HO 100/62/141–6 (PRO).

52. Howell and Howell, *State Trials*, vol. xxvi, col. 1117.

53. Justiciary Papers, JC 26/294 (SRO)

54. McCance Collection D272/6 (PRONI); McSkimmin, *Recollections*, MS 12.F.36 (RIA).

55. A. MacNeven to Lord Downshire, 10 December 1796, D607/D/387 (PRONI); Lord Hillsborough, 9 January 1797, Rebellion Papers, 620/28/75 (NAI). Interestingly, this development prefigures the 'quarter-master' role which the west of Scotland reputedly played during the Anglo-Irish War of 1919–21.

56. Elliott, *Partners in Revolution*, pp. 51–74.

57. For biographical background, see ibid., pp. 98–106.

58. *Glasgow Courier*, 12 January 1797.

59. *Northern Star*, 30 December–2 January 1797.

60. Diary of John Galt, 13 January 1797, D. 561/1 (PRONI).

61. For a report of the initial Scottish landing, G. Dallas, 20 September 1797, Melville Papers, 54A–55B, National Library of Ireland (NLI).

62. *Northern Star*, 7–10 and 17–21 April 1797 for coverage of the Peace Petition movement in the Scottish cities.

63. L. McNally to E. Cooke, 5 Feburary 1797, Rebellion Papers, 620/36/227 (NAI).

64. For fundraising, see Rebellion Papers, 620/18/3 (NAI), Boyle and Higgins's spy reports.

65. Madden, *Antrim and Down*, p. 169 for McCabe's activities.

66. Madden, *United Irishmen*, ser. 3, vol. i, pp. 250–1. See Smyth, *Men of no Property*, pp. 161–2, for a discussion of the content of this printed material.

67. *Dublin Evening Post*, 15 September 1796.

68. Rebellion Papers, 620/35/130, A. Newton's information, 9 February 1798 (NAI).

69. *Report from the Second Committee Enquiring into the Condition of the Poorer Classes in Ireland*, p. 456.

70. J. Lapslie to R. Dundas, 22 March 1798, Laing MSS II 650–1 (University of Edinburgh). Lapslie had been one of the main prosecution witnesses in the trial of Thomas Muir. The Earl of Eglinton had similar worries over the Irish in Ayrshire, RH 2/4/80/69–74 (SRO). Packmen and pedlars generally in Scotland were liable to come under suspicion, see JC 26/296 (SRO) for the committal of William Craig, a packman on a charge of seditious practices.

71. *Report from the Second Committee Enquiring into the Condition of the Poorer Classes in Ireland*, p. 147; Minutes of the Hibernian Society, 1792–1824, TD 200.7, Strathclyde Regional Archives (SRA).

72. Handley, *The Irish in Scotland*, p. 133.

73. See JC 26/295 (SRO) for Craigendallie, and W. Scott to R. Dundas, 22 August 1797, Melville MSS GD 51/5/29 (SRO). For Murdoch, see his declaration 17 April 1799 in RH 2/4/83 f. 172 (SRO).

74. Earl of Eglinton to R. Dundas, 12 March 1797, Laing MSS II 500 (University of Edinburgh).

75. Walker, 'The Protestant Irish', pp. 48–9.

76. *Statistical Account for Scotland*, vol vi, p. 520. Judging from the names of its members, Gourlay, Weir, Meinzes and the like, the Glasgow Hibernian Society was also a Protestant body. It was not exclusivist in terms of ethnicity, Scots were welcome to join providing they had been resident three years previously in Ireland or if they were married to Irishwomen.

77. See Elliott, *Partners in Revolution*, p. 146.

78. For the radical reaction, see *Northern Star*, 15–17 , 20–24 and 24–7 March 1797. The paper's presses were finally broken up by the Monaghan Militia on 19 May and it ceased publication.

79. In Coleraine, the leaders of the local United Irishmen were being arrested, and 'their associates either dragged to prison or having to fly and leave their families and properties to the risk of danger': John Galt's Diary, 31 May 1797, D. 561 (PRONI). The cheapest passage was on 'Bye Boats', carrying goods, livestock and passengers, and costing only 6d. or 9d.: Report of the Sheriff of Wigtown, RH 2/4/80 f. 124 (SRO).

80. T. Kennedy to Earl of Eglinton, 9 February 1797, Laing MSS II 500 (University of Edinburgh).

81. See Wells, *Insurrection*, pp. 28–43.

82. Lord Grenville to Lord Pelham, 15 June 1797, Rebellion Papers, 620/31/96 (NAI).

83. Lord Grenville to R. Dundas, 9 May 1797, RH 2/4/80 f. 62 (SRO).

84. T. Kennedy to Earl of Eglinton, 9 February 1797, Laing MSS II 500 (University of Edinburgh).

85. See J. Durham to R. Dundas, 14 September 1797, Laing MSS II 629 (University of Edinburgh).

86. *Report from the Committee of Secrecy of the House of Commons* (1799), p. 29.

87. Earl of Eglinton to R. Dundas, 27 November 1797, Laing MSS II 500 (University of Edinburgh). His information was passed on to the Viceroy's office, Rebellion Papers, 620/33/94 (NAI). As the authorities feared, Reid maintained contact with United colleagues back in Ulster, writing to the Down County Committee in February 1798: Black Book of Rebellion, McCance MSS D. 272/1 (PRONI).

88. J. Durham to R. Dundas, 14 September 1797, Laing MSS II 629 (University of Edinburgh).

89. T. Whinnery to Lees, 1 June 1797, Rebellion Papers, 620/31/11 (NAI). Portpatrick was not the only possible destination. 'I also find', he reported, 'that people are flying in great numbers from this town and the whole Northern District, and taking their passage *from hence* in vessels bound for Whitehaven, Liverpool and every part of England and Scotland, by this means people who have been principally concerned in disturbing this Kingdom will escape justice . . .'

90. Census details, RH 2/4/80 ff. 69–74 (SRO).

91. R. Dundas to Lord Grenville, 7 July 1797, RH 2/4/80 f. 122 (SRO).

92. Report of the Sheriff of Wigtown, 2 August 1797, RH 2/4/80 ff. 124 and 140 (SRO).

93. Lord Grenville to Lord Pelham, 15 June 1797, Rebellion Papers, 620/31/96 (NAI); Earl of Galloway to R. Dundas, 16 June 1797, RH 2/4/80 f. 110 (SRO); R. Dundas to J. King, 9 May 1797, RH 2/4/80 f. 67 (SRO).

94. W. McConnell to R. Dundas, 3 July 1797, RH 2/4/80 f. 126 (SRO); J. Durham to R. Dundas, 14 September 1797, Laing MSS II 629 (University

of Edinburgh). Durham particularly suspected lime sloops from Larne of conveying fugitives, and also suggested masters were smuggling people ashore in small boats. For sample of the type of passport *bona fide* travellers required, see Lowry MSS D. 1494/18 (PRONI).

6

United
1796–1797

When a nation finds itself in this dread abyss of misery, and would
be delivered, let them unite, resist the oppression, and discard the
oppressors; for no government, however powerful in appearance, or
rigorous in effects, can oppose with success the united wisdom and
energy of a determined people.

George Mealmaker, *The Moral and Political Catechism of Man.*[1]

The organisational effects of United Irish involvement in Scotland are as
perplexing and opaque today as they were to the Lord Advocate and the
Home Office in the late 1790s. This is inevitable, given the nature of
underground political activity and the fact that this was now largely the
business of artisans and weavers, rather than the urban élites who had
led the Friends of the People. In the early part of 1797, the authorities
were still groping for information, but thanks to the usual voluntary
contributions from local supporters of government, the picture was becoming clearer that roots were being put down.

Demonstrating that the cross-border exchange of information was
occurring on an informal level, one Ulster correspondent, writing to the
Glasgow Courier, was admirably abreast of developments:

Let me tell you, while your neighbour's house is on fire, to take
care of your own. A vast number of United Irishmen have fled
into your country. Some of the highest *Up Men* in Belfast have . . .
taken homes. They have several Societies established as far back as
February last [1797] and therefore the magistrates of Scotland ought
to be on their guard against them. They will put the peasantry *up*
in the Western Counties particularly, before you know what you
are doing; they go abroad under the pretence of seeking work,
service and selling linens, remnants and such like, and their lure

among them, I understand is very fascinating, and has been for some time.[2]

In May, the flow of amateur reports was complemented by information from the official intelligence network that secret oath-based societies in correspondence with 'the disaffected in Ireland' had indeed been established in the south-west.[3] Thus armed, the Lord Advocate was 'fully convinced that mischief was going on', but at the same time he remained frustrated by the impenetrable secrecy of the new radical procedures. The best weapon to tap into these was continued co-operation between Edinburgh, Whitehall and Dublin, which mirrored the increasing co-ordination of their opponents in the underground movement.[4]

The shadowy new organisation to which government intelligence referred was the United Scotsmen. This group was to bear the hopes of radicals and the apprehensions of the Scottish authorities for the next five years. They have also received a fairly rough handling in subsequent historical debates, ranging from Whiggish dismissal as 'small scale' and 'venial', to lionisation in other accounts as class warriors, and anti-colonialists into the bargain. More subtle and judicious analyses of their development, however, are less inclined to equate significance with numerical strength, or to stress the 'prophetic' dimension of radical activity in a historicist fashion.[5] The potential strengths and intrinsic weaknesses of the United Scotsmen are best appreciated by treating them on their own terms, and by giving full attention to their external linkages.

The influence of Irish radicals on the United Scotsmen can be assessed under three main headings: structure, ideology and diffusion.

STRUCTURE

The Lord Advocate was correct to stress 'how exactly' the United Scotsmen had copied the proceedings of the United Irishmen, for it is in terms of their formal organisation that they bear the closest correspondence.[6] The marked similarity of their tests, resolutions and constitutions is not coincidental, but marks a conscious remoulding of Scottish radicalism in the Irish image.[7] George Mealmaker and other activists justified the move to an oath-bound society on the grounds that secrecy and mutual recognition of initiates were essential in a climate of government repression which had closed off the constitutionalist route.[8] In these conditions, recourse to the new-style Irish Constitution, when it was presented by the Ulster delegates in Glasgow in the summer of 1796, was a logical step. The shift to covert tactics appeared to be one of the secrets behind the radical movement's rapid numerical progress in Ireland the previous year. Its drawbacks were less apparent, but in practice the centralised, hierarchical structure of parochial, county, provincial and national committees was already proving less resistant to spy infiltration than the horizontal, cellular structure of the Defenders.[9] Unfortunately for the Scots, this alternative model was not an available option. Individual Defenders probably arrived as part of the forced migration of 1797, but organisationally theirs was not an outward-looking movement on the scale of the United Irishmen; besides, its blend of Catholicism and nationalism was highly unsuitable for Presbyterian Scottish palates.[10]

IDEOLOGY

A more tentative comparison is possible in terms of ideology. This also had tactical implications. We know less about the development and tensions in the United Scotsmen's thought than about those of their prolific Irish counterparts. The seminal texts for the Scottish case are the Society's *Resolutions and Constitution*, and Mealmaker's *The Moral and Political Catechism of Man, or a Dialogue between a Citizen of the World and an Inhabitant of Britain*.[11] While these were essential components in the armoury of United agents, it is less certain how accurately their principles were received and reinterpreted by grass-roots members. One member admitted that he 'did not know precisely what was the object of the society', beyond a vague nod towards 'French principles and French rules'.[12]

Once official hysteria is set aside, the *Catechism* is rather a sober document. Its advocacy of universal suffrage and annual parliaments place it firmly in the tradition of the more advanced sections of the Scottish Friends of the People. Indeed, its demands do not seem to have moved beyond those of the earlier 'Glasgow Society of United Scotsmen', formed in November 1793 and represented at the British Convention.[13] There are French flourishes in Mealmaker's Rousseauist conception of natural equality. Otherwise, the pamphlet is a good example of the type of red-blooded Painite beliefs which Whiggish moderates in the Friends of the People sought to combat. As in United Irish thought by this point, the general republican tone is clear: the rule of the privileged caste of kings and lawgivers rests merely on 'a mutual compact betwixt the governors to support each other and the tendency of the weak towards division and exploitation, through the devices of ignorance and priestcraft'.[14]

There are more specific parallels in political ideology. The concept of 'Uniting', the common cause of British and Irish radicals against the common foe, and the rejection of man-made barriers between peoples were the first and most obvious. As expressed in the *Resolutions*:

Mankind are naturally friends to each other; and it is only the corruptions and abuses in government that make them enemies.

We profess ourselves friends to mankind, of whatever nation or religion. National and party distinctions have been created and supported by tyrannical men, on purpose to maintain their unjust usurpations of the People.

There is one political principle at least which seems to have received practical implementation from members. For as far as their limited resources would allow, the Scots, like their Irish colleagues, attempted to extend their organisation and combine their activities with fellow radicals. The higher committee sitting in Glasgow, for example, intended sending four delegates to London, Ireland and 'the North Country', and a levy was made of local societies, such as Pollokshields, for the purpose.[15] On this occasion, money was difficult to find and certainly no delegate was sent to the Ulster committee, but representatives were reported to have played a role in communicating the United system to the north of England, with suspected links in Westmorland and Cumberland.[16]

Secondly, Mealmaker's document also makes much of the lawful right of resistance against tyranny, a constant in United Irish calculations. He argued powerfully that: 'when one part of a nation tyrannises over another by wicked councils, or one set of men over another, laying grievous yokes upon their persons, property and consciences, in such cased resistance is a necessity and moral virtue and may only be blamed if there is no possibility of success'. On the best Scriptural authority, no act could be titled 'rebellion', 'when the will of the majority of the People is consulted and acted upon'. Although Lord Eskdale, presiding over Mealmaker's eventual trial for sedition, was repelled by the thought of the right of resistance being 'left to the determination of some poor ignorant people in Cupar', this was another theme in Mealmaker's philosophy which seems to have found resonance among the United Scottish rank and file.[17] As in Ulster, albeit on a less ambitious scale, in 1796 and 1797 military preparations seem to have been proceeding in some Scottish localities. United men in the north of Glasgow were reported to be arming and exercising, acting on instructions that 'it was proper for them to go into the Militia or Volunteers in order to exercise'.[18] Attempts at winning over individual soldiers in the Renfrewshire Yeomanry and Perth Volunteers were also proceeding.[19] This was another popular United Irish pastime and it was indicative of problems to come for the Scots that they made little headway here. On the contrary, Scottish regiments were much in demand for Irish service precisely because of their reliability.[20]

Thirdly, there was a measure of agreement between the two bodies on ecclesiastical issues. The United Scotsmen's opposition to lay patronage and the forcing of ministers on congregations had been prominent in their *Resolutions,* but was toughened in the *Catechism* into Mealmaker's outright disestablishment stance. This was couched in the deist termino- logy of 'reasoning factors' created by the 'Supreme Being', a step beyond the Friends of the People who had avoided such a divisive position. This development was matched by the rising prominence in the Irish Society of leaders such as Tone, Lord Edward Fitzgerald and Arthur O'Connor, who were proud to state they were 'free thinkers' on matters of religion.[21]

Fourthly, while taking on board most of Paine, Mealmaker did not tackle the question of social reform. The goal of an equalisation of property is explicitly rejected in favour of the customary radical advocacy of economic individualism. Similarly, the *Resolutions* protest detestation of 'all riots and tumults'. This corresponds to the views of the socially conservative sections of the United Irish leadership, such as MacNeven, who claimed 'a horror of social revolution', and wished to channel and control popular expectations, using the Defender alliance.[22] Yet, this was only one tendency in the Irish movement; there was also a powerful critique of the social order available from figures like Thomas Russell and his associates, 'ferociously anti-aristocratic, but essentially bourgeois in perspective'.[23] In Scotland, Mealmaker's formulations on this subject may have been equally contested by grass-roots members, but no evidence has survived of a similar coherent militant leavening.

Indeed, it is unwise to force too close an identity of thought and action between the Irish and Scots. In the first place, the principles of 'common cause', 'lawful resistance' and disestablishment were not simply one-way borrowings from the former to the latter. The first was independ- ently rooted in the experiences of Scottish radical politics of the first half of the decade, though the specific oath-bound form of uniting was new. The second, a fusion of Lockean and Covenanting thought, had originally been a *Scottish* export to Ulster, energised by the social and political constraints on Presbyterians in that Province. The third, meanwhile, was to be expected from a communicant of the Scottish Relief Synod, such as Mealmaker. Seceders seem to have had a significant presence generally in United Scots ranks, a group which had little affection for the Church of Scotland 'by law established'.[24]

Important ideological distinctions also existed between the two sets of radicals, which reflected the differing political contexts of Scotland and Ireland. One was the role accorded to the institution of parliament in their philosophies. The authorities were convinced that the United Scots- men's limited immediate aims masked their basic intention 'to overturn the government of the country, by alienating the minds of the people and inciting them to resistance'.[25] In reality, despite the *Catechism*'s excited stress on popular sovereignty and its call for a national convention to redraft the constitution, and despite even the arming of local Societies, the Scots seem to have persisted longer in their belief in the efficacy of a reform of parliament than the Irish. The oath taken by the Renfrewshire United men in 1797, for example, was not some bloodthirsty Defender production, but a pledge to 'persist in Parliamentary Reform without the hopes and fears of rewards or punishments'.[26] In contrast, for Irish radicals the veniality and corruption of their own legislature had been bywords since the 1780s. The years 1793–5 had further undermined its legitimacy, with the defection of the parliamentary Whig opposition to support the prosecution of war with France, and London's increasingly unconcealed control of Irish affairs. This background greatly assisted the shift in May 1795 towards a more literal conception of popular sovereignty, which set the United Irishmen on the road to insurrectionary solutions.

Linked to this position was also the persistent gap between Scottish and Irish radicals over the significance given to issues of national determination. In Ireland, in the course of the 1790s, contempt for parliament grew hand in hand with a critique of the very nature and existence of the English connection. By mid-decade this had received a dubious boost from the infusion of the Defenders' brand of sectarian nationalism. In Scotland, although the 1799 *House of Commons Committee of Secrecy Report*, claimed it had detected an attempt to withdraw from the Union and create a separate republic, the rationale of 'a distinct society of United Scotsmen' probably owed more to logistics and geographical realities than to conscious nationalist convictions. After all, the concern was to overturn national barriers rather than erect new ones. The substitution of 'Britain' or 'North Britain' for Ireland in the original oath is itself revealing; evidently, the aim of the old British Convention to bind Scottish and English radicals in a popular front was not to be abandoned simply because of the recent organisational innovations.

DIFFUSION

While United Irish delegates were responsible for introducing their system into Scotland in 1796, the shape of Irish influence in their later development is more problematic. The official account reveals a clear pattern of spatial diffusion. Glasgow and Ayrshire were the first strongholds by the spring of 1797. From there, the system was spread by 'emissaries' to Renfrew, Lanark, Dumbarton, Fife and Perth during the summer. The government legal sources, on which one must rely, also suggest that Irish involvement in this process was considerable. We have, for example, the Thornliebank cotton spinner John Jarve's testimony that he 'never saw any but of the lowest order, and mostly Irishmen'.[27] There is also the official dispatch of Ilay Campbell of Dunbartonshire that Irishmen had been active in disturbances there, 'as they are the great pomoters of mischief everywhere'.[28] To these can be added the frequent reports from the Lord-Lieutenant of Ayrshire, the Earl of Eglinton, on the role of the Irish in the unsettled state of the south of his county. Yet, these observations need careful handling. Jarve, himself implicated in the Society, was under judicial examination, and when he made his statement 'appeared very much frightened'. In this situation, it may have been expedient to play down local involvement; it was, in fact, a Scot – David Coulston – who had been instrumental in founding the Thornliebank Society. In Campbell's case there seems to be a general paternalistic concern to paint local unrest as being the work of 'throngs not belonging to the district'. The consistent intelligence from south Ayrshire is much more difficult to challenge, especially as it predates official hysteria over 'contagion', which equated Irishness with disaffection. It is highly likely that the Maybole societies, in particular, had an important Irish component, as borne out in subsequent prosecutions against their members.[29] The question is how typical south Ayrshire was. As one of the earliest centres of Irish settlement, and a major magnet for the latest refugee wave, it may not be appropriate to extend its experience a priori to the rest of Scotland. Even in this case, the Irish were not Eglinton's only local difficulty, home-grown irritants were also at hand in the form of a 'cursed set of seceders in some parishes, that are real bad subjects, seditious and democratical'.[30]

Drawing together the fragmentary evidence on offer, some of the organisers and foot soldiers of the United Scotsmen undoubtedly *were* Irish, either formal missionaries, spontaneous refugees, or domiciled residents. The Irish weaver James Craigendallie was reported to be 'a great man among them at Perth'. A United man himself, 'he felt every friend to the cause ought to be so'.[31] Another Irishman, Edward Doherty, 'a true democrat and fine fellow', was also busy communicating United signs in Perthshire, and may be the character arrested, 'going drunk through the streets of Crieff, singing . . . also having been much around Auchterarder, a democratic nest, as well as Dunning'.[32]

Distinctively Irish tactics were also employed. These activists did not only rely on Mealmaker's earnest *Catechism* to win recruits. As had been discovered in Ireland, the more accessible medium of songs and ballads could be equally effective in popularising radical principles.[33] Part of Craigendallie's success was attributed to his 'being very zealous as a Songster [and] a Poet', though unlike Doherty he preferred to keep his 'guilloteening songs' for a more discreet audience.[34] Similarly, the song *Burk's Address* [sic] was circulated by another Irish activist, Archibald Dearny, among the United Scotsmen in Ayrshire.[35]

Another familiar Irish tactic employed in Scotland was the use of Freemasons' Lodges as a cover for underground activities. In an increasingly fashionable thesis, Masonry has itself been credited as an influence in the general growth of secret societies in Ireland from the 1760s and particularly in the foundation of the United Irishmen in particular.[36] Certainly by the 1790s the Craft had acquired a reputation for advanced political principles, and the United Irishmen felt comfortable in making the most of the lodges as fronts and recruiting grounds. Scotland offered good opportunities to extend the surrogate method, with an extensive network of lodges, which were believed to be more 'popular and radical' than elsewhere.[37] As usual, details are scanty. There is little to support Burke's or Abbé Barruel's visions of an all-embracing masonic conspiracy, for distinguished loyalists – such as Sir James Stirling, the Lord Provost of Edinburgh – were also lodge members.[38] Nevertheless, by 1797 some connection apparently had developed between some freemasons and democrats at grass-roots level. The available evidence relates to southwest Scotland. In Galloway, a local priest wrote that:

> masons are uncommonly active in recruiting, having frequent and numerous meetings. They scruple at nobody, however worthless, which shews no good design – masons give out the story that Robespierre passed a decree giving no quarter to the English, but the Inniskilling Dragoons when surrounded, their commanding officer gave Mason's signs, and both parties ceased fire and retired.[39]

A more definite link with the United system was uncovered in Maybole. Here, Irish masons, reputedly members of the United Irishmen, joined with some local Scots in the course of 1796 to form a break-away lodge, 'Maybole Royal Arch'. The ostensible purpose was to instruct members in the 'higher degrees' of Royal Arch and Knight Templar, not normally available in ordinary Masonic lodges, but these degrees provoked immediate suspicions 'on the grounds that they were mediums through which, under a pretended connection with Freemasonry, it was sought to propagate the infidelity and political principles of the French Revolution, and to evoke sympathy for the democrats in Ireland in their endeavours to effect their national independence'.[40] The result was an unusual trial for sedition in September 1800, which revolved around certain 'impious and abominable ceremonies' such as drinking porter out of a human skull; the length of time taken to bring the case to court helped produce a 'not proven' verdict.[41]

Just as Scotland did not form the limit of the United Irishmen's cosmopolitan world-view, neither did Irish missionising comprise the sum total of external influences on Scottish radicals. The intended dispatch of representatives to England in 1797 was one indicator that bilateral links had survived from the days of the British Convention. The ailing London Corresponding Society continued to foster the connection with like-minded Scots, such as the Edinburgh bookseller Alexander Leslie.[42] The presence of an English agent had been suspected in Perth in 1795, and in May 1797 one Jameson arrived, apparently delegated by the London Corresponding Society to make contact with old Friends of the People centres like Linlithgow.[43]

The situation becomes more complicated. Concurrently with the Scots, English democrats had also become bound to the United system by agents from Ulster. Manchester, as Elliott suggests, became 'England's Belfast', with a large number of recruits, particularly from the local Irish community, sworn in by November 1796.[44] In London by the summer of the following year, organisational and ideological change was also rejuvenating the remnants of radicalism, so that when the exiled Ulster leaders Coigley and McMahon arrived in the capital, they already had a useful infrastructure of contacts and were later able to add Liverpool to the system. The authorities thought that Scotland too received agents from these reconstituted centres, and acting on information from Manchester they arrested Ulsterman George Murdoch, a blacksmith, who had migrated through Liverpool and Manchester *en route* for Edinburgh.[45] It was later revealed that plans for a correspondence with Scotland had been laid and that information was to be communicated by relays of special messengers, but the government had swooped before this could be put into effect.[46]

In short, extraneous factors were vital in the spread of the United Scotsmen – vital, but not the whole story. The impression is that radical developments also possessed a greater *internal* momentum than elsewhere on the British mainland. Not all agents were Irish – or English. One of the most widely travelled missionaries, Archibald Grey, was a Scot who moved through Irvine, Kilwinning, Stirling, St Ninians, Alloa and Kincardine to gain recruits. In St Ninians his handiwork was still evident in November 1797, with 'oaths taken upon the Irish plan'.[47] The movement's most charismatic organiser, Angus Cameron, was also a Scot, a native of Lochaber, as was its chief ideologist, Mealmaker of Dundee.

Mealmaker's case is the most revealing. His pedigree in Scottish radical politics was long and impressive. He had written the Perth reformers' Address, which had resulted in Revd Palmer's trial and transportation. As secretary of the Dundee Friends of Liberty, he had been a delegate at the Second Scottish Friends of the People Convention and the Third British Convention, and had been arrested and imprisoned in the subsequent 'Reign of Terror' in 1794.[48] This individual biography is indicative of a broader pattern of continuity in the evolution of the new radicalism. Looking again at the United Scotsmen outposts in the 1799 *House of Commons Committee of Secrecy Report*, some of these were also centres for the Friends of the People. This impression is reinforced by Burns's geographical breakdown of the 26 United Scottish societies mentioned in official sources: 4 in Ayrshire, 2 in Stirling, 1 each in Renfrew, Dumbarton, and Lanark, 5 in Forfarshire and 8 in Fife.[49]

This was not 'continuity' in the mechanistic sense envisaged in the *House of Commons Committee of Secrecy Report*, which viewed the two organisations as part of a uniform conspiracy to overthrow the Constitution. This became something of an obsession with the Scottish authorities and led them, almost certainly, to overstate the role of the propertied class in the latest incarnation of radicalism.[50] Whereas the United Irishmen had retained a diverse class base, despite the outflow of middle-class members in the spring of 1796; in Scotland, the defection of the Edinburgh lawyers and Foxite gentlemen from the cause began earlier and was more complete. The United Scotsmen drew instead on the traditional radical work groups who had formed the rank and file of the Friends of the People. Weaving parishes, such as Thornliebank, Cupar, Kilwinning and Maybole, were heavily represented, and the tradition of journeymen artisans with their high degree of labour mobility also helped the process of geographical diffusion.[51]

Burns goes as far as to suggest that the prime historical function of the movement was 'to keep alive these groups experience of political activity gained in the early 1790s'.[52] If this was the case, then we might add that United Irish activity had its own galvanising role in the process. It was not that the Irish presumed to graft on an alternative leadership, ideology or membership base, but rather that they offered a systematic new method of organising radical activity and disseminating ideas. In this way, they were able to draw in the remnants of the Friends of the People and give them a new direction and sense of belonging to a wider radical community.

As to be expected, the adoption of underground United tactics did not go unchallenged by some sections of the Scottish movement. Robert Sands, like Mealmaker an ex-delegate to the British Convention, disapproved of it as 'a villainous scheme', and was one of a number of Perth radicals who resisted Craigendallie's attempts to make them 'United' by holding separate meetings.[53] How far these divisions were general in Scotland we do not know, but Wells's claim that remodelling on the Irish pattern 'was achieved at the expense of Scottish democratic unity' seems rather sweeping when set against the available evidence.[54] Nor was this simply an 'Irish' problem rooted in inter-ethnic tensions; the Scots and Irish seem to have stood on both sides of the divide at Perth. A more plausible source of friction was simply resentment of innovation by some of the key figures who had kept the flame of radicalism alive in the difficult days following the British Convention. This became reinforced by 'great apprehensions' against taking secret oaths when a specific measure, the Act of 37 Geo II imp. 120, was passed against them in August 1797.[55]

OPPORTUNITIES AND CONSTRAINTS

Another key component in understanding the United Scotsmen's path of development is their interaction with the broader dimensions of popular discontent in Scotland.

One understandable misconception of the Lord Advocate and his associates surrounded the role of individual human agents in inciting the popular mind to disaffection and disloyalty. Thus, in Dumfries unrest was the work of 'the wilful misrepresentations of wicked and designing people'; in Dumbarton, of 'a few individuals whose principles stand in opposition to all Government'.[56] For Robert Dundas the enemy were basically 'the emissaries of sedition', and he relished trapping these creatures almost as much as the propertied turncoats of the early nineties. Not surprisingly, the 'emissaries' themselves, like the able McCabe, favoured this estimation of their capabilities. When Cuthbert and Potts returned to Belfast in 1796, supporters were quick to boast that 'they had been busy inoculating in Scotland . . . distributing constitutions, and the Scots were adopting them very fast'.[57]

Like most variants of the conspiracy thesis, the notion that subversive ideas can be simply 'inoculated' into passive recipients is highly flawed. It neglects that before such ideas can succeed, they must be 'practically adequate' or, in other words, both credible and coherent with the actual experience of the intended audience. The point is that in Scotland by 1797 certain aspects of popular experience *were* beginning to develop in a manner which suggested a more receptive climate for the United evangelism.

International and domestic events were again decisive in this process. First, the war was going badly for Britain. Its continental allies Prussia and Austria had deserted it, and even its 'Wooden Walls' – the invincible Navy – was suspect. Attempts to capitalise on Jervis's victory off Cape St Vincent in February 1797 did little to raise public morale after the humiliation of the Bantry Bay episode, and news of the fleet mutinies at Spithead and the Nore in April and May gave an edge to loyalist misery.[58]

In contrast to Pitt's declining diplomatic and military position, the stabilising Directory regime had given France mastery of Europe and was turning its face towards Britain as its last remaining enemy. Rapid and dramatic reversals of fortune for 'the Old Corruption' appeared imminent.

Already, the shocks of war and fears of invasion had combined with the alarming rise in the national debt to threaten the nation's financial stability. The confidence of the City of London snapped, the value of consols was stripped away and a run on the banks was only halted by Pitt's desperate order to the Bank of England to suspend gold payments. Such panic measures fuelled the sense of impending doom, but did little to mitigate the resultant trade depression which struck hardest at the constituency of craftsmen and textile workers to which Scottish radicals made their appeals.[59] By June 1797, to take one local example, the Glasgow Hibernian Society's funds had sunk so low that payments to sick members had to be suspended for the next nine months.[60]

An even more direct and significant boost for United Scots activity came from the disturbances against the implementation of the Scottish Militia Act, flaring up in August and September of that year.[61] This episode is emblematic in a wider sense. Militia riots were not the preserve of the Scots, and a previous outbreak had also swept through Ireland in the spring and summer of 1793. Closer comparison of the two cases reveals some of the chronic limitations which faced the United Scots in their attempts to construct a mass movement on the Irish scale.[62]

The authorities in Ireland and Scotland shared the same basic motivation in raising a militia through compulsory service. Their action formed part of a larger initiative to extend the supply and enhance the flexibility of the forces available for peacekeeping and home defence. In Ireland, the Militia was also intended to replace the politically suspect Volunteers and was organised on a county basis, officered by local Protestant gentry and comprised largely of Catholic conscripts, who were selected by ballot. Brushing aside worries over 'men of doubtful principles' gaining arms, a similar ballot-based system was introduced in Scotland, naturally without the accompanying religious stratification.[63]

The contours of resistance in the two countries also broadly corresponded. Both sets of disturbances were widespread and socially inclusive. In Ireland, all four provinces were involved and almost every county; in Scotland, riots ranged over seventy counties from New Galloway to Strathtay. Rioters were not drawn simply from the lowest social groups, but included artisans and shopkeepers, as well as weavers and colliers in the manufacturing villages. Their immediate grievances were also similar. The ballot with its associations of compulsion and rumours of forced overseas drafts raised most hostility, but this was reinforced too by fears that the age limits of 19–23 in the Act selectively targeted the economically active, whom families and communities could ill-afford to loose.

Perhaps the most obvious and dramatic contrast between the riots lies in the degree of violence which attended them. The Irish Militia riots were distinguished both by the brutal force employed by troops to suppress them, and by the readiness of mass formations of rioters to open fire on the military in response. 'In just eight weeks,' comments Bartlett, 'as many as 230 lives had been lost . . . over five times the number of casualties sustained in the previous thirty years of agrarian disturbances'.[64] In Scotland the worst incident was the Tranent 'massacre', where soldiers of the Pembrokeshire Cavalry fired on a crowd. The eleven fatalities on this occasion were the only ones in the whole series of disturbances.[65]

This simple numerical fact hints at a much deeper divergence in the underlying causes of the riots, re-emphasising the distinctiveness of social and political life in the two countries. The Irish Militia riots were evidence not only of pre-existing, deep-seated fissures in Irish society, but also of the alienation which was actively growing between lower-class Catholics and the Irish Ascendancy. The forms of the riots, which have been viewed as the final bankruptcy of the Irish 'moral economy', was related to the previous year's mass campaign for Catholic emancipation. On the one hand, Whitehall's eagerness in forcing the Relief Acts of 1792 and 1793 through the Irish parliament undermined Protestant morale and heightened their fear and hatred of the Catholic masses. At the same time, these concessions raised the popular expectations of Catholics, who believed that in place of further sweeping gains they had been betrayed by the imposition of conscription and the accompanying anti-Catholic hysteria. In the short term, their resistance to the Act met with some success. The ballot was discreetly withdrawn, and the government was forced to supplement the Militia with volunteers and even recruits from outside Ireland. The longer-term legacy was more grave. The deep distrust felt by Catholics was further fuelled by the savagely coercive response of the authorities to the anti-Militia protests and was later to be channelled through the Defenders and the United Irishmen. Thus, argues Bartlett, 'the 1793 riots helped create the atmosphere of fear and repression that made the '98 possible and some sort of '98 inevitable'.[66]

For some of its representatives, the Scottish administration was in a similar crisis of hegemony. The commander of the Scottish military district, Adam Gordon, wrote to the Home Secretary of 'The very disorderly and very turbulent state in which many parts of Scotland are actually in . . . if this bad spirit should become general and spread to all and to distant parts of Scotland – all of the force I can command here

will be inadequate to force a compliance . . .'.[67] The military situation
was indeed delicate. The dispersed nature of the riots led to logistical
difficulties in dispatching troops quickly; most regulars were guarding
the south coast of England; and the worry of democratic infection hung
over the Volunteers. These problems were only resolved by the import
of a large number of English troops. At one stage, the transfer of a
cavalry regiment from Ireland was even contemplated.[68]

Yet, official nervousness in this instance should not divert attention
from the greater resources of political stability and social homogeneity
at the government's disposal in Scotland.[69] Unlike Ireland, this permitted
a more subtle and effective strategy in which determined military intervention to curtail unrest was combined with active attempts to explain and
win acceptance for the provisions of the Militia Act. These techniques
were urged on the Lord Advocate by the Duke of Portland, but were
also in harmony with the experience and advice of officials in some of
the most disturbed districts.

The military dimension of the response to the riots consciously followed
'the most unquestionable and satisfying example of Ireland'. Regiments
of regulars were to be used to bolster Volunteer morale, and to scour
the country 'to prevent the disaffected from ever collecting in such
bodies as to carry their threats into execution . . .'[70] It was also vital,
believed Portland and Dundas, not to waver on the implementation of
the Act itself. Its suspension would strike at the heart of the political
order, 'too probably endangering the general submission and obedience
to the laws upon the maintenance of which the Constitution and National
Power depends'.[71]

Equally, they realised that 'it was not possible to coerce the whole of
Scotland, if the spirit and example already shown should carry along
every country'.[72] The solution had two parts. First, convinced as usual
that the 'emissaries of sedition' were at work, the leaders of the riots
were to be peeled off, 'to undeceive the multitude and punish the seditious'.[73] Accordingly, only the ringleaders in local incidents were usually
arrested, with few or even no arrests in some of the most militant areas
such as Stirling or Lanarkshire.[74] There were examples of harsh sentencing,
notably from Lord Braxfield, but early excesses proved counter-productive, with juries preferring to acquit, and the bulk of trials were not
generally severe.

To this approach was attached a belated educational campaign. This
followed the type of diagnosis offered by Deputy Lord-Lieutenant Veich
of Dumfries, who suggested that opposition to the Militia did not spring
from 'a spirit of disaffection or disloyalty in the inhabitants, but in some
instances arising from a misapprehension from a total ignorance of the

Act and its intent'.[75] 'Prudent explanation' became a priority, and the Home Secretary advised that the Lord-Lieutenant's post up notices on church doors, clearly setting out the provisions of the Act, and that public meetings be held to bring the people 'to listen to the detection of falsehoods', making them 'sensible of the fatal consequences of resisting the law of the land'.[76]

The combination of these measures had a positive effect. In some areas the local gentry also eased the situation by subscribing to funds to provide paid substitutes for those unlucky in the ballot.[77] At Beith, previously 'the mother of all mischief', the Earl of Eglinton was able to meet personally with former rioters, now anxious to stress that they were 'good and loyal subjects to King and Constitution', and magnanimously promised them pardons.[78] By mid-September, Dundas was writing confidently that the threatened rebellion had vanished very rapidly, and that local magistrates were beginning to recover from 'that state of trepidation into which I was hurt and alarmed to see they had fallen'.[79]

The greater flexibility of power relationships in Scotland and the evidence of paternalistic survivals do not mean that the 1797 Militia riots were 'non-political'. Some centres of unrest in Ayrshire, where Liberty Trees were planted and 'the people were very bad indeed', were old democratic centres.[80] Although much less bloodthirsty and destabilising than in Ireland, the wave of popular protest against the Militia Act does suggest a measure of frustration developing between governed and governing, for the moment contained by well-tried methods.

The United Scotsmen seemed initially wrong-footed by the public expressions of this frustration. Despite protest at times appearing 'previously methodised' and 'systematic', there is no evidence that the wave of unrest was deliberately fermented. Once matters were underway, the terrain seemed more favourable for political radicals to try to mould immediate popular discontent into support for major constitutional change. The integration of specific grievances with a broader political programme, it was doubtless hoped, would extend United organisation and lay the basis for the future rising which might be required to secure their vision.[81] Striking in this respect was the energy of the ubiquitous Angus Cameron, who was circulating in disturbed parishes and encouraging armed resistance.[82]

This strategy had some success and may have contributed to the eastwards spread of the movement and the extension of its presence into rural areas, but to put this in perspective, the Societies at their height probably never attracted more than a few thousand members, active and nominal.[83] For all the efforts of activists, like Cameron, the men and women who had taken part in the Scottish Militia riots were not an alienated and brutalised population ready to rise, nor was the comparative mildness of official measures in the aftermath the stuff of which campaigns of mass politicisation are made. By the end of 1797, even those background factors which had previously favoured the Society had dissipated. Trade was reviving, especially in textile areas, and the fortunes of war were turning. The French had been unable to capitalise on the fleet's immobilisation during the spring mutinies, and at last the government had a naval victory to celebrate with Admiral Duncan's defeat of the Dutch fleet at Camperdown in December. The hero of the hour was fêted, not only by the Scottish administration and the government press, but by a rising wave of popular loyalism.[84]

There was a further blow. The United Scotsmen's activity during the riots may possibly have assisted their diffusion, but was achieved at the cost of the secrecy which had protected the movement to date. In this the radicals gratified the Lord Advocate, who had realised back in May that their proceedings were impossible to penetrate, unless they acted 'with more boldness'.[85] Competition between the 'ideological' demands of developing their membership base and the 'practical' impulses of a secret society had similarly beset United Irishmen from 1795 onwards.[86] Now, government surveillance in Scotland also assumed a more focused and determined air, making use of inside information. It was hoped the London Corresponding Society agent, Jameson, now working for the Glasgow Lord Provost, would reveal the names of the main leaders in Glasgow and Edinburgh.[87] Even Cameron, who had been arrested on charges of mobbing and rioting, may have been allowed to escape trial in return for information.[88] A full, systematic campaign to crush the movement was pre-empted by the arrest of George Mealmaker at Dundee in November, after an approach from a bogus 'confidential person', but arrests followed in Perth, Dundee and Edinburgh.[89] Within weeks, the deepest confidences of the Society were available to newspaper readers: 'the oaths of secrecy similar to the United Irishmen, their system of communicating intelligence, and even their tactics of studiously trying to gain over the military'.[90]

On this inauspicious note, the first phase of the history of the United Scotsmen drew to a close.

SCOTLAND ABROAD

The Society of United Irishmen acted as a 'catalyst' in Scottish radicalism in the true scientific sense, influencing its process of development, without being much altered in itself. Although the Scots were apparently unable to send their own representatives, news of the extension of the United system to Scotland and elsewhere in mainland Britain flowed back through

Irish agents from 1796 onwards to raise the spirits of the frustrated Ulster committees, as indeed had been the original intention.[91] At a county meeting at Downpatrick, County Down, in October 1797, one speaker – Dr David Thompson of Ballyrush – had just returned from Scotland. He was able to show his colleagues a Scottish constitution which was 'word for word as is the Irish, only the words North Britain put in for Ireland,' and inform them that he had been present at a National Meeting in May in Edinburgh, when the number of United Scotsmen returned was 2,871; he had also been present in September when a further 653 were enrolled.[92]

In a similarly practical vein, the Societies were well enough abreast of events in Scotland to use them in attempts to subvert Scottish troops in Ireland. A typical handbill distributed to soldiers proclaimed: 'Let the Scottish soldiers . . . recollect the same considerations (and recollect the recent massacres at *Tranent*) for the redress of which Scotsmen are now united, and them if they can, let them condemn *us* for struggling for liberty, of which we sincerely wish them to partake . . .'.[93]

The case of the Scots as 'junior partners' in the alliance is more complex. We have seen that the Irish influence was more in terms of organisational remodelling than of ideology or personnel. As with the Friends of the People, the new breed of Scottish radicals also looked to the greater political experience of the Irish and to the inspiring example of a mass movement in the making. Mealmaker's trial revealed that meetings were assured of thousands of reformers like themselves meeting in Ireland and England, and agents in Thornliebank and Cupar impudently carried with them copies of the 1797 *Report of the Committee of Secrecy of the House of Commons of Ireland*, where the Scots could read of the United Irishmen's new military format and of 100,000 men organised in Ulster alone.[94]

As repression in Ulster intensified, this identification with events in the Province brought its own problems. The hanging of the young Antrim farmer William Orr in October 1797, for administering the United Irish Oath to two Fifeshire Fencibles, gave the Irish Societies their most potent symbol of martyrdom. An influx of new members followed, or as one ballad had it: 'Thy blood to our Union more energy gave'.[95]

In Scotland, the effect was the opposite. With Scottish radicals already more isolated by their lack of numbers than the Irish, Orr's fate confirmed earlier worries over the implications of their new oath-bound form. Radicals in Dunfermline now ceased to meet, 'in consequence of their observing from the newspapers, that a person had been convicted of administering unlawful oaths'.[96] In Maybole, some members regretted ever having become involved in 'the dangerous business, since matters were going on ill in Ireland or attended with bad consequences there'.[97]

As radicals had already found in supporting the Revolution in France, this was the cost of an alliance with a developing political movement. The issue is whether the United Scotsmen had any real alternative. In the absence of the discipline and secrecy of the United system, the Scots would no doubt have continued to meet in a private and fairly purposeless fashion. The example of the Perth radicals who had refused to enter the system was not encouraging. Their meetings were quickly penetrated by an informer, who, finding 'nothing very bloody' about their songs, toasts and speculations about French politics, wished he had joined the United set instead.[98]

As well as bestowing a more cohesive structure, the Irish alliance linked the Scots into the international revolutionary movement, and thus implicitly held out the prospect of external aid in the shape of French military intervention. This was imperative, given the movement's embarrassingly obvious failure to attract a mass membership at home, but it was also to confer a sense of mission, noticeably absent in the Perth dissidents, sustaining the United Scotsmen in the years of adversity which lay ahead. As with the Irish alliance, however, this pro-French strategy was not cost-free.

One of the most pressing problems sprang from the United Scotsmen's lack of numerical muscle, and whether this would be sufficient to raise French interest. A simple tactic, common throughout the radical movement, was to boost paper membership, with a United Scots delegate in Paris, Thomas Graham, claiming that 200,000 of the Scottish people were ready to rise.[99] More modestly, a French agent in Altona, Hamburg, was given to understand that 60,000 United Scotsmen, 'all armed' were mustered in the Glasgow and Paisley area.[100] Another approach was to increase genuine recruitment by whatever means came to hand, sometimes regardless of the new member's degree of political conviction. Again, Freemasonry was used as a reference point. One likely recruit at Glasgow was asked if he wished to be a Mason. Replying that he already was one, he was told that this was 'some new masonry', which they could instruct him in. It related to the news of the country and contained 'more news than was to be found in the newspapers'.[101] Craigendallie likewise pushed the esoteric attractions of 'belonging'. Membership was sold as signifying special zeal and attachment to the cause, conferring mysterious benefits on the initiate: in his own words, 'The Union was going on rapidly everywhere and the advantages were such as none could conceive till they joined'.[102] One of these advantages was held to be protection in the event of an invasion. As with the Galloway Masons, the signs of the

United system were said to 'save a man's life if the French were coming here, for the Frenchmen would know you to be a friend of them'. More perceptive observers realised this was nonsense, as the signs changed every three or four weeks.[103] If cajoling was not effective, then threats of the 'new Robespierreian system', where deserters and traitors, 'were never more heard of again' could be tried. If even threats failed, then drink might always find the way to a new recruit.[104]

These desperate measures had already been pioneered on a much greater scale in Ireland, where they had the counter-productive effect of attracting 'the most violent and unstable elements in the community, while driving off more restrained radicals.[105] In Scotland, the tactics were never successful enough to promote similar structural tensions, but the introduction of nominal and uncommitted members was liable to damage the secret operation of the movement. Such uncertain defenders of the cause were also likely to melt away at the first signs of government interest in the Societies.

A second difficulty with the reliance of French aid was a basic lack of information as to the precise intentions of the United Scotsmen's 'deliverers'. This could be serious enough to dispel the initial optimism which had been raised by international linkages. This was also a chronic problem for Irish radicals. Although they were effective negotiators, United Irish leaders in France do not seem to have realised the need for frequent communication with a home movement which was attempting to keep hopes of an invasion alive in the face of the government counter-offensive. Starved of news, divisions over the timing of any rising increased and the agents Lowry and Tennent worried that 'indifference towards France might be the result'.[106] If this was the case with the United Irishmen, who had their own delegates to the Directory, how much more frustrating and debilitating was the situation of the Scots, who had to rely on scraps of intelligence at second hand through the underground network. In these circumstances, it was hardly surprising that some United Scotsmen adopted an 'attitude imposante' and considered sending representatives to Paris to press for an invasion attempt.[107]

Even more serious were the effects that any alliance with the French might have on popular sentiments in Scotland, the very sentiments which the United Scotsmen hoped to mobilise. The French Revolution, as Dickson notes, had boosted popular conservatism, as well as popular radicalism.[108] A war of ideas followed, in which a series of powerful messages reached down the social order. Ordinary French people were portrayed as victims of a revolution built on speculative theorising which threatened private property and Christianity. To this, the British liberties were contrasted: parliamentary monarchy, the rule of law, and a constitution which was the product of historical precedent and sound common-sense. These messages were disseminated through a host of official and unofficial channels, newspapers, penny tracts, and sermons. Yet antipathy to the French was no more the product of a conspiratorial governing élite, than radical principles flowed from 'the emissaries of sedition'. The popular Irish Catholic identification with France as a traditional ally had little parallel in Scotland, where downright anti-Gallicism after the English model had a more common currency. British military reversals, as suggested, may have driven some into the radical camp, but for others they confirmed that France was bent on universal domination as of old. Loyalist fears were expressed in busy preparations to resist French aggression, as at Glasgow in January 1797, where 'alarms of an invasion had no effect . . ., but to increase the spirit of loyalty and to add considerably to the number of Volunteers'.[109] This became a general pattern and even in the most radical parishes, such as Maybole, Auchterarder and Perth, Volunteer corps flourished and local farmers offered their services to transport the military.[110] At Thornliebank, a penitent John Jarve even credited the Volunteers with the responsibility for 'the great change in the sentiments there, and one of the causes of the plans of the United there being broke'.[111]

Typically of popular culture in the 1790s, this new pugnacious spirit was soon channelled into song. The *Courier* reported a new ballad being sung in loyal circles:

> They say that this country is all gone to staves,
> That our rulers are nothing but scoundrels and knaves,
> That the only thing left to effect our salvation,
> Is to bow to the French and submit at discretion.
>
> Ah *Be-gar*, say the French – we are *de* Great Nation,
> And will be very sure *be-give* you *de* vexation,
> Unless that your Despots get our of *de* way,
> And allow us *de* freedom *de* world to sway.
>
> Very well Mr Nick Frog, then come your ways over,
> The nearest I think is from Calais to Dover,
> We'll teach you fine things, 'mong others we trust,
> The grand vulgarism of *biting the dust*.[112]

If this was not enough, fundamental problems also arose with the actual mechanics of building links with the French. Scottish radicals now discovered that when military aid was at stake, expediency could win out over international brotherhood as the United Irishmen's role as mediators between Scotland and France became plagued by contradictions.

The official and popular mind in France had a long-established interest in Scottish affairs, independent of any encouragement from the Irish colony at Paris. This drew on an amalgam of cultural sources, ranging from memories of the Jacobite risings and Ossianic romanticism, to a selective reading of the historians Hume and Robertson. The impression received from all this – of a historic nation bearing uneasily the yoke of English oppression – seemed to gain confirmation from the reports of a confusing variety of spies, dispatched by the chaotic French intelligence services in the early 1790s, and from the successive Scottish democratic conventions which were extensively, if hyperbolically, covered in the French press.[113]

Already by January 1793, Scotland and Ireland were being presented to the French National Convention as enjoying an identity of interest, as two oppressed nations 'always restive, and secretly in revolt against the injustice of the dominating race . . . [with] the hope of ultimately regaining their entire independence . . .'.[114] Therefore, when the Directory adopted its more aggressive military posture at the end of 1795 to achieve 'the extermination of England', not only were the two suffering kingdoms accorded an important role, but their efforts were to be co-ordinated. The agent Jean Mengaud was subsequently dispatched in the Spring of the following year to discover the peoples' disposition to rebellion and, if the Scots were not already in communication with the United Irishmen, he was to facilitate this.[115]

For their own part, while their strategy of seeking French assistance was still taking shape, the Irish shared this 'inclusive' view. This was clear from the Scottish dimension which had automatically entered Wolfe Tone's Washington memoir to Ambassador Adet in August 1795. Tone's mind was soon to change as the competition for French military resources intensified over the next two years. By April 1796, he was protesting that a force was being considered for Scotland, and remained convinced that 'nothing will ever be done there unless we first begin in Ireland'.[116]

The United Irishmen were in an even more awkward position after Ireland's failure to rise at the time of the Bantry Bay expedition. Over the next six months, there was little popular enthusiasm in France for another attempt, and instead attention shifted towards the campaign in Italy. When interest eventually did revive, it became obvious that any Irish venture was liable to be subsumed in a general British invasion strategy. The attractions of a major attack on the British mainland meant that as far as Tone and his colleagues were concerned, the potential for disaffection in England and Scotland was being given greater weight than the actual mass movement the Irish had constructed, and the incipient rebellion in that country. They were also faced by the realisation that the active missionising of the Ulster committees, and their claims for successful recruiting on the mainland, might have in reality damaged the United Irishmen's position by pointing French interest elsewhere.[117]

These doubts were temporarily put aside in the summer of 1797, as the Dutch Republic offered the Directory its fleet for another Irish expedition, anxious to redeem itself after previous military disasters in Ceylon and Surinam.[118] Instead, Tone was cheated again, as foul weather, internal bickering and a superior British naval force kept its ships confined off the bleak North Sea island of Texel. The Irish option was closed off and the thoughts of the Dutch commander General Daendels inclined towards more imaginative alternatives.

Daendels's heart was originally set on a landing at Harwich or Great Yarmouth, with a triumphal march either west to London or north to Edinburgh and Glasgow and possibly on to Ireland, but plans for a direct attempt on Scotland also began to crystallise. When the United Irish agents Alexander Lowry and John Tennent arrived at Texel in early August, Daendels closely questioned them 'as to what they knew of the state of the public mind in Scotland, and the possibility of meeting support from the patriots in that country'.[119] The Irishmen's response was 'very rational', as Tone archly suggested, in sharp relief to the morale-boosting pronouncements usually made for domestic consumption. From their information:

> It seems that emissaries have been sent from the north of Ireland to that country, to propagate the system of United Irishmen; and that they have to a certain degree, succeeded in some of the principal manufacturing towns, such as Paisley and Glasgow, where societies are already organised, and by last accounts they have even advanced so far as to have formed a provincial committee: nevertheless they observed these facts rested on the veracity of agents sent from the north, the Scotch having sent none of their body in return; that they could not pretend to say whether the Scotch patriots were up to such a decided part, as to take up arms in case of an invasion, but their opinion rather was they were not so far advanced.[120]

This brutally honest assessment, made in advance of the boost received from the Militia Riots, failed to deflate Daendels, and between 9 and 21 August he composed an invasion plan, which he himself admitted was 'bisarre' at first sight.[121] A total of 15,000 troops were to land at Leith. They would move into the interior of Lowland Scotland and gain mastery of all the country between Edinburgh and Glasgow which was supposedly bare of regular troops. Meanwhile, five or six frigates and a flotilla of smaller craft were to round the north of Scotland and gain control of the

Firth of Clyde, where the land contingent would re-embark for the north of Ireland. Still, some of the Irish agents' realism had penetrated. Daendels did not flatter himself that the Scots would greet his arrival by planting the Tree of Liberty, though the presence of 'comités d'insurrection' in correspondence with Ireland raised the possibility that the country was as liable to take up arms *for* rather than *against* them. Even if this was not the case, the population might be persuaded to remain neutral if the invading army conducted itself sensibly.

This unconvincing plan also survived the scepticism of Tone, who, realising that an ancillary strike at Ireland was better than nothing, on 14 September took a copy to General Hoche's headquarters in Prussia to win his support. By this time, it had grown into two debarkations totalling 30,000 troops, including French regulars, 25,000 of whom might cross to England and force a passage, while 5,000 were destined for Ireland; a leading command was projected for General Macdonald, the son of a Scottish Jacobite.[122]

A dubious Hoche promised to consider the plan, but his health was visibly declining, and his death from rapid consumption a week later meant the loss of a possible advocate.[123] Even more final was the Texel fleet's destruction on 11 October at Camperdown. On hearing the news of this engagement, the fugitive United man at Kirkoswald, Major Reid, was heard to exclaim 'Damn it!, then we will have no invasion this season'.[124] His prediction was entirely accurate.

The Dutch invasion plan had surprise on its side. The Scottish authorities knew quite well the flimsy naval force which protected Scotland's east coast, and worried how to concentrate their ground troops at points vulnerable to the enemy.[125] On the other hand, as Woods suggests, its complexity, with successive embarkations and debarkations, meant that there was much that could go wrong. Daendels almost certainly exaggerated the ease with which he could manœuvre 30,000 men in the Scottish interior, sustaining themselves off the land without antagonising the local population.[126]

Its military weaknesses aside, the very fact that the interest of the French and their allies in Scotland adopted this practical expression and that the United Scotsmen could be seriously considered as a bridgehead for invasion again underlines that Scottish radicalism cannot be analysed by exclusive reference to domestic horizons.[127] Soon it was to become all too clear that the movement was actually growing over-dependent on its external linkages, its priorities driven by the intensification of internal splits among its Irish allies and by the vagaries of French foreign policy. At the turn of the year, the auspices still seemed favourable. In November, the formation of the *armée d'Angleterre* under Bonaparte, 'the democrats' child and champion', revived invasion hopes, but even more encouraging was the arrival in Paris of Thomas Muir. At last, it seemed, Scotland would have an independent voice to press home its cause, and one which could speak from the moral high ground.

NOTES

1. RH 2/4/83 ff. 27–40 (SRO).
2. *Glasgow Courier*, 22 June 1797.
3. Earl of Eglinton to H. Dundas, 16 March 1797, Melville MSS GD 51/5/29 (SRO).
4. R. Dundas to J. King, 6 May 1797, RH 2/4/81 f. 212 (SRO).
5. Brims, 'The Scottish Democratic Movement', pp. 566–7.
6. R. Dundas to Duke of Portland, 13 January 1798, RH 2/4/83 f. 21 (SRO)
7. For the United Scotsmen's Tests and Constitution, see *House of Commons Committee of Secrecy Report* (1799), app. 15, pp. 67–9; for the United Irishmen's, see MacNeven, *Pieces of Irish History*, pp. 76–8, 99–103.
8. Howell and Howell, *State Trials*, vol.,xxvi, cols 1135–79; D. Cameron Declaration, RH 2/4/81 f. 201 (SRO).
9. Smyth, *Men of no Property*, p. 114.
10. For suggested Defender entry, see J. Dalrymple Hay to Earl of Galloway, 10 June 1797, HO 100/72/451 (PRO). To complicate matters, the term 'Defender' was often used loosely to apply to any of the disaffected in Ireland. Elliott, 'The Origins and Transformation of Early Irish Republicanism', p. 420 does note that Defender representatives met with the French in London in 1792, but this may have been a chance encounter.
11. *Resolutions* in RH 2/4/83 ff. 23–6 (SRO); *Catechism* in ff. 27–40.
12. J. Jarve Declaration, 13 April 1798, RH 2/4/84 f. 210 (SRO).
13. Responding indignantly to anti-constitutional slurs, this body proclaimed 'their firm and unalterable intention to pursue every legal measure to obtain a reform in Parliament, fully convinced that universal suffrage and annual parliaments are the only means that can be used to secure the liberty and happiness of this nation', *Glasgow Advertiser*, 11–15, 15–18, 18–22, 25–9 November 1793. There is no apparent organisational link between the United Scotsmen and this original Glasgow body.
14. RH 2/4/83 f. 30 (SRO).
15. D. Coulston Declaration, JC 26/294 (SRO).
16. PC 1/44 A.161 (PRO); R. Dundas to J. King, 18 April 1798, RH 2/4/83 f. 170 (SRO); *House of Commons Committee of Secrecy Report* (1799), p. 27; Tone, *Life of Theobald Wolfe Tone*, vol. ii, p. 432.
17. Howell and Howell, *State Trials*, vol. xxvi, col. 1177.
18. J. Jarve Declaration, 13 April 1798, RH 2/4/84 f. 210 (SRO).
19. Ibid.; A. Macdonald Declaration, April 1798, JC 26/295 (SRO).
20. The conscription element in the Irish Militia laid it open to subversive influence, see Elliott, *Partners in Revolution*, p. 127 for the problems of the Monaghan Militia in this respect. 'Scotch Fencibles' were requested speedily for delicate operations such as the escort of United prisoners: M. Wainwright to J. Pelham, 7 May 1797, Rebellion Papers, 620/30/29 (NAI). See also *Edinburgh Advertiser*, 30 May–2 June 1797 for the resolutions of the Perthshire Fencible Regiment, stationed at Galway, pledging themselves against any attempt by the United Irishmen to spread sedition in their ranks.

21. Smyth, *Men of no Property*, p. 84; Elliott, *Wolfe Tone*, p. 105 on Tone's deism.

22. MacNeven, *Pieces of Irish History*, pp. 177, 203. The *Northern Star*, 24–8 March 1796 also subscribed to the doctrine of self-help. In its 'Friendly Advice to the Industrious Poor', it suggested that heavy taxation was only one cause of poverty, for some men were 'taxed twice as much by their folly, three times as much by their drunkenness and four times by their laziness as they are taxed by government'. Dog-keeping by the poor was also frowned upon.

23. Smyth, *Men of no Property*, pp. 166–7.

24. Burns, 'Industrial Labour and Radical Movements', p. 215.

25. Howell and Howell, *State Trials*, vol. xxvi, col. 1177.

26. D. Coulston Declaration, JC 26/294 (SRO).

27. J. Jarve Declaration, 13 April 1798, RH 2/4/84 f. 210 (SRO).

28. I. Campbell to R. Dundas, 26 August 1797, RH 2/4/80 f. 194 (SRO).

29. J. Kennedy Declarations, August and 2 December 1799, JC 26/298 (SRO).

30. Earl of Eglinton to H. Dundas, 26 June 1798, Melville MSS GD 51/1/899 (SRO).

31. W. Murray to R. Barclay, 27 December 1797, Laing MSS II 639 (University of Edinburgh); W. Scott to H. Dundas, 22 July 1797, Melville MSS GD 51/2/29 (SRO).

32. Melville MSS, ibid.

33. Smyth, *Men of no Property*, pp. 161–2. In 1795–6, the United Irishmen had produced two ballad collections, *Paddy's Resource* and *The Irish Harp New Strung*. The former contained over a hundred 'liberty songs' and toasts.

34. W. Scott to H. Dundas, 22 July 1797, Melville MSS GD 51/2/29 (SRO).

35. J. Kennedy Declaration, 2 December 1799, JC 26/298 (SRO).

36. Beames, 'Peasant Movements: Ireland', pp. 85–8; A. T. Q. Stewart, *A Deeper Silence*, pp. 164–78. For an official history of Irish Freemasonry, see Lepper and Crossle, *History of the Grand Lodge*, p. 296.

37. A quasi-Masonic influence pervaded the early Scottish trade-union movement, see Campbell, *The Lanarkshire Miners*, pp. 59–60. Masonic links also existed with the United Societies in Manchester, Goodwin, *Friends of Liberty*, pp. 339–440; Thompson, *Making of the English Working Class*, p. 170.

38. Stirling was Scottish Grand Master in 1798, *Glasgow Advertiser*, 23 November 1798.

39. J. Robertson to R. Dundas, January 1798, Laing MSS II 641–2 (University of Edinburgh). Again indicating Freemasonry's ideological diversity, Galloway Masons loyally celebrated the British fleet's victory at Camperdown in 1797: Smith, *Freemasonry in Galloway*, p. 12.

40. Murray Lyon, *History of the Lodge of Edinburgh*, pp. 322–9.

41. JC 26/307 (SRO) for further details of declarations and testimony. The case also received coverage in the *Glasgow Advertiser*, 22 September 1800 and *Glasgow Courier*, 25 September 1800. Beyond this, it would be intriguing to know whether the Scottish lodges also assisted the missionising strategy by providing contacts and hospitality, as seems to have been the case in Ireland – McCabe, McCracken and Samuel Kennedy were all lodge members. Unfortunately, Scottish Grand Lodge Records are imperfect for the 1790s and it is possible that the names of Irish masons joining local lodges were not passed on to the higher authority. Extant local records were also checked for the names of prominent United Scotsmen, but with a negative result. Again, this is not conclusive proof that men like Mealmaker or Grey did not have Masonic links. (I am grateful to Andrew Reith at the Scottish Grand Lodge Library for this information.)

42. Place MS 27815, ff. 5, 16, 17, 136 (British Library). For Leslie, see Meikle, *Scotland and the French Revolution*, p. 155.
43. W. Scott to R. Dundas, 7 May and 26 June 1797, RH 2/4/80 ff. 75, 116 (SRO).
44. Elliott, *Partners in Revolution*, p. 145. The key figure here was James Dixon, like Craigendallie an Irish weaver, resident in the city from 1788.
45. R. Dundas to J. King, 18 April 1798, RH 2/4/83 f. 170 (SRO).
46. J. Dixon evidence, 7 May 1798, PC 1/42 A43 (PRO).
47. JC 26/294 (SRO); W. Murray to R. Dundas, 20 November 1797, Laing MSS II 500 (University of Edinburgh).
48. Narrative of the Arrest, Examination and Imprisonment of George Mealmaker, RH 2/4/83 ff. 41–9 (SRO).
49. Burns, 'Industrial Labour and Radical Movements', p. 205; Howell and Howell, *State Trials*, vol. xxvi, col. 1152.
50. R. Carmichael to R. Dundas, 7 and 9 August 1797, RH 2/4/80 ff. 144–6 (SRO). A watch was kept on Lord Wycombe, who had travelled from Scotland to the north of England and then to Ireland. Lord Sempill's visits to a suspected house in Glasgow were also noted, J. McDowell to R. Dundas, 25 November 1797, RH 2/4/80 f. 240 (SRO).
51. Note the case of David Coulston. A printfield worker, he tramped from job to job, from Thornliebank to Glasgow, on to Campsie, and back to Thornliebank, in the space of a few years, JC 26/294 (SRO).
52. Burns, 'Industrial Labour and Radical Movements', p. xii.
53. Spy Report, 13 August 1797, RH 2/4/80 f. 148 (SRO).
54. Wells, *Insurrection*, p. 73.
55. Brims, 'The Scottish Democratic Movement', p. 560.
56. H. Veich to the Duke of Queensberry, 3 September 1797, RH 2/4/81 ff. 55–7 (SRO); I. Campbell to R. Dundas, 26 August 1797, RH 2/4/80 f. 194 (SRO).
57. Statement to Secrecy Committee Ireland, 4 April 1797, Add. MSS, Pelham Papers, 33119* (British Library).
58. *Edinburgh Advertiser*, 6–9 June 1797 for contemporary reaction; Wells, *Insurrection*, pp. 79–109 for the fullest account.
59. This was keenly felt after two years of relative prosperity 1794–6, Murray, *The Scottish Handloom Weavers*, p. 50.
60. Meeting of 6 June 1797, Minutes of the Hibernian Society, TD 200.7 (SRA).
61. *Glasgow Courier*, 6 June 1797 on the initial 'leave to embody a Militia in Scotland'. The Bill was finally passed on 19 July. Overviews of the Militia riots are provided in Burns, 'Industrial Labour and Radical Movements', chap. 4; and Logue, *Popular Disturbances in Scotland*, pp. 116–27. See also *Edinburgh Advertiser*, 7–11 July, 3–8 August, 8–12 September 1797; *Glasgow Courier*, 24 August 1797 for riots in Cadder and Dunse, 26 August for Kirkpatrick and Campsie, 29 August for Strathhaven, 30 August for Tranent and 2 September for Dumfries and Galloway.
62. For Ireland, see Bartlett, 'An End to the Moral Economy', pp. 41–64.
63. J. Craig to R. Dundas, 18 May 1797, RH 2/4/80 f. 80 (SRO). Craig's worries were mainly for the large manufacturing towns, though in the event rural areas were the worst effected.
64. Bartlett, 'An End to the Moral Economy', p. 58.
65. 'Narrative of Events at Tranent', RH 2/4/81 f. 49 (SRO).
66. Bartlett, 'An End to the Moral Economy', p. 44.
67. A. Gordon to Duke of Portland, 23 August 1797, RH 2/4/80 f. 154 (SRO).
68. *Glasgow Courier*, 3 September 1797; Duke of Portland to Duke of Montrose, 28 August 1797, RH 2/4/80 f. 212 (SRO).

69. The government had no 'Catholic question' to wrestle with. A policy of official aid and conciliation had been adopted towards Scotland's small Catholic community, for which their leaders 'were fulsomely grateful, as if it had given them opulence and power into the bargain': Duke of Portland to J. Hippisey, 27 July [1795], Laing MSS II 580 (University of Edinburgh).

70. Duke of Portland to A. Gordon, [September 1797], RH 2/4/80 f. 154 (SRO).

71. Duke of Portland to Duke of Montrose, 28 August 1797, RH 2/4/80 f. 212 (SRO).

72. R. Dundas to Duke of Portland, 30 August 1797, RH 2/4/80 f. 248 (SRO).

73. The Lord Advocate felt that sentencing should distinguish between those charged with simple Riot and Tumult against a specific Act, and those guilty of the 'higher crime' of sedition: R. Dundas to Duke of Portand, 30 August 1797, ibid.

74. Duke of Portland to R. Dundas, September 1797, RH 2/4/81 f. 187 (SRO).

75. H. Veich to the Duke of Queensberry, 3 September 1797, RH 2/4/81 ff. 55–7 (SRO).

76. Duke of Portland to Duke of Montrose, 28 August 1797, RH 2/4/80 f. 212 (SRO); for examples of posters, see RH 2/4/80 f. 229 (SRO): Montrose; RH 2/4/81 f. 4 (SRO): West Lothian. Note also the *Glasgow Courier*'s 'mission to explain', 24 August 1797.

77. Burns, 'Industrial Labour and Radical Movements', p. 200.

78. Earl of Eglinton to R. Dundas, 9 September 1797, RH 2/4/81 f. 69 (SRO).

79. R. Dundas to J. King, 13 September 1797, RH 2/4/81 f. 131 (SRO).

80. J. Gordon to R. Dundas, 23 August 1797, RH 2/4/80 f. 180 (SRO); Earl of Eglinton to R. Dundas, 27 August 1797, RH 2/4/80 f. 200 (SRO).

81. Brims, 'The Scottish Democratic Movement', vol. 2, pp. 560–6.

82. Campbell to R. Dundas, 16 October 1797, Laing MSS II 501 (University of Edinburgh); Howell and Howell, *State Trials*, xxvi, cols 1165–80; Declaration of James Menzies, April 1798, JC 26/294; JC 3/49 (SRO) for sentence of fugitation.

83. An Irish visitor in May had the number enrolled at under three thousand, Lowry MS D. 1494 (PRONI). See above p. 168.

84. *Glasgow Courier*, 17 October and 21 November 1797 for examples of local celebrations.

85. R. Dundas to J. King, 6 May 1797, RH 2/4/84 f. 212 (SRO).

86. See Curtin, 'The United Irish Organisation in Ulster', pp. 209–22.

87. J. Orr to R. Dundas, 18 November 1797, RH 2/4/81 f. 230 (SRO). His information turned out to be 'paltry'.

88. Logue makes this suggestion, *Popular Disturbances in Scotland*, p. 122. This would be an interesting turn of events, as Cameron later re-emerges in connection with the United Britons and as a projected United Scottish agent to France and as a member of a possible 'Scotch Directory', see below pp. 181, 186.

89. JC 3/4 (SRO) for criminal letters on Mealmaker. *Glasgow Courier*, 14 November 1797 for his arrest and *Scots Chronicle*, 10–14, 14–17 December for subsequent arrests.

90. *Glasgow Courier*, 7 December 1797.

91. For lack of Scottish delegates, see Tone, *Life of Theobald Wolfe Tone*, vol. ii, p. 432. On information from Irish agents, McNally to Cooke, 7 February 1797, Rebellion Papers, 620/36/227 (NAI); Newell's Reports, 21–9 July 1796, HO 100/62/141–6 (PRO).

92. Lowry MS D. 1494 (PRONI); For Thompson, Black Book of Rebellion, McCance Collection, D. 272/1 (PRONI).

93. *House of Commons Committee of Secrecy Report* (1799), app. xxx, p. 221.

94. Howell and Howell, *State Trials*, xxvi, cols 1147, 1159; D. Coulston Precognition, August 1798, JC 26/294 (SRO); W. Henderson Precognition, April 1798, JC 26/295 (SRO).

95. *Glasgow Courier*, 5 October 1797 for Scottish coverage of the Orr case.

96. Howell and Howell, *State Trials*, xxvi, col. 1185.

97. J. Kennedy Declaration, 11 April 1798, JC 26/298 (SRO).

98. Howell and Howell, *State Trials*, xxvi, col. 1154; W. Scott to H. Dundas, 22 July 1797, Melville MSS GD 51/5/29 (SRO); Spy Report, 13 August 1797, RH 2/4/80 f. 140 (SRO).

99. Elliott, *Partners in Revolution*, p. 142.

100. Extract d'une lettre d'Altona du Ministre de la Marine, 19 Brumaire [1798], AF III 26, f. 30.

101. J. Jarve Declaration, 13 April 1798, RH 2/4/84 f. 210 (SRO).

102. W. Scott to H. Dundas, 22 July 1797, Melville MSS GD 51/2/2 (SRO).

103. Ibid.

104. Alexander Macdonald admitted he was 'somewhat intoxicated' when persuaded to take the United Scotsman oath, Declaration, April 1798, JC 26/295 (SRO).

105. Curtin, 'The Transformation of the United Irishmen', p. 491.

106. Elliott, *Partners in Revolution*, pp. 152, 161.

107. Extract d'une lettre d'Altona du Ministre de la Marine, 19 Brumaire [1798], AF III 26, f. 30.

108. Dickinson, 'Popular Conservatism and Militant Loyalism', pp. 103–25.

109. I. Campbell to H. Dundas, 14 January 1797, RH 2/4/80 f. 3 (SRO)

110. *Glasgow Courier*, 25 February 1797 on Maybole, where a local minister planned to use volunteer cavalry to counter invasion; 23 March on the formation of a company at Auchterarder; RH 2/4/80 f. 18 (SRO) on Perth developments.

111. J. Jarve Declaration, 13 April 1798, RH 2/4/84 f. 210 (SRO).

112. *Glasgow Courier*, 27 January 1798.

113. Meikle, *Scotland and the French Revolution*, p. 166n.

114. *Moniteur*, 3 January 1793, quoted ibid, p. 164.

115. Ibid., p. 169.

116. Tone, *Life of Theobald Wolfe Tone*, vol. ii, p. 90.

117. Elliott, *Partners in Revolution*, p. 160.

118. Scharma, *Patriots and Liberators*, pp. 280–2.

119. Tone, *Life of Theobald Wolfe Tone*, vol. ii, p. 132.

120. Ibid., p. 432.

121. MS 706, fos. 32–6, National Library of Ireland (NLI); see Woods, 'A Plan for the Dutch Invasion of Scotland', pp. 108–14.

122. Tone *Life of Theobald Wolfe Tone*, vol. ii, p. 442.

123. The *Glasgow Courier*, 3 October 1797 rejoiced: 'The Directory has lost its favourite . . . the great champion of usurpation and tyranny.'

124. Earl of Eglinton to R.Dundas, 27 November 1797, Laing MSS II 500 (University of Edinburgh).

125. J. Stirling to R. Dundas, 21 February 1797, RH 2/4/78 f. 35 (SRO); H. Dundas to R. Dundas, 7 March 1798, Laing MSS II 500, 646 (University of Edinburgh).

126. Woods, 'A Plan for the Dutch Invasion of Scotland', pp. 113–14.

127. As for a Scottish dimension in French strategy, the Directory's agent in Altona suggested 'Il faut attaquer votre enemie partout et par tous les moyens'. Extract d'une lettre d'Altona au Ministre de la Marine, 19 Brumarie [1798], AF III 26, f. 300.

7

Rebellion
1798

'Scotland is Irish all over'.

Arthur O'Connor to Roger O'Connor, 13 February 1798[1]

Ye Croppies of Wexford, I'd have you be wise,
And not go to meddle with Mid-Lothian boys,
For the Mid-Lothian boys, they vow and declare,
They'll crop off your heads as well as your hair.
Remember at Ross and at Vinegar Hill,
How your heads flew about like chaff in a mill,
For the Mid-Lothian boys, when a croppy they see,
They blow out his daylights or tip him cut three.

Scottish soldiers song of the 1798 Rebellion[2]

SCOTLAND'S ADVOCATE?

Thomas Muir was received by the French in a burst of excitement and concern. Just as their country was turning its attention to the conquest of the final enemy, Muir appeared in their midst, like one of their favourite 'héros chantés par Ossian', a singular victim of English oppression in whose honour public banquets, illuminations and stirring laudations were elaborately arranged.[3] Radicals at home also rejoiced, especially since rumours of his death had been circulating from the previous summer.[4] Nor had the Dublin Irishmen forgotten their friend, as Arthur O'Connor's *Press* exhorted the French Directory 'in the name of the generous people whom they govern, to fulfil every duty of hospitality towards the Apostle of Liberty'.[5]

Yet, sadly for Muir, his subsequent year in France, also the last year of his life, was to be spent in self-aggrandisement, bickering and disappointment. This was the embarrassing coda to a revolutionary career, rather than a new beginning. This outcome was only partly due to

Muir's own physical and mental deterioration, but also reflected the frictions and humiliations inherent in émigré politics.

Muir's life after he was removed from Edinburgh resembled an adventure novel.[6] He had escaped from Botany Bay after two years, sailed to the American west coast and travelled inland via Acapulco and Vera Cruz to Havannah. He was then dispatched as a prisoner of war to Spain, but *en route* his ship was intercepted by a British squadron and he was badly wounded in the skirmish. After a period of imprisonment, he was repatriated as a French subject.[7] These events had cost Muir dearly. He was ill and exhausted, and the loss of an eye and part of a cheekbone had left him permanently disfigured. Already on his travels he had found it necessary to rewrite recent history and accord himself an exaggerated role at its centre; now, after the adulation of his initial welcome subsided, he was to discover that for a foreign exile in Paris egotistical propaganda became a way of life.[8]

The Paris of 1798 was hardly the internationalist capital of the *Girondins* in which Muir had triumphed five years before. Although the foreign minister Charles Delacroix gave strong signals that unconditional support would be forthcoming for Scotland and Ireland, the priorities of the Directory regime were now dominated by the sordid realities of money and power. Thus, in accepting Delacroix's recommendation that Muir be welcomed 'as one who had dared to maintain the Lamp of Liberty', the Directory added the ominous postscript to 'recommander d'économie'.[9]

An increasingly rigid social hierarchy was also now in place and the nation resounded to spy-mania and denunciations of fiscal corruption. Initially, Muir was well enough regarded to be named as a minister in a projected 'Scotch Directory', but to find an enduring position in this tarnished new order he had to prove his worth.[10] A major problem was his isolation from events at home. Muir had left the Scottish political scene almost five years before, and was now forced to rely on occasional visitors to Paris for information on developments such as the Militia riots and the United Scotsmen. Some contacts were less than reliable. Typical was the Scot Robert Watson, an ex-London Corresponding Society official, already well practised in the art of inflating radical numbers. Arriving in September 1798, he proceeded to establish his position as self-appointed English republican agent to France and as a close collaborator with the Irish.[11] He was full of the news that 50,000 were ready to rise in Scotland, and led Muir to believe that the fugitated United Scotsmen Cameron and Kennedy would soon visit and prove useful agents. Other Scottish visitors were more circumspect, like the Swords brothers of Glasgow, who testified to Muir's initial prosperity, but also relayed the telling anecdote of a drunken squabble between Muir and that other exiled 'Apostle of Liberty', Thomas Paine.[12]

Besides conviviality, Muir's energies and frustrations were to find a voice in appeals for money and in bombastic memorials addressed to the new foreign minister, Tallyrand, calling for French intervention in Scotland.[13] The two were connected, since Muir assured his hosts that money would be received 'in the name of the Scottish people', and would be paid back 'with interest and enthusiasm' in the event of a successful invasion.

The memorials were remarkable for their shaky grasp of political realities. Muir now fully embraced a nationalist position regarding Scotland's past and future. The artisans of Scotland, he explained, inspired by the French example, had held a convention in 1792, not to be confused with the 1793 British Convention, which was 'a miserable plaything of the English government'. But the cause of liberty had advanced since then and any French invasion could expect the assistance of 'fifty thousand Scottish highlanders, and one hundred thousand Scottish patriots in all'.[14] Muir's nationalism had also acquired a competitive edge and he was anxious to dismiss the popular misconception in France that the English lower classes would welcome an invasion.[15]

Fifty thousand highlanders' were, in fact, eight times the number which had risen in the 1745 Rebellion. It was enough that such expansiveness threatened to discredit all refugee intelligence in French eyes, but soon more immediate problems with Muir's embassy became evident. Despite his intention to press Scotland's special case for aid, Muir also became entangled with the acrimonious affairs of the United Irishmen in Paris. Again, fraternity came off a poor second amid personal power struggles and the scramble to win French favour.

The advent of Napper Tandy from America in June 1797 had rapidly opened up divisions in the Irish colony. The ugly but charismatic Tandy paraded around the city, much as he had in Dublin, painting himself as 'un ancien militaire' and 'un très riche proprietaire', and challenging the horrified Wolfe Tone and Edward Lewins as sole United Irish agents in Paris.[16] It was to his camp that Muir gravitated during the course of 1798, symbolised by their joint hosting of a St Patrick's Day banquet. This would have been enough to rouse the enmity of Tone, but Muir also attempted to expound his own definition of 'fraternity' by claiming patriotic leadership of the Scottish and Irish peoples for himself. Drawing on his links with the Dublin Society in 1792 and 1793, which had done something to bring on his subsequent sufferings, he proclaimed: 'I am a United Irishman, I am a Scotsman. I can speak in the name of two nations . . .'.[17] Within weeks of his arrival he was already putting this commission into practice, intervening in the admission of new Irish refugees to France to the detriment of Tone's hard-won authority in this delicate area.[18]

Tone and an Irish deputation were forced to call on Muir to dissuade him from his ambitious advocacy, but following a discussion lasting almost three hours, he refused to give way, telling them pertly that he knew as much of their country as they did, and had as much confidence from the United Irishmen as they had. Communication was broken off.[19]

Tone's waspish diagnosis of Muir's situation was contained in his observation that, 'of all the vain, obstinate blockheads that ever I met I never saw his equal'. Personal considerations may indeed have encouraged the Scot's support for Tandy, believing he could be manipulated in a way Tone and Lewins certainly could not. Tone was less likely to admit that other Irish exiles such as Coigley, and the British radicals Watson and John Ashley were also drawn to the Tandy faction in the face of his own secrecy and lack of communication.[20]

There also seems a more poignant compulsion bringing together Muir and Tandy. This can be gleaned from their shared fondness for public posturing and high-profile propaganda, tactics which in the past had similarly bound Muir to Hamilton Rowan. Steeped in the politics of bombast and enthusiasm, both were fast becoming historical curiosities. Now, in 1798, the future of radicalism was not to be dictated by pronouncements in the *Moniteur*, but by the quiet, disciplined work of professional revolutionaries like Tone or William Putnam McCabe, and above all by the momentum of popular unrest and government reaction back in Ireland.

'ALL ONE PEOPLE ACTING FOR ONE COMMON CAUSE'

While the émigré community in Paris was fragmenting, democrats at home were pressing to reconstruct the revolutionary alliance across the three kingdoms. This differed in form and method from previous attempts. The year 1797 had seen the co-opting of remnants of grass-roots British radicalism through the spontaneous initiative of the Ulster committees, but the first two months of 1798 were dominated by frantic efforts by London and Dublin leaders to effect union at executive level. There had been shadowy references among Scottish radicals to a 'national' or 'secret committee' of seven members co-ordinating revolutionary work in 1797. The intention now was to make this a reality.[21] In this way, the component national strands of the democratic movement were to be bound under a cohesive vanguard and given a sense of direction previously lacking.

On his return from Paris *en route* for Ireland in early January, James

Coigley had already encountered this determination among London democrats. Here the United Britons, a militant outgrowth of the fading London Corresponding Society, had come together with United Irishmen in the capital to form a 'central committee', 'to draw together the Bond of Union with all country places and with Ireland, Scotland and America'.[22] Composed of representatives from England, Scotland, and Ireland, this 'congregated delegation' appointed Benjamin Binns and William Bailey to accompany Coigley back to Dublin. Both were to carry an Address from the London Corresponding Society to 'the Irish Nation', promising open political support and a fraternal greeting from the United Britons to the United Irishmen, to prepare the way for the co-ordination of further covert activity.[23]

Enthusiasm for the alliance was not only a British preserve. On the contrary, the major inspiration to forge the new executive union came from tensions and divisions within the United Irish Society. The bone of contention was still whether the Irish should risk an independent rising. Arguing the case in favour were O'Connor, Fitzgerald and Neilson, who drew their support mainly from lower-class radicals across a broad north–south spectrum. Opposing them and counselling delay until French assistance arrived were a 'more narrowly political group' of propertied Dublin figures, such as Thomas Emmet.[24] Ostensibly, January and February were months of renewed optimism, as the French ports seemed to swell with invasion preparations, but the lack of communication about their allies' precise intentions, and frustration over the deteriorating domestic situation, only sharpened these national leadership splits.

At one level these splits might be interpreted as early precursors of more modern tactical debates over the role of 'spontaneity' and 'organisation' in revolutionary situations: one party stressing the role of mass activity in effecting change, the other stressing the value of planning and direction from a central leadership cadre. What is more certain in the Ireland of the 1790s is that Emmet's position reflected a visceral fear, and unwillingness, to mobilise, in Pakenham's words, 'the primitive forces of the countryside in an ideological struggle'.[25] The desperate search for external assistance was preferable to placing the United Society's trust in their own countrymen, thus risking the destruction of property and the whole social order.[26]

The militants' desire for a reinvigorated British alliance was of a different nature. Their concern was principally to use developments on the mainland to force their case for an unassisted rising in Ireland in the Society's internal counsels. They were obviously alive to the strength that the diversionary implications of any British rising leant to their arguments, but they also drew more generally on the propaganda potential of external links. Their strategy operated on two levels. On the one hand, the United Britons Address was discussed privately at a full meeting of the Irish National Committee on 14 July at which provincial delegates were given copies to take back to their own members. These were well received in Ulster. At Shane's Castle, County Antrim, in February, the audience of the Ulster Provincial Committee was informed that 'even more flattering' than communications from France was the dispatch of three delegates from the United Britons to the National Committee, and that 'from this moment they were to consider England, Scotland and Ireland all one people acting for one common cause; they were legislators now chosen from the three kingdoms as an executive for the whole'. The Address itself was then circulated, with a strong nudge towards the militant position that 'this made it certain we should now obtain our liberty though the French never should come here'.[27] Similar scenes followed in the Armagh and Londonderry County Committees.[28]

Complementing the private communication of this deeply secret intelligence, the militants' propaganda weapon, *The Press*, also undertook a public campaign, using news of the British alliance to bolster popular morale. The Address from the London Corresponding Society was duly published with its stirring promise of solidarity against a common enemy:

> What are fifty, nay a thousand slaves,
> To the nerve of a single arm,
> That strikes for Liberty?[29]

By this time, Binns and Coigley had already returned separately to Britain, and during February the practical details of the Union were hammered out in London and transmitted to the provincial societies in Manchester and the north.[30] News of the Union in the form of an address composed by Thomas Crossfield, president of the London Corresponding Society, was to be carried to France on Coigley's next mission. Unfortunately for Coigley, he was to be accompanied by Arthur O'Connor, who had been attracting the authorities' attention since his arrival in London the previous December. O'Connor's concern for his enormous collection of luggage sat uneasily with his role as a confidential agent, and after a series of delays – while he tried to secure a suitable income for his stay in Paris – he, Coigley, Binn's brother John and two associates were arrested on 28 February at the King's Head Tavern in Margate, while attempting to secure a passage to France. As they awaited trial, a wave of arrests seized back the initiative for the government.[31] The London movement was easily broken by the taking of some twenty prisoners, brazenly meeting at their accustomed haunts on 18 and 19 April; swoops on Manchester, Leicester and Birmingham followed. By these determined measures the latest incarnation of the common radical cause was strangled at birth.

The Scottish dimension of the Bond of Union was implicit in the versions offered to the Irish for private and public consumption. *The Press*, for example, communicated tantalising developments in Scotland to its readers, but was handicapped by the lack of detailed intelligence.

> The United business in Scotland has increased to such a height as to attract the attention of the government in no small degree. The Highlands which hitherto had been the habitation of prejudice and oppression, have added numbers to the fraternity, to the great alarm of the Highland noblemen and chieftains. There is talk of the United Scotsmen being FORTY THOUSAND in number; from the extreme caution of the people however, there is no method of acquiring certain information, respecting their numbers, or anything else relative to them.[32]

The message of broadly organised disaffection was also repeated in the Address to the French, which was found in Coigley's pocket at Margate, and which was to prove enough to hang him: 'Already have the English fraternised with the Irish and Scots, and a delegate from each now sits with us. The sacred flame of liberty is rekindled, the holy obligation of brotherhood is received with enthusiasm . . . Disaffection prevails and a United Britain burns to break her chains'.[33]

Meanwhile, in his personal correspondence, Arthur O'Connor assured his brother that 'Scotland was Irish all over,' and that it was easy to learn that the people were looking for a change.[34]

Whether the Scots really were willing or able to be full participants in the revolutionary alliance was quite another matter. For even the authorities were well aware that there was 'much exaggeration' generally in the reports of the O'Connor party.[35] In the first place, London, rather than Scotland, was inevitably closer to the heart of the new insurrectionary strategy, as an attack on the nerve centre of government would have the greatest value as a diversionary device. Indeed, serious barriers of communication would have to be surmounted before the Scots could be genuinely integrated into any combined revolutionary effort. Links with Ulster were a great deal more feasible than with the British capital over 500 miles away overland; the United Scotsmen had already experienced difficulties in funding agents to travel any further south than Cumberland. It may be that the 'Scottish delegate' sitting in London was the elusive Angus Cameron, on the run from Scotland since 1797. Certainly, his evangelism among the Militia rioters in Strathtay and the north would explain the reports in *The Press* and elsewhere of Highland recruitment to the United cause.[36] In these circumstances the Scots were forced to rely on 'runners', such as the Ulsterman George Murdoch, who reached Scotland via Lancashire in April 1798, only to be cooly picked up and interrogated by the Scottish authorities.[37]

Murdoch's fate was symptomatic of further problems encountered by Scottish radicals in the face of increasingly well-informed and able government officers. The real work of dispersing the Societies had begun earlier than in England, with the premature arrest of Mealmaker and his associates in November 1797. Mealmaker was brought to trial in January, and his sentence of fourteen years' transportation provoked an admirable display of defiance.

> He was to be another victim to the Pursuit of a Parliamentary Reform; but he could easily submit and go to a distant country, where others had gone before him; he did not fear it. His wife and children would still be provided for . . . the young Mealmakers would be fed by that God who feeds the ravens.[38]

Nevertheless, this sentence acted as an unambiguous warning to less stout-hearted reformers, and the trial itself gave the government an excellent opportunity to display its knowledge of the organisation and function of their 'secret' societies.[39] Thanks to 'the daily disclosures of what is going forwards with the United Scotsmen', the Lord Advocate decided to take no chances with the convicted, and prescribed transportation from Scotland as soon as possible.[40] The English mass arrests of April were also replicated north of the border, with Glasgow, Cupar and Ayrshire targeted.[41] Among those arrested were Archibald Grey of Irvine and the Glasgow activists Coulston and Jarve, their examinations over the next few months providing yet more detail on the business and progress of the Union.

Besides these well-tried security measures, Scottish radicals also had to contend with their familiar problems in attracting mass support. O'Connor's 'FORTY THOUSAND' was less ridiculous than Thomas Muir's 'hundred thousand patriots', but was still woefully wide off the mark. Continuing invasion scares, with the prospect of a visit from Bonaparte and the *armée d'Angleterre*, maintained the momentum of popular patriotism. Although worries had been expressed over the effects of proposed pay cuts, the Volunteers continued to spearhead the recovery of loyalist self-confidence in January.[42] Glowing reports came in from formerly 'most democratical' counties, such as Renfrewshire, boasting the local corps' uniform spirit of loyalty and determination to 'defend their country against foreign invasion and to quell domestic insurrection'. They were accorded more credit for checking 'those dangerous principles of new-fashioned liberty, equality and democracy . . . than all the acts in parliament . . . and all the exertions of a watchful and wise administration'.[43]

It is a credit to their persistence that, even after these reversals in the first months of 1798, some cells in the old radical centres continued with political activity. In Dundee, attempts were made in February to subvert the local Volunteers.[44] In Glasgow, by early May plans, 'fresh imported from London', were being laid for reformers to form their own Volunteer Corps or infiltrate the city's existing First Corps, since no oath of admission was required, but these had soon to be given up since the prototype corps at Southwark had not been allowed to arm.[45] Instead, the Scots were forced to wait passively on the trials of O'Connor and Coigley, and the rest at Maidstone, which began on 21 May.[46] 'The internal plan of the country', reported the Glasgow spy Jameson, 'depends much on [these]. If the government are foiled, it will give the seditious a new resurrection, as after [the] trials of Hardy, Thelwell and all, they are waiting in awful suspense for the result.'[47] By the time the verdicts were eventually passed on 28 May, the fate of 'the Margate Five' was already being overtaken by more dramatic developments. The long-awaited rebellion in Ireland had at last broken out.[48]

'THE STORM INCREASES OVER POOR HIBERNIA'

The 1798 Rebellion was far from the controlled liberation struggle which enthusiasts had originally envisaged. For the nineteent-century historian Lecky, this was 'a scene of horrors, hardly surpassed in the modern history of Europe'.[49] Even through today's eyes, more accustomed to mass bloodletting, the '98 is still a ferocious and haunting episode, evidence of the deep-rootedness of sectarian conflict, which the United Irishmen had preferred to wish away.

The speed of Ireland's descent into rebellion was conditioned partly by news of the projected British alliance, but much more importantly by the interlocking effects of rumoured French assistance and of heightened government coercion. The United Irishmen were now forced to accept, as Tone had feared, that an Irish invasion would only be one dimension of a master strategy against the British Isles, but were willing to rationalise this as mysterious news reached the Dublin leadership that the French could be expected in April.[50] This was transmitted to the Ulster provincial committee in January by delegate Robert Hunter, who reasoned that 'the Directory would fit out a more formidable expedition in that they would invade the whole three kingdoms at once'.[51]

As similar information percolated through the subordinate layers of the movement the next month, the effect was a quickening of the pace of activity, with delegates drawn to constant meetings in Dublin.[52] Current membership returns still showed an impressive popular base of 279,894, on paper outnumbering government forces by four to one. Middle-class recruitment in the capital was reported to be thriving, while economic distress – following a hard winter – assisted the consolidation of mass membership in strongholds such as Meath and Kildare, and the extension of the system to Wicklow, Wexford and Carlow.[53] Even with these favourable indicators, the leadership were unwilling to move to an immediate rising. On the contrary, as French support now appeared almost tangible, this strengthened the hand of Emmet and the Dublin moderates, and orders for United men to reserve their keenness for an actual landing remained in force.

This strategy might have had some relevance if the French had arrived in time, and if the authorities had been negligent or ill-informed enough to permit United military preparations to continue. Both were equally unlikely. Although there was apparently a genuine commitment from the Directory to assist Ireland, the specific dates which had been floated in front of the Irish National Committee were more probably the work of O'Connorite standard bearers in Paris than a reflection of Barras and his colleagues' real intentions. Unaware of the gravity or the potential of the Irish situation, the weight of French military power was being switched by the late spring to the Egyptian campaign, while the resources of the *armée d'Angleterre* were spent on more immediately rewarding projects in continental Europe.[54] It is difficult to escape the suspicion that Muir and Tandy's 'puffing themselves for their private advantage' had done little to assist the radical cause in this respect.[55]

The British government's conduct over the next few months was conditioned in part by their comprehensive knowledge of United Irish intentions, most complete in spy-ridden Ulster. News of the movement's internal splits and the possibility of a rising without waiting on the French had reached Dublin Castle via Hamburg as early as November 1797.[56] From then, with the aid of informers – such as the barrister and playwright Leonard McNally, whose company Thomas Muir had found most congenial on his Dublin visit – they were able to follow each stage of United preparations. Coupled with news of invasion preparations at the four Channel ports, this intelligence pointed to the need for stiff military measures and a possible pre-emptive strike. The government were strengthened in this resolve by the imprecations of the Irish loyalist party. A wave of rural violence in the Midlands and south, which notably included the assassinations of active magistrates like Colonel St George in Queen's County, gave life to old fears that Catholics were organising to dispossess and exterminate the whole Protestant population.[57] The morale of the Protestant gentry cracked and reaction assumed the form of local terror campaigns by the Irish Militia and Yeomanry. The Army commander-in-chief Sir Ralph Abercromby made a last desperate attempt to restore military discipline and check such practices as torture and summary sentencing, but the efforts of this 'Scotch beast', as Lord Chancellor Clare damned him, created a public storm in Dublin and Westminster, resulting in his resignation in April.[58] The appointment of General Lake as his successor, whose 'frisky methods' had subdued Ulster the previous year, now made unlicensed military authority the keystone of the official solution to the Irish crisis. Pitt's government was forced to line up behind those very Ascendency politicians whose fanaticism and eager loyalty it had become accustomed to treat with well-bred distain.

The exposure of United Irish rank and file to repressive techniques, hardly imagined even in the Insurrection Act, contrasted sharply with the government's squeamishness over the fate of the national leadership. Given the shyness of informers like McNally concerning public testimony, a debate unfolded between Whitehall and Dublin Castle over whether known conspirators could be apprehended without being brought to trial. The balance was tipped in favour of a pre-emptive approach by the acquisition of a new agent in the Castle's stable: Thomas Reynolds, a United colonel and kinsman of Lord Edward Fitzgerald. On the morning of 12 March, as the Leinster Directory met at the house of Oliver Bond to vote yet again on the timing of the rising, a party of Dunbartonshire Fencibles moved in to take up Provincial delegates and members of the Supreme Directory in the net.[59] There were heroic attempts at evasion, with the Dublin delegate eating sensitive papers, but the most significant escapee was the latecomer Lord Edward. Leadership now devolved upon him and the militant party, by default rather than by reasoned debate.

The United Irishmen's strategic development over the next few months has begun to be re-evaluated in a more positive light than previously. To some extent, this distances the new leadership from the former charges of 'prevarication' and 'disintegration', and underlines the notable resilience and flexibility of the United organisation in the wake of the March arrests.[60] There was little doubt that the common insurrectionary alliance with English and Scottish radicals, beloved of O'Connorite enthusiasts, was a vanished prospect. Independent of the defects of their mainland brethren, the government swoop had disrupted the Dublin leadership's external and internal communication lines, compromising contact even with their own provincial supporters. But, while disappointing in political terms, diversionary risings had become less important from the strategic viewpoint. As government terror in Leinster increased, it became clear that an independent attempt without French aid must be made immediately to have any chance of success. This would require the maximum effort to be made around Dublin to paralyse the functioning of government by a single knock-out blow.[61] Fairly consistent plans along these lines were in place as early as March: four United divisions were to seize key locations like the Castle and Customs House, while the divisions in neighbouring counties were simultaneously to disperse government troops and march into the capital in support of the rising. When these targets were achieved, the United men in the rest of the country were to engage the enemy. The fact that United organisation in Dublin was not as fully developed as elsewhere gives some rationale to the continuing postponements of rebellion over the next ten weeks.[62]

The United Irishmen's difficulty then was not a want of planning. On the contrary, the customary internal splits were soon opening up over the precise direction of the proposed *coup*. These were debilitating, not only removing some key figures, such as the Sheares brothers, but also permitting them to embark on ill-judged freelance efforts.[63] Even more fateful was the further wave of arrests on 19 May which included Lord Edward, the most prestigious and militarily experienced United leader. The arrests could not stop the momentum of events, but when the rising was eventually proclaimed on 23 May, the co-ordination of events became impossible. In Kildare, Carlow and Wicklow, where there had already been two months of spasmodic civil war, the rebellion swiftly degenerated into chaos and slaughter.

The required rising in the metropolis did not materialise, largely through the effects of arms raids and faltering rank-and-file confidence. Instead, the rebels were to achieve their greatest successes in Wexford. This was one of the largest areas of Protestant plantation outside Ulster, and in the 1790s their descendants still held the most profitable agricultural land. The unstable balance of sectarian relations implied in this situation ensured that the county also witnessed some of the worst of the sectarian slaughter, emblematic of the '98 Rebellion.[64] Here too, the local insurgents' lack of weaponry and trained leadership was particularly telling.

Under the improvised but inspired leadership of a Roman Catholic curate, John Murphy, the rebels looted Volunteer arms depots, massacred a Protestant clergyman and several of his congregation, and beat off a combined force of Militia and Yeomanry at Oulart Hill. Gaining recruits by the hour, they attacked and captured Enniscorthy on 28 May. Two days later, another government force making for Wexford was defeated, and the rebel army, now twenty thousand strong, occupied the town.

The rebels showed little military or logistical refinement, and mass wave tactics were used repeatedly against entrenched positions. The pike was the main weapon, used to ferocious effect especially against cavalry, but when in short supply a desperate array of billhooks, scythes and pitchforks were pressed into service. The very savagery of the initial outbursts and the refusal of the rebels to behave according to military textbooks panicked inexperienced and irregular troops, precipitating a series of government retreats in late May. Inevitably, the lack of seasoned men told also on the insurgents. The initial victories encouraged them to push forwards, spreading the revolt to Munster, but their effort stalled after the failure to capture New Ross in County Kilkenny. As the leadership haggled over tactics, government forces were able to chose their own ground to meet any renewed threats.[65]

The rebel leaders' lack of experience was also reflected in a wave of murder, arson and looting, for the United army was as uncontrollable in victory as adversity. Indeed, the revolt in the south had turned largely into a sectarian war. Rumours of an Orange offensive, once exploited by the United Irishmen to increase membership, gained apparent confirmation through the violence of Orange-dominated Militia and Yeomanry regiments. The massacre of Protestant prisoners was the result, with some of the worst incidents taking place at Scullabogue, where a locked barn full of women and children was set alight; and at Wexford, where loyalists were hung and piked on the town's bridge. Such horrors were to be repaid in kind as Crown forces recovered their poise in the first weeks of June.

Their confidence was assisted by the realisation that the Irish Militia had not deserted as feared and by the fact that only five southern counties had actually risen. Also encouraging was the course of the rebellion in Ulster. Curtin points out that the delayed rising in the north brought at least 27,000 United men into the field, despite the reports of sectarian murder and destruction of property south of the border, and thus cannot be viewed as a failure of mass revolutionary zeal.[66] Instead, the major difficulty stemmed from a lack of leadership, as senior officers split, resigned or even turned informer, rather than hazard their carefully built organisation without French assistance or the fall of Dublin at the very least. Direction devolved upon Henry Joy McCracken, but for all his courage and ability he could not render the Ulster rising any more than partial. In place of the co-ordinated tactics originally prescribed, Antrim rose on 7 June, and by the time Down followed on the 9th, the United offensive was already collapsing. The government was thus able to go on the offensive immediately, after a rebel defeat at Ballynahinch – the revolt in Ulster, so long dreaded in official circles – was over in under a week.

From here, spurred on by now almost hysterical Ascendancy politicians, the army moved in force into rebel-held country in the south. The back of the insurgents' strength was broken at the rout of Vinegar Hill on 21 June. Those bands who regrouped were to be extinguished in the savage mopping-up operation, which proceeded during the rest of the summer.

There remained one lingering hope. In all their exertions, the rebels – both north and south – had been sustained by their belief in the imminent appearance of the French. This too proved in vain as the Directory was still unaware of the severity of their plight. Three small and belated expeditions eventually set out under the Generals Humbert, Hardy and, most ignominiously, Napper Tandy. Together and severally these were unlikely to snatch back a United victory.[67] Only Humbert's attempt in August landed troops in any force, but the destination of these 1,000 French regulars was Killala in Connacht, the only province unaffected by rebellion and where United Irish hopes were slimmest. A gifted general, he pushed south and defeated British troops at Castlebar, but was eventually surrounded and captured on 8 September. General Hardy's force, which included Wolfe Tone, was a similar 'postscript', and although more substantial was thoroughly demoralised and under-resourced. His ships were defeated and captured by the British fleet at Loch Swilly in October. Confident as always of his ability to raise the Irish people, Tandy's expedition consisted of a single gun-running corvette, the *Anacréon*. The object of the voyage was to land as many native leaders as possible to reactivate the rising. They landed at Donegal on 17 September, but stayed less than two hours on hearing of Humbert's defeat. Tandy recognised an old friend in the local postmaster, drowned his disappointments, and was carried back on board insensible.

This is the basic litany of events in the United Irishmen's Rebellion. Men like Samuel Neilson had used the previous seven years trying to construct a truly national, cross-sectarian movement in Ireland, whilst at the same time stretching out their organisational precepts to democrats in Scotland and England. In a few short weeks in the summer of 1798, their careful work of making 'United men' seemed spent. The course and outcome of the rising were to affect Ireland's political development profoundly, but its repercussions were experienced on a wider scale. The bitterness of failure was also to test the resolve of sympathisers across the North Channel.

IS SCOTLAND UP?

As the rising in Ulster was expiring, some United Irishmen, employed on the packet between Donaghadee and Portpatrick, spread reassuring whispers that 'the people in Scotland were as hostile to government as those in Ireland and were up in great numbers'.[68] In reality, Scottish involvement in the United Irishmen's insurrection assumed quite a different form.

Scots actively participated in the events of the summer of 1798, but rather than as radical brothers in arms, they served as members of His Majesty's forces charged with extinguishing all manifestations of rebellion. Scottish troops, and Highland Fencible regiments in particular, formed a disproportionate number of the 30,000 strong regular force stationed in Ireland on the eve of the Rebellion, totalling thirteen out of twenty regiments.[69] Subsequent reinforcements drew heavily on Scottish military reserves, with the embarkation of regiments such as the Royal Scots and the Sutherland Fencibles greeted by enthusiastic local crowds.[70] These units were also to figure prominently in the major engagements of the campaign: the Argyll Fencibles, for example, at the battle of Ballynahinch; the Midlothian Fencible Cavalry at New Ross and Wexford.[71]

The possibility that the Scots might lend weight in this capacity had long been foreseen and feared by Irish radicals, and possibly gave an edge to fanciful accounts of the Highland Host's conversion to the democratic cause. Scottish troops had already proved themselves formidable adversaries during the disarming of Ulster in 1796 and 1797, and, as one Belfast United Irishman told the informer Newell, there were only three they were dreading: 'a bad harvest, the exportation of victuals, and the importation of Scotch soldiers'.[72]

There were few instances of Scottish soldiers being persuaded to take the United Oath, and their loyalty and steadfastness was considered a commonplace.[73] In these circumstances, the presence of the Scots became a propaganda issue for the United Irishmen. O'Connor's *Press* had already sensed the betrayal it implied, invoking Culloden and the Butcher of Cumberland against 'these Scottish soldiers who had become the journeymen of *other butchers* in similar scenes perpetrated upon this hapless country'.[74] Removed from the immediate events of 1798, the sympathetic historian Madden was more conciliatory and politic. 'Of all the King's troops in Ireland during the Rebellion of 1798, the Scotch', he commented, 'invariably behaved with the most humanity towards the people.' He considered this fact 'well worth of the attention of those of my countrymen . . . who indulge in occasional sallies against Scotch settlers'.[75]

The truth was somewhere between the two. Where under tight and level-headed command, Scottish troops could behave commendably, strictly adhering to the rules of war over the treatment of prisoners and non-combatants. The Scottish officers engaged in the disarming of Kildare, for example, were 'most humane', not doing any more than is absolutely necessary from their orders.[76] Where good leadership was lacking, the Scots rivalled the worst excesses of the terrified Irish Militia and Yeomanry. Thus, in the aftermath of the rout of government forces at Castlebar, the depredations of Frazier's Highlanders 'raised a spirit of discent and disaffection which did not before exist in that part of the country'.[77] Even for those who did not participate in the excesses, there was little sympathy available for an enemy who used vicious and unorthodox tactics. A far more credible emotion was the triumphalism expressed in the 'anti-Croppie' song of the Midlothian Fencible Cavalry, placed at the start of this chapter.

The level of home-grown involvement may help explain the interest displayed generally by the Scottish in the unfolding of the Irish Rebellion. The coverage of Scottish newspapers represents an interesting portent of the place that the Scottish military tradition was to have in the country's popular culture.[78] Considerable pride was displayed in Scottish valour. Typically, the advent of the Dumfries Cavalry was felt to be 'a great acquisition to the country at this time, from the spirit and readiness they evince against the insurgents', encountering a party of rebels at Rathfarnam, they had already 'cut them down in very short time'.[79] Later, reviewing the campaign as a whole, the armchair strategists at the *Glasgow Courier* were quite assured of the fact that 'Scottish regiments . . . had distinguished themselves by their activity and spirit in crushing the Rebellion and repelling the invasion.'[80]

This response was in marked contrast to the picture painted by Pakenham for England, which had committed a much less significant number of troops to the emergency. Here, he suggests, the Rebellion made little impact on public life that summer, as 'for most Englishmen, Ireland remained a closed book, and its current disturbances were no more alarming than a rebellion in some distant part of Africa'.[81]

The geographical proximity of Scotland to the Irish unrest also had a galvanising effect on the Scottish authorities. Coupling this with the experience gained during the previous refugee influx to their shores in 1797, they considered that there was little room for a disengaged attitude, realising 'how tenty we ought to be this side of the water'.[82] The refugee crisis built up slowly. Ladies and bishops were the first to fly, but within weeks the exodus from Ireland became more general.[83] Since fighting was initially concentrated in the south-east, the south Wales ports and the Isle of Man became the first recipients of the fugitives. At Milford Haven, 1,500 had soon landed and the inhabitants were busy raising contributions for their relief.[84] The situation was transformed by the spread of the revolt to Ulster. At once, the short sea routes to Scotland were exploited, and 'peaceable inhabitants' of the northern counties began to escape in vast numbers.[85] By the second week in June, Campbeltown was fast filling with refugees from Antrim, while the more familiar reception point of Portpatrick was so crowded that there was no shelter left; one gentleman nevertheless reported that he had slept sounder on the floor there than he had for weeks past in his own country.[86]

The refugees were of all classes and descriptions. Most were of the 'lower orders', but the startled gentry were also included. One enterprising Scot had even taken the step of advertising desirable properties for sale in the *Dublin Evening Post* at the height of the crisis.[87] Despite a proclamation issued to prevent persons leaving Ireland without a passport, the all-consuming problem for the Scottish authorities remained how to separate the 'genuine' – in other words, 'loyalist' refugees – from those who had been involved in the planning and execution of the Rebellion.[88] Here class was of only limited use as a distinguishing variable, since distinguished citizens had been represented on both sides of the conflict. Indeed, the figure of the genteel fugitive with something to hide had become familiar enough to be portrayed in Galt's *Annals of the Parish* in 1821. The tactics of stopping and searching boats arriving at Portpatrick were again employed, but the screening process was not helped by the casual sale of passports at Donaghadee.[89] Given 'the circumstances of the times and the numbers landing in all directions', legal niceties were again neglected and swarms were sent back regardless of their situations. As the General in command of the operation well knew:

> Some of these might be forced to fly [*sic*] their country for protection, and were to be truly pitied, but many were of bad and of very suspicious characters, and I could not possibly tell the good from the bad. Being sent back to Ireland in safety, they were under the protection of the King's troop and would of course be treated according to their merits.[90]

All this failed to take account of those still landing unofficially along the coast. In a three-day period from 13 June, around seventy Irishmen who had landed in this clandestine manner were returned.[91] While a week later, the ever-vigilant Earl of Eglinton reported that a further nine suspects had been discovered on the Carrick shore and taken to Ayr by the Volunteers.[92] These were only palliative measures, for, as local officers in the south-west knew, 'many worthless characters [had] got into the little bays and creeks and escaped into the interior of several counties in the district'.[93]

Besides these obvious security concerns, wider Scottish interest in the Rebellion was also stimulated by the legacy of long-standing educational linkages. Leading figures in the events of 1798, like T. A. Emmet, W. S. Dickson, Thomas Ledlie Birch and James Porter, had been educated at Scottish universities and were doubtless known personally to many upstanding local citizens; consequently a vicarious fascination surrounded their fate. The arrest and court martial of Birch, for instance, who had obtained his MA from Glasgow University in 1772, caused a much greater stir in the Scottish press than the United Scotsmen's arrests in the spring.[94]

These embarrassing ex-students prompted their *Alma Matres* to behave with circumspection. The University of Edinburgh publicly announced its determination not to admit into its classes any students dismissed from Trinity College Dublin for having been members of treasonable societies, while they continued under sentence of expulsion.[95] Student clubs were also cautious, with Emmet's name being erased from the membership of the Speculative Society in Edinburgh in November 1798, on the grounds that he had, 'acknowledged himself as privy to carrying on a treasonable correspondence with France . . .'.[96] This, however, was also coupled with a proposal to sever connections with the Trinity College History Society, and the result, as Cockburn notes, was to throw the club into convulsions which introduced 'the whole politics of the day'.[97] The debate drew in older conservative members, like the future Lord Advocate Charles Hope, who tried to browbeat their younger Whiggish counterparts. After a season of agitation, almost resulting in a duel, the Dublin link was salvaged.

The controversy surrounding the Emmet episode helps highlight the complexity of Scottish attitudes to the Irish crisis. Unthinking condemnation was admittedly the position of the staunchest pro-government press, whose indignation at the outbreak had been heightened by their own over-confident predictions of Irish loyalty only a few months before. In November 1797, the *Courier* had happily informed readers that, 'for the honour of Ireland we think it will be seen . . . that the leaven of disaffection will disappear, wherever our gallant fellow subjects shall have an opportunity of engaging the common enemy'.[98] When, contrary to this forecast, tension in the southern counties increased in the spring, their coverage of Irish affairs became synonymous with the brief routine reporting of violent incidents, wrenched out of any social or historical context. Their treatment of the actual rising did not stray far from the official dispatches, and was injected with polite notes of optimism.[99] In essence the '98 was presented as 'A real Popish rebellion', and this image proved a most persistent one in Scotland.[100]

More measured was the approach of the *Glasgow Advertiser*, which had enjoyed radical pretensions in the 1790s. Now chastened, it still aspired to a thoughtful and 'enlightened' audience.[101] Its reporting in the early part of the year was at first unusual for its attempts to understand the developing crisis, and in its unwillingness to accept the Irish authorities' version of events. It believed that 'the hideous system of Marat' had been forced on the 'innocent and unresisting Irish peasant', but credited official brutality and unscrupulous informers with a large portion of the country's distress.[102] Challenging Lord Clare's view that army outrages were not ascribable to government, the *Advertiser* commented indignantly that 'If government had not planned, authorised and directed those terrible proceedings, how in God's name can it account for or reconcile its supineness, indifference or insensibility.'[103]

In his crude sociological diagnosis of Ireland's ills, its correspondent also expounded the views of the 'moderate', caught between two 'extremist' camps.

> the system of terror prevails on both sides; and to the middle is to have one's loyalty wickedly and artfully misrepresented . . . The tie which unites landlord and his tenant in many places is broken. The great and deplorable calamity of this system is that society is broken down; and the mild persuasion of the honest and independent man is lost to the wholesome operation of unbiased justice.

There were three main evils: military attacks were not dissipating, but antagonising the peasantry; the non-payment of rents was acting as an 'engine of social dissolution'; and the declining state of cultivation of the land would have grave economic consequences. 'Abuses were present also in the polity in the form of placemen and pensioners', and 'in the sufferings of the multitude through exemplary punishment, that sent the leaders away untried'.[104]

The judicious tone contained here was to shift as open rebellion broke out, and as violence spread and intensified. Coverage began to revolve around 'the dreadful list of murder', and became as routinised and staccato as the mainstream loyalist newspapers. Now 'the savages of the West' were condemned, along with 'the murderous machinations of those depraved and cruel wretches who disgrace the Irish character'.[105] The slaughter at New Ross and Wexford and the burnings at Scullabogue were related in horrifying detail, and a new, impending massacre of Protestants in Dublin credulously sketched. Here Roman Catholic children were to be distinguished by a red ribbon round their wrists, and even Catholic women were to be involved in the killing of Protestant women and innocent children.[106] The government were urged on in the prompt execution of whatever measures they thought necessary to 'check the rebellion's progress and the dreadful effusion of human blood'.[107]

It was not until the arrival of Lord Cornwallis as viceroy and commander-in-chief in June, that some of the paper's liberal footing was recovered. Feeling comfortable with his mixture of firm measures and selective conciliation, blessings were poured on the head of this man through whose agency 'Ireland had ceased to be a Golgotha, and her people rescued from the poignard of the assassin'. His victory over Humbert was duly celebrated:

> Then drink to Cornwallis and brave General Lake,
> Long may they make discord and anarchy shake,
> Till firmly established, still more to increase,
> Hibernian Olive may blossom in peace.[108]

If the *Advertiser*'s difficulties are suggestive of the liberal dilemma when confronted by the Rebellion in Ireland, what finally of committed political radicals grouped around the United Scotsmen? Clearly the determination of some democrats was strengthened by an attempt which, for all its shortcomings, had brought thousands more men into the field than could ever be realistically hoped for in Scotland, and which in the process had thoroughly terrified the British and Irish authorities. In June, sympathisers in Glasgow tried to persuade troops not to leave for Ulster by thrusting 'very seditious papers' under the barracks gate, and succeeded in spreading 'worrying misrepresentations'.[109] Meanwhile in Ayrshire, suspected Irishmen in the Volunteer Corps fired on the troops who had previously escorted their fugitive countrymen from the Carrick coast.[110] Others, like the weavers David Black and James Paterson, were less active in their defiance, but vindicated the Rebellion by representing 'the Irish insurgents as people groaning under oppression, and struggling in defence of their just rights'.[111]

These few cases form the limit of our knowledge, but this is probably significant in itself. For all the rebels' reckless bravery, the Rebellion was a massive defeat. It is likely this simple fact damaged the United Scotsmen's morale and credibility as much as the spring round-up of activists.[112] The movement was already sorely pressed by government surveillance and by the consciousness of their own weakness. Now, the Irish Rebellion brought home to them what could be the result once 'Revolution' moved from the idealised abstract to the concrete. One lesson was the failure of the French to provide more than token military assistance, but even more sobering was the savagery of the conflict and the spectre of sectarian murder, almost inconceivable after the messages of universal brotherhood emanating from Ireland over the past seven years.[113]

It is possible that the Rebellion claimed a final victim. Napper Tandy's departure on his mission to liberate Ireland had left Thomas Muir in sole command at the United Irish club in Paris. Although this now attracted a new wave of refugees, the French were losing their trust in the émigré community as a valuable conduit for intelligence.[114] Once more left behind by events, and with hopes of French aid to his own country fading fast, Muir moved out to Chantilly.[115] There he died and was buried in January 1799.

The *Advertiser*'s vision of a society 'broken down' during the course of the '98 Rebellion was an unconsciously accurate analysis of the crisis in the social order which climaxed in Ireland that summer. It was true that this was a crisis within definite limits: the largely Catholic Militia, raised at the cost of widespread violence only a few years before, did not desert *en masse*; and after a few weeks the victorious authorities felt able to countermand Ascendancy die-hards and couple military coercion with more creative measures to diffuse unrest. Yet, there is little doubt that the gulf between Irish and Scottish experience, which had been increasingly evident from the middle of the decade, was now complete. Scotland lacked the corrosive bitterness of social relations which had caused the Wexford explosion, and its landed gentry, despite the Lord Advocate's fears during the Militia riots, were still distinguished by their poise and cohesion. The question of why Scotland did not rise is easily answered. If the United Scotsmen had made such an attempt, they would have been crushed with ease.

The United Irish Society outlived its Rebellion, but the effects of failure were profound. Most of the leading cadre were either dead or imprisoned; Wolfe Tone, Muir's old adversary, had cut his own throat after his request for a soldier's death by the firing squad had been refused him. Among the new generation of leaders, the debilitating wrangling over the timing of another rising ceased since a French invasion now seemed indispensable for success. Yet, although popular disaffection persisted, the unique moment in which this had been joined to the exigencies of French military strategy had passed and with it the United Irishmen's best chance of success.

These developments were paralleled in Scotland, where the dependence on external support had been an even greater factor in radical calculations. Scottish ranks had become thinner, but a leaven of determined revolutionaries remained to pursue the physical force option, however unpromising the opportunities over the next few years. In this they were to be assisted by the latest wave of migration from Ireland. Yet, the contribution of these new arrivals was also to be circumscribed by the experience of rebellion. For the Scottish authorities, the Irish had assumed the status of a security problem, whose activities were to be closely monitored, while in the popular mind the atrocities of the '98, related so faithfully by the Scottish press, promoted the identification of Irish ethnicity with 'violence' and 'treachery'. The conduct of some fugitives in Scotland did little to dispel this negative ideological climate.

NOTES

1. Rebellion Papers, 620/35/139 (NAI).
2. Marquess of Midlothian's notebook, MS 5750 (NLS).
3. *Moniteur*, 12 Frimair an VI [2 December 1797].
4. *Edinburgh Advertiser*, 30 May–6 June 1797.
5. *The Press*, 16 December 1797.
6. It was actually dramatised by Ronald Mavor in the play *Muir of Hunters-hill* (1963).
7. Mackenzie's account is unreliable here, *Life of Thomas Muir*; more useful is Bewley, *Thomas Muir of Huntershill* which draws on unpublished Spanish sources.
8. In his memorandum to the Spanish Viceroy Branciforte in July 1796, he wrote of three million Irish Catholics, turning their eyes to the Friends of the People Convention in Scotland and transmitting 'a solemn and pathetic address'. William Drennan would not have appreciated this interpretation of events. Pratt Insh Papers, Dep. 344 (NLS).
9. Arch. Aff. Etr. Corr. Pol. Espagne 649 ff. 405–6, Delacroix to Directory, 10 July 1797, Pratt Insh Papers, Dep. 344 (NLS).
10. Secret intelligence sent to the British government, January 1798, *Dropmore* MS, iv, 69, 70 (British Library). Other famous names from the early 1790s, Lord Lauderdale and Colonel Macleod MP were also included, as was the United Scotsman Angus Cameron.
11. AAE Corr. Pol. Angl. 592 f. 220. For Watson's memoranda to the French from September 1798 to October 1800: AAE Corr. Pol. Angl. 592 f. 220, 593 ff. 18, 532–7; AN GG¹ 72 ff. 114–15. See also Thompson, *Making of the English Working Class*, p. 190.
12. Meikle, 'Two Glasgow Merchants in the French Revolution', pp. 149–58. Again, indicative of the cohesive social world of the eighteenth-century gentleman was the fact that one of the brothers had attended Glasgow University with Muir. The Swords' case is discussed extensively in RH 2/4/8 ff. 240–95 (SRO).
13. Almost immediately, Muir had intimated that he had few wants, but he required 'lodging not unworthy of my former status and which is not capable of inviting the wretched criticism that patriots have no standing in France', Muir to Delacroix, 29 December 1797, AAE Corr. Pol. Angl. 592 f. 144. Later, he requested a *Domaine National* to the value of 15,000 F. to free him from further claims on the Directory's humanity, AAE Corr. Pol. Angl. 590 ff. 321–2.
14. AAE Mémoires et Documents (Angl.) II ff. 153–72.
15. Mémoire de Muir sur l'État d'Angleterre, AAE Corr. Pol. Angl. 592 f. 161.
16. Tone, *Life of Theobald Wolfe Tone*, vol. ii, p. 462.
17. *Moniteur*, 15 Nivose An VI [4 January 1798].
18. *Glasgow Advertiser*, 26 February 1798. Some Irishmen landed at Bordeux were freed on Muir's recommendations and enjoyed the best of treatment.
19. Tone, *Life of Theobald Wolfe Tone*, vol. ii, p. 463.
20. Elliott, *Partners in Revolution*, pp. 170–1.
21. The earlier 'national' committee had been mentioned by witnesses at Mealmaker's trial, Howell and Howell, *State Trials*, xxvi, cols 1136, 1147.
22. B. Binns Responses, MS 873/451 (TCD); Rebellion Papers, 620/18A/14 (NAI).
23. *House of Commons Committee of Secrecy Report* (1799), app. IX, pp. 58–60 for L. C. S. Address; app. VIII, pp. 56–8 for United British.
24. Cullen, 'The Internal Politics of the United Irishmen', pp. 194–5.
25. Pakenham, *The Year of Liberty*, p. 91; Emmet himself was the first to admit this: MacNeven, *Pieces of Irish History*, p. 33.

26. Elliott, *Partners in Revolution*, p. 176.
27. *Secrecy Report [Ireland]*, 1798, app. XIV, pp. 146–7.
28. L. McNally to E. Cooke, 25 February 1798, HO 100/75 ff. 130–2 (PRO); *Secrecy Report [Ireland]*, 1798, app. VI, pp. 77–8.
29. *The Press*, 23 January 1798.
30. Wells, *Insurrection*, pp. 129–30.
31. See reports in *Glasgow Advertiser*, 5 March 1798 and *Edinburgh Advertiser*, 6 March 1798.
32. *The Press*, 3 February 1798.
33. PC 1/42A.143 (PRO); B. Binns to R. Madden, 24 May 1843, Madden MS (TCD).
34. Rebellion Papers, 620/35/139 (NAI).
35. *House of Commons Committee of Secrecy Report* (1799), p. 21.
36. Meikle, *Scotland and the French Revolution*, pp. 191–2n.
37. R. Dundas to J. King, 18 April 1798, RH 2/4/83 f. 170 (SRO).
38. *Glasgow Advertiser*, 13 January 1798; the trial was also followed in *The Press*, 23 January 1798.
39. Howell and Howell, *State Trials*, xxvi, cols 1135–64.
40. R. Dundas to J. King, 13 February 1798, RH 2/4/83 ff. 165–6 (SRO).
41. *Glasgow Advertiser*, 16 April 1798; *Glasgow Courier*, 14 April 1798.
42. R. Dundas to J. King, 10 February 1798, RH 2/4/83 ff. 126–9 (SRO).
43. W. McDowell to R. Dundas, 26 January 1798, RH 2/4/83 f. 98 (SRO)
44. R. Dundas to Duke of Portland, 10 February 1798, RH 2/4/84 ff. 126–7 (SRO).
45. Jameson's intelligence, RH 2/4/84 ff. 218, 226 (SRO).
46. *Glasgow Advertiser*, 23 April and 25 May 1798; *Glasgow Courier*, 17 April and 21 May 1798.
47. Jameson's intelligence, RH 2/4/84 f. 226 (SRO)
48. Although there was enough secret evidence to convict the five accused, the government's sources were too valuable to reveal in open court. O'Connor had the advantage of Erskine as his council; and Fox, Sheridan and Gray as character witnesses. He was acquitted, but immediately rearrested and dispatched to Ireland to face charges there. Found with the incriminating French Address on his person, Coigley was less fortunate, and was convicted of high treason. He was hanged on 7 June.
49. Lecky, *A History of Ireland*, vol. 4, p. 265.
50. Earl of Camden to Duke of Portland, 16 January 1798, HO 100/75/32–3 (PRO).
51. Meeting of the Provincial Committee at Armagh, 14 January 1798, McClelland MS MIC. 507 (PRONI). The news would have been particularly welcome to Hunter, a moderate who was unwilling to risk the carefully constructed United organisation in Ulster in a premature rising. Meanwhile in Paris, Lewins was also prepared to make the best of things, assuring Director Barras that the formation of a coastal army under Bonaparte's command would 'greatly encourage the many English and Scottish republicans', as well as guaranteeing Barras's promise of assistance to the Irish Executive Committee, McPeake Papers, T. 3048/G/6 (PRONI).
52. Earl of Camden to Duke of Portland, 26 February 1798, HO 100/75/128–34 (PRO).
53. Ibid.: McNally's Enclosure, 20 February 1798.
54. Elliott, *Partners in Revolution*, p. 214.
55. Tone, *Life of Theobald Wolfe Tone*, vol. ii, pp. 462–3.
56. Earl of Camden to Duke of Portland, 6 January 1798, HO 100/75/6 (PRO).
57. *Glasgow Courier*, 19 February 1798; *Glasgow Advertiser*, 20–3 February 1798.
58. Pakenham, *The Year of Liberty*, pp. 150–6. For some outside the charmed

circle of the Dublin Ascendancy, Abercromby's treatment was outrageous. See, for example, J. Hewitt to W. Fawcett, Melville MSS GD 51/1/327 ff.1–8, (SRO). Hewitt, a government supporter in Ulster, was furious over Abercromby's savaging by 'that Puppy' John Foster in the Irish House of Commons.

59. *Glasgow Courier*, 22 March 1798. Other leaders such as Emmet and MacNeven were arrested in a simultaneous operation. The total haul was 16 senior men, *Dublin Evening Post*, 13 and 15 March 1798.

60. The most compelling narrative of the 1798 Rebellion is still Pakenham's *Year of Liberty*, but for recent reinterpretations of United strategy on the eve of rebellion, see Graham, 'An Union of Power', pp. 244–54, and Curtin, 'The United Irish Organisation in Ulster', pp. 209–221.

61. Graham, 'An Union of Power', pp. 250–1.

62. The new executive was actively involved in these preparations. This included Samuel Neilson whom Pakenham dismisses as a harmless drunk. Neilson was reported to have traversed Ulster and Munster early in 1798 rallying support: ibid., p. 252.

63. Cullen, 'The Internal Politics of the United Irishmen', p. 195. Neilson and Fitzgerald supported a *coup* based on the United Irishmen's own resources, the Sheares brothers relied on the Militia declaring for the rebellion.

64. Furlong, *Father John Murphy*. Wexford had also been a major flashpoint during the 1793 Militia riots: 18 people were shot in a single incident, p. 18.

65. Ibid., p. 106.

66. Curtin, 'The United Irish Organisation in Ulster', pp. 218–19. For the classic account, see Dickson, *Revolt in Antrim and Down*; also McSkimmin, *Annals of Ulster*.

67. Elliott, *Partners in Revolution*, pp. 214–40.

68. R. Carmichael to R. Dundas, 31 June 1798, Laing MSS II 500 (University of Edinburgh).

69. *Glasgow Advertiser*, 15 January 1798. These were the Aberdeen Fencibles, the First and Second Battalions, the Breadalbane Fencibles, the Reay Fencibles, the Loyal Tay Fencibles, the Second Battalion, the Argyllshire Fencibles, the Caithness Legion, Frazier's Fencibles, Lord Elgin's Fifeshire Fencibles, the Inverness Highlanders, the North Lowland Regiment, the Perthshire Fencibles, the Ross-shire and Caithness Fencibles, and the Dunbartonshire Fencibles.

70. *Glasgow Courier*, 14 and 21 June 1798.

71. General Nugent to General Lake, 13 June 1798, Rebellion Papers, 620/38/129 (NAI); Marquess of Midlothian's notebook, MS 5750 (NLS).

72. Frazier MSS II/24 (NAI).

73. Four Breadalbane Fencibles were found guilty of taking the Oath and were sentenced to serve abroad in the 60th Regiment: *Glasgow Advertiser*, 13 July 1798. In contrast, the men of the Tay Fencibles spontaneously agreed to subscribe a portion of their pay to the War Fund: *Glasgow Courier*, 29 March 1798.

74. *The Press*, 18 November 1798.

75. Madden, *United Irishmen*, ser. 3, vol. iii, p. 283n.

76. T. Moore, *The Life and Death of Lord Edward Fitzgerald*, vol ii, p. 95.

77. J. Taylor to Lord Castlereagh, 31 August 1798, Cornwallis Correspondence II, p. 396 (PRO).

78. On this theme, see Wood, 'Protestantism and the Scottish Military Tradition', pp. 112–36.

79. *Glasgow Advertiser*, 14 June and 16 July 1798.

80. *Glasgow Courier*, 30 October 1798.

81. Pakenham, *Year of Liberty*, pp. 233–4.

82. J. Carmichael to R. Dundas, 29 November 1798, Laing MSS 666–7 (University of Edinburgh).

83. E. Cooke to W. Wickham, 12 June 1798, HO 100/81/61 (PRO).

84. *Edinburgh Advertiser*, 15–19 June 1798; Handcock, 'Reminiscences of a Fugitive Loyalist', EHR (1886), pp. 536–44.

85. *Glasgow Courier*, 14 June 1798.

86. *Edinburgh Advertiser*, 12–16 June 1798; J. Carmichael to R. Dundas, 29 November 1798, Laing MSS 666–7 (Edinburgh Univ.).

87. *Dublin Evening Post*, 14 June 1798. The Irish correspondent of the *Glasgow Advertiser* explained their state of mind over the past months. 'There was not a man fitted for civilised society who did not meditate on emigration, and who did not intent to seek in another climate, that peace and security, which there was not a prospect of Ireland affording them for many many years': *Dublin Evening Post*, 16 August 1798.

88. *Dublin Evening Post*, 26 May 1798.

89. J. Carmichael to General Lake, 21 June 1798, Rebellion Papers, 620/38/203 (NAI).

90. General Drummond to R. Dundas, 26 June 1798, Laing MSS 500–1 (University of Edinburgh). Some of those sent back were later hanged.

91. J. Carmichael to General Lake, 21 June 1798, Rebellion Papers, 620/38/203 (NAI).

92. Earl of Eglinton to R. Dundas, 20 June 1798, Melville MSS 51/5/29 f. 38 (SRO); *Glasgow Advertiser*, 22 June 1798.

93. General Drummond to R. Dundas, 26 June 1798, Laing MSS 500–1 (University of Edinburgh).

94. *Glasgow Advertiser*, 29 June 1798; see also *Glasgow Courier*, 16 June 1798 for the sensational sentence of hanging on Dickson.

95. *Edinburgh Advertiser*, 26–9 June 1798.

96. *History of the Speculative Society*, p. 8.

97. Cockburn, *Memorials*, p. 67.

98. *Glasgow Courier*, 25 November 1797.

99. For example, see *Glasgow Courier*, 29 March and 29 May 1798 on developments in Carlow and Dublin. The illumination of Belfast was seen as a testament to Ulster's loyalty, the Antrim rising began the next day: *Glasgow Courier*, 7 June 1798.

100. W. S. Dickson, *The Narrative of the Confinement*, p. 115–6, for Dickson's attempts to persuade a Scotsman otherwise.

101. The arrest of Arthur O'Connor had resulted in a sympathetic biographical sketch. He was a man who 'always kept the best company in Ireland': *Glasgow Advertiser*, 16 March 1798.

102. *Glasgow Advertiser*, 22 January and 12 February 1798. Spies it believed were evidence of 'that vindictive spirit which like jealousy makes the meat it feeds on'.

103. *Glasgow Advertiser*, 19 February 1798.

104. Ibid., 20 April 1798.

105. Ibid., 19–23 April 1798 for disturbances in Queen's County and Rathmines.

106. Ibid., 8 and 11 June 1798.

107. Ibid., 6 June 1798.

108. Ibid., 15 October 1798.

109. R.Dundas to Duke of Portland, 24 June 1798, RH 2/4/83 ff. 366–7 (SRO).

110. Earl of Eglinton to H. Dundas, 20 June 1798, Melville MSS GD 51/5/29 f. 38 (SRO). While the original capture of the fugitives was reported in the papers, this incident was not.

111. Howell and Howell, *State Trials*, vol. xxvi, col. 1183. This vindication formed an important part of the indictments for sedition made against these men in September 1798. Paterson was fugitated, Black sentenced to five years transportation.

112. Brims, 'The Scottish Democratic Movement', vol. 2, p. 573.
113. Most of the rebels' victims were Episcopalians, but common Protestant-ism was likely to outweigh this. The strength of Scotland's own commit-ment to the Reformed Faith, which also permeated the democratic movement, can be reckoned from reaction to Bonaparte's deposition of the Pope in April 1798. The *Glasgow Advertiser* offered an appropriate elegy:

> Look up John Knox frae 'mang the deid,
> Look up and shake your auld grey heid,
> Behaud the whore of Babylon,
> Fled frae mighty Rome

114. Elliott, *Partners in Revolution*, p. 239.
115. Bewley, *Thomas Muir of Huntershill*, p. 182.

8

Diaspora
1799–1806

I am a Paddy and a Croppy too and wish to God the Croppies
would do in Scotland, what they have done in Ireland.
                                    Theophilus McAllister, March 1799[1]

Theophilus McAllister had left his native Ireland in February 1796.
Three years later, he was apprehended in Irvine by the Scottish authorities
after a tavern brawl. His seditious talk in front of two Fencible soldiers
had prompted one of them to draw his bayonet, saying he would put it
through McAllister if they were in Ireland. This incident, trivial in itself,
indicates the extreme polarisation of popular political opinion at the
beginning of the new century, with McAllister's defiant outburst standing
as an eloquent statement of the bitterness and frustrations of those
whose radicalism had survived the '98 Rebellion.

The confused state of the remnants of radical organisation in Ireland
and on the mainland was also reflected in the latest production of the
House of Commons Secrecy Committee in 1801, with its quest for a
mythical 'British executive'.[2] In Scotland too, the new Lord Advocate
Charles Hope admitted that although the local Societies' numbers were
not formidable, their secrecy certainly was, and for all the efforts of his
spies who attended their meetings he could never penetrate their executive
committee which he knew sat in Glasgow.[3] The obscure and partial
nature of the available evidence still presents enormous methodological
difficulties today. This is particularly the case in trying to estimate the
influence of the 'Irish disaffected' in Scotland. Official links between the
two movements were now quite overshadowed by the efforts of individual
enthusiasts, drawing strength from the ever-swelling Irish migration flow.
Contact thus became more sporadic and haphazard in the new century.
This informal process was doubly distorting. On the one hand, new

arrivals, with an active United background, were generally more cautious and temperate than McAllister, and hardly likely to boast their impeccable insurrectionary credentials in the face of a rising spirit of loyalism. This is an understandable tendency which may understate their actual involvement in subsequent political agitation in Scotland. Conversely, the Scottish administration tended to exaggerate the threat posed by this ethnic group by consistently failing to distinguish between the diverse political and confessional allegiances of Irish migrants. Instead, they preferred to treat all Irishmen as 'Croppies' by definition, and as such immediately suspicious and threatening to the public peace.

In these difficult conditions, E. P. Thompson's modest aim to 'reconstruct what we can' is very appropriate.[4]

THOSE WHO CAME

Sociologists of international migration have recently come to emphasise the 'conjunctural fluidity' implicit in the categories of political refugee and economic migrant.[5] Early nineteenth-century observers of the latest wave of Irish settlement in Scotland were equally alive to the intertwining of political and economic motivations for population movement. In many areas of the south-west, post-Rebellion arrivals joined the 'considerable immigration of Irish poor', which had been in motion from the 1780s. In Ayr, Kilmarnock and Renfrewshire, local ministers and manufacturers were in agreement that the '98 had given a powerful impetus to in-migration, which was perceived to have become constant from around 1800.[6]

Clearly, the new dawn promised by the attempts of Viceroy Cornwallis to forge 'an alliance between the government of the country and the affections of the people' had failed to materialise.[7] By January 1799, the Scottish newspapers were citing numberless accounts of robberies and murders culled from their Dublin and Belfast counterparts.[8] In the countryside that year, rent rises accompanied a slump in employment, snow fell in the late spring and after a wet summer the harvest failed. Emigration to the mainland was the predictable response, rising soon to an average of 50,000 a year.[9]

At the same time, there was also widespread recognition that the unsettled state of their own country contrasted with widening employment opportunities across the North Channel. This situation reflected both the prosperous state of Scottish manufactures and the impulse to agricultural improvement offered by high grain prices. The classic logic of 'push and pull' after 1798 was powerfully expressed by the cotton spinner Peter Ewart in his evidence to the Parliamentary Committee on the Irish Poor.

Many persons who had been implicated in the events of that unhappy period were naturally ready to seek an asylum in parts of England and Scotland, where they were not known and where they could, as it were, begin a new life. It happened likewise that the Rebellion was also coincident with the first attempts to introduce the spinning of cotton by power in the West of Scotland; and there existed among the native working classes of that country a strong objection to factory labour so that the master spinners of Paisley and Glasgow were glad to employ the Irish as being the only persons who would work with them; there were, likewise, many plain weavers . . . who having been brought up to linen weaving in their own country, easily turned their hands to another branch of the same trade.[10]

For those with an active involvement in the Rebellion, the extra-legal attentions of the soldiery and magistrates offered an additional pressing reason to leave Ireland. McDowell suggests that the results of judicial repression through the ordinary courts from mid-1798 to the end of 1799 reflected 'a policy of measured severity', but this has to be taken with General Lake's candid admission that his troops' determination to destroy everyone they considered a rebel 'to be beyond description and wanting correction'.[11] Elsewhere it has been suggested that casualties during the Rebellion and its aftermath numbered some 30,000 as a best estimate, of which probably fewer than 4,000 were government troops or loyalists.[12]

Scotland was not an automatic choice for refugees. America, for so long 'the Lamp of Liberty' to middle-class United Irish leaders, appeared a more congenial place of asylum, lying beyond the bounds of British jurisdiction. Unfortunately, self-exile was expensive, with the costs of settling a family of four reaching perhaps fifty guineas.[13] Nor were the American authorities enthusiastic over this troublesome cargo, for, as Rufus King – the American Minister in London – commented, he could not persuade himself that 'the malcontents of any country will ever become useful citizens of our own'.[14]

France also beckoned the ideologically committed, after years of assurances that the relief of patriot exiles would be treated as a moral obligation. *Émigrés* from the lower classes, including artisans and small farmers, now followed in the wake of Wolfe Tone and Arthur O'Connor. In practice, their welcome was not always enthusiastic, as the French authorities and the remaining United Irish representatives struggled to construct an *ad hoc* refugee policy.[15] Automatic entry could no longer be guaranteed, and the pensions eventually given to successful applicants in January 1800 abruptly ceased during peace negotiations with the British eighteen months later.

It was Scotland, however, which remained the obvious reversible destination for those whose speedy exit was imperative. Its appeal was to
men like James Agnew Farrel, the Larne United leader, whose nerve had
failed at the last moment, and who remained concealed until affairs
calmed down and he was able to return now under a general amnesty.[16]
More commonly, Scotland represented the poor man's best option for
permanent settlement. The costs of the necessary documentation and
conveyance between the two countries remained open to opportunistic
abuse, but even so Scottish exile remained cheap, and particularly attractive
when the chance of forging 'new lives', as Ewart had grasped, was taken
into consideration.[17]

This is not to infer that all Irish migrants arriving at Portpatrick and
the western ports were ex-rebels. Economic distress, social dislocation
and political instability could affect rebel and loyalist alike. It is also
possible that many of those with past United links felt comfortable as
simple 'economic migrants', and were less than willing to resume revolutionary careers in their new environment. Indeed, in Ireland it was
becoming apparent that 'loyalty' was becoming something of a movable
feast.

Although the subtleties and complexities were to be lost on the Scottish
authorities, the political allegiances of the Ulster Presbyterian population
were on the brink of a historic realignment. More acute Irish commentators were already aware of this by 1799, noting that the term 'United
Irishmen' was losing its popular currency in Ulster, as sectarian boundaries
assumed an increasingly fixed quality. As a revived Defenderism began
to capture Catholic disaffection, there was a consequent increase in the
ranks of the Orange Institution. Orangeism was of course Ireland's own
pugnacious vehicle for popular loyalism. This zealous and apparently
uncontrollable plebeian movement, with its stress on conditional loyalty
for 'the King and his heirs, as long as he or they support the Protestant
ascendancy', was initially viewed with deep distrust by the authorities
until the Orangemen's military service during the 1798 Rebellion.[18] By
June of the next year, Chief Secretary Castlereagh was commenting
approvingly that 'the Protestant dissenters in Ulster have in a g[rea]t
degree withdrawn themselves from the Union, and become Orangemen
. . . the Province of Ulster comprises at this moment a numerous body of
determined Loyalists'.[19] In some areas this process had been underway
for at least two years, the most striking fact about 'this astonishing
increase of Orangemen' for one observer being that 'immense numbers
of them are in Belfast'.[20] Significantly, the Orangemen were themselves
aware of the dangers inherent in their rapid growth and worried that
this might conceal infiltration from those of a dubious political past.

With this in mind, local lodges evolved an esoteric system of 'higher degrees' to delimit the new recruit's involvement until he had established his loyalist credentials.[21]

It was no coincidence that the transplantation of Orangeism into Scotland was also bound up with the post-Rebellion migration wave. The first lodge was established at Maybole in 1799, possibly by a company of the Ayrshire and Wigtownshire Militia returning from service in Ireland.[22] The subsequent diffusion of the Order through the west of Scotland would have been impossible, however, without the contribution made by Protestant Irish settlers. Maybole, a booming weaving centre, had been a popular destination for this group since the early 1790s. The same is true of Thornliebank and Pollokshaws, originally radical strongholds, but also centres of Orange activity by the 1820s. In the wake of the '98, it is even possible that the framework of lodges provided a familiar social and cultural reference point, not only for loyalists of long standing, but also, as in Ireland, for those formerly disaffected Protestants who had become disillusioned by the sectarian colouring which the United Irishmen's Rebellion had eventually assumed. For this group, membership of the Orange Institution, the very bulwark of Protestant Loyalism, was a talisman of future good conduct.

'THE ONLY SAFE PLACE'

If voluntary emigrants to Scotland presented a complex profile of motivation and political inclination, there was one group of new arrivals from Ireland in 1799 whose pedigree was not in doubt. These were the Irish state prisoners, the survivors of the central leadership of the United Irishmen's Society who were dispatched to Fort George in Nairn in April. Their case reveals the anxiety which still animated Westminster and the Scottish authorities over political contagion from Ireland, but also indicates the destructive gap in experience and understanding between Irish radicalism's leadership and rank and file.

The situation of the state prisoners was the product of negotiations between the government and the captured United leaders which had begun towards the end of July 1798.[23] After the execution of the Sheares brothers on 24 July, some of the most prominent prisoners in Dublin's Newgate and Kilmainham Jails informed the authorities that in return for the reprieve of Michael Byrne and Oliver Bond, and for additional concessions, including their own voluntary exile, they would make a full confession. After a short delay, during which Byrne was executed, the United offer was eventually accepted, and Bond's trial was dropped.[24] The irony was not lost on some contemporaries that while this high-level haggling was being conducted, their ordinary members in much of the country at large were suffering the worst extremes of military coercion. Even loyalists queried the motivation of a government which sought to crush the United conspiracy by 'killing 25,000 followers and pardoning 80 leaders'.[25]

At first, the 'Newgate Treaty' seemed a handsome bargain for both sides. The prisoners avoided a series of dangerous prosecutions, with Emmet and MacNeven given a platform to project their self-definition as moderates driven to extremes by the denial of their reasonable aims. Meanwhile, the government, which might have found it difficult to mount watertight evidence in some of the United Irish cases, was given the opportunity to silence critics of its repressive policies, and isolate and discredit the United leadership once and for all. Inevitably, not all of these hopes were fulfilled.

Some second-rank figures were allowed to accept banishment, but the project to export the main United men to America was aborted when the Federalist President Adams considered them too dangerous to admit. The government then decided that from among these prisoners 'men of sufficient talent and consequence to render their place of exile a matter of national importance should be detained for the duration of the War'. This group included Emmet, O'Connor, Neilson and Thomas Russell – for all of them this was nothing less than a betrayal. Despite their confinement, they proceeded accordingly to orchestrate a United revival with their customary bitterness.[26] Incensed at Dublin's laxness, and aware that the resultant agitation might well spill on to the mainland, the Home Office now resolved to deal with the threat after its own fashion and assumed responsibility for the Irish state prisoners' future detention.

This was the essential background to the transportation of the exotic cargo to Scotland. Soon it became apparent that Westminster's concern over its novel security problem was shared by the Scottish administration. After the initial issue of who was to pay for their subsistence and attendance was settled, 'proper warrants' were dispatched to Edinburgh to calm the Lord Advocate's legalistic worries over his authority to detain the state prisoners. The Scottish authorities then assiduously set about finding a suitable place of confinement.[27] In the forefront of this task was the United Irishmen's former adversary Sir Ralph Abercromby, now the general in command of the Scottish military district. He surveyed a variety of sites; these included the castles of Edinburgh, Stirling and Dumbarton, all 'very improper places' with slovenly security; and also the Bass Rock, where state prisoners before the Union had been held; but he finally settled on Fort George on the Moray Firth as 'the only safe place'. This site was 'remote, had no connection with any town or disaffected county, it had large accommodation, a resident Governor and Fort Major, a healthy situation and a respectable garrison'.[28]

The same extreme caution surrounded the conveyance of the state prisoners to their new residence. In late March, sixteen Dublin United leaders set sail for Gourock, picking up an additional four prisoners from Belfast, including W. S Dickson and William Tennent, one of the original founders of the United Irishmen.[29] From the moment of their landing on Scottish soil on 30 March, they were surrounded by a *cordon sanitaire*. On the beach, soldiers from the Rutland Light Dragoons and the North Yorks Militia were drawn up in two lines. This ceremony completed, the prisoners were conducted into four coaches and proceeded to Greenock, still under military escort.[30]

In one sense, the authorities' anxiety was not unfounded. The United leaders appeared flattered and quite unabashed by this attention. 'They all wore a very *modest* Jacobinical smile on their faces', reported the *Edinburgh Advertiser*, 'and on coming into town they let down such of the coach windows as were up that they might be seen'.[31] Nor was the 'spirit of sedition quenched in them'. MacNeven had followed one of the waiters serving them dinner at Greenock Town Hall, enquiring the number of troops in Paisley, Glasgow and the vicinity, and asking as to the state of people's minds in Scotland, 'are they all loyal?' The waiter's reply, that they were 'all loyal to a man', struck him with astonishment.

The state prisoners may even have entertained the hope that the Scottish Friends of Liberty would come to their assistance.[32] The next day, their convoy galloped through Renfrew, Govan, and the Gorbals of Glasgow, where, according to Dickson, 'not only the roads, but the adjoining fields were perfectly crowded with people, who kept pace . . . for many miles'. On their approach to Glasgow, 'The multitude became so great that escort seemed to have some apprehension of a rescue, though the conduct of the crowd was perfectly peaceable.'[33]

In fact, the response of the Scottish crowds to these celebrities probably owed as much to curiosity as to outright enthusiasm or hostility. The *Advertiser* found this hardly surprising since these were 'the hellish authors of the diabolical series of rebellion, devastation and murder that now disgrace our Sister Kingdom', but the bizarre spectacle presented by the prisoners was enough by itself to arouse public excitement. Arthur O'Connor was still resplendent in his green United uniform, with the rest 'completely cropped with mustachios *après la mode Française*'. To the crowd at Hamilton, 'they appeared more *Frenchmen* than *Irishmen*', while on the route north it was commented that they must be '*very great men*', or they would not be escorted by such a large retinue, since a troop of horse had not been spotted in the Highlands since 1746.[34]

After a journey of over 200 miles, the party finally arrived at Fort George, 'within sight of the Scottish Alps, and Culloden with all its recollections'.[35] The prisoners' subsequent treatment there was, as Samuel Neilson had grudgingly to admit, as liberal as could be expected.[36] General James Stuart, into whose charge they passed, quickly gained their respect as a fellow gentleman 'by birth education and manners', and was to intervene regularly on their behalf over the more stringent restrictions imposed by the Home Office.[37] The Governor's principal objects remained 'the security of the prisoners and the prevention of any intercourse with the Publick [sic]', but his obvious concern for his charges secured them a growing number of privileges. They had separate apartments, and were allowed to take part in sea-bathing and a variety of sports for a large part of their day. Their food was 'varied and remarkably good', and the Revd Dickson, whose love of the table would have done justice to a Scottish Moderate divine, lovingly recounted, 'their very fine salmon twice or thrice a week, other fish both round and flat, beef, mutton, pork, veal, lamb . . . plenty of garden stuffs and sallading, . . . young ducks and peas', not to mention their wine, porter and ale, which were also 'unfailingly good'.[38]

This abundance stands in stark relief to the experiences of the less socially and politically prestigious United prisoners being transported from Ireland during the same period. Hundreds were pressed into the British Navy or sent to serve in the Army in the disease-ridden West Indies.[39] Others were sent to Emden in January 1799, for service in the Prussian forces or to work in mines, while the remainder followed the well-travelled route to Botany Bay. Of the consignment aboard the *Atlas* and the *Hercules*, 127 out of 320 died of maltreatment and neglect before they could reach the penal colony.[40]

Despite their material advantages, the Irish state prisoners remained deeply alienated and unhappy, believing that the government had failed to honour its part of the Newgate bargain. The first letter in what was to become an avalanche of complaints, demands and self-justifying memorials arrived at the Home Office at the end of April.[41] The Ulster prisoners, and William Tennent in particular, were the most persistent and aggrieved correspondents, since they had not even been party to the original 'Treaty' and felt they were being held illegally without trial.[42]

As the men's confinement lengthened, with no apparent end in sight as long as the war with France continued, it became apparent that their frustration and resentment were also being turned on each other. Far from being the forcing ground for new strategies, their years in Scotland served to heighten the fissiparous tendencies of the United Irish leadership, and eventually hastened the disintegration of their carefully constructed movement.

THE SOCIETIES

While internal conflict was a welcome by-product of Scottish captivity, the government's original intention of isolating and neutralising the United Society's top leaders was also achieved. Yet, victory here was not complete, for before their departure from Dublin in March, Russell and O'Connor had already set in motion a reorganisation of the Society. The elaborate hierarchy of committees, which had evolved through the 1790s, had been shattered by the failure of the Rebellion. In contrast, the hallmarks of the new United military structure were to be exclusivity and a conscious detachment from the active cultivation of grass-roots support. New members would be accepted only on personal recommendation and after a careful vetting procedure. The lower committees through which the rank and file had elected their officers were not re-established. In their place, a compact new national executive was empowered to select a vanguard of 'generals', who in turn would select the next leadership level. So deep was the secrecy felt to be required, that the lower ranks were only to be filled on the eve of the next French invasion. No written communication or visible organisation was permitted, and arms would be distributed at the last moment, when the arrival of the French would be sufficient to signal a general rising. The French would deal with the Crown forces in orthodox military style, while the Irish people would disrupt lines of communication with guerrilla tactics. Until their arrival, the United organisation would be kept primed by the activity of a few travelling agents, though unlike in 1795–6 these would not engage in mass recruitment.[43]

While this plan had the merits of simplicity and extreme discretion, it rested, as Elliott suggests, on two false premises: first, that the French would quickly embark on a further invasion attempt; and second, that the Irish people would be willing to rise spontaneously. Despite the combination of the hopeful stirrings in the Channel ports and reassurances that the French had plans for a summer expedition, the final collapse of the Directory in 1799 and Bonaparte's assumption of power had signalled the end of Ireland as a realistic calculation in French strategy. Instead, it became one of a number of possible destinations for the next naval strike, competing with the more exotic attractions of the West Indies, Louisiana, Malta, Egypt and Surinam. While the Society's confidence in popular insurrection initially seemed better founded, as disaffection and rural violence were becoming endemic in Irish society, it still required assiduous local leadership to shape this towards political goals. In the absence of this guidance, Defenderism, rejuvenated and with a heightened sectarian content, was the likely beneficiary.[44]

At the heart of the United Irishmen's strategic miscalculation was the leadership's continuing distrust of the *menu peuple*; in this sense, there had been little movement beyond the extreme caution of Emmet and MacNeven. The lower classes were to be deployed in a highly controlled fashion to assist a political *coup*, without any attempt at imaginative understanding of their motivation and limitations.

Perhaps rooted in the same distrust was also the desire to extend the new organisation to the British mainland, an initiative which was apparently accorded equal priority with reorganisation efforts in heartlands such as Wexford and Wicklow. Assisted by the flow of rebel fugitives from the previous winter, over 15,000 United men were reported to be organised in the Irish rookeries of London, with a further 8,000 in Manchester.[45]

There is every reason to believe that Scotland too was the target of this instinctive expansionism. The most likely conduit for the new system was the familiar figure of William Putnam McCabe. In compiling his sketch of this character, Madden could not resist appending the line from *Richard III*, 'He was the covertest, sheltered traitor that ever lived'. Certainly in the midst of the '98 and in its aftermath, this seasoned revolutionary had been required to put his skills of disguise and impersonation to full use. Following his arrest in attempting to free Lord Edward Fitzgerald, he had persuaded his guards from the Dunbartonshire Fencibles to sign a petition demanding his release on the grounds that he was a visiting Scottish weaver, 'a decent and industrious lad, well-known and respected in Glasgow'.[46] After a series of similar hair-breadth escapes, he arrived in London in 1799, bringing plans for diversionary activities to assist the French invasion of Ireland. He remained until the summer, when he left for Edinburgh.[47]

McCabe settled in Scotland, ostensibly as a respectable citizen. For the next two years, he worked in a blacksmith's shop in order to pick up knowledge of machine building. He was also the latest in the long line of Irish radicals to enjoy the benefits of Scotland's open educational system, attending lectures on chemistry and mechanics. In 1801 at Glasgow, he married a Scottish widow, 'a lady remarkable for her beauty'. Yet, the old McCabe was still in evidence, and in the same year he narrowly escaped the clutches of the Scottish authorities by sheer effrontery. On walking down Princes Street, he was arrested by the police, despite protestations that he was a native of Edinburgh and not an Irish refugee. When the officer persisted, McCabe put his hand into his breast coat pocket and pulled out a small pistol, saying 'Very well, sir; since you think I am Irish, I will show you an Irish toothpick'. The police made no further attempt to detain him, and McCabe went shortly afterwards to France.[48]

Beyond this we know nothing of McCabe's political activities, nor of how the new United system was transmitted and received in Scotland. Thanks to the tireless efforts of Colonel Fletcher of Bolton, an early pioneer of the Orange Institution in England, we have some information on Lancashire and Yorkshire, which McCabe had visited at the end of 1800 and again in July 1801. Here, McCabe appears to have enlightened local leaders of the latest developments in revolutionary strategy in Ireland, and a military organisation remarkably similar to the new Irish model was soon in existence, with participation from long-standing local democrats and Irish fugitives alike.[49] In Scotland, by comparison, the absence of written communications between radicals is compounded by the authorities' own problems in intelligence gathering; one of their best informers had recently fled south to avoid his creditors and he proved difficult to replace.[50]

The temptation is to seize on any scraps of information available. For example, Madden states that McCabe was able, 'even in that time the war with France was at its height, to scatter abroad discontent', visiting 'London, Nottingham, Paisly [sic], Glasgow, Stockport and Manchester, and each exhibited as proof of his presence, symptoms of popular discontent, not infrequently of open violence'.[51] When this is matched with the fact that during the spring of 1800, during McCabe's residence in Scotland, Paisley and Glasgow *were* marked by serious food riots – which some friends of government believed 'were fermented by those persons who on all occasions are disposed to disturb public tranquillity' – it is easy to make the connection that the official Irish United leadership, through the medium of McCabe, were orchestrating or at least sanctioning the latest wave of disturbances on the mainland. The authorities were also quick in making this link, especially when at Paisley one of the main suspects taken up had left Ireland during the Rebellion, and was 'generally considered as of bad and seditious principles and conduct'.[52]

With closer acquaintance, the picture which emerges of the 1800 riots is a more complex one, which again emphasises the opportunities and constraints for radical political activity in Scotland. Despite being less widespread than the Militia riots, the disturbances of 1800 were severe, and in some areas necessitated military intervention.[53] February and March saw disorders in Ayrshire, Renfrewshire and Glasgow, and in Edinburgh in May meal mobs kept the local Volunteers under arms for twenty-four hours. Further outbreaks in Pollokshaws, Ayr and Glasgow followed in November and December.[54] While the Earl of Eglinton was convinced that 'meal was only the pretext', and that the riots were a cloak for sedition, other, more discerning, commentators realised that they were witnessing the conjunction of genuine economic grievances with conscious attempts at politicisation, or, as McDowell explained to the Lord Advocate, 'the spirit of 1794 had burst forth, and politics is mixed with the present scarcity to excite the disaffected to tumult and insurrection'.[55]

So extreme was the food crisis in 1800, it seems inevitable that unrest would have been present in some form, even without the intervention of 'the wicked views of bad and designing people'. The failure of the harvest in 1799 and the problems of importing cereals from the world market during wartime had caused a scarcity of supply which was reflected in dramatically rising food prices for British consumers.[56] The crisis was serious enough to produce an industrial recession, especially in the textiles and tertiary sectors, with the Ulster linen industry, dependent on British markets, being dealt its death blow. Despite this interweaving of fortunes, popular reactions in Ireland and Scotland varied considerably. In the former, with significant numbers of the rural poor close to the margins of subsistence, food crises tended to dampen unrest, with emigration acting as a safety valve; in Scotland, the share of money wages devoted to food was so great as to leave little slack to deal with price rises. In some areas these climbed from week to week. In East Lothian between 1798 and 1800, prices rose by 146%, in Fife by 180%, while in Edinburgh, a peck of grain which had cost 1s. in January 1799 was fetching 3s. 7d. by April 1800, a rise of 358% in eighteen months.[57] In rural areas, where the population depended on the local market for their food supply, and in the growing urban areas, where fears of shortages and price rises energised the mob, direct action to control the supply and pricing of staple cereals seemed both expedient and legitimate.

While there is little doubt of the power of rumour and the potential for agitation in these circumstances, it is much less plausible that United Irish organisers like McCabe were the fountainhead for such tactics. In the first place, participation in these volatile and high-profile developments, and the direct contact with the masses this would involve, was most out of keeping with the obsessive secrecy and remoteness of the revived United organisation. Nor would active missionising among the lower orders in the west of Scotland harmonise with McCabe's personal agenda. Scotland served him as a convenient bolt-hole, where he could develop new technical skills. While the discreet communication of the new Irish tactics to the higher committees in Scotland and England was compatible with current United policy and would not compromise McCabe's sequestered existence, any incautious foray into the front line would do so immediately.

This is not to deny Irish involvement in the meal riots. The case of the rebel fugitive at Paisley has been noted. It may also be significant that some of the worst outbreaks of rioting occurred at Kilmarnock. Here, many Irishmen were reported to have arrived after 1798 in consequence of the Rebellion; ironically, given his view of the 'refugee problem', they had found work in Home Secretary Portland's coalmines.[58] As was becoming clear in London and the northern English cities, impatience at the inactivity imposed by the United Irishmen's formal policy of delay was liable to drive some recent Irish migrants to revive the spirit of disaffection through their own efforts.[59]

The impetus to radicalise existing discontent also arose spontaneously from local Jacobin cadres. The well-tried technique of publishing seditious handbills was employed in Ayrshire, Renfrewshire and Glasgow; the authorities were anxious to pursue William Paton, a Saltmarket printer, who had composed and published one example, suggesting Glasgow's inhabitants rally at Glasgow Green.[60] By the end of 1800, the Lord Advocate had grown suspicious that a secret correspondence was still being maintained between England and Scotland.[61] One possible mechanism for keeping the old lines of communication open was the relief fund for the English state prisoners arrested in 1798, whose network of collectors included Ayrshire.[62] Indeed, Scottish radical tactics in the meal riots appear to owe more to the ideas of the early Spenceans, who were believed to have instigated bread riots in London in 1800 and 1801, than to the exclusivist principles of United Irish organisation. Followers of Thomas Spence, this group rejected the goal of a centralised disciplined underground and instead placed their faith in the spread of agitation at grass-roots level, which, they believed, would make disaffection amorphous enough to escape official detection.[63]

Objective conditions were, however, less favourable than elsewhere on the mainland. While prices in the south escalated without respite, leading to a 'hypercrisis' by the end of the year, in Scotland the tendency was towards rapid fluctuations, eventually on a downward trend. Here, recovery was evident by 1801, though prices remained higher than the preceding twenty years.[64]

The Scots also had to reckon with paternalistic responses to emergency relief. These were most effective in rural areas and in the smaller towns. Maybole had a particularly cohesive response to meet the necessitous state of the poor, with a committee appointed to meet weekly until a relief scheme had matured, and having the power to assign grain and collect subscriptions. 'By these exertions of benevolence', reported the *Glasgow Courier*, 'as much meal . . . and money to buy meal was secured as will enable to secure the poor of that parish to purchase their meal at as cheap a rate as they used to in the years of plenty'.[65] Urban centres proved more resistant to traditional relief mechanisms, but in Glasgow alternatives were provided in the shape of soup kitchens at Calton and the Trongate, following a similar scheme in Dublin under the patronage of Viceroy Cornwallis.[66] The alternative was self-help. This was preached by the *Courier*, offering rice recipes 'for the consideration of the cottager', but was also put into practice by working men's benefit clubs, like the Hibernian Society, which purchased grain for distribution among their members.[67]

Finally, there remained the threat of official repression. Handicapped by their lack of information on current Societies, the Scottish authorities were nevertheless eager to strike in exemplary fashion, even if prosecutions involved events which had already receded into radicalism's heroic past. From 1799, for example, there had been a determined attempt to root out activists in Ayrshire. Neatly complementing the charitable impulses of local notables, Maybole was the focal point of these official tactics, with a round-up of United Scotsmen members in the vicinity.[68] Again in September 1800, after a delay of five years, two local residents were tried under the Seditious Oaths Act, accused of using Freemasonry as a cover for treasonable activities.[69] The case had taken so long to come to court that one of the accused, John Andrew, had in the interim abandoned his former political principles, and 'had been heard to speak in favour of the government and Mr Pitt's abilities'.[70]

'THE BOYS IN THE MORNING'

On Robert Dundas's elevation to Chief Baron in 1801, the post of Lord Advocate of Scotland had been filled by Charles Hope. Conspicuously lacking a great legal mind, Hope was another 'Party man', a violent and energetic Tory, whose public speaking voice, according to Lord Cockburn, was surpassed by Mrs Siddons alone.[71] His personal bundle of enthusiasms and obsessions was destined to put a fresh stamp on the office and on government policy towards disaffection. Above all, he was a warrior *manqué*, whose martial spirit had originally led him to serve as a private in the First Regiment of Edinburgh Volunteers. His official correspondence with the Home Office was fairly cursory, except where military matters were concerned, for he considered any attempt to subvert the Volunteers as the gravest offence. At the same time, Hope's 'strategic' perspective gave a more precise and measured appreciation of the radical threat than his predecessor's. He realised that actual numbers in the Societies were not impressive, but that vigilance was still essential, as these determined activists could be employed to effect in the event of any French invasion attempt. Consequently, it was the degree of external threat which was largely to determine the Lord Advocate's course of action at each juncture.

This was clearly demonstrated in the spring of 1802, when at last worthwhile intelligence reached him from Fife that United Scotsmen cells were regrouping and a rising was intended.[72] Hope trusted his informant, who had 'a complete knowledge of the villainy of his associates', and whose information, more importantly, corresponded with similar he had received from 'other quarters'.[73] The Fife agent's information does offer a persuasive insight into the activities of United survivors in the most adverse circumstances, suggesting both their willingness to look beyond local problems and experiences and how this was reflected in the continuation of external links.

In the beginning of the year, a centralised leadership was still operating from Glasgow. This was now eager to take stock of the underground movement's strength and to lay concrete plans for the future, while restraining impetuous spirits in the mean time.[74] A letter reached the Fife United Scotsmen 'in the form of a parable', saying that 'trade was brisk and increasing and they would know the number in the district who would risk their fortunes upon a new branch of trade'. In other words, membership returns were requested; these were to be highly specific, with special lists of those who were 'learned', meaning those with military experience who were familiar with the drill manual. In response, information was being collated in the weaving villages and other old radical strongholds. The figure of 1,000 reported for Auchtermuchty and Strathmingo, whose combined population was only 2,000, seems an obvious exaggeration, but other returns have a more credible ring and indicate the survival of a determined radical cadre at local level; 93 were still United in Auchterarder, 59 in Dunning, 133 in Crief, 29 in Foulis and 483 in Perth. One 'very active hand' in Perth was the Irishman Robert Winluck, one of those who had originally opposed James Craigendallie's plan to remodel the town's societies on United principles.[75] Evidently, while the vicissitudes of the previous five years had caused some to recant, for others insurrection now seemed the only option, with all other routes for political change cut off.

Secrecy was imperative. No books were to be kept for fear of discovery and it was a general rule to burn all letters after they had been read. Still, the democrats could not help rejoicing in their prospects as now they shifted from a simple reliance on foreign assistance. 'Peace or war', reported the agent, 'were equally favourable to their views. For if it was peace, numbers of the Fencibles and Militia, and especially the Volunteers, would join them, 'being truly United'; by their assistance they expected to get hold of arms and military stores. It would be no great matter to take possession of Edinburgh Castle, 'which had already been reconnoitred, as some of the invalid soldiers there were United'. If it was war, 'there must be a struggle in France betwixt those who are for and those against, and that is the time to strike the blow in Britain and Ireland'.

In order to maximise their own resources, arms were being gathered in a good many different places, including ten foot pikes in Auchterarder. To convey these, the traditional Irish method had been adopted of pretending to assemble for a funeral. Indeed, the central leadership had to restrain rank-and-file enthusiasm. The burning of a local landowner's plantation was to be followed by similar incendiary tactics, but the order came from Glasgow 'to desist from every outrage or disturbances and to carry on quietly until further directions, and above all to take care not to call the attention of the Sheriff or Justices of the Peace by their conduct'.

This astonishing confidence and willingness for independent action was based firstly on local evidence. The rumour that the Crown forces had been breached was corroborated by three individuals in the Fife Militia who said 'the whole regiment, except seven stupid fellows were United, some were so when their names were taken as Militiamen, and many were made since . . .'. Many of the Dundee Volunteers, the whole of the Second Battalion of the Perth Volunteers, and over seventy of the Strathmingo Volunteers were also 'all United'.

Similar accounts of the Militia's dubious loyalty had been emphasised by United leaders in Ireland to bolster morale before the '98 Rebellion. Significantly, the Fife radicals were also in contact with a cell of United Irishmen in the Forth Dragoon Guards, who had been garrisoned at Auchtermuchty. Again it is highly unlikely that these soldiers were acting under instructions from the official Irish leadership, but nevertheless their individual participation in the village's radical meetings had the immediate effect of drawing local activities into the broader framework of resistance. The main thrust of the dragoons' message was that their Irish brethren were impatient for their co-operation. A letter to Private John Caddel from his brother in Dublin was read at Auchtermuchty the day before the regiment decamped. 'The Boys in the Morning', it stated, 'are as strong and numerous, as well-affected as ever, and that is these boys are as numerous in England and Scotland as they are in Ireland, the King's troops will not be a bite to them'. The letter was quickly burned 'as the safest thing'.

This was not the Fife men's only external link. More formal contact was also in evidence with the south through the medium of 'persons who pass as riders carrying a good deal of information backwards and forwards', and the Societies were aware that 'in England they have a new plan of government'. The quickening of activity indicated in the Fife case certainly fits coherently with the revival of the United British organisation, which had followed the release of the English state prisoners in March 1801, and which was proceeding in London and the north of England in the first half of 1802.[76]

In short, the Fife spy's belief was that an an insurrectionary attempt would be made in 3–4 weeks. Whereas Robert Dundas in this situation might have been provoked into hasty action, Hope's response was judicious and restrained. He counselled vigilance, but 'taking care at the same time not to betray a premature knowledge of their schemes, because partial discoveries induce the disaffected to change their mode of proceeding and correspondence, and put us to new trouble to detect them, without in the smallest degree tending to their ultimate disappointment'.[77] This policy strongly contrasted with the swoop on George Mealmaker in November 1797, which had allowed other members of the United Scotsmen's leadership to escape, and with Whitehall's strike in England in 1799 when radical reorganisation was still at an early planning stage. Hope's insight in this instance lay in distinguishing between 'the wishes of the leaders of the disaffected' from the conditions under which these could be realistically achieved. He was encouraged in his analysis first by signs of the economic revival underway from the autumn of 1801. Secondly, by spring 1802 the threat of French invasion had receded with negotiations underway between Britain and France, which were soon to result in the Treaty of Amiens.[78] Yet, he remained circumspect, and as a safeguard advocated close co-operation between the civil and military authorities. His information was transmitted to the sheriffs of Lanark and Perth, and he suggested to the Home Secretary – who approved of his cat-and-mouse tactics with the reformers – that for the present, Volunteers 'composed of the higher orders' need not be disbanded, but that proper security measures be adopted to store the arms of corps which had been stood down.[79]

This approach was well chosen. In London, the underground revival continued through 1802, feeding off the deep alienation of Irish migrants in the riverside and East End parishes and the grievances of recently demobilised soldiers and sailors. Their restlessness and impatience for action led to plans for a rising in the capital which was to set a larger movement in the provinces in motion. The embryonic conspiracy was shattered by the arrest of the veteran radical Colonel Despard and his associates in November.[80] In Scotland, despite an outbreak of rioting in Perth in September directed against the reduction of the Army and Navy, the visible precautions surrounding Volunteer arms and the general level of surveillance prescribed by the Lord Advocate seem to have produced a new period of quietness and retrenchment in the Societies. It was not until the following year, with the renewal of the war with

France in May and a new rebellion in Ireland in July that the Scottish again began to regroup. Now, Charles Hope was forced to reconsider his strategy, and his perception of danger suddenly sharpened as his eyes turned to the growing Irish community in the west of Scotland.

1803: THE ENEMY WITHIN

After various alarms that the prisoners at Fort George would apply to a Scottish court to resolve their anomalous status and obtain a release, the Peace Treaty with France at last removed the major pretext for their confinement; they were allowed to enter permanent banishment in June 1802.[81] Governor Stuart reported that most proposed going to America, but that the prisoners were by now on very bad terms, with several, including Arthur O'Connor, refusing to speak to the others.[82]

The pull of France, and the opportunities offered by the continuing instability of Anglo-French relations, proved too tempting for the main leaders, Emmet, Russell and O'Connor. Still bickering, they arrived separately in Paris, where, despite their distrust of Bonaparte and their growing reluctance to rely solely on French aid, they renewed negotiations with the First Consul. These apprehensions partly lay behind their modest demand for 10,000 troops to invade Ireland, an underestimate which also reflected their imperfect knowledge of conditions at home, where there had been an unaccustomed calm over the previous two years. Here, like McCabe in Edinburgh, fugitive leaders had been quietly pursuing respectable careers, and both the Defenders and the United Irishmen appeared snuffed out.

This situation rapidly changed with the collapse of the Treaty of Amiens and the imminent renewal of war. From spring 1803, the authorities grew more aware of United regrouping. The key directing roles were filled by Thomas Emmet's younger brother Robert, Thomas Russell, recently returned from France, and the ubiquitous McCabe who was now busy organising the *émigré* community in Paris. The 1799 plan of minimal formal organisation was now adopted. Discretion and mobility were at a premium and surprise was to be the rebels' main weapon. Once again, a rising in Dublin, following a modified scheme of McCabe's, was to be the signal to rouse the counties. Russell was also convinced that Ulster would rise spontaneously despite the sea-change in political attitudes there since the '98.

Although the desire for independent action had been developing among sections of the United movement, voiced most powerfully in Russell's rallying call that 'the Irish people should begin at once and free themselves', northern radicals could not resist stretching out to their old allies in Scotland and England. The Irish authorities were well aware from the report of the Belfast spy Samuel Turner that one Witherspoole, from the neighbourhood of Castlereagh in County Down, had visited Scotland, returning with reports that 'they are doing well there, and would assist us if a Rising would take place'. By May, 'Scotch reports' had again become a regular feature at United Irish meetings, but these were given verbally, hampering Turner's attempts to procure further information.[83] Indeed, the United Irishmen had more cause for concern over the torpor of their usual areas of strength in the north of England, where agents were reported to be anxiously travelling in June and July.[84]

The promise offered by the political situation in Scotland was not entirely the product of Witherspoole's obvious enthusiasm. In April 1803, the Lord Advocate reported that the Societies in Scotland were 'all alive again', and their activities in centres like Perth continued to be carefully monitored, though their central leadership was as impenetrable as ever.[85] External communication was a particular source of concern and Hope ordered the interception of letters to and from suspects like Robert Winluck, who was said to be 'deeply connected with the United Scotsmen, and in close correspondence at present with Ireland'.[86] Disaffection also had a more practical outlet in incidents of wilful fire-raising against government officials during the summer.[87]

What precise form Scottish assistance was to assume is unclear. Rather unsatisfactory intelligence was volunteered from a prisoner held in Carlisle Gaol that Edinburgh Castle had been reconnoitred by United men, but similar stories had been circulating around the Fife societies since the previous spring.[88] It may be that a diversionary thrust *was* envisaged, featuring a simultaneous attempt on the centres of government administration in Dublin and Edinburgh. The obvious precedent for this concerted strategy was Robert Watt's ill-fated escapade in the Scottish capital nine years before.

Perhaps just as well for the eager Scottish democrats, their services were never called upon. The rising in Dublin turned out to be a premature affair, set in motion before preparations for co-ordinated external assistance, or even for that matter broad-based support within Ireland, were satisfactorily completed. Communications with France had been disrupted as war approached, and Emmet and his associates became more convinced of the need for their own insurrectionary strategy. Afraid that Dublin Castle had been alerted to their intentions, and still convinced that the rural masses would rise at the seizure of the capital, they dispensed last-minute instructions to their supporters and moved on 23 July. It soon became clear that the *élitist* model of United organisation was collapsing amid its contradictions, as confusion and indecision caused the rising to stall almost at once. Emmet and the Dublin leaders were easily surrounded after a series of misadventures; Russell's attempts in Ulster similarly met with disappointment. By October, both he and Robert Emmet had been tried and executed, and had entered into United martyrology.

Although Emmet's attempt was emphatically an abortive one, it renewed the loyalist passion for revenge in both its popular and official dimensions. The identity of confessional and political identities was further reinforced, with Orangeism receiving a major boost and even a measure of governmental approval. Both Whitehall and the Irish authorities were deeply embarrassed by the outbreak, each blaming the other for the failure of its intelligence services which they believed had made the whole episode possible.

The situation in Scotland was rather different. Unlike the '98 Rebellion, the events in Dublin that summer made little mark on the consciousness of the Scottish public; the press reported the rising in a clinical fashion, relying exclusively on official dispatches.[89] In contrast, the Scottish administration was drawn in immediately, for by late July the west coast ports and their hinterlands were already fast filling with arrivals from Ireland. While Ulster had not risen as Russell had expected, drilling and arming had proceeded in parts of Antrim and Down even after the Dublin collapse. This along with a revival of Defenderism contributed to the generally disturbed state of the north.

The latest migrants were doubtless the usual mixture of fugitives, loyalists and employment seekers, but anticipating instructions from the Home Office, customs officers were ordered by the Lord Advocate to take 'the same measures which had been followed during the former Rebellion' against all Irishmen.[90] Charles Hope was better placed in this situation than his English counterparts, who were experiencing great difficulty in monitoring the flow of Irish into Liverpool and other major cities.[91] Relations with Dublin had not soured to the same extent and useful information was still being exchanged between law officers in the two kingdoms.[92] Familiar problems of selectivity remained though. Those coming in from open boats were 'plainly fugitives', and typically Lord Eglinton rounded some up at once, but the question was how to deal with 'those who pretend they have come over for work and have passports'. There was no evidence against them 'although they may be notorious rebels and well known in Ireland'.[93] Like his predecessor, Hope was willing to resort to extra-legal measures, but now these assumed a more deliberately coercive aspect. Besides sending the Irish back in custody or dealing with them as vagrants, he was convinced that pressing some into the Navy would serve as a salutary example and soon stem the migration flow at source.[94]

The note of desperation in Hope's correspondence was prompted by new fears of a French invasion, with undisguised naval preparations in Brest and the western ports from late June. If this blow took place, he reasoned, what would be the reaction of those 'instinctive rebels' in Scotland, the Irish population, whose numbers had been growing rapidly in the last decade, apparently in geometric ratio with the blossoming of disaffection in their own country. This anxiety was not the product of Hope's military mania alone. Similar concerns over the concentration of Irish settlers in the south Ayrshire manufacturing villages had already been voiced at the time of the Militia riots. More recently, Lord Redesdale, the Irish Lord Chancellor, while considering the lessons of Emmet's Rebellion, had forcibly stated his belief that there were 'Irishmen in London and more in Scotland, who continued the connection with their own country that the purpose of mischief called for'.[95]

By August 1803, the Lord Advocate believed he had local corroboration of just such a connection. Information had arrived from a Glasgow Volunteers private that 'several concealed Irish Papists' had entered into the regiment merely for the purposes of mischief, namely to get arms into their hands and to subvert some of their countrymen. These men 'were all in the former Rebellion and [were] now keeping up a daily correspondence with traitors there'.[96] This news of an attempt to tamper with his beloved Volunteers struck Hope deeply. Although the present case concerned only nine Irishmen, his anxiety was sharpened by the Lord Provost's estimate that there were not less than 10,000 Irish in Glasgow and the immediate vicinity, and 'almost all of the most suspicious character, and very many of them known to be old rebels, not in the least reformed'. He was now convinced of the magnitude of the security threat implicit in the very presence of this community.

> They both excite me in terms of a very great uneasiness on this subject as they are persuaded that if a French force were to appear on the West Coast of Scotland, that these Irish would rise to a man, all over the West of Scotland, where there is both a very trifling, even including the Volunteers, most of whom have not yet got arms.[97]

Hope was aware that repatriation was not a practical option, stressing to the Home Office his awareness of the danger of 'ordering these people to leave the country'. However much he might have preferred the simple re-export of his 'security problems', his alternative prescription was for a mixture of exemplary punishment and increased surveillance. Recognising 'the unpopularity of having recourse to measures out of the ordinary course of law', he still strongly urged the necessity of giving magistrates more power to apprehend and detain suspicious persons.[98] An increased military presence was, of course, for Hope the ultimate deterrent.

By these means, by selecting a few of the principle people among them we shall probably be able to confound and defeat the designs of the rest. At present in the case of the renewal of the disturbances in Ireland, or of a descent on the east coast, I really conceive the tranquillity of the West of Scotland to be in great danger. Besides sounding among the Glasgow magistrates, this is the view of Lord Elgin, and General Wemyss. An obvious measure is to increase the Volunteer establishment in Glasgow, Renfrew and Ayr.[99]

As the invasion scare grew by late autumn, Hope's general excitement and his apprehension of 'the enemy within' grew apace. Looking to the example of Ireland over the past few years, he begged the Home Office for the discretionary authority to proclaim Martial Law, which would leave civil courts open for ordinary offences but ensure that 'immediate examples' could be made of scoundrels disposed to assist the invader. In the mean time, he busied himself with contingency plans which would make it certain that 'if the enemy does come, he will find us a tough morsel'.[100]

The Lord Advocate was commended by the Home Secretary for his zealous exertions, but the challenge of an invasion attempt, which he seems almost to have welcomed, never materialised.[101] Bonaparte's preparations dragged on slowly and were still incomplete by the next year. In December 1803, part of the French force assembled in the Channel sailed to the West Indies, thus depriving Hope of his chance to lead the Scottish resistance in a death-or-glory stand. He was promoted to Lord Chief Justice and died in his bed in 1831.

The official perception of the Irish in Scotland as a threat to domestic peace was destined to outlive Charles Hope, despite flaws in his original formulation of the 'problem'. His key misconception stemmed not from any overestimate of the growing numerical strength of this group. The Provost's estimate of 10,000 Irish in the Glasgow area in 1803 can be set beside the 1821 Census figure of 25,000 of Irish birth for the city itself.[102] Instead, like most Scots, Hope failed to detect the effects of sectarian polarisation in Ireland, which had been set in motion in earnest by the events of the '98 Rebellion and further boosted by Emmet's rising. Characteristically, he remained blind to the significance of the fact that his informant on the nine 'concealed Irish Papists' was himself an Irish *Protestant*. While some Protestants continued to support the radical cause, clearly the deep political and religious conflicts which were once more coming to dominate Irish society had also been transplanted as part of the migration process. Yet, the blanket identification of Irish ethnicity with violence and rebelliousness was to persist, unchallenged by any evidence to the contrary. Even as the Protestant loyalist community became strident and visible, chiefly through the medium of the Orange Order, the official reaction was one of dogged impartiality in the face of what were perceived as confusing and pointless party squabbles, as 'unwelcome as some of the Irish themselves'.[103]

The Lord Advocate of Scotland was not alone in regretting the failure of the French to challenge the preparedness of Crown forces. Although Bonaparte was to gaze fitfully over plans for another invasion over the next decade, even after the destruction of his fleet at Trafalgar, the increasingly despotic tendencies of the new French regime displaced any lingering traces of the altruistic internationalism which in the past had sustained democrats in hard times.

In Scotland, radicals again went to ground, with the United Scotsmen disappearing from government correspondence from this point onwards. In Ireland, the United movement now rapidly and finally disintegrated, and the abiding popular grievances of that country were left to find a voice in repeated Defender revivals. In Paris, the surviving United Irish leaders had also grown embittered and disillusioned, passing their exile in straightened circumstances. These remnants of a once proud mass movement gained a brief encouragement from Bonaparte's formation of an Irish Legion in 1803 to provide a supply of Irish officers as part of his invasion preparations, but in the longer term this initiative placed the survival of their Society entirely at his discretion. Besides the dictates of high politics, United ambitions were also blighted by the legacy of Fort George. The dispute between Thomas Emmet and Arthur O'Connor, which was originally grounded in policy differences, had become viciously personalised during the years of confinement and almost resulted in a duel.[104] The internecine warfare between their opposing camps both embarrassed the French and impeded any sustained revival. Neither the Irish Legion nor the Society of United Irishmen survived beyond the summer of 1806.

It was now clear that when Scottish radicals again regrouped in the conditions of extreme dislocation which accompanied the end of the Napoleonic Wars, they would have to exploit their own accumulated resources of experience and ideas in the struggle to build a democratic movement.

NOTES

1. JC 26/298, (SRO).
2. See *Reports from the Committees of the House of Commons* 1803–6), x, p. 800.

3. C. Hope to Lord Pelham, 4 August 1803, RH 2/4/88 f. 231 (SRO).
4. Thompson, *The Making of the English Working Class*, p. 542.
5. Kay and Miles, 'Refugees or Migrant Workers?', p. 14.
6. *Report from the Second Committee Enquiring into the Condition of the Poorer Classes in Ireland*, pp. 64, 143 for Ayrshire examples; p. 130 for Renfrewshire.
7. *Glasgow Advertiser*, 15 October 1798.
8. *Glasgow Advertiser*, 6 August 1799; *Glasgow Courier*, 1 January 1799; see also *Dublin Evening Post*, January 1799, and Rebellion Papers, 620/5/59 f. 3 (NAI).
9. Handley, *The Irish in Scotland*, pp. 153–4.
10. *Report from the Second Committee Enquiring into the Condition of the Poorer Classes in Ireland*, pp. 64.
11. McDowell, *Ireland in the Age of Imperialism*, pp. 632–7.
12. Pakenham, *Year of Liberty*, p. 392.
13. Rudé, 'Early Irish Rebels in Australia', p. 22.
14. *Correspondence of Rufus King*, vol. ii, pp. 639–45, quoted in Pakenham, *Year of Liberty*, p. 657.
15. Elliott, *Partners in Revolution*, p. 267.
16. MS Book, *The Oakboys, the Hearts of Steel, the Volunteers and the United Irishmen of Larne and Neighbourhood*, D. 2095/18 (PRONI).
17. J. Arbuckle to A. Gordon, 12 April 1799 on the abuse of passport procedures, Rebellion Papers, 620/48/18 (NAI). Passports had been required since May 1798 for travel between Ireland and Great Britain, under a proclamation of April 1799 they were also required for those travelling in the opposite direction, Dublin *Freeman's Journal*, 26 May 1798.
18. McFarland, *Protestants First*, pp. 36–7.
19. Lord Castlereagh to Duke of Portland, 3 June 1799, HO 100/87/5–7 (PRO).
20. Senior, *Orangeism in Ireland and Great Britain*, p. 83.
21. McFarland, *Protestants First*, p. 37.
22. Ibid., pp. 48–69.
23. McDowell, *Ireland in the Age of Imperialism*, pp. 655–7.
24. Bond later died in captivity, after bursting a blood vessel. Foul play was suspected, and William Drennan attended his post-mortem, but it transpired that the evening before his death Bond had consumed two sheep's heads and four bottles of wine: *Glasgow Courier*, 14 September 1799.
25. R. Johnson to Lord Downshire, 18 [August] 1798, D607/F/351 (PRONI), quoted in Elliott, *Partners in Revolution*, p. 209.
26. Elliott, *Partners in Revolution*, p. 247.
27. R. Dundas to Duke of Portland, 6 March 1799, RH 2/4/85 ff. 7–9, (SRO). The Lord Advocate was quick to emphasise to the Home Office that the question of financial responsibility was particularly important since no funds for maintenance existed in Scotland.
28. R. Abercromby Memorandum, 6 March 1799, RH 2/4/85 ff. 11 (SRO). Dumbarton was particularly objectionable as it lay open to the Irish Channel and its garrison consisted of 'a few old invalids'. Edinburgh was already crowded with French prisoners of war.
29. *Edinburgh Advertiser*, 22–6 March 1799. The Dublin prisoners were: S. Neilson, T. A. Emmet, J. Sweetman, T. Russell, A. O'Connor, R. O'Connor, E. Hudson, J. Chambers, J. Cuthbert, G. Cumming, J. Cormick, M. Downing, E. Sweeny, W. MacNeven, S. Wilson and W. Dowdall. The Ulster prisoners also included R. Simms and R. Hunter: General Drummond to A. Marsden, 12 January 1801, Rebellion Papers, 620/10/120/2 (NAI).
30. *Edinburgh Advertiser*, 2–5 April 1799; W. S. Dickson, *The Narrative of the Confinement*, p. 113.

31. *Edinburgh Advertiser*, 2–5 April 1799.
32. Ibid.
33. W. S. Dickson, *The Narrative of the Confinement*, p. 118–19.
34. *Edinburgh Advertiser*, 2–5 April 1799; W. S. Dickson, *The Narrative of the Confinement*, p. 120.
35. Ibid., p. 132.
36. See Neilson's Correspondence in Madden, *United Irishmen*, ser. 3, vol. iii, pp. 243–304.
37. W. S. Dickson, *The Narrative of the Confinement*, p. 156; Madden, *United Irishmen*, ser. 3, vol. iii, p. 283n. Stuart was, in fact, a brother of the Earl of Moray and thus of higher social status than most of the United leaders. J. Stuart to Duke of Portland, 22 April 1799, RH 2/4/85 f. 50 (SRO). The Home Office had originally wished solitary confinement, which Stuart thought would give rise to unnecessary trouble and expense.
38. W. S. Dickson, *The Narrative of the Confinement*, p. 139. Not surprisingly, the State Prisoners were expensive to maintain, with their expenses soon outstripping the £212 per month originally estimated: J. Stuart to Duke of Portland, 1 June 1800, RH 2/4/86 f. 85 (SRO). The transfer of money from the Home Office to Governor Stuart to meet these costs became a bone of contention: J. Stuart to Duke of Portland, 13 October 1800, RH 2/4/86 f. 132 (SRO).
39. See Account Written by Andrew Bryson on his Transportation to the West Indies, T. 1373/56 (PRONI), and Rebellion Papers, 620/47/138–40, 620/56/170 (NAI).
40. Rudé, 'Early Irish Rebels in Australia', pp. 17–35, and see Reece, *Exiles from Erin*, pp. 10–26.
41. S. Wilson to Duke of Portland, 27 April 1799, RH 2/4/85 f. 63 (SRO). See also R. O'Connor to J. Stuart, 11 June 1799, RH 2/4/85 f. 93 (SRO); J. Stuart to Duke of Portland, 8 September 1799, RH 2/4/85 f. 13 (SRO); W. Tennent, R. Hunter and R. Simms to J. Stuart, 12 March 1799, RH 2/4/87 f. 19 (SRO); J. Stuart to C. Hope, 31 December 1801, RH 2/4/87 f. 143 (SRO).
42. Memorial of W. Tennent, Rebellion Papers, 620/16/117/1 (NAI); Memorials and Requests for Items, D 1748/A/3/9 f. 26 (PRONI). His chagrin was obvious. 'There never was any charge exhibited against him, consequently the reason for his imprisonment remains in the heart of the government.'
43. Elliott, *Partners in Revolution*, p. 248.
44. *Charlemont* MSS II 354 (HMC) for the revival of Defenderism in Ulster.
45. PC 1/4/A 152–3 (PRO).
46. Madden, *United Irishmen*, ser. 3, vol. iii, p. 296.
47. Ibid., p. 321; Rebellion Papers, 620/7/74/1, 8 & 22 and 620/46/104 (NAI).
48. Madden, *United Irishmen*, ser. 3, vol. iii, p. 353.
49. Rebellion Papers, 620/49/11 (NAI); Madden Papers, MSS 873/767 (TCD).
50. R. Dundas to J. King, 30 March 1800, RH 2/4/86 f. 280 (SRO).
51. Madden, *United Irishmen*, ser. 3, vol. iii, p. 332.
52. J. McDowell to R. Dundas, 10 November 1899, RH 2/4/86 f. 283–5 (SRO).
53. For involvement of Banffshire Volunteers at Paisley, see Duke of Fife to Duke of Portland, 6 March 1800, RH 2/4/86 f. 181 (SRO).
54. Earl of Eglinton to R. Dundas, 13 November 1800, RH 2/4/86 f. 274–5 (SRO); C. Hope to R. Dundas, RH 2/4/86 ff. 219–20 (SRO); *Glasgow Courier*, 18 February, 1 May, 28 October, 1 November, 8 November 1800.
55. J. McDowell to R. Dundas, 10 November 1899, RH 2/4/86 f. 283–5 (SRO).

56. See R. Wells, *Wretched Faces*, pp. 35–52.

57. Logue, *Popular Disturbances*, p. 26.

58. *Report from the Second Committee Enquiring into the Condition of the Poorer Classes in Ireland*, p. 143.

59. Elliott, *Partners in Revolution*, pp. 257, 285.

60. *Caledonian Mercury*, 17 May 1800; Earl of Eglinton to R. Dundas, 13 November 1800, RH 2/4/86 f. 274–5 (SRO).

61. R. Dundas to J. King, 3 December 1800, RH 2/4/86 ff. 291–2 (SRO).

62. R. Oliphant examination, 2 June 1801, HO 30/9/58–148 (PRO).

63. Thompson, *Making of the English Working Class*, p. 672–4.

64. Wells, *Insurrection*, pp. 179; Logue, *Popular Disturbances*, pp. 18–53.

65. *Glasgow Courier*, 6 February 1800; at Kilmarnock, weekly collections were taken at church doors and distributed amongst poor householders: *Glasgow Courier*, 15 March 1800; at Saltcoats, Ardrossan and Stevenston £120 was raised, including a contribution from the local Volunteer corps: *Glasgow Advertiser*, 13 March 1800.

66. *Glasgow Advertiser*, 14 February 1800; *Glasgow Courier*, 15 March 1800.

67. *Glasgow Courier*, 6 February 1800; see Minutes of the Hibernian Society, 22 November 1800, TD 200.7 (SRA).

68. J. Kennedy declarations, 11 April, n.d. [August] and 2 December 1799, JC 26/298 (SRO); see also *Glasgow Courier*, 21 September 1799 for Kennedy's fugitation and the decision not to proceed with the prosecution of William Neilson of Kilwinning. Another who regretted the error of his ways was Archibald Grey of Irvine. Grey had been assumed to be in Hamburg and active in the Philosophical Society there. He had, in fact, been in hiding in Strathhaven and attempted to construct a deal with the authorities in which he would surrender the names of his superiors to secure a pardon: C. Hope to Lord Pelham, 25 May 1802, RH 2/4/87 f. 186 (SRO).

69. *Glasgow Courier*, 22 September 1800; *Glasgow Advertiser*, 25 September 1800; *Edinburgh Advertiser*, 19–23 September 1800.

70. *Glasgow Courier*, 22 September 1800.

71. Ormond, *The Lord Advocates of Scotland*, vol. 2, p. 205; Fry, *The Dundas Despotism*, pp. 244–5.

72. C. Hope to Lord Pelham, 2 April 1802, RH 2/4/87 f. 153 (SRO).

73. Ibid.

74. Examination, RH 2/4/87 f. 155 (SRO) from which the subsequent account is drawn.

75. W. Murray to R. Barclay, 27 December 1797, Laing MSS II 639 (University of Edinburgh); W. Scott to H. Dundas, 22 July 1797, Melville MSS GD 51/2/29 (SRO).

76. J. W. to Henry Dundas, 24 March 1801, Melville MSS 1041 f. 85 (NLS). The United Britons were said to be expanding, using the Freemasons, trades societies and benefit clubs as a cover, and forming a plot to overthrow the government; Reports March to July 1802, HO 42/65 (PRO); Howell and Howell, *State Trials*, xxviii, cols 342–423.

77. C. Hope to Lord Pelham, 2 April 1802, RH 2/4/87 f. 153 (SRO).

78. *Glasgow Courier*, 1 and 3 April 1802.

79. Lord Pelham to C. Hope 7 February 1802, RH 2/4/87 f. 160 (SRO). *Glasgow Courier*, 8 and 13 May 1802 for standing-down of the Greenock, Loyal Carrick and Glasgow Volunteers. The latter corps was hailed:

> Ye firm supporters of your Country's cause,
> Who rose for Order, Liberty and Laws,
> With Saviour 'hand upheld a Monarch's Throne,
> And crushed the noxious deeds by discord thrown.

80. Elliott, 'Irish Republicanism in England', pp. 204–21.

81. After the liberation of the English State Prisoners, the Irish had eagerly awaited their turn. Originally committed under the Duke of Portland's warrant, they believed they could use Scots Law to force either a trial or their immediate release. The authorities decided to play a waiting game, hoping that any Scottish court would have them transported back to Ireland or enforce their continued confinement at Fort George.

82. J. Stuart to Lord Pelham, 30 June 1802, RH 2/4/88 f. 185 (SRO).

83. M. McDonagh, *The Viceroy's Postbag*, p. 275. Witherspoole was eventually arrested in October: Rebellion Papers, 620/10/121/15 (NAI).

84. Rebellion Papers, 620/65/126/10 and 620/66/67/33 (NAI); HO 47/20 (PRO).

85. C. Hope to Lord Pelham, 4 August 1803, RH 2/4/87 f. 231 (SRO).

86. C. Hope to Lord Pelham, 4 August 1803, RH 2/4/87 f. 231 (SRO); C. Hope to R. Trotter, Postmaster, 5 August 1803, RH 2/4/87 f. 23 (SRO). Hope was aware of the irregularity involved in opening mail, but invoked his position as Lord Advocate.

87. C. Hope to Lord Pelham, 13 August 1803, RH 2/4/88 f. 251 (SRO).

88. J. Curwen, 10 October 1803, Rebellion Papers, 620/12/141/38 (NAI).

89. See, for example, *Glasgow Courier*, 29 to 30 July and 2 August 1803.

90. C. Hope to Lord Pelham, 29 July 1803, RH 2/4/88 f. 219 (SRO). Meanwhile, magistrates were to 'make strict enquiry regarding all foreigners and strangers including Americans and Irishmen now in their different districts'.

91. HO 42/712 and 79/6 (PRO).

92. C. Hope to Lord Pelham, 29 July 1803, RH 2/4/88 f. 219 (SRO). The contents of a letter found on a suspect apprehended in Paisley, implicating 'the whole Masonic Order' in Tyrone, were speedily passed to the Viceroy's office.

93. C. Hope to Lord Pelham, 6 August 1803, RH 2/4/88 f. 243 (SRO).

94. Ibid.

95. Redesdale Papers, T 3030/6/6 (PRONI).

96. C. Hope to Lord Pelham, 4 August 1803, RH 2/4/88 f. 231 (SRO). The suspects were to be watched but not apprehended for the present as they were considered too cautious to have preserved the letters they had received from Ireland.

97. Ibid.

98. Ibid., for an example of Renfrewshire magistrates' prompt action against an Irishman 'of suspicious character'.

99. Ibid.

100. C. Hope to C. Yorke, 15 October 1803, RH 2/4/88 f. 329 (SRO). If Edinburgh could no longer be defended, the different boards of revenue were to be removed to a place of safety to allow the collection of taxes to go on unimpeded in the unoccupied areas. If the French pushed on to Glasgow, every sloop and boat on the west coast was to be burnt to prevent the enemy passing over to Ireland.

101. C. Yorke to C. Hope, 18 October 1803, RH 2/4/88 f. 334 (SRO).

102. *House of Commons Select Committee on the State of Ireland* (1825), p. 823.

103. McFarland, *Protestants First*, p. 52.

104. Emmet left for America at the end of 1804 and pursued a distinguished legal career. O'Connor was appointed a General of Division by Bonaparte and became his trusted adviser on Irish affairs: Madden, *United Irishmen*, ser. 3, vol. iii, pp. 141–77, 247–8; McDermott, 'Arthur O'Connor', pp. 48–69; for the Irish Legion, see Elliott, *Partners in Revolution*, pp. 331–40.

CONCLUSION

A United Legacy
(1807–1820)?

Craig Calhoun argues that the major social foundation for radical protest was the traditional community, based either on locality or on a craft, and that it was not until 1830 that this pervasive localism was breached and community was overtaken by class as a populist concept.[1] Remembering the vibrancy of democratic cells in the industrial villages of Scotland, it would be wrong to dismiss this stress on the local and the communal. However, it has been a major theme of this book that political consciousness also drew strength from a broader vision of the task of reform.

Well before Calhoun's date for the demise of localism, there had developed an internationalist dimension to radical activity, expressed in the hard-won alliance between the Irish and Scottish democratic movements. Originally this alliance had been based on an alternative version of 'community' – the 'ideological community' between Presbyterian Ulster and Scotland, which provided a framework for intellectual and cultural interchange. From the early 1790s practical links were also constructed both from principle and expediency. Middle-class radicals in Ireland looked out to their 'brother-friends' in Scotland, often before seeking solidarity with their own Catholic countrymen. For the Scots, the self-confident spirit of Irish politics was an inspiration to their own growing organisation. Yet Scotland was not Ireland. Greater social homogeneity, a more organic process of economic development, and a muted tradition of political protest meant a more hostile terrain for democratic mobilisation. In addition, the strategy of mutual assistance imposed its own costs, attracting the fury of the peculiarly repressive Scottish legal system.

As the tide turned against open, constitutionalist campaigning, the habit of cross-fertilisation could not be unlearned. As early as 1794 and 1795, the United Irishmen were contemplating covert communication and expansion across the North Channel. By the time the new United system took root in Scotland a few years later, buttressed by repeated migration waves, it was now embraced by plebeian radicals, weavers and artisans. Again the import of Irish methods was controversial, but for activists like James Craigendallie and Archibald Grey to be 'United' was to be bound in a cohesive brotherhood which kept radical ideas alive for better days. Above all, contact with the United Irishmen provided the vital mediating link between democrats in Perth, Maybole and Irvine, and the very fountainhead of liberty and reason in revolutionary France.

Although marginalised in some historians' accounts, this linkage greatly exercised the minds of contemporary officials who were unwilling to equate the size of the revolutionary movement with the threat that it posed. The strategic concerns of Lord Advocate Hope have already been traced, but these merely anticipated the strictures of a more illustrious friend of government, George Canning, who thundered against:

> the trite and futile argument that our would-be reformers and revolutionists are few in number. This may be, and it will be a consolation when the attempt shall have been suppressed; but it is no security against its success if we omit to take rigorous measures for its suppression. When was a revolution effected in any state but by an active and enterprising minority.[2]

Here a rather incongruous but instructive parallel can be drawn between the 'revolutionary minority' of the late eighteenth century, and another small and determined political group of the twentieth, the Communist Party of Great Britain. Both shared a universalist conception of politics and earned the fear and contempt of government. Their self-perception as part of an international movement, as participants in a historic mission initially achieved in only one part of the world, ensured that they survived through many vicissitudes. There was also a key distinction. In the more modern example, the fascination with 'workers' power' in the Soviet Union and the belief in its eventual world-wide triumph motivated the Party beyond other considerations. For almost seventy years the existence of the Soviet state represented not only an achievement in itself, but a source of confidence that similar victories might be secured elsewhere.[3] For early political radicals in Scotland, disillusionment set in much more swiftly, as the Revolution in France descended through the corruption and cynicism of the Directory into the despotism of Bonaparte in the space of a decade. From an early stage, the Scots were forced into an awareness that to break out of their restricted power base and recruit mass support, they had to be a truly 'native' movement, in the sense that their doctrines and organisation had to be anchored in the realities of social and economic development in early industrial Scotland.

This did not imply the death of an internationalist vision. Throughout Britain, this lasting legacy of 1790s Jacobinism grew more expansive with the new century. For the Leeds croppers who plotted insurrection in 1817, 'the recent news from the Brazils seemed to cheer them with greater hopes than ever'.[4] In Scotland, the outward-looking impulse extended beyond the continuing engagement with developments in England, which has understandably tended to absorb historians' attention.[5] The connection with the Irish 'Sister Kingdom' was also trenchantly maintained in three major respects. First, the expressions of solidarity and common cause, which had so alarmed the Scottish administration in the early 1790s, were now a commonplace in radical literature. Second, on a more practical level, Scottish radicals were to return repeatedly to the distinctive United system of oath-bound organisation whenever circumstances seemed to demand it. Third, Irish personnel continued to be involved in Scottish political and industrial movements.[6]

The first tangible evidence that links still existed between the disaffected in the two countries appeared in July 1807, when a set of 'Defender' documents, including an oath, constitution and a rambling history of the Society, were discovered in Kilmarnock.[7] There was much bloodthirsty talk of 'Death or Liberty' and arming as a protection against tyrants; expenses were to be raised to send a delegate to Ireland 'to get intelligence of what was going on elsewhere'. The town had been a centre for Irish migration from 1798, and the Society may have been an offshoot of the 'Regenerated Defenders' who were active in the counties of Down, Antrim and Armagh from December 1806.[8] The Scottish authorities were cautious but not unduly panicked by these revelations. This was an appropriate response as the Irish movement was essentially a retrospective phenomenon, an obscure junction of surviving Defenderism and the lingering United spirit, still clinging to faith in another French invasion.[9]

September 1811 saw further disclosures, and the new Lord Advocate Archibald Colquhoun informed the Home Office that the organisation seemed to extend to England and Ireland where it had originated. It confirmed official suspicion of the Irish community to learn that many in Scotland were members of it, as well as some natives.[10] The Society had a system of inner circles and a hierarchy of oaths, which made its proceedings impossible to penetrate, and still lived in hope of assistance from 'abroad or Ireland'. This was expected to arrive in November, but within months the Lord Advocate could satisfy himself that there was no immediate danger of the public peace being threatened; he adopted the usual monitoring measures in case the association should ever 'attempt to reduce itself into a more regular form'.[11]

Before the next year had ended, another challenge emerged. This was more formidable for the authorities as it was located firmly in the main-stream of Scotland's social and political development. It arose from a burst of trade-union activity in the western manufacturing districts. In 1809, a combination had been formed among operative weavers in Glasgow and the vicinity, which soon caused employers concern that its objectives were to 'cramp and fetter the masters in the employment of their time . . . to raise the price of labour; and in other respects to bring the masters under the control of the leaders of the Combination . . .'.[12] Almost instinctively, the new association corresponded with different associations in England and Ireland.[13] The latter initiative was understandable, as Ulster was suffering from similar fluctuations in cotton manufactures with half of the factories in the Belfast area idle by 1814.[14] Personal ties may also have been instrumental; the operative weavers in the west of Scotland included, in the Lord Advocate's view, 'a considerable body of Irishmen, disposed to riot and tumult', but fortunately kept quiet and peaceable by their native Scots colleagues.[15] Local Irish support was certainly evident towards the end of 1812 when 40,000 weavers eventually went on strike after a series of legal wrangles over wage rates. The Hibernian Society, still in existence in Glasgow's East End, was one of a variety of groups which contributed to their strike fund.[16]

The extent of mutual support and the sophisticated organisation of the weavers' combination in over seventy associations alarmed the authorities, ever watchful for 'seditious and traitorous designs'.[17] Not only was the government unwilling to intervene to establish minimum wages, the Lord Advocate blatantly supported the manufacturers' case and was as determined as they to crush the weavers' movement by the arrest and trial of its leaders.[18] This calculated use of the Combination Acts and the repeal shortly afterwards of the Statute of Artificers, empowering magistrates to fix the price of labour, signalled the end for the paternalism which had characterised the Scottish workplace and community relations, and ushered in a new, more sharply antagonistic phase of social conflict.

The application of the Combination Acts in Scotland was not enough to check industrial organisation or the communication which had developed between Scottish and Irish trade unionists; by 1814, the Calico printers' organisation had established links with Belfast, Carrickfergus and Dublin, but was suppressed like its predecessor in 1812.[19] Episodes like these only fed the growing conviction that the apparatus of the state and the legal system were operating in a manner fundamentally hostile to the interests of working people. This was further strengthened by the passage of the Corn Law in 1815. The immediate response was recourse to the tradition of spontaneous riot, with outbreaks in Perth, Dundee and Glasgow. But in the conditions of extreme industrial crisis which followed the close of the war with France, the outrage of the Scottish crowd also began to be translated into more sustained political protest.[20] There were two decisive moments in this process, the agitation of 1816–17 and 1819–20; in both, the principle of solidarity of radicals throughout the British Isles and the more specific United legacy continued to be invoked.

External contacts were most visible in the influence which the post-war revival of English radicalism exhibited in Scotland. Major Cartwright's two-month tour of the north in 1815 led to the formation of a variety of local Hampden clubs and drew in established reformers such as Captain Johnstone and William Moffat from the Friends of the People era.[21] The southern radical press, particularly Cobbet's *Weekly Political Register,* were also influential, and by 1816 Scottish radicals had embarked on a campaign of mass public meetings and petitions for parliamentary reform.[22]

These open tactics were not the only option. When it became obvious that the government was implacably opposed to any reform measure and economic distress intensified in a series of slumps, the alternative was to follow the underground insurrectionary path. For this, an organisational blueprint and a body of experienced personnel lay ready to hand in the industrial communities of the west of Scotland.

In late 1816, the authorities discovered from their informer, the weaver Andrew Richmond, that secret committees were meeting in Glasgow, Ayrshire, Dumbarton and Stirling, drawing in 1812 activists and even survivors from the 1793 Societies.[23] 'The constitution of Masonry and Masonic signs' were employed as security devices, but the need was apparently felt for a more disciplined approach. Accordingly, when delegates from Manchester and Carlisle visited the Glasgow committee, 'copies of the arrangements of the Irish insurgents and of the traitors in Scotland in 1795' were compared, with the Irish model emerging triumphant. Richmond originally reported that this was because it promised 'a regular and disciplined force' to allow the process of arming to commence in earnest, but later suggested that some of the Glasgow leaders also had personal familiarity with the United Irish system, using their prior knowledge to hammer out its detailed implementation.[24] There may be some substance to the latter claim as some of those involved in the new organisation were Ulster migrants; the committee met in the house of the weaver Hugh Dickson, who had left County Tyrone in 1800, his colleague Andrew McKinlay, another weaver, was a native of County Armagh, who had come to Scotland in 1799.[25]

McKinlay appears as a key driving force behind the secret initiative, producing a copy of the oath from 'the Irish Treason Trials' and declaring it would serve as an oath of fidelity.[26] Yet, events had moved on since 1798 and the searing experience of the sectarian disintegration of the United Irishmen's Rebellion had clearly left its mark. On this occasion the old oath was not to be an inclusive 'Bond of Union', for McKinlay decreed that Roman Catholics were not to be allowed into the association, 'because priests had preached against all interference in political matters and auricular confession made the associated afraid that Roman Catholics might be the means of betraying them'.[27]

It had not only been the democratic movement who had learned from the experiences of the past thirty years, but the authorities too were now also able to anticipate challenges to the political order more effectively. Thus, the resurfacing of the United Oath was a powerful signal of danger, and when on 26 February 1817 the Lord Advocate Alexander Maconochie in his maiden speech read it to a packed House of Commons, its promise to pursue political reform by 'physical strength' if necessary, it greatly assisted the government's case for the suspension of Habeas Corpus.[28]

The round-up of twenty-five Glasgow suspects, including Dickson and McKinlay, had begun the day before, and they were quickly committed on charges of sedition and taking unlawful oaths.[29] Again, much was made at the trials of the notorious oath, 'which was in almost similar terms with the oath taken by the United Irishmen which led to dreadful consequences in Ireland . . .', but the Lord Advocate's parliamentary prowess was not matched by his forensic ability. Some minor figures were convicted, but the embarrassing revelation that the Crown had promised to reward the star prosecution witness allowed the case against McKinlay to collapse.[30]

Following these unsuccessful trials, there was initially little agitation at local level, but instead 'a great deal of private association for political purposes'.[31] By late July 1819, amid a further trade depression and savage wage cuts, the resurgence of political reform pressure could not be mistaken in the west of Scotland. Despite fears of 'Manchesterising' in the wake of the Peterloo massacre, Scottish reformers began to gather in large open-air demonstrations.[32] At these events it was again clear how far the expansive concept of brotherhood had become entrenched in Scottish radical rhetoric. Along with placards bearing the battlecry 'Remember Manchester' and poles bearing the cap of liberty was one banner with the legend:

> Rose, Thistle and Shamrock blended,
> May the Rose of England never blow,
> May the Thistle of Scotland never grow,

> May the Harp of Ireland never play,
> Till Hunt, the Champion, wins the day.[33]

This latest revival of political radicalism drew lessons from earlier episodes and stood out in terms of its level of organisation and mobilisation of mass support across a variety of trades. A high value was placed on propaganda and the movement was able to sustain its own newspaper the *Spirit of the Union*. 'Union Societies' were also formed after the English example of Joseph Brayshaw; bound up with the principles of moral force, passive resistance and the goal of mutual education for their working-class members, they spread rapidly in 1819.[34]

As in 1816, however, public campaigning soon reached its limits as the national government responded with a further wave of repressive legislation to curtail public assembly and the radical press.[35] Now the Union Societies began to display the covert characteristics more commonly associated with the 'United' label, and Scottish reformers split between constitutionalist and physical-force leaderships. By the end of the year, those Unions which had opted for the latter were organised in the familiar form of a series of hierarchical committees where business was conducted with great regularity and secrecy.[36]

Even hostile commentators were forced to admire 'the constant and very quick communication with one another, equal if not superior to the established posts of the country'. In Paisley, for example, knots of radicals gathered at the different street corners in confident expectation of the latest news from England.[37] English ambassadors also visited the town, bearing a large Staffordshire plate broken in pieces. These were given to delegates about to be sent south and when all of them were present there the plate would be complete again.[38]

An Irish dimension was also evident to agitation in 1819–20. This involved the usual encouraging rumours, such as the intelligence from Dublin that 500,000 radicals had gathered in the city and driven a troop of Scots Greys to mutiny.[39] The reports which began to reach the Irish administration by the end of 1819 also suggested that the concert of reformers in the three kingdoms was assuming a more substantial shape. One informant, claiming eighteen years' knowledge of radicalism in Ulster, stated from undoubted authority that Corresponding Societies had been formed in Belfast for the specific purpose of communication with the disaffected in Scotland and England.[40] Equally alarming was the report of another 'loyal subject (tho' a female)' that the signal for a general rising was to be the seizure of the Lord-Lieutenant and Council in Dublin.[41] Renewed attempts at missionising were going ahead with a courier distributing around two hundred letters from 'the reformers at

Belfast' to the Irish in Paisley and Renfrewshire.⁴² Piecing this information together, and mindful of the uneasy state of the mass of the manufacturing population in the western districts of Scotland, it was considered 'necessary for public service' that the police of the north and east coast of Ulster be immediately acquainted with these circumstances.⁴³

Fears of a simultaneous insurrection also preoccupied the Scottish authorities. Just as Lord Advocate Hope had believed almost twenty years before, the presence of a growing Irish population in the west was considered inherently destabilising. The Duke of Hamilton explained the effect on the 'well disposed' people of north Lanarkshire. His part of the country was:

> unfortunately surrounded by idle Irishmen, weavers and colliers, who created a general uneasiness; and if any means were to be carried into effect to separate the good from the bad, or to maintain order and public justice, it is required that the civil power and the peaceable part of the population should know how and where to find support and protection.⁴⁴

Hamilton did not trouble himself to specify whether the 'idle Irish' were Protestant or Catholic, but the latter group were a great source of concern, not least to their own Bishop Andrew Scott who regarded them with some contempt 'as keen in their passions and easily inflamed'. They were 'very numerous, very poor, and had nothing to loose in a revolution', and were 'easily flattered by reformers with the hope of ameliorating their circumstances by a revolution'. Indeed, their grievances, he believed, were 'being deliberately magnified to enlist them in the ranks of the treasonably disaffected', a fate from which only improved pastoral care could save them.⁴⁵

We do not know how far such attempts actually produced recruits, for it is no easier to quantify the extent of Irish political involvement in this period than it was for the late 1790s. What is more certain is that the success or failure of the Scottish democratic movement did not rest on these strategies. The reformers continued to be dogged by tactical divisions over whether intensified propaganda and open campaigning were preferable to armed insurrection. The latter temporarily won the day; on 2 April, manifestos posted throughout the west called for a strike the next day in support of the formation of a Provisional Government. Unlike Mealmaker and his colleagues in the United Scotsmen, the radicals of 1820 were no longer battling in isolation. The breadth of support for their positions is indicated by the 60,000 who obeyed the strike call. Glasgow, Paisley and other centres were immobilised, as weavers, factory workers, miners and other workmen took part. The armed rising, however, failed to materialise, apart from a skirmish at Bonnymuir where a small party of enthusiasts were easily dispersed. This defeat reflected both the lack of any effective English attempt, which radicals had widely expected, and the ability of government to muster sufficient troops to deflect armed confrontation by force if necessary. The Lord Advocate continued to employ coercive tactics to make the most of 'the Radical War'. Forty-seven men were arrested on charges of high treason, of whom eighteen were transported and three – Wilson, Baird and Hardie – were brought to the scaffold.

Another figure caught up in the events of 1820 to his cost was William Putnam McCabe. With an anti-Irish spirit already well in place in official circles, it was discovered that this proven revolutionary had been resident in Glasgow for the previous five months. This most unwelcome link with the past was quickly put under house arrest, even though a search of his papers revealed nothing related to politics and he was plainly sick and dying.[46] He was examined under oath, but the magistrates were eventually satisfied that he had no connection with the radical leaders in Ireland and Scotland, and he was allowed to proceed to Paris. He died on 6 January 1821. Characteristically, this arch-intriguer left his friends in doubt as to whether he had made a deathbed conversion to Catholicism or died 'firmly attached to his former early principles'.[47]

The Scottish administration's caution in the case of McCabe is understandable given his revolutionary career, but it also stemmed from the basic misconception that unrest was still the work of old 'Jacobines' and 'emissaries of sedition', when it was plain by this point that its real source was the country's experience of rapid social and economic change.

The continuity which we have traced in the Irish–Scottish alliance in the previous fifteen years must be approached with caution. This was a transitional period for the two countries. Their fates continued to diverge in a way that was profoundly to influence the nature of political protest in each society. This process ultimately had its roots in the social and economic differentiation which had marked the preceding two centuries, and thus was difficult to grasp immediately. Indeed, when the legislative Union between Ireland and Great Britain was formally established in January 1801, it was the model of the previous 'Scotch Union' which was held up as an indication of the benefits to which the Irish might aspire. For the government the Union was the solution to a comparable security problem, but for liberals, like William Drennan, the prospect of political *and* social assimilation was not unwelcome.

By the Union with England the middling and inferior ranks of

people in Scotland gained a complete deliverance from the powers
of the aristocracy which oppressed them. By the Union with Great
Britain the greater part of the people of all ranks of Ireland would
gain an equally complete deliverance from a much more oppressive
aristocracy; an aristocracy not founded like that of Scotland in the
natural and respectable distinction of birth and fortune, but in the
most odious of all distinctions, that of religious and political prejudices . . . Without a Union with Great Britain, the inhabitants of
Ireland are not likely to consider themselves a people.[48]

In reality, the Irish Union was far from being an integrative force. It did
not cause the country's economic decline; structural problems of land
tenure and demography were already deeply entrenched and Irish public
finances had been destabilised by the lengthy war effort. It did, however,
subordinate Ireland to the needs and interests of the British economy in
the latter's crucial period of expansion and industrialisation. The result
was an intensification of Ireland's structural dependence and the uneven
development of productive forces *within* the country. While Ireland had
appeared to be on the verge of an industrial revolution in the course of
the eighteenth century, it was only in Ulster with its developed textiles
sector that free trade with Britain led to industrial expansion. While
industry concentrated on the north-east, the Union prefigured a century
of rural stagnation and impoverishment for most Irish peasants in the
south and west.

Nor was the Union able to soothe sectarian tensions or neutralise
popular politics. The original intention had been to couple it with a
measure of emancipation, thus diluting Irish Catholicism into the British
context and rendering it a harmless minority interest, but the alliance of
the Crown, the Irish Ascendancy and British ultra-conservative opinion
blocked this and ensured that the 1801 Act became 'a Union with the
Protestant party in Ireland'. This fact was to shape subsequent political
discourse in Ireland and became emblematic of the confessional battlelines
which lay at the heart of social and political life. By definition, Protestants
became 'Unionists', while the dispossessed rural masses and the Catholic
middle class mobilised from the 1820s under Daniel O'Connell's banner
of Emancipation and Repeal. Rapidly, Irish politics were becoming the
politics of nationalism, and Irish nationalism was becoming defined in
exclusively Catholic terms.

In a southern economy where the forces of industrialisation and modernisation were retarded, these developments drew as much on local
peasant grievances and methods as the pioneering mass techniques of
O'Connell's Catholic Association. The 1790s legacy of an organised

peasant underground movement also assisted the persistence of agrarian unrest as a force in its own right, requiring special coercive legislation for the next thirty years. A bewildering variety of new secret societies developed in the new century, ranging from Rockites, Shanavests to Whitefeet and Terry Alts. Of these, the most persistent were the Ribbon-men, another direct offshoot of Defenderism, emerging in the years 1811–13 often as a direct response to Orange harassment. In the 1820s the Society assumed an agrarian form and evolved ideologically as one of the most concentrated expressions of intense Catholic nationalism.[49]

Scotland's destiny was quite distinct. Here the inference which can be drawn from the agitation of 1812–20 is that popular alienation was already finding expression in class rather than nationalistic or sectarian forms. Scotland was fast developing as an industrial society on a more solid and broad-based foundation than Ireland. The outstanding feature of this process was initially the growth of factory-based textile production centred on the Clyde Valley, which in turn created the basis for the rise of heavy industry in the 1830s. The new market created by these develop-ments rejuvenated the agricultural system, with Scottish rural society displaying a flexibility and stability which reduced the social tensions evident in Ireland and elsewhere in Britain in the first half of the century.[50]

Political protest in Scotland was centred in the new manufacturing districts and its backbone was formed not only by domestic workers and artisans, but also by the growing number of factory-based operatives. The forms of this protest were also coherent with a modernising society, with working-class activity displaying flexibility and variety. In the imme-diate aftermath of the Radical War, political radicalism briefly subsided, but trade unionism received a powerful stimulus from the repeal of the Combination Acts in 1824. Popular political societies soon also recovered with the agitation surrounding the Whig Reform Bill in 1830–2 and were to flourish with a vengeance in the Chartist agitation of the next two decades.

For Scottish radicals, the question of 'fraternal links' now revolved around the integration of the Irish in Scotland into their campaigns. By 1841, as Ireland's economic woes and Scotland's industrial development grew in tandem, the number of Irish-born in the country had grown to over 126,000, of whom perhaps as many as a quarter were Protestant.[51] The difficulty was that this population was not ideal material for the construction of a progressive alliance. In the first place, they had brought with them their own sectarian traditions; by the early 1830s Bishop Scott could testify to their lack of representation in trade unions and combinations, and the organisation of many in secret societies of Orange-men and Ribbonmen.[52]

The Protestant community was perhaps more easily assimilated on the grounds of their shared religion with the majority of the Scottish population. The '98 tradition of Presbyterian radicalism had not yet been entirely eclipsed. Some Orangemen in Scotland were involved in anti-reform activity in 1831, but other lodges were disbanded because the political credentials of their members were suspect and the Orange leadership remained concerned at the taint of 'revolutionary and republican notions' among the rank and file.[53] Yet, even when involved in radical movements or trade disputes, as the example of Andrew McKinlay in 1816 suggests, their anti-Catholicism could reinforce the native antipathy to Irish migrant labour and fuel the sectionalism which was coming to characterise Scottish labour relations.[54]

The Catholic Irish remained even more preoccupied with the unfolding of nationalist politics at home. The political life of their community was dominated by their unswerving loyalty to Daniel O'Connell and the Catholic Association.[55] This did not rule out expressions of fellow-feeling from some quarters in Scotland, such as Peter Mackenzies's *Loyal Reformers Gazette*, particularly after the passage of the Catholic Emancipation Act in 1829, but their lack of engagement with Scottish affairs helped restrict opportunities for concerted action for decades to come.

All this was a long way from the death of 'puerile antipathies' and the dawn of 'The Manhood of Nations' which the original alliance between the Society of United Irishmen and the Scottish Association of the Friends of the People had seemed to promise. A final vignette from the reform agitation of 1832 illustrates how far political relationships had been transformed. In the procession in support of the Reform Bill, the Irish now walked as a separate body, as 'the United Irish' or 'the United Irish Reformers', bearing banners on which were portraits of Wolfe Tone and Robert Emmet.[56] These were no longer the heroes of secular radicalism, but the icons of an evolving Catholic nationalist cult. Scottish democrats had acquired their own pantheon in the shape of Muir, Mealmaker and the 1820 martyrs; in the process, they had also discovered their own 'radical tradition', a tradition in which the formative influence of Irish precepts and personalities was yet due its place.

NOTES

1. Calhoun, *The Question of Class Struggle*.
2. P. J. V. Rollo, *George Canning*, London, 1965, p. 165, quoted in Wells, *Insurrection*, p. 265.
3. Thompson, *The Good Old Cause*, p. 58.
4. Ibid., p. 91.
5. For a full discussion of relations with English reformers, see Roach, 'Radical Reform Movements in Scotland'. Fraser, in *Conflict and Class*,

also stresses these links to counter nationalistic interpretations of the content of Scottish political activity in 1819–20; see pp. 108–10.

6. Wells, *Insurrection*, p. 264 for parallel developments in England.
7. RH 2/4/92 ff. 70–4 (SRO).
8. Elliott, *Partners in Revolution*, p. 342.
9. One figure reported to be still active in the Regenerated Defenders in Ireland was Dr Thompson of Antrim, who had visited Scotland as a United Irish Delegate in 1797, A. Colquhoun to Lord Sidmouth, 6 September 1811, RH 2/4/98 f. 336 (SRO).
10. A. Colquhoun to Lord Sidmouth, 6 September 1811, RH 2/4/98 f. 336 (SRO).
11. A. Colquhoun to Lord Sidmouth, 19 February 1812, RH 2/4/98 f. 337 (SRO).
12. *Glasgow Herald*, 15 March 1813; Letterbooks of the Association of Master Cotton Spinners, 12 October 1809, T-MJ/99 (SRA).
13. *Glasgow Herald*, 15 March 1813.
14. *Glasgow Chronicle*, 13 February 1816.
15. A. Colquhoun to Lord Sidmouth, 4 December 1812, RH 2/4/98 f. 330 (SRO).
16. *Glasgow Herald*, 15 March 1813. The Society loaned £15 to the strikers. This may be the payment referred to in Minutes of the Hibernian Society, 24 and 25 November 1812, TD 200.7 (SRA). See RH 2/4/99 ff. 612–24 (SRO) for the weavers' demands and local magistrates' responses.
17. A. Colquhoun to Lord Sidmouth, 4 December 1812, RH 2/4/98 f. 330 (SRO). Their anxiety intensified when it emerged that the veteran radical Maurice Margarot, who had been transported after the British Convention in 1793, had returned to Scotland and had been in touch with old friends: A. Colquhoun to Lord Sidmouth, 4 November 1812, RH 2/4/99 f. 455 (SRO).
18. They were sentenced to eighteen months imprisonment, *Glasgow Herald*, 15 March 1813; see also *Glasgow Herald*, 30 November 1812 for the strike in Lanarkshire.
19. AD 14/14/1816 (SRO).
20. Meikle, *Scotland and the French Revolution*, p. 220; *Glasgow Chronicle*, 9 November 1816 and 22 December 1817 for typical protest meetings over economic distress.
21. Meikle, *Scotland and the French Revolution*, p. 221; A. Maconochie to Lord Sidmouth, 22 December 1816, RH 2/4/112 f. 627 (SRO) for a reaction to the Clubs; see also *Scots Magazine*, LXXVIII (1816), p. 873.
22. *Glasgow Chronicle*, 12 November 1816 for Glasgow's petition to the Prince Regent.
23. A. Maconochie to Lord Sidmouth, 25 December 1816, RH 2/4/112 f. 729 (SRO). The Spencean Philanthropists were also reported to have a Glasgow outpost: *Glasgow Chronicle*, 22 December 1817; *Hansard*, XXXV, cols 411–18.
24. Richmond, *Narrative of the Condition of the Manufacturing Population*, p. 183.
25. AD 14/17/18 (SRO).
26. A. Maconochie to Lord Sidmouth, 26 December 1816, RH 2/4/112 f. 722 (SRO). McKinlay's position was possibly assisted by the receipt of a letter from Dublin which assured the Scots they were backed by thousands in Ireland, 'who were ready to go all lengths to the cause', A. Maconochie to Lord Sidmouth, 25 December 1816, RH 2/4/112 f. 729 (SRO).
27. A. Maconochie to Lord Sidmouth, 26 December 1816, RH 2/4/112 f. 722 (SRO).
28. Omond, *The Lord Advocates of Scotland*, p. 234.
29. *Glasgow Chronicle*, 25 September and 8 March 1817.

20. *Glasgow Chronicle*, 3 June 1817; Howell and Howell, *State Trials*, xxxiii, col. 355.

31. Parkhill, *The History of Paisley*, p. 43.

32. *Glasgow Chronicle*, 6 September 1819 for Peterloo reaction; for public meetings, *Glasgow Chronicle*, 14 August, 5 October 1819; *Spirit of the Union*, 30 October, 13 November and 11 December 1819.

33. *Spirit of the Union*, 30 October 1819.

34. Roach, 'Radical Reform Movements in Scotland', pp. 157–9; *Glasgow Chronicle*, 11 November 1819.

35. *Glasgow Chronicle*, 7 December 1819 for the passage of the Seditious Meetings Act.

36. Parkhill, *The History of Paisley*, p. 45.

37. Report, 2 March 1820, RH 2/4/131 f. 214 (SRO); see also J. Hamilton to A. Maconochie, 1 March 1820, RH 2/4/131 f. 216 (SRO).

38. Parkhill, *The History of Paisley*, p. 50.

39. *Glasgow Chronicle*, 27 November 1819.

40. F. McNeil to C. Grant, 26 October 1819, State of the Country Papers 2084/9, (NAI).

41. Maria L.-M., 20 September 1819, State of the Country Papers 2076/11 (NAI).

42. J. Wedderburn to the Lord-Lieutenant, 21 November 1819, State of the Country Papers 2084/11 (NAI).

43. Ibid.

44. *Glasgow Chronicle*, 9 December 1819.

45. A. Scott to A. Maconochie, 23 August 1819, RH 2/4/126 f. 526 (SRO).

46. J. Reddie to C. Grant, 18 March 1820, Rebellion Papers, 620/14/215/1–2 (NAI).

47. Madden, *United Irishmen*, ser. 3, vol. iii, p. 358. He may, of course, have been lying about his lack of political involvement during his Scottish stay, but his latter years had been clouded by a wrangle over a law suit and he had been in very poor health for some time.

48. *Glasgow Courier*, 19 January 1799; see also *Courier* for 12 February for extracts from Daniel Defoe's *History of the Union* (1707).

49. Elliott, *Partners in Revolution*, pp. 355–7.

50. Devine, 'Stability and Agrarian Change in the Eastern Lowlands of Scotland', pp. 331–46.

51. Handley, *The Irish in Scotland*, p. 89.

52. Ibid., p. 161.

53. McFarland, *Protestants First*, p. 59.

54. Clarke and Dickson, 'The Making of a Class Society', p. 174.

55. Handley, *The Irish in Scotland*, p. 316–18.

56. *Scotsman*, 22 December 1832, quoted in Handley, *The Irish in Scotland*, p. 315. Daniel O'Connell's portrait was, of course, also prominent.

Education of Presbyterian Ministers and Probationers with Involvement in the 1798 Rebellion

MINISTERS

Robert Acheson (E)
John Arnold (S)
Thomas Alexander (G)
Samuel Barber (G)
James Boyle (G)
Thomas Ledlie Birch (G)
William Steel Dickson (G)
James Davidson (G)
Henry Henry (G)
Adam Hill (S)
Joseph Jackson (U)
Sinclair Kelburn (G, E, D)
Futt Marshall (No Info.)
Benjamin Mitchell (U)
Arthur MacMahon (G)
John McNeish (No Info.)
James Porter (G)
Robert Scott (G)
James Simpson (G)
Robert Steele (No Info.)
William Sinclair (G)
John Smith (G)
John Wardlow (No Info.)

PROBATIONERS

William Adair (G)
James Hull (G)
John Miles (G)
John Pinkerton (No Info.)
Reuben Rodgers (G)
Charles Wallace (G)
Archibald Warrick (G)

KEY

D: Dublin (Trinity College)
E: University of Edinburgh
G: University of Glasgow
S: Scotland
U: Ulster (Strabane)

Address from the Society of United Irishmen in Dublin, 1792

We take the Liberty of addressing you in the Spirit of Civic Union, in the Fellowship of a just and common Cause. We greatly rejoice that the Spirit of freedom moves over the Face of Scotland; that Light seems to break from the Chaos of her internal Government; and that a Country so respectable for her Attainments in Science, in Arts, and in Arms, for Men of literary Eminence, for the Intelligence and Morality of her People, now acts from a Conviction of a Union between Virtue, Letters, and Liberty, and now rises to Distinction; not by a calm, contented, secret Wish for a reform in parliament, but by openly, actively, and urgently *willing* it, with the Unity and Energy of an embodied Nation. We rejoice that you do not consider yourselves as merged and melted down into another Country, but that in this great national Question you are still Scotland – the Land where Buchanan wrote, and Fletcher spoke, and Wallace fought.

Away from us and from our Children, those puerile Antipathies so unworthy of the Manhood of Nations, which insulate Individuals as well as Countries, and drive the Citizen back to the Savage. We esteem and we respect you. We pay merited honour to a Nation in general well educated and well informed, because we know that the Ignorance of the People is the Cause and Effect of all civil and religious Despotism. We honour a Nation regular in their Lives and strict in their Manners, because we conceive private Morality to be the only secure Foundation of public Policy. We honour a Nation eminent for Men of Genius, and we trust that they will now exert themselves, not so much in perusing and penning the Historian. May we venture to observe to them that Mankind have been too retrospective, canonized Antiquity, and undervalued themselves. Man has reposed on ruins, and rested his Head on some Fragments of the temple of Liberty, or at most amused himself in pacing the Measurement of the Edifice, and nicely limiting its Proportions; not reflecting that this Temple is truly Catholic, the ample Earth its Area, and the Arch of heaven its Dome.

We will lay open to you our Hearts; – our cause is your cause. If there is to be a Struggle between us, let it be which Nation shall be foremost in the Race of Mind; let this be the noble Animosity kindled between us, who shall first attain that free Constitution, from which both are equidistant, who shall first be the Saviour of the Empire.

The sense of both countries with respect to the intolerable abuses of the constitution has been clearly manifested, and proves, that our political situations are not dissimilar; that our rights and wrongs are the same. Out of 32 countries in Ireland, 29 petitioned for a reform in parliament, and out of 56 of the royal burghs in Scotland, 50 petitioned for a reform in their internal structure and government. If we be rightly informed, there is no such thing as popular election in Scotland. The people who ought to possess that weight in the popular scale, which might bind them to the soil, and make them cling to the constitution, are now as dust in the balance, blown abroad by the least impulse, and scattered through other countries, merely because they hang so loosely to their own. They have no share in the national *firm*, and are aggrieved not only by irregular and illegal exaction of taxes: by misrule and mismanagement of corporations; by misconduct of self-elected and irresponsible magistrates; by waste of public property; and by want of competent judicatures; but, in our opinion, most of all, by an inadequate parliamentary representation – for, we assert, that 45 commoners, and 16 peers, are a pitiful representation for two millions and a half of people; particularly as your commoners consider themselves, not as the representatives of that people, but of the councils of the burghs by whom they are elected.

Exclusive charters in favour of boroughs monopolize the general rights of the people, and that act must be absurd which precludes all other towns from the power of being restored to their ancient freedom.

We remember that heritable jurisdictions and feudal privileges, though expressly reserved by the act of union (20th art.), were set aside by act of parliament in 1746; and we think that there is much stronger ground at present, for restoring to the mass of the people their alienated rights, and to the constitution its spirit and its integrity.

Look now, we pray you, upon Ireland. Long was this unfortunate island the prey of prejudiced factions and ferocious parties. The rights or rather duties of conquest were dreadfully abused. Very lately, the part of the nation, which is truly colonial, reflected that though their ancestors had been victorious, they themselves were now included in the general subjection; subduing only to be subdued, and trampled upon by Britain as a servile dependency. When therefore the Protestants began to

suffer what the Catholics had suffered and were suffering; when from
serving as the instruments they were made themselves the objects of
foreign domination, then they became conscious they had a country;
and then they felt – an Ireland. – They resisted British dominion, renounced colonial subserviences, and following the example of a Catholic
parliament just a century before, they asserted the exclusive jurisdiction
and legislative competency of this island. A sudden light from America
shone through our prison. Our volunteers arose. The chains fell from
our hands. We followed Grattan, the angel of our deliverance, and in
1782 Ireland ceased to be a province, and became a nation. But, with
reason, should we despise and renounce this revolution, as merely a
transient burst through a bad habit; the sudden grasp of necessity in
despair, from tyranny to distress, did we not believe that the revolution
is still *in train*; that it is only the herald of liberty and glory, of Catholic
emancipation, as well as Protestant independence; that, in short, this
revolution indicates new principles, foreruns new practices, and lays a
foundation for advancing the whole people higher in the scale of being,
and diffusing equal and permanent happiness.

British supremacy changed its aspect, but its essence remained the
same. First it was force, and on the event of the late revolution it became
influence: direct hostility shifted into systematic corruption, silently drawing off the virtue and vigour of the island, without shock or explosion; –
corruption, that glides into every place, tempts every person, taints
every principle, infects the political mind through all its relations and
dependencies; so regardless of public character as to set the highest
honours to sale, and to purchase boroughs with the price of such prostitu-
tion; so regardless of public morality, as to legalize the licentiousness of
the lowest and most pernicious gambling, and to extract a calamitous
revenue from the infatuation and intoxication of the people.

The patriots won reform, but the revolution itself was nominal and
delusive. – The wheel merely turned round, but it did not move forward,
and they were as distant as ever from the goal. They resolved – They
convened – They met with arms – They met without them – They
petitioned. But all in vain – for they were but a portion of the people.
They then looked around and beheld their Catholic countrymen. Three
millions – we repeat it – three millions taxed without being represented,
bound by laws to which they had not given consent, and politically lead
in their native land. The apathy of the Catholic mind changed into
sympathy, and that begot an energy of sentiment and action. They had
eyes, and they read. They had ears, and they listened. They had hearts,
and they felt. They said – 'Give us our rights as you value your own.
Give us a share of civil and political liberty, the elective franchise and

the trial by jury. Treat us as men and we shall treat you as brothers. Is taxation without representation a grievance to three millions across the Atlantic, and no grievance to three millions at your doors? – Throw down that pale of persecution, which still keeps up civil war in Ireland, and make us one people. We shall then stand, supporting and supported, in the assertion of that liberty which is due to all, and which all should unite to attain.

It was just – and immediately a principle of adhesion took place for the first time among the inhabitants of Ireland – All religious persuasions found in a political union their common duty and their common salvation. In this society and its affiliated societies, the Catholic and the Presbyterian are at this instant holding out their hands and opening their hearts to each other, agreeing in principles, concurring in practice. We unite for immediate, ample, and substantial justice to the Catholics, and when that is attained, a combined exertion for a reform in parliament is the condition of our compact, and the seal of our communion.

British supremacy takes alarm. The haughty monopolists of national power and common right, who crouch abroad to domineer at home, now look with more surprise and less contempt on this 'besotted' people. A new artifice is adopted, and that restless domination which, at first, ruled as open war, by the length of the sword; than as covert corruption, by the strength of the poison: among parties, among persuasions, among families, nay, to make the passions of the individuals struggle like Cain and Abel, in the very home of the heart, and to convert every little paltry necessity that accident, indolence, or extravagance bring upon a man, into a pander for the purchase of his honesty and the murder of his reputation.

We will not be the dupes of such ignoble artifices. We see this scheme of strengthening political persecution and state inquisition, by a fresh infusion of religious fanaticism; but we will unite and we will be free. Universal emancipation and representative legislature is the polar principle which guides our society and shall guide it through all the tumult of factions and fluctuations of parties. It is not upon a coalition of opposition with ministry that we depend, but upon a coalition of Irishmen with Irishmen, and in that coalition alone we find an object worthy of reform, and at the same time the strength and sinew both to attain and secure it. It is not upon external circumstances, upon the pledge of man or minister, we depend, but upon the internal energy of the Irish nation. We will not buy or borrow liberty from America or from France, but manufacture it ourselves, and work it up with those materials that the hearts of Irishmen furnish them with at home. We do not worship the British, far less the Irish constitution, as sent down from heaven, but we consider it as human workmanship, which man has made, and man can mend. An unalterable constitution, whatever be its nature, must be despotism. It is not the constitution but the people which ought to be inviolable, and it is time to recognize and renovate the rights of the English, the Scotch, and the Irish nations. – Rights which can neither be bought or sold, granted by charter, or forestalled by monopoly, but which nature dictates as the birthright of all, and which is the business of a constitution to define, to enforce, and to establish. If government has a sincere regard for the safety of the constitution, let them coincide with the people in the speedy reform of its abuses, and not by an obstinate adherence to them, drive that people into republicanism.

We have told you what our Situation was, what it is, what it ought to be; our End, a National Legislature; our Means, an Union of the whole People. Let this Union extend throughout the Empire. Let all unite for all, or each Man suffer for all. In each Country let the People assemble in peaceful and constitutional Convention. Let Delegates from each Country digest a Plan of reform, best adapted to the Situation and Circumstances of their respective Nations, and let the Legislatures be petitioned at once by the urgent and unanimous Voice of England, Scotland, and Ireland.

You have our Ideas. Answer us, and that quickly. This is not a time to procrastinate. Your illustrious Fletcher has said, that the Liberties of a People are not to be secured without passing through great Difficulties, and no Toil or Labours ought to be declined to preserve a Nation from Slavery. He spoke well; and we add, that it is incumbent on every Nation who adventures into a Conflict for Freedom, to remember it is on the Event (however absurdly) that depends the estimation of public Opinion; Honour and Immortality, if fortunate; if otherwise, Infamy and Oblivion. Let this check the Rashness that rushes unadvisedly into the Committal of national Character, or, *if that be already made*, let the same Consideration impel us all to advance with active, not passive, Perseverance, with manly Confidence and calm Determination, smiling with equal scorn at the Bluster of official arrogance, and the Whisper of private Malevolence, *until we have planted the flag of Freedom on the summit and are at once victorious and secure.*

Address to the Delegates for Parliamentary Reform, 1793

Associated for the purpose of promoting union among Irishmen, restoring three millions of brethren to the rights of citizenship, and effectuating a radical and complete reform of parliamentary representation for the people of Ireland, we cannot behold, with indifference, the vivid glow of patriotism which brightens the face of other nations, and the irresistible elasticity, with which man, long bent down into a beast of burden, shakes off the yoke of despotism and resumes his form erect, in neighbouring kingdoms. We exult in the triumph of humanity which regenerated Gaul exhibits; and the revival of the long-dormant valor, which made the Cæsars tremble, and in earlier times, filled Rome itself with suppliant mourners. We accompany with raptures, the steps of freemen traversing the mountains of Savoy, erecting the standard of liberty on the strongholds of despotism, and uniting the great family of God in the bonds of fraternity. In the fruitful plains of Belgia we hail prospects equally grateful to the enlightened eye, and flattering to the liberal heart. The arm of despotism palsied – her hosts discomfited – her throne tottering to ruin – and her motley train of slaves and sycophants, with all her proud abettors, plunged in despair, or meditating, with fell revenge, a last convulsive struggle in her cause.

But our raptures and our triumphs might be ranked with the transports of children, did we dwell for ever, as with the stare of foolish wonder, on these the glories of another land; while even the fainter brightness which opens on our own, and sister kingdoms, shines unnoticed. Thank God! there too we see the light of political knowledge widely diffused; and the seeds of liberality vegetating with vigor in the genial warmth of restored fraternity, and united patriotism. With us, that knowledge hath already assumed the form of language, and, in humble respectful petition, presented the claims of a proscribed nation at the bar of the legislature. We are sorry to say these claims were not treated with deference, or decency. We were not discouraged, but reanimated by their rejection. The chaos of Irishmen, as a voice of Omnipotence, was instantly moulded into a body, its members arranged, and the frame organized. Nor were vigor and harmony ever characterized in greater perfection, than in the representation of that body now exhibited in the metropolis of the kingdom. – And as it reflects the image of the original, we *know* it will speak its voice – the people's voice! – *the only 'Sure Divine' Law of Nations!*

We know too, that voice *shall* be heard. Irishmen have willed it, and they *must* be free. The violations of their constitution, the perversion of its principles, the abuse of its powers, and the avowed influence of venality and corruption, must be swept away together; not, we hope, by the awful experiment of contested revolution – may Heaven avert the dreadful necessity! but, by a *voluntary, immediate,* and *radical reform.*

While this is the object of our desires, our actions, and our union, and we are unalterably determined, by peaceable and constitutional means, to obtain it, we reprobate the mean idea of enjoying it exclusively. Liberty is the desire of *all* nations! The birth right of *all* men! To preserve it, with watchful jealousy, is the first political duty! To recover it, when arrested by the hand of tyranny, the highest pinnacle of human glory. That all men may assert, reclaim, and enjoy it, is, therefore, the fervent prayer of our hearts!

That Scotland, for ages, the asylum of independence, and equally renowned in arms and arts; that Scotland, the modern nurse of literature and science, whose seminaries have supplied the world with statesmen, orators, historians, and philosophers; Scotland, whose penetrating genius, has forced its way into the repositories of nature, unveiled her hidden mysteries, and brought forward all her richest treasures for the healing of the nations! Scotland, where a Reid and a Beatty broke the spells of an annihilating philosophy, which had reduced the universe to a *shadowy idea*; who held her up to ridicule; and presented creation anew, in her native substantiality and solid glories, to the fight of all men! That this same Scotland should have so long forgotten her degraded state, as a nation, slept over her political insignificance, or silently acquiesced in the mockery of a popular representation, among the senators of another people, hath long filled us with inexpressible astonishment. And, when we reflected on our relation of fellow-subjects, or, as our Catholic brethren have more properly denominated us, *fellow slaves!* and the more solemn ties of religion and blood by which many of us are connected with you, we candidly own our astonishment was not free from a mixture of regret: for, however humiliating our own situation may have been, the Protestants and reformed among us, in the scale of freedom, were much superior to the Scottish people.

What your state, as a people, was, previous to the day which set upon your independence, and blotted your name from among the nations of the earth, we presume not to delineate. What your state, from that day, has been, and now is, we know, and ye, *the delegates for promoting a reform*, must feel. Delineation of it is, therefore, unneccesary. We only say – and we say it, with confidence, Scotland as a nation, or part of a nation, has no people! *The idea therefore of a parliamentary representation of a Commons of Scotland* is only a *political fiction!* a fiction too bold, that we are astonished at the audacity, which first presumed to hold it out as a reality. And when we consider that a whole nation implicitly swallowed the *idea* as a *reality*, we cannot be surprized that the genius of a Hume should invert the position, and endeavour to impose the reality of the universe, upon a *credulous sceptical* world, as an idea only.

Your eyes, brother-friends of a reform, are now opened to the deception; your tongues are loosed, and your pens ready. While with your eyes ye behold the necessity and importance of the political regeneration which you have united to promote, let your tongues make it familiar to the ears, and your pens present it to the eyes of your brethren, *whose fathers were a people*. We are assured of your abilities, your learning, and your eloquence; your patriotism we doubt not; and on your perseverance we rely with confidence. Nor can we suppose, for a moment, that ye will ever suffer the whisper of malice, or the frowns of office to deter you from your pursuit. It is worthy of men – worthy of you – And ye will not abandon it! Ye will never disappoint your brethren by disgracing yourselves! We know the conflict is arduous. But, where the public good is the end, and the means are legal, every step is safe; . . . Success sure, tho' slow, and the reward immortal.

Bibliography

PRIMARY SOURCES: MANUSCRIPT
England
British Library Additional Manuscripts

Pelham Papers, 33101–22
Place Papers, 27808–9, 27813–18

Public Record Office (PRO)

Cornwallis Papers:
  PRO 30/11/270
Home Office:
  HO 79/1, 6, 10, Ireland, secret entry books
  HO 100/34–179, Irish Correspondence
  HO 42/22 Letters and Papers of George III, 1792–1814
Privy Council:
  PC 1/23/A.38, London Corresponding Society, 1794–6
  PC 1/28/A.62, Corresponding Societies, 1795
  PC 1/38/A.123 and 1/40/A.129–33, Corresponding Societies, 1797
  PC 1/41/A.136–9, Corresponding Societies. Treason, 1798
  PC 1/42/A.140–4, Corresponding Societies. Treason, 1798
  PC 1/43/A.152–3, Corresponding Societies. UI Societies in London, 1799
  PC 1/44/A.155, Corresponding Societies. Ireland, 1799
  PC 1/44/A.158–9 and A.161, Corresponding Societies. Irish Prisoners. United
    Englishmen, 1799
  PC 1/3514, 3526–35, 3552–3, Treason. Corresponding Societies, 1800–2
  PC 1/3564, 3581–3, Secret Information. Irish Insurrection, 1803

France
Archives des Affaires Etrangeres (AAE)

Correspondence Politique:
  Angleterre, 590, 592–3
Mémoires et Documents:
  Angleterre, 2, 9, 18, 19, 32, 48, 53, 56

Archives Nationales (AN)

Pouvoir Exécutif:
    AF III/206/943, 28–9, 30
Marine:
    AN GG¹ 72 ff. 114–15

Ireland
National Archives, Ireland (NAI)

Rebellion Papers, 620/1–67
State of the Country Papers, 1015/1–1017/66
State Prisoners' Petitions, 1796–9
Frazer MSS II/23–4

National Library of Ireland (NLI)

MS 6, Lake Correspondence, 1796–9
MS 45, 54A Melville Papers
MS 3212, Tone Letters

Royal Irish Academy (RIA)

MS 24.K.48, Memoirs of A. H. Rowan
MS 12.F.36, Recollections of the most important events which took place in the
    County of Antrim

Trinity College Dublin (TCD)

MSS 868–9, Sirr Papers
MS 873, Madden Papers
MSS 2041–51, 3805–9, Tone Papers
MS 4833, Sheares Letters
MSS 7253–6, Hope MSS

Northern Ireland
Public Record Office of Northern Ireland (PRONI)

D. 272 McCance Collection
D. 553 Drennan–Bruce Correspondence
D. 561 John Galt's Diary
D. 607 and 671 Downshire MSS
D. 1494 Lowry Papers
D. 2095/18 MS Book *The Oakboys, the Hearts of Steel, the Volunteers and the
    United Irishmen of Larne and Neighbourhood*
MIC 507 Cleland MSS
T. 759 Rebellion Papers
T. 765 Drennan Letters
T. 965/4 United Irish Press Cuttings
T. 1373/56 Account Written by Andrew Bryson on his Transportation to the
    West Indies
T. 3030 Redesdale Papers
T. 3048 McPeake Papers

Scotland
Edinburgh University

Laing MSS II 500–1, 650–1
Minutes of the Dialectic Society, vol. 1, 1791–4; vol. 2, 1794–1801
Stewart–Drennan Letters, 1807–8, D E. 1. 100², H5–8

Glasgow University

Francis Hutcheson, Letters to Thomas Drennan, 1737–46

National Library of Scotland (NLS)

Marquess of Midlothian's notebook, MS 5750
Melville MSS 7, 15, 45, 172, 1041
Pratt Insh Papers, Dep. 344

Scottish Records Office (SRO)

Arniston MSS RH 4/15/4
Grand Lodge of Scotland Miscellaneous Papers, GD/1009/16/1–5
High Court of Justiciary, Small Papers, 1789–1820 (JC 26)
Lord Advocate's Correspondence, 1789–1820 (RH 2/4)
Lord Advocate's Precognitions, 1800–1820 (AD 14)
Melville MSS GD 51
South Circuit Minute Books, 1792–1820 (JC 12)
West Circuit Minute Books, 1792–1820 (JC 13)

Strathclyde Regional Archives (SRA)

Letterbooks of the Association of Master Cotton Spinners, 12 October 1809, T-MJ/99
Minutes of the Hibernian Society, 1792–1824, TD 200.7

PRIMARY SOURCES: PRINTED
Contemporary Works

J. Abernethy, *Sermons*, London, 1748–51.
A. Barruel, *Mémoires pour servir l'histoire du Jacobinisme*, London, 1797.
J. Burke (ed.), *Poems and Songs of Robert Burns*, London, 1955.
The Case of John Simson, Professor of Divinity in the University of Glasgow, Glasgow, 1727.
Charlemont MSS: The Manuscripts and Correspondence of James, First Earl of Charlemont. HMC 12th Report, Appendix pt. 10; 13th Report, Appendix pt. 8, London, 1891–4.
D. A. Chart, *The Drennan Letters 1776–1819*, Belfast, 1931.
A Collection of Addresses transmitted by certain English clubs to the National Convention of France, London, 1793.
W. Cobbett, *Elements of Reform, or an Account of the Advocates of Parliamentary Reformation*, London, 1809.
T. Davis (ed.), *The Speeches of the Rt. Hon. John Philpot Curran*, Dublin, 1853.
The Declaration and Confession of Robert Watt, written, subscribed and declared by himself, the evening before his execution, for High Treason at Edinburgh October 15 1794, Edinburgh, 1794.
W. S. Dickson, *The Narrative of Confinement and Exile of William Steel Dickson D. D.*, Dublin, 1812.

W. Drennan, *Fugitive Pieces in Verse and Prose*, London, 1815.

Dropmore MSS: The Manuscripts of J. B. Fortesque Esq., preserved at Dropmore. HMC 13th Report, Appendix pt. 3; 14th Report, Appendix pt. 5, London, 1892–4.

W. H. Drummond (ed.), *Autobiography of Archibald Hamilton Rowan Esquire*, Dublin, 1840.

A Few Thoughts on Political Subjects Submitted to the Consideration of Manufacturers and Others in the West of Scotland, Edinburgh, 1792.

A. Fletcher, *Memoir Concerning the Origin and Progress of Burgh Reform in Scotland*, Edinburgh, 1819.

J. Galt, *Annals of the Parish*, Edinburgh, 1821.

F. Hutcheson, *Collected Works*, Hildesheim, 1969–70.

H. Joy and W. Bruce (eds), *Belfast Politics or, a Collection of the Debates, Resolutions and Other Proceedings of that Town in the Years 1792 and 1793*, Belfast, 1794.

J. Kay, *A Series of Original Portraits*, ed. J. Paterson and J. Maidment, Edinburgh, 1838.

J. Kirkpatrick, *Historical Essay upon the Loyalty of Presbyterians in Great Britain and Ireland from the Reformation to this Present Year 1713*, Belfast 1713.

J. Larkin (ed.), *The Trial of William Drennan*, Dublin, 1991.

J. Lawless (ed.), *The Belfast Politics enlarged; being a compendium of the political history of Ireland for the last forty years*, Belfast, 1818.

T. R. Malthus, *An Essay on the Principle of Population*, London, 1806.

W. Marshall, 'Thomas Muir', in *Glasgow Magazine*, July–Dec. 1795.

R. Meek, *A Biographical Sketch of the Life of James Tytler*, Edinburgh, 1805.

R. Musgrove, *Memoirs of Different Rebellions in Ireland*, Dublin, 1802.

N. Macleod, *Two Letters to the Chairman of the Friends of the People at Edinburgh*, Edinburgh, 1993.

W. J. MacNeven, *Pieces of Irish History*, New York, 1807.

T. Paine, *The Rights of Man*, Harmondsworth, 1969.

Proceedings of the United Irish Society of Dublin, Dublin, 1793.

The Proposed Reform for the Counties Impartially examined: with Observations on the Conduct of Delegates, Edinburgh, 1792.

A. B. Richmond, *Narrative of the Condition of the Manufacturing Population and the Proceedings of the Government which led to the State Trials in Scotland*, Glasgow, 1824.

T. Sommerville, *My Own Life and Times, 1741–1814*, Edinburgh, 1861.

W. T. W. Tone (ed.), *Life of Theobald Wolfe Tone*, Washington, 1826.

E. Topham, *Letters from Edinburgh Written in the Years 1774 and 1775*, London, 1776.

W. Whiston, *Memoirs of Samuel Clark*, London, 1730.

C. J. Woods (ed.), *Journals and Memoirs of Thomas Russell*, Dublin, 1991.

Newspapers and Periodicals

The Bee
Belfast Newsletter
Caledonian Chronicle
Caledonian Mercury
Dublin Evening Post
Edinburgh Advertiser
Edinburgh Evening Courant
Edinburgh Evening News

Edinburgh Gazeteer
Freeman's Journal
Glasgow Advertiser
Glasgow Chronicle
Glasgow Courier
Glasgow Mercury
Moniteur [reprint 1858–63]
Northern Star
Porcupine
The Press
Scots Magazine
Spirit of the Union

Official Documents, Parliamentary Proceedings, etc.

T. B. and T. J. Howell (eds), *A Complete Collection of State Trials*, London, 1809–28.

The Parliamentary History of England from the earliest period to the year 1803, London, 1806–20.

'Reminiscences of a Fugitive Loyalist in 1798', communicated by G. F. Handcock, *English Historical Review*, 1, 1886, pp. 536–44.

Report from the Committee of Secrecy of the House of Commons of Ireland, Dublin, 1798 [also including the 1793 and 1797 secret reports].

Report from the Committee of Secrecy of the House of Commons relative to the proceedings of different persons and societies in Great Britain and Ireland engaged in a treasonable conspiracy, London, 1799.

Report from the Committee of Secrecy of the House of Lords on the State of Ireland, London, 1799.

Report from the Committee of Secrecy of the House of Lords relative to a treasonable conspiracy, London, 1799.

Report from the Second Committee Enquiring into the Condition of the Poorer Classes in Ireland. Appendix G: Report into the Irish Poor in Great Britain 1336 (40), XXXIV.

Reports from the Committee of Secrecy of the House of Lords in Ireland, Dublin, 1798.

Reports from the House of Commons, printed by order of the House, London, 1803–6.

Reports from the Secret Committee of the House of Commons respecting Seditious Practices, London, 1794.

The Statistical Account for Scotland, Edinburgh, 1791–7.

SECONDARY SOURCES
Published Work

P. Adair, *A True Narrative of the Rise and Progress of the Presbyterian Church in Ireland*, Belfast, 1866.

J. R. R. Adams, *The Printed Word and the Common Man, Popular Culture in Ulster 1700–1900*, Belfast, 1987.

J. G. Alger, *Englishmen and the French Revolution*, London, 1889.

W. J. Anderson, 'David Downie and the Friends of the People', *Innes Review*, XVI (1965), pp. 165–79.

W. D. Bailie, 'William Steel Dickson, D. D. (1774–1824)', *Irish Booklore*, 2 (1976), pp. 239–67.

J. M. Barkley, *A Short History of the Presbyterian Church in Ireland*, Belfast, 1960.

T. Bartlett, 'An End to the Moral Economy: The Irish Militia Disturbances 1793', *Past and Present*, 99 (1983), pp. 41–64.

M. R. Beames, 'Peasant Movements: Ireland 1785–95', *Journal of Peasant Studies* 2 (1975), pp. 502–6.

J. C. Beckett, *Protestant Dissent in Ireland 1687–1780*, London, 1948.

P. Beresford Ellis and S. Mac A'Ghobhainn, *The Scottish Insurrection of 1820*, London, 1970.

C. Bewley, *Muir of Huntershill*, Oxford, 1981.

F. J. Biggar, 'The Northern Star', *Ulster Journal of Archaeology*, 2nd Ser., I (1895), pp. 33–5.

E. Black, 'The Tumultuous Petitioners: The Protestant Association in Scotland', *Review of Politics*, 23 (1963), pp. 183–211.

W. T. Blackstone, *Francis Hutcheson and Contemporary Ethical Theory*, Athens (Ga.), 1965.

J. Brims, 'The Covenanting Tradition and Scottish Radicalism in the 1790s', in T. Brotherstone, *Covenant, Charter and Party: Traditions of Protest and Revolt in Modern Scottish History*, Aberdeen, 1989, pp. 50–63.

—— 'Scottish Radicalism and the United Irishmen', in D. Dickson, D. Keogh and K. Whelan (eds), *The United Irishmen: Republicanism, Radicalism and Rebellion*, Dublin, 1993, pp. 151–66.

W. L. Brock, *Scotus Americanus*, Edinburgh, 1982.

P. Brooke, *Ulster Presbyterianism: The Historical Perspective 1610–1970*, New York, 1987.

T. Brotherstone, *Covenant, Charter and Party: Traditions of Revolt and Protest in Modern Scottish History*, Aberdeen, 1989.

C. Brown, 'Protest in the Pews', in T. Devine (ed.), *Conflict and Stability in Scottish Society*, Edinburgh, 1990, pp. 83–105.

R. Brown, *The History of Paisley from the Roman Period down to 1884*, 2 vols. Paisley, 1881.

J. Bullock and A. L. Drummond, *The Scottish Church 1688–1843: The Age of the Moderates*, Edinburgh, 1973.

K. Burgess, 'Scotland and the First British Empire 1707–1770s: The Confirmation of Client Status', in T. Dickson (ed.), *Scottish Capitalism: Class State and Nation from the Union to the Present*, London, 1980, pp. 89–136.

R. A. Cage (ed.), *The Working Class in Glasgow 1750–1914*, London, 1987.

C. Calhoun, *The Question of Class Struggle*, Oxford, 1982.

C. Camic, *Experience and Enlightenment: Socialisation for Cultural Change in Eighteenth-Century Scotland*, Edinburgh, 1983.

A. Campbell, *The Lanarkshire Miners: A Social History of their Trade Unions*, Edinburgh, 1979.

R. H. Campbell and A. Skinner (eds), *The Origins and Nature of the Scottish Enlightenment*, Edinburgh, 1982.

A. Carlyle, *Autobiography*, London, 1910.

G. E. Christianson, 'Secret Societies and Agrarian Violence in Ireland 1790–1840', *Agricultural History*, XLVI (1972), pp. 369–84.

I. Christie, *Stress and Stability in Late Eighteenth-Century England*, Oxford, 1984.

T. Clarke and T. Dickson, 'The Making of a Class Society: Commercialisation and Working Class Resistance, 1780–1830', in T. Dickson (ed.), *Scottish Capitalism: Class State and Nation from the Union to the Present*, London, 1980, pp. 137–80.

E. Cochrane, 'Scottish-Irish Trade in the Eighteenth Century', in L. Cullen and

T. Smout (eds), *Comparative Aspects of Scottish and Irish Economic and Social History 1600–1900*, Edinburgh, 1977, pp. 151–60.

H. Cockburn, *An Examination of the Trials for Sedition which have hitherto occurred in Scotland*, Edinburgh, 1888.

—— *Memorials of his Time*, Edinburgh, 1909.

K. H. Connell, *The Population of Ireland 1750–1845*, Oxford, 1950.

J. Coutts, *A History of the University of Glasgow from its Foundation in 1451 to 1909*, Glasgow, 1909.

W. H. Crawford, 'Ulster as a Mirror of the Two Societies', in T. Devine and D. Dickson (eds), *Ireland and Scotland 1600–1850*, Edinburgh, 1983, pp. 60–9.

—— 'The Belfast Middle Classes in the Late Eighteenth Century', in D. Dickson, D. Keogh and K. Whelan (eds), *The United Irishmen: Republicanism, Radicalism and Rebellion*, Dublin, 1993, pp. 62–73.

L. Cullen, *An Economic History of Ireland since 1600*, London, 1972.

—— *The Emergence of Modern Ireland 1600–1981*, London, 1981.

—— 'Incomes, Social Classes and Economic Growth in Ireland and Scotland 1600–1800', in T. M. Devine and D. Dickson (eds), *Ireland and Scotland 1600–1850*, Edinburgh, 1983, pp. 248–56.

—— 'The Internal Politics of the United Irishmen', in D. Dickson, D. Keogh and K. Whelan (eds), *The United Irishmen: Republicanism, Radicalism and Rebellion*, Dublin, 1993, pp. 181–8.

—— and T. Smout (eds), *Comparative Aspects of Scottish and Irish Economic and Social History 1600–1900*, Edinburgh, 1977.

—— T. C. Smout and A. Gibson, 'Wages and Comparative Development in Ireland and Scotland 1563–1780', in R. Mitcheson and P. Roebuck (eds), *Economy and Society in Ireland and Scotland 1500–1939*, Edinburgh, 1988, pp. 105–14.

N. J. Curtin, 'The Transformation of the Society of United Irishmen into a Revolutionary Mass Organisation, 1794–96', *Irish Historical Studies*, 24 (1985), pp. 463–92.

—— 'The United Irish Organisation in Ulster 1795–8', in D. Dickson, D. Keogh and K. Whelan (eds), *The United Irishmen: Republicanism, Radicalism and Rebellion*, Dublin, 1993, pp. 208–9.

T. S. C. Dagg, *The College History Society: A History 1770–1920*, Dublin, 1969.

T. M. Devine, 'Stability and Agrarian Change in the Eastern Lowlands of Scotland, 1810–1840', *Social History*, 3 (1978), pp. 331–46.

—— 'The English Connection and Irish and Scottish Development in the Eighteenth Century', in T. M. Devine and D. Dickson (eds), *Ireland and Scotland 1600–1850*, Edinburgh, 1983, pp. 12–23.

—— 'Unrest and Stability in Rural Ireland and Scotland, 1760–1840', in R. Mitcheson and P. Roebuck (eds), *Economy and Society in Ireland and Scotland 1500–1939*, Edinburgh, 1988, pp. 126–39.

—— 'The Failure of Radical Reform in Scotland in the Eighteenth Century: The Social and Economic Context', in T. M. Devine (ed.), *Conflict and Stability in Scottish Society*, Edinburgh, 1990, pp. 51–64.

—— (ed.), *Irish Immigrants and Scottish Society in the Nineteeth and Twentieth Centuries*, Edinburgh, 1991.

—— and D. Dickson (eds), *Ireland and Scotland 1600–1850*, Edinburgh, 1983.

A. Dewar Gibb, *Fortuna Domus, a Series of Lectures Delivered at the University of Glasgow in Commemoration of the Fifth Century of its Foundation*, Glasgow, 1952.

H. T. Dickinson, 'Popular Conservatism and Militant Loyalism 1789–1815', in

H. T. Dickinson (ed.), *Britain and the French Revolution 1789–1815*, London, 1989, pp. 103–25.

C. Dickson, *Revolt in the North: Antrim and Down in 1798*, Dublin, 1960.

D. Dickson, *New Foundations: Ireland 1660–1800*, Dublin, 1987.

—— and H. Gough, *Ireland and the French Revolution*, Dublin, 1990.

—— D. Keogh and K. Whelan (eds), *The United Irishmen: Republicanism, Radicalism and Rebellion*, Dublin, 1993.

T. Dickson (ed.), *Scottish Capitalism: Class State and Nation from the Union to the Present*, London, 1980.

I. Donnachie and C. Whatley (eds), *The Manufacture of Scottish History*, Edinburgh, 1992.

J. Donnelly Jr., 'Republicanism and Reaction in the 1790s', *Irish Social and Economic History*, 11 (1984), pp. 94–100.

M. Donnelly, *Thomas Muir of Huntershill*, Bishopbriggs, 1975.

—— 'Thomas Muir', in J. Baylen and N. Gossman (eds), *Biographical Dictionary of Modern British Radicals*, vol. 1, Sussex, 1979, pp. 330–4.

D. N. Doyle, *Ireland, Irishmen and Revolutionary America 1760–1820*, Dublin, 1981.

G. S. Draffen (ed.), *Yearbook of the Grand Lodge of Antient, Free and Accepted Masons of Scotland*, Edinburgh, 1954.

G. Duckworth and G. Langmuir, *Railway and Other Steamers*, Prescot (Lancs.), 1968.

J. Durkan and J. Kirk, *The University of Glasgow 1451–1577*, Glasgow, 1977.

J. Ehrman, *The Younger Pitt*, London, 1983.

M. Elliott, 'The "Despard Conspiracy" Reconsidered', *Past and Present*, 75 (1977), pp. 46–61.

—— 'The Origins and Transformation of Early Irish Republicanism', *International Review of Social History*, 23 (1977), pp. 405–28.

—— 'Irish Republicanism in England: The first phase' 1797–9, in T. Bartlett and D. W. Hayton (eds), *Penal Era and Golden Age: Essays in Irish History, 1690–1800*, Belfast, 1979.

—— *Partners in Revolution: The United Irishmen and France*, London, 1982.

—— *Watchman in Zion: The Protestant Idea of Liberty*, Belfast, 1985.

—— *Wolfe Tone: Prophet of Irish Independence*, New Haven (Conn.) and London, 1989.

—— 'Ireland in the French Revolution', in H. T. Dickinson (ed.), *Britain and the French Revolution 1789–1815*, London, 1989, pp. 83–101.

R. L. Emerson, 'Scottish Universities in the Eighteenth Century 1690–1800', *Studies in Voltaire and the Eighteenth Century*, 167 (1977), pp. 453–75.

M. Fallon, *Abraham Colles 1773–1843: Surgeon of Ireland*, London, 1972.

J. Ferguson, *Balloon Tytler*, London, 1972.

S. Ferguson, *Brief Biographical Sketches of Some Irish Covenanting Ministers who Laboured in the Latter Half of the Eighteenth Century*, Londonderry, 1897.

W. Ferguson, *Scotland:1689 to the Present*, Edinburgh, 1968.

W. J. Fitzpatrick, *The Secret Service under Pitt*, London, 1888.

D. Forbes, *Hume's Philosophical Politics*, Cambridge, 1975.

M. Foucault, *The Archaeology of Knowledge*, London, 1972.

R. F. Foster, *Modern Ireland 1600–1972*, Harmondsworth, 1989.

W. H. Fraser, *Conflict and Class: Scottish Workers 1700–1838*, Edinburgh, 1988.

M. Fry, *The Dundas Despotism*, Edinburgh, 1992.

M. Fry, 'The Whig Interpretation of Scottish History', in I. Donnachie and C.

Whatley (eds), *The Manufacture of Scottish History*, Edinburgh, 1992, pp. 72–89.

N. Furlong, *Father John Murphy of Boulnavogue 1753–1798*, Dublin, 1991.

P. Gibbon, 'The Origins of the Orange Order and the United Irishmen', *Economy and Society*, 1 (1972), pp. 135–63.

A. Goodwin, *The Friends of Liberty: The English Democratic Movement in the Age of the French Revolution*, London, 1979.

T. Graham, 'An Union of Power: The United Irish Organisation', in D. Dickson, D. Keogh and K. Whelan (eds), *The United Irishmen: Republicanism, Radicalism and Rebellion*, Dublin, 1993, pp. 244–54.

D. Guthrie, *The Medical School of Edinburgh*, Edinburgh, 1959.

T. Hamilton, *A History of the Irish Presbyterian Church*, Edinburgh, 1886.

J. E. Handley, *The Irish in Scotland*, Cork, 1943.

J. Hill, 'The Meaning and Significance of Protestant Ascendancy, 1787–1840', in W. E. Vaughan (ed.), *Ireland after the Union 1801–1870*, Oxford, 1989, pp. 1–22.

The History of the Speculative Society 1764–1904, Edinburgh, 1905.

D. B. Horn, *A Short History of the University of Edinburgh*, Edinburgh, 1967.

R. A. Houston and I. D. Whyte, *Scottish Society 1500–1800*, Cambridge, 1989.

M. Hutchinson, *The Reformed Presbyterian Church in Scotland*, Edinburgh and Glasgow, 1893.

J. Innes Addison, *The Matriculation Albums of the University of Glasgow from 1728–1858*, Glasgow, 1893.

R. W. Innes Smith, *English-Speaking Students of Medicine in the University of Leyden*, Edinburgh, 1932.

J. A. Jackson, *The Irish in Britain*, London, 1963.

R. Jacob, *The Rise of the United Irishmen 1791–4*, London, 1937.

F. G. James, *Ireland and the Empire 1688–1779*, Cambridge (Mass.), 1973.

T. Johnson, *The History of the Working Classes in Scotland*, Glasgow, 1946.

E. M. Johnstone, *Great Britain and Ireland 1700–1800*, Edinburgh, 1963.

D. Kay and R. Miles, 'Refugees or Migrant Workers? The Case of the European Volunteer Workers in Britain (1941–6)', *Journal of Refugee Studies*, 1 (1986), pp. 214–30.

R. Kee, *The Most Distressful Country*, Harmondsworth, 1972.

J. Kendal, 'The First Chemical Society, the First Chemical Journal, and the Chemical Revolution', *University of Edinburgh Journal*, 16 (1963), pp. 235–45.

P. Kivy, *Francis Hutcheson: An Inquiry Concerning Beauty, Order, Harmony and Design*, The Hague, 1973.

W. T. Latimer, *A History of the Irish Presbyterians*, Belfast, 1902.

D. Laye, 'The Wealth of the Greater Irish Landowners, 1750–1815', *Irish Historical Studies*, 1 (1974), pp. 15–30.

W. Leckie, *A History of Ireland in the Eighteenth Century*, London, 1892.

B. Lenman, *An Economic History of Modern Scotland*, London, 1977.

J. H. Lepper and P. Crossle, *History of the Grand Lodge of Free and Accepted Masons of Ireland*, Dublin, 1925.

K. J. Logue, 'Thomas Muir', in R. Menzies (ed.), *History is My Witness*, London, 1976, pp. 1–51.

—— *Popular Disturbances in Scotland*, Edinburgh, 1979.

A. Loughridge, *The Covenanters in Ireland*, Belfast, 1984.

A. Luce and T. E. Jessop (eds), *The Works of George Berkeley, Bishop of Cloyne*, London, 1953.

I. McBride, 'William Drennan and the Dissenting Tradition', in D. Dickson, D.

Keogh and K. Whelan (eds), *The United Irishmen: Republicanism, Radicalism and Rebellion*, Dublin, 1993, pp. 49–61.

J. McConnell (ed.), *Fasti of the Irish Presbyterian Church*, Belfast, 1951.

F. MacDermot, 'Arthur O'Connor', *Irish Historical Studies*, 15 (1966), pp. 48–59.

M. McDonagh, *The Viceroy's Postbag*, London, 1904.

R. B. McDowell, 'The Personnel of the Dublin Society of United Irishmen 1791–4', *Irish Historical Studies*, 2 (1940–1), pp. 12–53.

—— *Ireland in the Age of Imperialism and Revolution*, Oxford, 1979.

W. McEwan, *A History of Lodge St. John Maybole No. 11*, Maybole, 1981.

E. W. McFarland, *Protestants First: The Orange Institution in Nineteenth Century Scotland*, Edinburgh, 1990.

F. G. McHaffie, *The Short Sea Route*, Prescot (Lancs.), 1983.

P. Mackenzie, *Life of Thomas Muir*, Glasgow, 1833.

—— *Reminiscences of Glasgow and the West of Scotland*, Glasgow, 1865–83.

J. D. Mackie, *The University of Glasgow: A Short History*, Glasgow, 1954.

R. J. Mackintosh, *Life of Sir James Mackintosh*, London, 1835.

M. McNeil, *The Life and Times of Mary Ann McCracken 1770–1866*, Belfast, 1988.

S. McSkimmin, *Annals of Ulster from 1790 to 1798*, ed. E. J. Crum, Belfast, 1906.

R. R. Madden, *The United Irishmen, their Lives and Times*, London, 1857–60.

—— *Antrim and Down in '98*, Glasgow, n.d.

A. Malcolmson, *John Foster: The Politics of Anglo-Irish Ascendancy*, Oxford, 1978.

W. H. Marwick, *A Short History of Labour in Scotland*, Edinburgh, 1967.

W. L. Mathieson, *The Awakening of Labour in Scotland: A History from 1747 to 1797*, Glasgow, 1910.

H. W. Meikle, 'Two Glasgow Merchants in the French Revolution', *Scottish Historical Review*, 8 (1911), pp. 149–158.

—— *Scotland and the French Revolution*, Glasgow, 1912.

W. M. Metcalf, *A History of Paisley*, Paisley, 1909.

D. W. Millar, *Queen's Rebels, Ulster Loyalism in Historical Perspective*, Dublin, 1978.

—— *Peep O'Day Boys and Defenders: Selected Documents on the County Armagh Disturbances 1784–96*, Belfast, 1990.

R. Mitcheson and P. Roebuck (eds), *Economy and Society in Ireland and Scotland 1500–1939*, Edinburgh, 1988, pp. 126–39.

T. Moore, *The Life and Death of Lord Edward Fitzgerald*, Dublin, 1832.

V. Morgan, 'Agricultural Wage Rates in Late Eighteenth Century Scotland', *Economic History Review*, xxiv (1971), pp. 181–201.

J. B. Morrel, 'The University of Edinburgh in the late Eighteenth Century', *Isis*, 62 (1971), pp. 158–71.

N. Murray, *The Scottish Handloom Weavers 1790–1850: A Social History*, Edinburgh, 1978.

D. Murray Lyon, *History of the Lodge of Edinburgh (Mary's Chapel No. 1)*, Edinburgh, 1900.

S. Nenadic, 'Political Reform and the "Ordering" of Middle-Class Protest', in T. Devine (ed.), *Conflict and Stability in Scottish Society*, Edinburgh, 1990, pp. 65–82.

H. Nicholson, *The Desire to Please: A Study of Hamilton Rowan and the United Irishmen*, London, 1943.

Nomina eorum qui gradum medicinae doctoris in academia Jacobi Sextus Scotorum quae Edinburgi est adepi sunt, Edinburgh, 1846.

D. F. Norton, 'Francis Hutcheson in America', in *Studies in Voltaire and the Eighteenth Century*, 154 (1976), pp. 1547–68.

G. O'Brien, 'Franco-phobia in Later Eighteenth-Century Irish history', in D. Dickson and H. Gough, *Ireland and the French Revolution*, Dublin, 1990, pp. 40–51.

M. R. O'Connell, *Irish Politics and Social Conflict in the Age of the American Revolution*, Philadelphia, 1965.

C. O'Grada and J. Mokyr, 'New Developments in Irish Population History', *Economic History Review*, 37 (1984), pp. 473–88.

G. W. T. Omond, *The Lord Advocates of Scotland*, Edinburgh, 1883.

T. Pakenham, *The Year of Liberty*, London, 1972.

J. Parkhill, *The History of Paisley*, Paisley, 1857.

M. Perceval-Maxwell, *The Scottish Migration to Ulster in the Reign of James I*, London, 1973.

C. H. E. Philpin (ed.), *Nationalism and Political Protest in Ireland*, Cambridge, 1987.

C. Porter, *Irish Presbyterian Biographical Sketches*, Belfast, 1887.

T. P. Power and K. Whelan (eds), *Endurance and Emergence: Catholics in Ireland in the Eighteenth Century*, Dublin, 1990.

B. Probert, *Beyond Orange and Green: The Political Economy of the Northern Irish Crisis*, London, 1979.

J. Ramsey, *Scotland and Scotsmen in the Eighteenth Century*, Edinburgh, 1888.

B. Reece (ed.), *Exiles from Erin*, Dublin, 1991.

J. S. Reid, *History of the Presbyterian Church in Ireland*, Belfast, 1867.

E. Richards, 'How Tame were the Scottish Highlanders during the Clearances?', *Scottish Studies*, 17 (1973), pp. 35–50.

C. Robbins, ' "When it is that Colonies May Become Independent": An Analysis of the Environment and Politics of Francis Hutcheson (1694–1746)', *The William and Mary Quarterly*, 3rd ser., 11 (1954), pp. 214–51.

—— *The Eighteenth-Century Commonwealthman: Studies in the Transmission, Development and Circumstance of English Liberal Thought from the Restoration of Charles II until the War with the Thirteen Colonies*, New York, 1968.

G. Rudé, 'Early Irish Rebels in Australia', *Historical Studies*, 16 (1974–5), pp. 17–35.

C. Sarolan, 'The Golden Age of the University of Edinburgh', *University of Edinburgh Journal*, 1 (1925), pp. 45–53.

S. Scharma, *Patriots and Liberators: Revolution in the Netherlands 1780–1813*, New York, 1977.

W. R. Scott, *Francis Hutcheson: His Life, Teaching and Position in the History of Philosophy*, Cambridge, 1900.

H. Senior, *Orangeism in Ireland and Great Britain 1795–1835*, London, 1966.

A. W. Smith, 'Irish Rebels and English Radicals 1798–1800', *Past and Present*, 7 (1955), pp. 78–85.

J. Smith, *Lodge St. Andrew No. 179*, Dumfries, 1901.

—— *Freemasonry in Galloway*, Dumfries, 1920.

T. C. Smout, *A History of the Scottish People 1566–1830*, London, 1969.

J. Smyth, *The Men of No Property, Irish Radicals and Popular Politics in the Late Eighteenth Century*, Dublin, 1992.

N. M. Stern, 'The Bread Crisis in Britain 1795–6', *Economica*, 31 (1964), pp. 168–87.

D. Stevenson, *The Scottish Covenanters*, Edinburgh 1988.

A. T. Q. Stewart, ' "A Stable Unseen Power", Dr William Drennan and the

origins of the United Irishmen', in J. Bossy and P. Jupp (eds), *Essays Presented to Michael Roberts*, Belfast, 1976, pp. 80–92.
—— *The Narrow Ground: Aspects of Ulster 1609–1969*, London, 1977.
—— *A Deeper Silence: The Hidden Origins of the United Irishmen*, London, 1993.
D. Stewart, *The Seceders in Ireland, with Annals of their Congregations*, Belfast, 1950.
T. W. Stubbs, *The History of the University of Dublin*, Dublin, 1889.
P. Tesch, 'Presbyterian Radicalism', in D. Dickson, D. Keogh and K. Whelan (eds), *The United Irishmen: Republicanism, Radicalism and Rebellion*, Dublin, 1993, pp. 34–48.
M. I. Thomis and P. Holt, *Threats of Revolution in Britain 1789–1848*, London, 1977.
E. P. Thompson, *The Making of the English Working Class*, Harmondsworth, 1963.
W. Thompson, *The Good Old Cause*, London, 1992.
A. Thomson, *The Origin of the Secession Church*, Edinburgh, 1848.
H. Trevor-Roper, 'The Scottish Enlightenment' in *Studies in Voltaire and the Eighteenth Century*, 58 (1966), pp. 1635–58.
W. E. Vaughan (ed.), *Ireland after the Union 1801–1870*, Oxford, 1989.
J. Veich, 'Philosophy in the Scottish Universities', *Mind*, 2 (1877), pp. 207–34.
L. Vogt, 'Portpatrick–Donaghadee: The Short Sea Route', *Clyde Steamers*, no. 7, Autumn, 1971, pp. 23–7.
G. Walker, 'The Protestant Irish in Scotland', in T. M. Devine (ed.), *Irish Immigrants in Scottish Society in the Nineteenth and Twentieth Centuries*, Edinburgh, 1990, pp. 44–66.
R. Wells, *Insurrection: The British Experience*, Gloucester, 1983.
—— *Wretched Faces: Famine in Wartime England 1793–1803*, Gloucester, 1988.
C. Whatley, 'How Tame were the Scottish Lowlanders during the Eighteenth Century', in T. Devine (ed.), *Conflict and Stability in Scottish Society*, Edinburgh, 1990, pp. 1–30.
—— 'An Uninflammable People', in I. Donnachie and C. Whately (eds), *The Manufacture of Scottish History*, Edinburgh, 1992, pp. 51–71.
G. A. Williams, *Artisans and Sans-Cullotes: Popular Movements in France and Britain during the French Revolution*, London, 1968.
A. Williamson, *Scottish National Consciousness in the Age of James VI*, Edinburgh, 1983.
T. Witherow, *History and Literary Memorials of the Presbyterian Church in Ireland*, London and Belfast, 1879.
I. S. Wood, 'Protestantism and the Scottish Military Tradition', in G. Walker and T. Gallacher (eds), *Sermons and Battle Hymns: Popular Protestant Culture in Modern Scotland*, Edinburgh, 1990, pp. 112–36.
C. J. Woods, 'A Plan for the Dutch Invasion of Scotland 1797', *Scottish Historical Review*, 53 (1973), pp. 108–14.
J. D. Young, *The Rousing of the Scottish Working Class*, London, 1979.

Theses

R. Allen, 'Scottish Ecclesiastical Influence upon Irish Presbyterianism from the Non-Subscribing Controversy to the Union of the Synods', MA Thesis, The Queen's University of Belfast, 1940.
I. M. Bishop, 'The Education of Ulster Students at Glasgow University during the Eighteenth Century', MA Thesis, The Queen's University of Belfast, 1987.

J. Brims, 'The Scottish Democratic Movement in the Age of the French Revolution', Ph.D. Thesis, University of Edinburgh, 1983.

C. M. Burns, 'Industrial Labour and Radical Movements in Scotland in the
1790s', M.Sc. Thesis, University of Strathclyde, 1971.

R. Cassirer, 'The Irish Influence on the Liberal Movement in England 1798–1832,
with Special Reference to the Period 1815–32', Ph.D. Thesis, University of
London, 1940.

W. McMillan, 'The Subscription Controversy in Irish Presbyterianism, with
reference to its political implications in the late eighteenth century', MA Thesis,
The Queen's University of Belfast, 1958.

M. de la Poer Beresford, 'Ireland in French Strategy 1691–1789', M.Litt. Thesis,
University of Dublin, 1975.

W. H. Roach, 'Radical Reform Movements in Scotland from 1815 to 1822',
Ph.D. Thesis, University of Glasgow, 1970.

W. A. L. Seaman, 'British Democratic Societies in the Period of the French
Revolution 1789–99', Ph.D. Thesis, University of London, 1954.

D. H. Smyth, 'The Volunteer Movement in Ulster: Background and Development
1745–1785', Ph.D. Thesis, The Queen's University of Belfast, 1974.

J. Walvin, 'English Democratic Societies and Popular Radicalism 1791–1800',
D.Phil. Thesis, University of York, 1969.

Index

DATE DUE
